Thinking
for Yourself

Thinking for Yourself

DEVELOPING CRITICAL
THINKING SKILLS
THROUGH WRITING

Second Edition

Marlys Mayfield

COLLEGE OF ALAMEDA

Wadsworth Publishing Company
Belmont, California
A Division of Wadsworth, Inc.

English Editor: Angela Gantner
Editorial Assistant: Julie Johnson
Production Editor: Vicki Friedberg
Managing Designer: Donna Davis
Print Buyer: Randy Hurst
Permissions Editor: Peggy Meehan
Designer: Cynthia Bogue
Copy Editor: Jennifer Gordon
Compositor: G & S Typesetters, Inc.
Cover: Donna Davis
Cover Photo: Midnight Sun, Brooks Range, Alaska
Peter Arnold, Inc./Clyde R. Smith, Photographer

Printed in the United States of America   50

1   2   3   4   5   6   7   8   9   10—95   94   93   92   91

Library of Congress Cataloging-in-Publication Data

Mayfield, Marlys, 1931–
    Thinking for yourself : developing critical thinking skills through
writing / Marlys Mayfield.—2nd ed.
      p.   cm.
    Includes bibliographical references and index.
    ISBN 0-534-13812-8
    1. English language—Rhetoric.   2. Critical thinking.   I. Title.
PE1408.M3933   1991
808′.042—dc20   90-12817
                                        CIP

To my students
at Merritt College, 1965–1970,
and College of Alameda, 1970–1990,
whose questions led me.

BRIEF CONTENTS

C O N T E N T S

P A R T   I

Basics of Critical Thinking 9

Chapter 1   Observation Skills 11

Chapter 2   Word Skills 48

Chapter 3   Facts 83

Chapter 4   Inferences   113

P A R T I I

Problems of Critical Thinking 153

Chapter 7   Evaluations   203

Chapter 8   Viewpoints   227

Chapter 9   Research Skills 264

PART III

Forms and Standards of Critical Thinking 291

Chapter 10   Inductive Reasoning and Inductive Fallacies 293

Chapter 11 Deductive Reasoning and Deductive Fallacies 331

Chapter 12   Critical Analysis of Argumentation 384

FOREWORD

Marlys Mayfield's book does not preach critical thinking; it practices it. Instantly engaging and irresistible to read, it contains an abundance of superb examples showing the richness and complexity of the thought we engage in every day. These examples are then successfully linked to the course material in such a way that it soon becomes quite evident how mastery of these few concepts can powerfully affect the discourse in almost any field—evidence often sought but not often achieved in the teaching of critical thinking.

This book is also about the writing process—about the courage to keep questioning even at the risk of not getting the assignment done neatly and on time and about the truths that can show up on the page unexpectedly when that courage is exercised. It is not a book about how to write "argumentative essays," "convince" an audience, or "defend" one's conclusions, but about how to use the writing process to test one's own convictions and make sure they are worth promoting. It is not, in short, about how to *sell* the truth, but about how to find it.

Thinking for Yourself begins where the effort to find the truth must begin: in observation. And by thus grounding critical thought in perception, it manages to promote self-confidence even while it leads toward self-scrutiny, a delicate accomplishment that is crucial to the successful teaching of critical thinking.

Indeed, throughout the text, the underlying approach continually proves both psychologically astute and morally appealing, for it takes as the touchstone of critical thought the perceptions and opinions of the individual thinker. It recognizes that the point of instruction in this area is not that students should come to doubt their powers, but that they should come to know where they are responsible for the exercise of these powers and to understand how they may improve this exercise.

Thus in Part I, after developing care for what one observes (Chapter 1), Mayfield encourages similar care in the choice of words for talking about these observations (Chapter 2). Only then are facts discussed (Chapter 3), the placement of this topic subtly making the essential point that "facts" depend on words and perceptions. Inference (Chapter 4) is carefully distinguished from fact, and the groundwork is laid for the discussion of inductive argument.

Part II is similarly astute and respectful. Not content with a simple "fact/opinion" or "fact/value" split, in which opinions are dismissed as "mere" opinions and values are tolerated only as necessary evils, Marlys Mayfield reaffirms the value of the decision making and judging that students do daily, while inspiring them to do it better. Her readers will not become fence-sitters or skeptics, nor will they be able to fall back on "Well, it's all just a matter of opinion, anyway!"

Of particular value—and rarity—among critical thinking texts is the acknowledgment in Part II of the role of feelings and intuition. The text here appeals to the practical and makes immediate connections with most domains. And in such appeal, as well, the text is culturally accessible, honoring the "ways of knowing" not only of women and of students of color, but also of managers and employees—and indeed of all those whose hands-on experience of the world makes them skeptical of mere bookishness.

Having thus firmly established the locus of critical thinking in the individual writer as perceiver and doer, Marlys Mayfield then pursues formal thought. Her final chapters on research and formal argumentation successfully build a bridge into academic competence.

To have been drawn into this book and worked through its exercises—which come as naturally as responses in a conversation—is to have learned what cannot be unlearned: how to think more carefully, not only in class, but wherever else it matters.

NANCY GLOCK
California Community Colleges

PREFACE

"Wait! Wait! Listen to me! . . . We don't HAVE to be just sheep!"

Used with permission of Chronicle Features, San Francisco.

HISTORY OF THE TEXT

Critical thinking can feel like waking up. Sometimes it's in the momentous, and sometimes in the ordinary, but inevitably it's a discovery that we have been asleep.

Since 1987, the year of this book's first edition, the momentous aspect has accelerated beyond any historical precedent. In chain reaction explosions, one nation after the other has stood up to say, "We don't HAVE to be just sheep!" It would seem that no matter how long a people are suppressed, they will eventually assert their need to think for themselves.

This book originated through some acts of waking up. Its germination began with a nagging dissatisfaction with the way I had been teaching English composition for fifteen years. Like my colleagues, I knew that writing was clear when thinking was clear. And so, I wondered, why not focus primarily on the thinking process instead of the writing process? Why not use writing to show how we think, instead of thinking so much about how we write? It seemed to me that this approach would do more to improve writing in the long run. The problem then was that none of us knew how to teach thinking, or even if that were possible.

By the late seventies, I learned it was possible: a number of educators were demonstrating some new theories and curricula for teaching thinking. They included foremost the work of J. P. Guilford and Mary Meeker in California and that of Reuven Feuerstein in Israel. In 1980 I received a small grant to undertake a teaching internship in the Feuerstein method, called "Instrumental Enrichment." I chose this program because it is based on a clearly identified hierarchy of thinking skills and because it teaches students an awareness of their thinking processes. By 1982 I was teaching two new experimental college courses. The first was a remedial course in thinking skills based on the Feuerstein system. The second was an English college transfer course designed to fulfill the new California State University critical thinking course requirements. Since this requirement specified content but did not restrict critical thinking to any particular departments or types of courses, I decided to combine critical thinking with writing into one course, calling it Critical Thinking in Reading and Writing.

This book is based on the material I developed for that course. It was written chapter by chapter as I worked with my students, based on whatever they needed to know. And what they did not know often astonished me: the difference between facts and inferences; between reasons and conclusions; the meaning of assumptions, opinions, and evaluations; the significance of viewpoint. During this period I was also working with Wadsworth Publishing Company, whose editors and reviewers offered suggestions and assistance that continued to shape the book's content and organization. The end product became a unique text serving two purposes:

> To teach English composition through an emphasis on the thinking process, serving as a composition text.

> To teach critical thinking through writing applications, serving as a critical thinking course text.

Aside from a general updating of the text with new examples, cartoons, and photographs, the guiding purpose of the second edition revision has been to provide instructors with more flexibility and teaching options. For instructors who wish to emphasize critical reading, there are now more than twenty new reading selections to choose from. For those who want to assign a research paper, there is a new chapter on research skills. For instructors who want to try collaborative learning, each chapter offers assignments that allow this. Further flexibility lies in the text's organization, which permits selective use of the material. While the text contains sufficient material for a two-quarter or two-semester course, instructors can tailor the material to fit the requirements of a one-quarter or one-semester course.

The feedback of students and their instructors guided the growth of this edition. I collected feedback not only from my own students, but also from my Peralta Colleges colleagues, as well as from instructors all across the country. This has indeed become our collaboration.

APPROACH AND COVERAGE

1. This text teaches both critical thinking and composition by emphasizing awareness of the personal thinking process. From the training of personal awareness, it moves to the more advanced stages of analyzing the thinking of others.

2. This book begins on a more fundamental level than most other critical thinking books, yet proceeds to a more advanced level than most, requiring students to develop and demonstrate highly sophisticated analytical skills.

3. The first half of the text works extensively with critical thinking in *nonverbal* problems, using photographs, cartoons, descriptive assignments, and report assignments. The second half moves into the more traditional application of critical thinking to *verbal* problems, analyses, and arguments.

4. The text provokes its readers constantly to think in order to work their way through the materials. Its problem and writing

assignments force confrontation with the common tricks and defenses used to avoid thinking. Some of these include the use of glib phrases, stereotypes, fixed opinions, the disregard of instructions, the substitution of evaluations and imagination for facts, the use of unexamined assumptions, and the acceptance of false authority.

5. In its style and pedagogy, the text shows consistent concern for the interaction of the cognitive and affective domains of learning. It also addresses directly the problems of distinguishing between feelings that clarify thinking and those that hinder it.

6. The text uses practical, everyday examples, connecting the concepts learned about thinking to life's problems. Direct quotations taken from the media concerning political and social issues are used extensively to illustrate the ubiquity and influence of arguments in our lives as well as the need for standards by which to judge them.

SPECIAL FEATURES
AND FURTHER REVISIONS

1. Each chapter begins with *Discovery Exercises,* which provide opportunities for students to uncover principles about thinking for themselves. They also engage and motivate students by asking them to draw on their own experiences and the things that interest them.

2. A study of the table of contents shows that Parts I and II cover basic material not usually presented in such depth in critical thinking texts, while Part III still offers extensive treatment of the more traditional topics of critical thinking, such as inductive and deductive reasoning, logical fallacies, and the critical analysis of arguments.

3. Several tools for evaluating student progress appear in the text. Each chapter ends with a summary and a true-false chapter quiz. These quizzes can be used to provoke further learning through oral review, or they can be used as written examinations. The Instructor's Manual contains tests on Parts I and II, new written content questions and essay thought questions for each chapter, tests on dictionary skills, additional tests on logical fallacies and reasons and conclusions, and two additional final exams.

4. The *Writing Applications* are another special feature. They can be used in English courses or any other course that wishes to encourage additional composition writing. They are designed to

provide more practice of the skills learned in each chapter, as well as to promote mastery of more and more complex rhetorical forms, ranging from the narrative and definition essay to the argumentative essay. In this edition, several Writing Applications have been revised to improve student comprehension, and three new ones have been included. Additional student writing examples have been added to further clarify assignment directions and to show possibilities for relating critical thinking to writing.

5. Many essays and short stories (averaging two a chapter) have been added to the second edition and serve to illustrate each chapter's main idea. These selections are either literary or else offer additional information concerning propaganda and the media. The boxes that appear in most chapters offer additional short readings that can be used in warm-up discussions or as additional writing assignments.

6. The research skills chapter is new to this edition and is designed to be optional. Its placement as Chapter 9 allows students to begin a research project by the middle of their term using the concepts and skills learned through Chapter 8. The requirements of the chapter writing assignment should move student interest forward to the problems of evaluating and building arguments as discussed in the succeeding chapters.

7. The chapter on logical fallacies from the first edition has been divided into two parts and placed at the ends of Chapter 9, "Inductive Reasoning," and Chapter 10, "Deductive Reasoning." This spares students from having to remember so many logical fallacies at once.

8. The Instructor's Manual has been expanded to include not only more tests, but also more teaching support for the new instructor, offering a bibliography, charts, transparency masters, and suggested answers to all exercises and tests.

9. Although many optional choices appear in this text, there are, nevertheless, some core writing assignments and exercises designed to evoke learning experiences that must be completed before the text can be fully understood. Each of these develops a particular thinking skill in a gradient sequence. It is recommended that both instructors and students complete each of the assignments listed below. Please also note that each title is preceded in the text by a star as a reminder of its core significance.

* Introduction: The Thomas Family (p. 2)
* Observing the Familiar: Vegetables and Fruit (p. 20)
* Observing the Unfamiliar: Tool (p. 23)
* Finding Facts in Photographs (p. 99)

* Using Facts and Inferences to Describe a Photograph (p. 130)
* Articulating Hidden Assumptions Behind Arguments (p. 165)
* Observing Viewpoints in Magazines (p. 238)

ACKNOWLEDGMENTS

The ten years I have spent in the writing of these two editions have brought me many devoted helpers and illuminating advisers. First, I wish to thank the many reviewers who let me know what their students needed and what could best serve them. They include Gary Christensen, Macomb County Community College; Robert Dees, Orange Coast College; Yvonne Frye, Community College of Denver; Helen Gordon, Bakersfield College; Patricia Grignon, Saddleback College; Elizabeth Hanson-Smith, California State University, Sacramento; Ralph Jenkins, Temple University; Shelby Kipplen, Michael J. Owens Technical College; Eileen Lundy, University of Texas, San Antonio; Daniel Lynch, La Guardia Community College; L. J. McDoniel, St. Louis Community College, Meramec; Paul Olubas, Southern Ohio College; Sue Sixberry, Mesabi Community College; and Patricia Smittle, Santa Fe Community College.

Next, I must thank those Wadsworth staff members who gave me day-by-day support in the creation of this second edition. They include first and foremost my English editor, Angie Gantner, and her assistant, Julie Johnson; our production editor, Vicki Friedberg; our designer, Donna Davis; our permissions editor, Peggy Meehan; and my own assistant, Kristina Bear.

Also, of the many friends and colleagues who gave me their time, advice, encouragement, and inspiration, I wish to mention Dorr Bothwell, Helen Burgess, Ed Carlstedt, Bob Doerr, Marina Fenner, Jerry Fishman, Jon and Marjorie Ford, Gerald French, Walter Frey, Frank Gerbode, Maureen Girard, Hans Guth, Jerry Herman, Connie Kagen, Connie Missimer, John Pearson, Gabriele Rico, and Josephine Riordan. Finally, for their patient acceptance of all those evenings we shared take-out dinners among my papers on the dining room table, I want to thank my son and granddaughter, Mark and Claire Frey.

Introduction to
Critical Thinking

"How do people plead insanity? Who's gonna believe a crazy
person?"

This is a book about thinking that will constantly require you to think. Usually you will not be told ahead of time what to expect, nor will you be given the "right" answers afterward. Instead, you will be asked to think out problems *for yourself* before they are discussed either in the text or in class. In addition, you will always be asked *to observe the way you think* as you go.

Each chapter in this text starts with Discovery Exercises for you to think about alone before participating in a class discussion. The purpose of these Discovery Exercises is to engage you in some experiences that will demonstrate *how* you think. They will also give you an opportunity to discover some principles about thinking for yourself.

To illustrate what Discovery Exercises are, this introduction will begin with one. After you have completed the discussion and writing that follows, you can continue to read more in this introduction about the attitudes required to develop critical thinking skills, this particular text's definition of critical thinking, and the traits of a critical thinker.

Discovery Exercise

★ Learning How We Think

This is an exercise to be done in class. Look at the photograph on page 3. Based on what you see there, rate each of the following statements as either *true, false,* or *can't answer.* Write down your answers without discussing either the questions or your replies with anyone else.

_____ 1. This is graduation day for the Thomas family.

_____ 2. The father is proud of his son.

_____ 3. The sister looks up to her brother.

_____ 4. This is a prosperous family.

_____ 5. The son has just graduated from law school.

When you have finished this quiz, wait, without talking to anyone else about your choices, until the instructor calls you for discussion. At this point you will be asked to give your answers to each statement and to justify each choice.

After the Discussion

Review the following questions. Were many of these covered in class? Now consider those that were not covered, either through continuing the discussion or by pausing to write out your answers, depending on your instructor's directions.

Photo by Rick Fanthorpe-White. Used with permission of the photographer.

1. What are your definitions of the following terms?

   TRUE   FALSE   CAN'T ANSWER

2. Can a statement be rated *true* if it contains an assumption?

3. Is it possible to determine if a written statement is *true* if it contains ambiguous words or phrases?

4. Should a statement be rated *true* if it is highly probable?

5. What makes a statement true or false?

6. Did you find yourself reluctant to choose the option of *can't answer?* Why or why not?

7. Do you ever feel unclear about the difference between fact and fiction? Does the difference really matter?

8. How can we know whether or not something is true?

9. What did this exercise teach you?

LEARNING FROM SHARING HOW WE THINK

Your work on this last assignment took you from isolated thinking to sharing the results with others. In the course of the discussion, you may have been surprised to discover the divisions that occurred in the class on the basis of different perceptions and judgments. Perhaps you even decided to change your original decisions during the discussion.

If doubts and shifts of viewpoint left you feeling confused or unsettled, consider that feeling as something beginning to grow in you that could lead to new perspectives and understanding. The work ahead throughout this book should involve many cycles of clarity surrounded by confusion (or even embarrassment), which is what true learning entails. In any case, this assignment was meant to remind you of what it means to learn first from your own *experience*, rather than from what others have told you, and to involve you directly in thinking for yourself.

In the process of developing critical thinking skills, the only essential attitude is to be willing to *learn*—which also means being willing to say "I am confused," or "I am wrong," or even "I don't know." Most of us associate "I don't know" with irresponsibility or ignorance. But it can also mean a greater commitment to honesty, and with that, an allowance of a creative space for something new to enter in. Critical thinking, then, does not mean having all the answers, but simply being willing to be surprised, to discover, and to learn. And sometimes this requires humility— from instructors as well as students.

The method of learning that you followed in the first Discovery Exercise is what is called the inductive method, or that of deriving principles from experience. In this case, what you learned was not about the people in the photograph but something about the way you think and how your way is similar to, or different from, the ways of others. You also observed your thinking without disguising or altering it to fit any principles offered in advance by the text. If you had been given these principles first, do you think they would have concerned you as much as they do now?

If critical thinking is best developed by observing your own thinking process, sharing your thoughts with others, discovering principles for yourself, and maintaining an open, learning attitude, then what exactly *is* critical thinking?

WHAT IS CRITICAL THINKING?

Dictionaries tell us that we use the word *thinking* to mean more than nineteen different mental operations. These range from reasoning to solving problems, to conceiving and discovering ideas, to remembering, to daydreaming. Some of these forms are conscious, focused, and directed, while others are unconscious, automatic, and undirected. In this book, we will be using the word *thinking* in the sense of conscious mental activity.

As for the word *critical,* most of us associate that term with being negative or finding fault. Although that certainly is one way the word can be used, a critical view can also be one of appreciation. If we look to the original meaning of the word, we find it comes from the root form *skeri,* which means to cut, separate, or sift; thus, the original idea conveyed by the word was to take something apart, or to analyze it. Here in its core idea we do not find negativity, but a procedure for evaluating knowledge. Moreover, *critical* is also related to the Greek word *kriterion,* which means a standard for judging. Putting together these two original ideas, we see that the word *critical* means analyzing on the basis of a standard. Thus, *critical thinking is consciously observing, analyzing, reasoning, and evaluating according to a standard.*

Now, what is a standard? Well, that is mainly what this book is about. Standards for critical thinking measure what is true and what is not, what is reliable information and what is not; standards show us how we know if something is true, or if this information is dependable. Learning these standards can be both an exciting and a difficult process, requiring new learning as well as *unlearning.* When we "unlearn," we recognize and monitor whatever less-conscious mental habits we have that interfere with clear thinking.

Let us turn now to a more concrete description of the kinds of skills you will be developing through this book. And once you have finished studying this book, return here to see, with more experienced understanding, how far you have come.

TRAITS OF A CRITICAL THINKER

The critical thinking traits you will be developing as you work your way through this book relate to inductive reasoning and deductive reasoning. In *inductive reasoning,* a critical thinker:

1. Observes self in the process of thinking.
2. Stays alert to monitor and correct self in the process.
3. Develops the confidence that he or she can produce accurate and reliable information.
4. Can distinguish among thinking, sensing, and imagining, and can use each selectively.
5. Can suspend thinking, judgments, and evaluations for a sufficient length of time while observing to gain insights. Can recognize an insight when it occurs.

6. Can concentrate on a problem that requires observing for as long as it takes.

7. Knows how to identify and verify facts. Knows when more facts are needed and has the patience to seek them out.

8. Has the flexibility to imagine a wide range of inferences to account for a situation rather than settling for the first inference that comes to mind.

9. Does not confuse facts with inferences, or opinions and evaluations with facts. Recognizes assumptions and looks for hidden assumptions.

10. Develops the ability to distinguish the relevant from the irrelevant and to see relationships and patterns.

11. Can identify and articulate problems (incongruities, contradictions) and feels challenged to understand and solve them.

12. Persists until true understanding or communication of a problem, word, or situation is reached.

13. Checks for errors and has standards for the communication of ideas.

14. Has a growing capacity to observe phenomena with awareness and objectivity, and recognizes own tendency to passively absorb and react.

15. Has the ability to choose the most likely conclusion from a given set of facts and the one most consistent with these facts.

16. Understands that the process of induction produces a hypothesis.

In *creating arguments* through both deductive and inductive reasoning, a critical thinker:

1. Wants to be logical—to offer convincing evidence or valid reasons to define or advance a viewpoint.

2. Has some knowledge of standards for the construction of a valid and sound argument.

3. Understands the basics of semantics, or the relationship between language and communication.

4. Clearly defines words used in argumentation and uses the dictionary with persistence to arrive at word understanding.

5. Recognizes how feelings can affect viewpoint in self and others. Knows the difference between conscious and unconscious viewpoints.

In *analyzing arguments* through both deductive and inductive reasoning, a critical thinker:

1. Can identify words that are undefined, ambiguous, or disguised in neutral terms.

2. Can identify the argument's conclusion, then its reasons and evidence. Does not confuse the reasons with the conclusions or start arguing with the reasons rather than the conclusion. Can tell if the reasons are sufficient to back up the conclusion.

3. Is aware of the use of unfair techniques of persuasion, such as hypnotism, emotional appeal, commercial and political manipulation.

4. Recognizes how viewpoint shapes information and can identify or describe an orientation. Recognizes bias and slant.

5. Is aware of important missing information, such as definitions or evidence.

6. Works from a standard of truth, examining contradictions and questioning information or assertions that appear to be false.

7. Is willing to concede if own argument is untenable and will seek a position that can be supported, even if it is that of the opponent.

Some of the terms or concepts in this list of traits may be unfamiliar to you now, but by the end of the book you will understand them, and will have incorporated them into your thinking. So your goal is clear, and the time has come to start down the path toward it.

I

Basics of Critical Thinking

This first section of the book offers materials that will show you what thinking is and how it actually occurs inside you and inside others. These chapters will show you how thinking can be first observed, and then improved, through exercises that will ask you to become more alert to the life around you, to talk to others about what you see and think, and to work with the mirror of words and writing.

The chapters on observation skills and word skills work together to get you seeing more deeply and naming more accurately what you see. Both of these lead into the chapters on facts and inferences, where you will acquire some basic tools for organizing and analyzing your thoughts that will remain useful throughout your study of critical thinking.

Observation Skills

Used with permission of Chronicle Features, San Francisco.

Observation skills keep us alive, but we can't acquire them from mottoes—only from staying in spontaneous interaction with life. Perhaps this is what the Boy Scouts and their master depicted in the facing cartoon realized too late. The attitude of being prepared cannot be learned from signs or books—only from a willingness to stay awake, to be curious, and to be able to confront whatever happens. To quote a wise saying, "You don't have to stay awake at night to get ahead. All you have to do is stay awake in the daytime." But this does not imply that having observation skills means being tense and grim. They can also provide us with a lot of fun.

Because developing observation skills is an essential foundation for critical thinking, this chapter consists mainly of exercises that require you to observe. The opening Discovery Exercises are meant to show you how *you* observe and how that may be be different from how others observe. As you work your way through these exercises, you will begin to discover your own rules about how to observe better, and in this manner you will begin to guide your own progress.

Writing is used in this chapter to make your observation skills more visible and conscious. Although the Writing Applications will put your focus on observing *things,* you will also be observing *yourself* at the same time. To put it another way, you will be *observing how you observe* from the reflection of your writing.

This chapter also discusses the mental processes involved in observation tasks: sensing, perceiving, and thinking. It considers qualities and attitudes that you can cultivate to improve your observation skills. And it includes readings to stimulate thought about the observation process.

Discovery Exercises

Comparing Our Perceptions

In class, write a one-paragraph description of the photograph on page 13. Try to describe what you see in such a way that your readers will be able to visualize it even without the picture before them. Do not discuss your work with anyone else in class while you observe and write.

When you have finished, form groups of three or four and read your descriptions aloud to one another. As you listen, notice in what details your descriptions are similar or different. When your group has finished, signal to the instructor that you are ready for a full class discussion of the following questions.

1. How can our differences be explained?
2. How can we know what is correct and what is not?

Photo by John Pearson. Used with permission of the photographer.

In completing this exercise, you may have discovered the following principles:

1. What we see is what is familiar.
2. What is not familiar is hard to see.
3. Sometimes we distort unfamiliar situations to make them familiar.
4. When we perceive, we must decide what is relevant and what is irrelevant. This in turn also affects what we see.

What Does Observing Feel Like?

The word *observe* comes from the Latin prefix *ob*, which means in front of, together with the root word *servare,* meaning to keep or hold, to watch, to pay attention. When we observe, therefore, we hold something in front of us. The word *watch,* a synonym for *observe,* comes from the Old English word *waeccan,* which means to stay awake and is derived from the Indo-European root *weg,* which means to be strong. When we watch, therefore, we stay *strong* and *awake.*

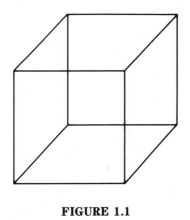

FIGURE 1.1

In this exercise, look at Figure 1.1. Observe the cube by watching it, looking at it intently, and staying "strong and awake" in your concentration. Then answer these questions for yourself:

1.   What happens to the cube as you observe it?
2.   Can you describe what observing feels like when you do it?

Observation and Insight

Study the cartoons on pages 15–16 carefully. Write down what you see and how you learned what the cartoons had to tell you. Notice how you (1) decode the information, (2) discover relationships between the people and the elements in the cartoons, (3) experience an insight or revelation (usually accompanied by laughter) when you understand its meaning.

USING OBSERVATION SKILLS TO DEVELOP NEW KNOWLEDGE

You have learned how careful observation can help you see details that you might otherwise have missed, details that can help you unlock problems or arrive at insights. Careful observation can also enable us to make

From *Totally U.S.* by Simon Bond. Copyright © 1988 by Polycarp Ltd. Used with permission of Harper & Row, Publishers, Inc.

discoveries and learn new things. The reading that follows illustrates this process. It is the story of a kind of trial its author went through that tested his capacity to do graduate research in science. Samuel H. Scudder (1837–1911) was an American naturalist who attended Lawrence Scientific School at Harvard, where he studied under the great biologist (then called a naturalist) Professor Jean Louis R. Agassiz. Pay close attention to the story because after you have finished reading it, you will be asked some questions about it. Then you will be asked to undertake a similar investigation of familiar objects.

"Have you seen a Frisbee?"

Used with permission of Richard Guindon.

"Now I *know* we're being followed!"

From *I Paint What I See.* Copyright © 1971 by Gahan Wilson. Used with permission of
Simon & Schuster, Inc.

LOOK AT YOUR FISH

Samuel H. Scudder

It was more than fifteen years ago that I entered the laboratory of   1
Professor Agassiz, and told him I had enrolled my name in the Scientific
School as a student of natural history. He asked me a few questions
about my object in coming, my antecedents generally, the mode in
which I afterwards proposed to use the knowledge I might acquire, and,
finally, whether I wished to study any special branch. To the latter I
replied that, while I wished to be well grounded in all departments of
zoology, I purposed to devote myself specially to insects.

"When do you wish to begin?" he asked.   2

"Now," I replied.   3

This seemed to please him, and with an energetic "Very well!" he   4
reached from a shelf a huge jar of specimens in yellow alcohol. "Take
this fish," he said, "and look at it; we call it a haemulon; by and by I will
ask what you have seen."

With that he left me, but in a moment returned with explicit instruc-   5
tions as to the care of the object entrusted to me.

"No man is fit to be a naturalist," he said, "who does not know how   6
to take care of specimens."

I was to keep the fish before me in a tin tray, and occasionally   7
moisten the surface with alcohol from the jar, always taking care to replace the stopper tightly. These were not the days of ground-glass stop-
pers and elegantly shaped exhibition jars; all the old students will recall
the huge neckless glass bottles with their leaky, wax-besmeared corks,
half eaten by insects, and begrimed with cellar dust. Entomology was a
cleaner science than ichthyology, but the example of the Professor,
who had unhesitatingly plunged to the bottom of the jar to produce the
fish, was infectious, and though this alcohol had a "very ancient and
fishlike smell," I really dared not to show any aversion within these sacred precincts, and treated the alcohol as though it were pure water.
Still I was conscious of a passing feeling of disappointment, for gazing
at a fish did not commend itself to an ardent entomologist. My friends at
home, too, were annoyed when they discovered that no amount of eau-
de-Cologne would drown the perfume which haunted me like a shadow.

In ten minutes I had seen all that could be seen in that fish, and   8
started in search of the Professor—who had, however, left the Museum;
and when I returned, after lingering over some of the odd animals
stored in the upper apartment, my specimen was dry all over. I dashed
the fluid over the fish as if to resuscitate the beast from a fainting fit,
and looked with anxiety for a return of the normal sloppy appearance.

This little excitement over, nothing was to be done but to return to a steadfast gaze at my mute companion. Half an hour passed—an hour—another hour; the fish began to look loathsome. I turned it over and around; looked it in the face—ghastly; from behind, beneath, above, sideways, at a three-quarters' view—just as ghastly. I was in despair; at an early hour I concluded that lunch was necessary; so, with infinite relief, the fish was carefully replaced in the jar, and for an hour I was free.

On my return, I learned that Professor Agassiz had been at the Museum, but had gone, and would not return for several hours. My fellow students were too busy to be disturbed by continued conversation. Slowly I drew forth that hideous fish, and with a feeling of desperation again looked at it. I might not use a magnifying glass; instruments of all kinds were interdicted. My two hands, my two eyes, and the fish: it seemed a most limited field. I pushed my finger down its throat to feel how sharp the teeth were. I began to count the scales in the different rows, until I was convinced that that was nonsense. At last a happy thought struck me—I would draw the fish; and now with surprise I began to discover new features in the creature. Just then the Professor returned. 9

"That is right," said he; "a pencil is one of the best of eyes. I am glad to notice, too, that you keep your specimen wet, and your bottle corked." 10

With these encouraging words, he added: 11

"Well, what is it like?" 12

He listened attentively to my brief rehearsal of the structure of parts whose names were still unknown to me; the fringed gill-arches and movable operculum; the pores of the head, fleshy lips and lidless eyes; the lateral line, the spinous fins and forked tail; the compressed and arched body. When I finished, he waited as if expecting more, and then, with an air of disappointment: 13

"You have not looked very carefully; why," he continued more earnestly, "you haven't even seen one of the most conspicuous features of the animal, which is as plainly before your eyes as the fish itself; look again, look again!" and he left me to my misery. 14

I was piqued; I was mortified. Still more of that wretched fish! But now I set myself to my task with a will, and discovered one new thing after another, until I saw how just the Professor's criticism had been. The afternoon passed quickly; and when, towards its close, the Professor inquired: 15

"Do you see it yet?" 16

"No," I replied, "I am certain I do not, but I see how little I saw before." 17

"That is next best," said he, earnestly, "but I won't hear you now; put away your fish and go home; perhaps you will be ready with a better answer in the morning. I will examine you before you look at the fish." 18

This was disconcerting. Not only must I think of my fish all night, studying, without the object before me, what this unknown but most visible feature might be; but also, without reviewing my discoveries, I must give an exact account of them the next day. I had a bad memory; so I walked home by the Charles River in a distracted state, with my two perplexities. 19

The cordial greeting from the Professor the next morning was reassuring; here was a man who seemed to be quite as anxious as I that I should see for myself what he saw. 20

"Do you perhaps mean," I asked, "that the fish has symmetrical sides with paired organs?" 21

His thoroughly pleased "Of course! of course!" repaid the wakeful hours of the previous night. After he had discoursed most happily and enthusiastically—as he always did—upon the importance of this point, I ventured to ask what I should do next. 22

"Oh, look at your fish!" he said, and left me again to my own devices. In a little more than an hour he returned, and heard my new catalogue. 23

"That is good, that is good" he repeated; "but that is not all; go on"; and so for three long days he placed that fish before my eyes, forbidding me to look at anything else, or to use any artificial aid. "Look, look, look," was his repeated injunction. 24

This was the best entomological lesson I ever had—a lesson whose influence has extended to the details of every subsequent study; a legacy the Professor had left to me, as he has left it to many others, of inestimable value, which we could not buy, with which we cannot part. 25

A year afterward, some of us were amusing ourselves with chalking outlandish beasts on the Museum blackboard. We drew prancing starfishes; frogs in mortal combat; hydra-headed worms; stately crawfishes, standing on their tails, bearing aloft umbrellas; and grotesque fishes with gaping mouths and staring eyes. The Professor came in shortly after, and was as amused as any at our experiments. He looked at the fishes. 26

"Haemulons, every one of them," he said; "Mr. —— drew them." 27

True; and to this day, if I attempt a fish, I can draw nothing but haemulons. 28

The fourth day, a second fish of the same group was placed beside the first, and I was bidden to point out the resemblances and differences between the two; another and another followed, until the entire family lay before me, and a whole legion of jars covered the table and surrounding shelves; the odor had become a pleasant perfume; and even now, the sight of an old, six-inch, worm-eaten cork brings fragrant memories. 29

The whole group of haemulons was thus brought in review; and whether engaged upon the dissection of the internal organs, the prepa- 30 ration and examination of the bony framework, or the description of the various parts, Agassiz's training in the method of observing facts and their orderly arrangement was ever accompanied by the urgent exhortation not to be content with them.

"Facts are stupid things," he would say, "until brought into connec-   31
tion with some general law."

At the end of eight months, it was almost with reluctance that I left   32
these friends and turned to insects; but what I had gained by this outside experience has been of greater value than years of later investigation in my favorite groups.

STUDY QUESTIONS

1. Why did Agassiz keep saying "Look at your fish!"? What was he trying to teach Scudder?

2. How would you describe the stages in Scudder's process of looking? What happened at each stage?

3. How did Scudder change personally in the course of his "trial"?

4. Do you think Agassiz's method of teaching was effective or wasteful?

Writing Applications

★ **Observing the Familiar: Vegetables and Fruit**

Expect to spend at least an hour at home on this exercise. Select one familiar vegetable or fruit that you have seen and handled many times: a potato, an onion, a tomato, an orange, or an apple. Take this fruit or vegetable as your specimen for study just as Scudder took his fish. You can use a knife and cutting board for inspection and exploring, but nothing else. Moreover, you should also keep to Scudder's restrictions by not talking about your work with anyone else or reading any materials on your subject. Take your time observing, taking notes, and if you wish, making drawings. Prepare a three- to four-page description of your fruit or vegetable that shows you have used *all* your senses in exploring your subject and have discovered *everything* you can about what will become your new intimate friend.

As you work, also write down the stages you find yourself going through in completing this task. When did you become bored? Excited? Angry? Show your awareness of your own inner process the way Scudder did of his.

When you have finished the first draft of your description, read it over and ask yourself the questions that follow. They are meant primarily as a checklist of reminders for revision before completing your final draft. Once you return to class, exchange your paper with a partner and consider these questions a second time as a guide for critiquing one another's work.

1. Did you use all your senses fully? Which ones did you seem to prefer? Which did you neglect?

2. Did you really stay with the task of recording the physical and actual details that you noticed while examining the fruit or vegetable, or did you tend to write more about what you *thought* or had heard about your object? Were you mainly describing the object itself or the images in your mind that you associated with this object? Were you trying so hard to be literary that you forgot to be concrete?

3. Did you spend the time necessary to find the most accurate words to describe taste, texture, and sound sensations?

4. Did you make an exhaustive physical description of the object? Or did you invent diversions from the task such as (a) giving a history of the fruit or vegetable, (b) supplementing a very brief description with an elaborate story, (c) eating it before you were finished, (d) writing a lengthy complaint about the assignment, or (e) insisting there was not much to observe?

5. Did you write down what was going on inside yourself as you wrote—feelings, attitudes, resistances, mood shifts, insights? If you forgot to include mention of your own process, rethink it through and add it now.

STUDENT WRITING EXAMPLE

This observation of a banana is not offered as a model for you to imitate like a recipe. Rather, it is meant to demonstrate how one student became absorbed in her work and solved the problem of *staying sensitive both to her subject and herself at the same time.* Read it as a reminder of what the assignment is asking you to do; then forget it and begin your own assignment.

OBSERVATION OF A BANANA

This fruit is crescent-shaped, and has ridges surrounding its outer surface. At first it looked smooth and rounded, but now I can see it is five-sided. Three of its ridges are further apart. Its shape fits nicely into the palm of my hand and lends itself to being cradled, for it has a resting position about it. It is long and lean, and curves into a happy smile.

The bottom of this fruit has a capped tip. The tip is dark brown in color, and has a protrusion that is scablike in texture. The circumference of this cap is hexagonal, and has an inner growth plate that is circular. This growth plate has several smaller plates, each fitting into the other, decreasing in size.

Emanating from this caplike structure are many hues. As I examine the fruit's color, and look at it longer and longer, I begin to see more and more colors. The different hues blend into tones and hues of yellow, ranging from yellow-green, green, blue-green, burnt umber, burnt sienna, to black. Shadows made by my hand fall on one side of the fruit's surface, changing the shades of yellow to a neutral tone of gray. The opposite side of the fruit is away from direct lamp light, and like the dark side of the moon, it is colorless. In contrast, the surface that is well lighted has a clear, crisp, lemony yellow appearance.

Along the length of the body of the fruit are brown bruise spots. There are different types of bruises on its surface; some are deep pits, and others are merely surface scars, while others are specks that seem to be caused by ripening. A water stain has soiled the green area leaving an irregular ring the color of instant coffee. It is at this point that the body of the fruit blends into its stem. The stem is a thin stalk, short, brown in color, and woodlike in texture. I am reminded of a decaying tree limb.

I feel the fruit in contact with my skin, almost as though I were touching flesh. It feels cool against the greater warmth of my hand. I am curious to know why it is cool, since it has not been refrigerated. I bring it up to my nose to smell it. It has a light springtime fragrance, and smells sweet, mild, and clean.

It takes some measure of force to break open the seal of its protective layer. There is a snapping, then a cracking sound, like the opening of a beverage can. It takes three downward motions to separate the outer layer from its source. This downward movement creates the sound of a zipper opening and closing.

Once inside the fruit itself, I can compare the outer layer of its peel to the inner layer. The outside surface of the fruit is sleek, and smooth, but it's not glossy, nor is it waxed. The inner part of the fruit's peel is fibrous, and pale yellow in color. It has many long threadlike fibrous strands clinging to the interior surface of the fruit. (Oh! I almost took a bite, but then I quickly remembered my purpose.) The edible part of the fruit is covered with thousands of lines. These lines intersect each other in a manner that reminds me of the global lines of longitude and latitude.

I begin to worry as I notice the fruit is starting to turn brown. The longer I study it, and expose it to the air, the faster it ripens. With this thought I begin to rush and forget to observe myself as I take a bite. Then, as though waking, I notice the inner surface of the banana is a deeper shade of cream. I become angry with myself for leaving teeth marks to spoil my view of its surface.

Taking a kitchen knife, I cut off a slice of fruit. It is a nice clean cut, and I can see into its heart. I cut another slice, and another, with each slice yielding the same results: a center holding four tiny brown specks. I make a cut lengthwise to observe the specks from a different angle, and

I see two parallel lines of brown specks coursing the length of fruit. The specks are minute seeds. I taste to see if I can feel them in my mouth. I cannot distinguish their texture from the soft cream of the whole. As I chew, I hear no crunch; in this fruit, there is no need to spit any seeds out. What a wonderful fruit to eat!

Now the banana is gone, transformed into a bloated pressure in my stomach. The peel lies limply across my sticky fingers, draped open like the petals of a flower. I stand up to toss it in the sink, but pause, remembering this is an exercise in observation, to take one last look. I see a brown splinterlike projection surrounded by a small star-shaped fleshy section; it is the last remnant of edible fruit. How fitting it is to start my examination with a crescent-shaped fruit, and to end it with a star.

Observing the Familiar: A Shoe

Often we don't really observe familiar objects that we see and touch every day. Look down at the shoes you are wearing now. Your assignment is to write, in class, a one-paragraph description of your shoes. Employ as many of your senses as you can to give a complete physical description.

When you have finished, hide your shoes while you read what you have written to a classmate. Ask him or her to draw a rough sketch of your shoes while you read. Afterward compare the sketch to your shoes. How close is their impression to the reality of the shoes?

If their impression and your description are far apart, answer the following questions:

1. What did you forget to describe?
2. What did you have trouble communicating?
3. Were you hampered by the lack of a technical vocabulary? Did you omit some of the details you observed because you lacked the right words? Did you attempt some imaginative metaphors, such as "My shoe is a boat"?
4. Did you neglect physical details, concentrating more on memories about the shoes? If so, did interest in your memories distract you from the task of directly perceiving your shoes in present time?

Now write a revised description of your shoes.

★ Observing the Unfamiliar: A Tool

Bring to class some household tool whose function may be unfamiliar and difficult for most people to identify. This could be a cooking implement, a highly specialized tool for some craft, a cosmetic tool, or any interesting item from your kitchen drawer or tool chest. Carry this object to class in a paper sack so that no one else can see it, and hand it to the instructor to put in a box on your arrival in class. Do not discuss what you have brought with anyone else.

Sitting at your desk with your eyes closed, take the tool given you by the instructor or someone assisting. Put the object on your lap under your desk. Spend at least fifteen minutes exploring your subject with your hands, getting to know its shape and texture by touch. Set aside your concerns about how to label your tool, or any worry about its function. Your mind will want to identify and categorize it immediately according to some mental stereotype. "Oh," it will say, "that is just a bottle opener. All bottle openers are the same. I want to work with something else." When this happens, just notice what your mind is doing and go on exploring the object as though you were a child, enjoying its touch, its smell, temperature, and taste (if you dare!). *Remember this is not a guessing game* whose purpose is to label an object, but an opportunity to explore a common object, using your senses to gain information. Get all the information you can without looking. Try even to guess its color. Take mental notes as you go along.

When the instructor gives you the signal, put the tool on top of your desk and open your eyes. Are you surprised? Do you think your exploration of the item would have been as full of discoveries if you had been told what it was?

Now spend at least fifteen minutes observing the visual details of your object and taking notes. Get all the information you can now from seeing; put it together with what you learned without your sight.

Read your notes and show your object to a neighbor. Take turns listening to each other's notes and making suggestions for improvement, based on these questions:

1. Were all senses used?
2. Did he or she forget to mention color or texture or temperature?
3. Was something obvious overlooked or not mentioned?

If you still cannot name the object or determine its function, ask around the room for its owner. See if his or her explanation helps you to see more than you did before, once you have come to understand the purpose of your object's design.

At home, putting all your information together, write a one- to two-page description, consisting of several paragraphs, that shows your full exploration of the object. Organize your information so that it is in a logical order that a reader can follow. In a final paragraph, describe what it was like for you to go through this assignment. Were there different stages in your process? Did you feel frustrated or anxious when you couldn't label your object?

STUDENT WRITING EXAMPLE

STUDY OF AN OBJECT

Julie Kelley

My first reaction to the object was one of disappointment. I knew what it was right away, and I was hoping to experience more of a challenge. I was holding a lid with a screen on it. I thought it was probably the lid of a jar with alfalfa sprouts growing in it, or a jar filled with fresh rosemary and basil, or a jar that was some kind of flour sifter. Moving along, I found that my disappointment didn't last long because I was anxious to get started.

The first words that I jotted down on my notebook were simply, "rough, round, and rim." "Rough" referred to the texture of the screen, "round" expressed the shape of the object, and "rim" was the object itself.

I rubbed the screen with my fingers and decided that it felt just like the screen that covers my grandmother's front porch. As I continued to rub it, my fingers became numb and sore.

I became very irritated as the girl in front of me wouldn't take her object out of her plastic sack and the noise was driving me crazy. I looked at the girl next to me, who was obviously feeling the same way I was, and we both began to laugh. The girl in front of us got the hint and took her object out of the bag.

My observations were very disorganized. I jumped from one thought to the next in no apparent fashion. My next piece of data that I had scribbled was that the rim felt about a half of an inch wide.

At that point, I discovered that the screen popped out of the rim with barely any effort at all. The edge was sharp and I could feel the little tiny tips of every wire. I began to explore the outer rim. I even drew a cross section of what I was feeling. While pushing my fingernail into a space I discovered at the bottom of the rim, I pushed too hard and bent my finger-nail backwards. It was painful. I wanted to close my eyes and go to sleep, but I didn't.

The screen became a very challenging feature. I figured it was about four inches in diameter, but for the life of me I couldn't figure out the pattern that the wires made. I made another drawing. Geometrically speaking, what I drew couldn't have been possible. I became curious enough to use the devious part of my brain to find a solution. I don't know if this was cheating or not, but it felt like it could have been. I pressed my fingers really hard on the screen for a long time, and then I brought my fingers up and looked at the imprint that the screen had left on my fingers. Ah ha! The wires were simply horizontal and vertical. Rather than weaving small individual circles, the manufacturer just made big sheets of horizontal and vertical wires and cut out the desired shapes.

The screen was slightly larger than the diameter of the rim so that it could be pushed into a dome. Yet, too much pressure could make it pop out in the center. I also figured that a person would have to twist the lid one-and-a-half times to get it on a jar snuggly. I figured that out by running my finger up around the ditch in the inside of the rim, using another finger as a marker of the place to where I began.

"Sigh!" That was all I wrote at that moment.

The rim was cool, suggesting to me that maybe it was metal. Aluminum, was my guess. I pictured it silver in color.

Boredom swept over me. I was also feeling tired. Suddenly I got a craving for a chocolate milkshake. Disregarding my desire, I faithfully continued to explore the lid.

Oh my goodness! It took me that long to discover a very prominent feature. On the outside of the rim, all the way around the whole thing, were a lot of little ridges running parallel to one another. How could I have missed those protrusions? I felt embarrassed. I then tried to count the ridges, but they were too small.

The instructor then called, "Time's up!" I was surprised because it didn't feel like thirty minutes to me; it felt much shorter.

My first visual reaction was "Wrong color." The rim was dull gold. It looked old and worn with age. I had pictured it newer looking. My nose could smell it now that it was above my desk. It smelled the way pennies smell when they are held in sweaty palms for a while.

The screen part was silver. Ah! a "Silver Screen." My sense of humor didn't want to sit still anymore. Some of the gold was wearing off, especially in the inside where the pointy screen was scraping it away from people taking it on and off a jar.

I couldn't figure out why the wires didn't unravel. It didn't look like there was anything holding them together. As I tried to figure that out, I became dizzy from staring at it.

The actual shape of the rim was slightly bent, and it wasn't the perfect circle I thought it was.

I then felt mixed emotions, one of happiness because of the silence I felt in the room, and another feeling of nausea because I had put too much perfume on and it was making me sick.

As time passed I began to fidget. The screen was making a popping noise as I pushed it in and out. Before long I realized I was annoying the girl next to me. "Sorry!"

"Bored and tired," was my next entry. Then I looked up as the instructor, who had been out of the room, entered and indicated the experiment was over.

I realized how much had transpired in this time. There were low points and high points, but no matter where I was mentally or emotionally, I always kept writing. And I was surprised the assignment was not as horrible as I had anticipated at the beginning.

Used with permission of Julie Kelley.

Reviewing Observation Skills You've Learned

Write a paragraph beginning with the following statement: In the course of doing these writing exercises, I have learned the following about my observation skills . . .

THE OBSERVATION PROCESS: SENSING, PERCEIVING, THINKING

When you worked with your shoes, your tool, and your fruit or vegetable, you went through a process of collecting data without preconceptions, arranging them in some kind of order, and drawing some conclusions about their patterns and meaning. As you learned in the Introduction, this is the process called inductive reasoning. If we observe our own mental processes as they are involved in tasks of reasoning, we can learn to recognize different parts of the process. This helps us make finer discriminations in tracking their appearance and disappearance, as well as in understanding their potential.

So what *are* the parts of this reasoning process? When we are collecting data without preconceptions, we are *sensing;* when we are arranging them in some kind of order, we are *perceiving;* and when we are drawing conclusions about their patterns and meaning, we are *thinking. Sensing* and *perceiving* are sometimes confused in popular usage; both are used to refer to a process of experiencing new information through the senses from the world outside or inside ourselves. To use computer language, both *perceiving* and *sensing* are used to refer to means of receiving data input. But to fully understand our observation processes, we need to make a distinction between the terms.

Sensing occurs through sense organs such as the eyes and skin. When these organs become activated by stimuli, such as by a bright, warm light, they send this information through the nervous system to the brain. When we sense something, we *feel* it; we feel the presence of something and have a certainty about that presence. When we sense, we do not yet have the words to identify or explain what is happening to us, because in order to find words, we have to think. *And when we start to think, we usually cut ourselves off from our sensations*. It is difficult, if not impossible, to both sense and think at the same time. If someone asks you to go outside and see how warm the day is, you have to stop talking and thinking to consciously feel the air temperature on your face and skin. In order to take a good reading, you need to keep an internal silence.

Perceive comes from the root words *percipere*, meaning to receive, *per* meaning thoroughly, and *capere*, meaning to catch, seize, or hold.

The etymology of this word shows us how perception works. When we perceive something, we catch and hold it in consciousness until we can grasp its meaning. Sensing comes before perceiving. Sensations have to be held in consciousness long enough to be interpreted by perception. This makes perceiving closer to thinking than to feeling. When we perceive something, we use memory to synthesize all our information in preparation for giving it a name.

For example, consider the process we go through when we taste an unfamiliar food, such as Swedish sweet rolls. When we take a first bite, our tastebuds *sense* the new food and then relay to our brain the message "unfamiliar taste." And so we pause to give this new taste another round of sensation, giving it more attention this time. Our nose also may relay "pleasant but unfamiliar fragrance." Now we begin to *perceive,* or to hold these sensations together in awareness in order to interpret (explain) them. The word *spice* may come to mind; we consult our spice memory file, catalogued according to spice characteristics. This taste and smell may be similar to—but yet different from—those of cinnamon and cloves. Should we ask a friend "What spice is in this food?" the reply will be "It's *cardamom.*" We can then put a new experience into our spice memory file under its name for future reference.

Thinking follows perceiving. So what is thinking? Philosopher Alan Watts once said that the word *think* comes from the European word *tong,* which is related to the word *thing.* When we think we *thing-a-fy:* we make "things" of nature and of events with our perceptions. We name, classify, manipulate, and order what we see. Psychologist Jean Piaget defined thinking as "an active process whereby people organize their perceptions of the world."

These definitions are only two of many that have been offered. As you learned in the definition of critical thinking in the Introduction, dictionaries describe more than nineteen different mental operations under the word *thinking.* In this text, our main concern is with thinking in the sense of *conscious problem solving.* A suitable comparison might be to say that the brain is our computer, while thinking is its programming and operation. The question remains as to what or who is the programmer or operator, and that might be best described as our conscious selves.

Following from these definitions, the observation process you've gone through in this chapter's exercises might arbitrarily be divided into the following stages:

1.   We take in our data from sensing.

2.   We perceive in our data patterns of similarities, differences, and identities that suggest categories of order. We decide *what* belongs with *what.*

3.   We draw comparisons in our data and from our memories about what we see and sense.

4.   We apply logical reasoning and standards to the material.

5. We imagine explanations and meanings concerning the data.

6. We assess what is missing and not known, and devise strategies for obtaining more data or explanations if needed.

7. We formulate ideas and words to communicate our discoveries to others.

8. We check for errors in our information, our language, and our form of communication.

BARRIERS TO OBSERVATION

Understanding the stages in the observation process can help us recognize conditions that threaten to hinder the process. For instance, as you may have felt in reading "Look at Your Fish" or in the process of describing your shoes, one problem with careful observation is that it *seems to take so much time*. Our inward experience can move through predictable stages—ranging from interest, to discovery, to communication, to boredom, followed by a clear determination to stop. However, as we have seen, more persistence and concentration can awaken a new cycle of interest, with more discoveries, followed by boredom and restlessness again. Yet, each time the cycle is renewed, deeper and deeper levels of understanding can be achieved. Experiencing—even suffering through—such a process can teach us that we have a far greater capacity to discover than we knew; it can show us that we do not need to depend on outside sources as much as we had assumed and that we *can* become our own most reliable source of information.

So to begin the process of observing, we have to maintain a willingness to spend time and to persist through boredom, restlessness, uncertainty, and discomfort. We also have to cultivate a willingness to listen. We know, from our discussion of the observation process, that sensing requires first listening in silence, then dialogue with our information and thoughts. Here is how Alan Watts explains, in his film *Buddhism, Man, and Nature,* the importance of suspending thinking while we are sensing:

> If you were to hear what anyone else has to say, you sometimes have to stop talking. And thinking is just talking inside your head. So if you are going to have anything to think about, you sometimes have to stop thinking. Just as if you would have anything to talk about, you have to sometimes stop talking and listen. The secret of the Buddhist view of life is to spend some time every day in which you don't think, but just watch. In which you don't form any ideas about life, but look at it. Listen to it. Smell it. Feel it.

This brings up something else that can get in the way of clear observation: undirected thinking. Undirected thinking functions like a radio that broadcasts on and on by itself. Yet, in order to get sensory input, we have to shut the thing off. As we have mentioned, conscious directed thinking organizes, compares, arranges, categorizes, and produces from perceptual experience. On the other hand, *undirected* thinking—such as daydreaming or free associating, which says, "This reminds me of this, which reminds me of that"—is a kind of false or pseudothinking that will operate even without purpose or conscious consent. At times it may even be extremely difficult to turn off, except through a lot of physical activity or some form of meditative practice. How many times have you said, "I just couldn't stop thinking and go to sleep"? In any case, we cannot engage in active directed or concentrated thinking unless we can succeed in turning off the pseudothinking mechanism. If we forget to consciously operate our computer, it will still go on like a robot with no one in control.

Undirected thinking will not only tend to talk to itself, but also to mechanically evaluate and categorize incoming data. And unless held back by our will, undirected thinking will not wait for sufficient information before rushing into evaluations and decisions. Samuel Scudder, you will remember, concluded he had learned *everything* possible about his fish after the first ten minutes.

But persistence in observing and sensing may reveal that we are seeing something totally *new* for which we have no established pigeonhole in our mental filing system. To give a historical example, what we now call quasars (an acronym for quasi-stellar radio sources) were originally categorized as stars within our own galaxy. However, further spectroscopic observations showed them to be immense distances away from the earth, far out of our galaxy, but with such vast outpourings of energy that they are visible to us. They had been incorrectly categorized as stars, misplaced under a familiar category. Thus, a new name had to be invented to reflect their nature (which still remains ambiguous to us).

Discovering new information through observation may lead to discomfort, so we may resist recognizing new information. In ordinary life, when new information suggests that we may have to exert ourselves to study the situation more deeply, our first reaction may be one of inertia. We try first to see if this new data can be assimilated into old categories of experience: "I haven't been able to get a decent job since I left high school; maybe I just need more luck."

If a problem persists, then we are forced to review the situation. We have to ask whether this problem really does fit into our existing mental scheme of categories, explanations, and solutions. In this case, the young man who wants a decent job may have to waive wishing for better luck and consider more training or college. When such problems become insistent enough to interrupt our lives, we are forced to rearrange or erase what we already know, to accommodate new data into new frames of reference.

Let's look again at Jean Piaget's definition of thinking as "an active process whereby people organize their perceptions of the world." At one point he described this process as involving both *assimilation* (or the simple addition of new information to old) and *accommodation* (when

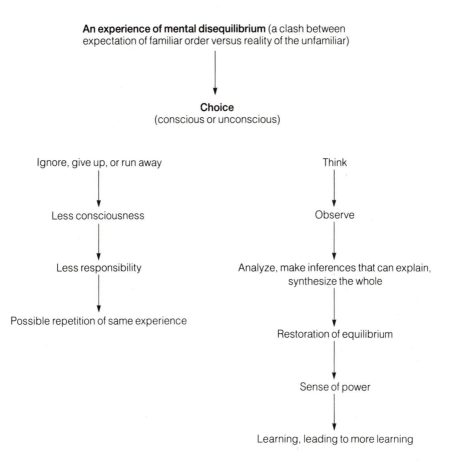

An experience of mental disequilibrium (a clash between expectation of familiar order versus reality of the unfamiliar)

Choice
(conscious or unconscious)

Ignore, give up, or run away   Think

Less consciousness   Observe

Less responsibility   Analyze, make inferences that can explain,
                                          synthesize the whole

Possible repetition of same experience

                                          Restoration of equilibrium

                                          Sense of power

                                 Learning, leading to more learning

FIGURE 1.2

The Thinking Process

we must change our intellectual organization in order to adjust to a new idea). When our mental scheme of things cannot grasp or easily categorize some new data, we undergo a mental sense of disequilibrium or confusion. This is an extremely uncomfortable feeling that we may not recognize as coming from the learning problem itself. Indeed, we may look for someone or something else to blame for our discomfort. We are only aware of a strong desire to get rid of this awful, uncomfortable feeling. But if we persist and succeed in concentrating on the actual problem, we will find an accommodation of understanding that will restore our equilibrium. And this restoration will not occur if we run away from the problem, but only when we return to actually confront it. Seen from another perspective, the mental discomfort of disequilibrium can actually help us persist in our efforts to find truth, for the reward of having arrived at truth is a sense of equilibrium (see Figure 1.2).

CONSCIOUS PROBLEM SOLVING
THROUGH OBSERVING

Wizard of the Upper Amazon is the true story of a Peruvian boy who was captured by a remote tribe of forest Indians in South America. In the years he lived with them, he was trained with the others in observation skills. Keen use of the senses was essential for their survival. Since they hunted in the jungle, they needed alert vision to spot game through its thick plant growth and camouflage, as well as acute hearing and smell to follow in pursuit. Part of their education came from scouting and hunting stories shared around the campfire in the evenings. Each would share what he had learned about their surroundings that day: where a tree was bearing new fruit, where a jaguar was seen near the howler monkeys, where droppings on the ground indicated the presence of partridges.

From F. Bruce Lamb, *Wizard of the Upper Amazon: The Story of Manuel Cordova-Rios.* Berkeley: North Atlantic Books, 1971.

The process of gathering and organizing new information also requires the discovery of the right words with which to communicate what we have learned. We may even have to invent new words, as in the case of quasars. We may have to spend considerable time with dictionaries, the encyclopedia, even in questioning other people. And again, this will require will and persistence over a temptation to conclude "That's not really what I mean, but I'll just put down any old thing and get it over with."

Clearly, all stages of the observation process find their major barriers *within ourselves.* Overcoming such barriers can only be managed through a thorough and conscious awareness of their existence exactly as they appear. When we are *aware* of our own forms of apathy or resistance and when we *acknowledge* such feelings, they tend to lose their power over us. But when we ignore or fight our resistances, they can become more powerful than ever. Only the rewards of achievement can sometimes pull us through all the temptations to get off course.

THE REWARDS OF SKILLED OBSERVATION

Sensitive, accurate observing requires an alertness to inner processes and a carefully built foundation of self-understanding. Anyone who does creative work—whether in writing, in the sciences, in the arts, or in the ordinary tasks of work and living—possesses these skills.

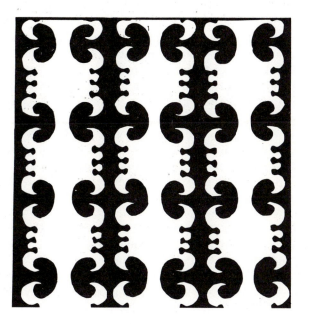

FIGURE 1.3

Can you see in this design the interaction between positive and negative space described in "The Innocent Eye"? Is either less important than the other?

The following reading, "The Innocent Eye," is taken from a book on art design. It suggests what you may have discovered for yourself through the writing exercises you completed in this chapter: that although observing may require self-control and patience, it is nevertheless a process that can lead us to rapture, power, and wonder (see Figure 1.3).

THE INNOCENT EYE

Dorr Bothwell

Creative observation of our surroundings revives in us a sense of 1 the wonder of life. Much of this discovery involves the recovery of something that we all once had in childhood. When we were very young we were all artists. We all came into this world with the doors of perception wide open. Everything was a delightful surprise. Everything, at first, required the slow, loving touch of our tongues and our hands. Long before we could speak we knew the comfort of our mother's warm body, the delightful feel of a furry toy. Smooth and rough surfaces, things cold and hot surprised and enchanted us. Touch by touch we built up our store of tactile impressions, keenly sensed in minute detail.

Later on, this tactile sensing was transferred to our eyes, and we 2 were able to "feel" through the sense of vision things beyond the grasp of our hands. This kind of seeing was not the rapid sophisticated eye sweep of the well-informed. This kind of seeing was a slow, uncritical examination in depth. The more we looked the more lovely and surprising things appeared, until we were pervaded by that wordless thrill which is the sense of wonder.

None of us has lost our store of tactile memories. Nor have we lost 3 our sense of wonder. All that has happened is that we have substituted identifying and labeling, which can be done very rapidly, for the tactile sort of feel-seeing which requires much more time and concentration. For example, if you were asked to look at the edge of your desk and estimate its length, it would only take you a few seconds to flick your eyes back and forth and say it is so many inches long. But suppose you were asked to run the tip of your finger along the edge of the desk and count every tiny nick? You would press your finger along the edge and move it very, very slowly, and your eye would move no faster than your finger. This slow, concentrated way of feeling and seeing is the first step towards regaining our sense of wonder.

There was a time when man moved no faster than his feet or the 4 feet of some animal that could carry him. During that period the artistic or creative spirit seemed to have free expression. Today, in order to be creative and yet move smoothly and efficiently through our fast-paced world, we must be able to function on two different speed levels. The mistakes we have made, often with tragic results, is to try to do *all* our living at the speed our machines have imposed upon us.

In order to live at this speed we must scan the surface of things, 5 pick out salient aspects, disregard secondary features; and there is certainly nothing wrong in this if we are driving on a busy freeway. But when we allow this pressure to invade every aspect of our life, we begin to "lose touch," to have a feeling that we are missing something, and we are hungry for we don't know what. When that happens, we have begun to suffer from aesthetic malnutrition. Fortunately, the cure for this condition is very pleasant, and although it takes a little self-discipline at the beginning, the results are worth the effort.

When we see as design artists, we become especially aware of the 6 interaction between positive and negative space. In architecture we are suddenly aware of the spaces between the windows, at the ballet we notice how the spaces between the dancers open and close, and in music we realize that rhythm is made by the shapes of silence between the notes.

Everywhere we look we see this principle in action. Trees are not 7 silhouetted against blank air, but hold blue spangles between their leaves while branches frame living shapes of sky. Space seems to be pulled between the leaves of a fern. We delight in the openings between the petals of a flower or the spokes of a wheel. This endless exchange between form and space excites us. Once more we feel in touch with our world; our aesthetic sense is being fed and we are comforted. . . .

We may have been taught that butterflies are lovely and toads are 8 ugly, so we admire the butterfly and shrink away from the toad without really examining it to find out if what we had been taught is true. Or we are taught that flowers are good and weeds are bad, so we pull up the latter without a glance. To the artist's eye there is no good or bad. There is just the inappropriate. In the garden, weeds are not appropriate, but in the vacant lot they offer a world of enchantment. And after we have learned to see the beauty in weeds, even though we have to pull them out of the garden, we can first admire their design.

When no preconceived ideas keep us from looking and we take all 9 the time we need to really "feel" what we see—when we are able to do that—the universe opens up and we catch our breath in awe at the incredible complexity of design in the humblest things. It is only when this happens that we regain our sense of wonder.

> From Dorr Bothwell and Marlys Mayfield, *Notan: The Dark Light Principle of Design*. New York: Dover, 1991. Used with permission of Dorr Bothwell.

STUDY QUESTIONS

1. What do you think of the statement, "When we were young we were all artists"?

2. Do you understand what the author is talking about when she speaks of the "aesthetic malnutrition" that comes from the high-speed living that makes us "lose touch"?

3. Describe what is meant by the "interaction of positive and negative space."

4. Explain what is meant by the statement, "To the artist's eye, there is no good or bad. There is just the inappropriate." Did you ever find, in the course of writing your descriptions, that you were so turned off by your judgments of an object that you had trouble contacting the object fully? Did you find any change in your attitude as you continued to work for a long period with the same object? Have you ever experienced the same thing with

people, moving from prejudice at the start to appreciation through sustained contact?

CHAPTER SUMMARY

1. Changing our critical thinking habits requires us to first observe our own thinking process so we can recognize our strengths and our weaknesses.

2. Careful observation can help us see details that contain the key to unlocking problems or arriving at insights. It can also help us discover new knowledge.

3. Observation is a process of sensing, perceiving, and thinking. Sensing is collecting data through the sense organs. Perceiving is holding sense data in consciousness until we grasp its meaning. Thinking is conscious problem solving.

4. Careful observation requires us to stay conscious, take our time, give full attention, suspend thinking in an attitude of listening, both assimilate and accommodate new knowledge, become aware of emerging insights, and persist in spite of boredom or discomfort. It requires us to face our own barriers and resistances.

5. The rewards of cultivating observation skills are self-understanding, creativity, rapture, power, and wonder.

Chapter Quiz

Rate each of the following statements as *true* or *false*. Justify your answer with an example or explanation to prove and illustrate your understanding. *Do not omit this part of the test. True/false* answers can be guessed. But when you defend your answer by example or explanation, you demonstrate not only your memory and understanding but also a higher order thinking skill of applying what you have learned to life. The first question is answered for you.

False   1. Observation skills are learned mainly through book learning.

   Support for Answer. On the contrary, observation is learned from participation, which is more active and spontaneous than reading. Samuel Scudder learned observing through the active coaching of his teacher Agassiz, as well as from his own efforts, curiosity, and persistence in studying his fish.

_____   2. The standard academic study of all of the physical sciences requires observation skills whether in the field or laboratory.

_____ 3. In thinking, the correctness of our conclusions usually depends on the clarity of our perceptions.

_____ 4. Observation skills can be developed by observing how you observe.

_____ 5. An insight is an experience of understanding that can occur spontaneously after we observe something intently for a while. One illustration of this experience is the story of Archimedes, who, while in his bath, discovered the means of measuring the volume of an irregular solid by the displacement of water.

_____ 6. Agassiz was simply too busy to give his student all the assistance he needed.

_____ 7. _Perception_ and _sensation_ are synonyms.

_____ 8. It is difficult to feel sensation and to think at the same time. If we want to feel whether or not a pair of new shoes fits properly, we have to pay attention.

_____ 9. Scientific observation can bring us new knowledge that does not fit our expectations or our familiar categories.

_____ 10. _Assimilation,_ according to Piaget, is an experience of easily understanding something that readily fits into our preexisting schemes or world view.

_____ 11. The word _thinking,_ according to the dictionary, has only one meaning.

Writing Applications

First Option

Describe an experience in which your safety, welfare, or survival depended upon your ability to observe a situation or problem clearly. This could involve a danger in city life, in camping or sports, or perhaps a life decision _where observation skills were crucial._ Write from three to five pages, telling your story as a narrative. Remember, the theme that should tie your story together is the theme of observation. Be sure to note and emphasize in your story where you observed and where you did not, and what the consequences were.

Second Option

Making use of memory and any written or photo journals you might have, write a travel story as a narrative in three to five typed pages. (See Carl Franz's story on pages 42–46 for a model.) Emphasize how this experience affected your senses. Strive to make your audience see and feel as you did. If you wish, adopt the point of view of a travel advisor (as Franz does), by recommending what a traveler might do or avoid doing when traveling the same route.

Review of Assignment Guidelines

1. *Form:* A story or narrative
2. *Theme:* (a) How observation skills helped me survive
   (b) A travel account conveying sensory information
3. *Length:* Three to five typed pages

Readings

THE ULTIMATE TRACK

Tom Brown, Jr.
William Jon Watkins

The account of Tom Brown, Jr.'s growing up in the "wilderness" of New Jersey is taken from the first chapter of his book. Brown now has a tracking, nature, and wilderness survival school in the same state. As you read, ask yourself, how does tracking teach observation skills?

Stalking Wolf was an Apache tracker. He had come to New Jersey   1
to be near his son who was stationed there. His grandson, Rick, was my best friend, and Stalking Wolf taught both of us how we could teach ourselves to track, to stalk, to live in the woods, and to survive there. He gave us the questions that would lead us to our answers, but he never told us an answer. He taught me to see and to hear, to walk and to remain silent; he taught me how to be patient and resourceful, how to know and how to understand. He taught me to see invisible things from the trail that all action leaves around itself. He taught me how to teach myself the mystery of the track. . . .

The vision of the world given me by Stalking Wolf has become a   2
window into time. The more tracks I see, the clearer the picture of the animal becomes until I can see him moving as he moved a minute, an hour, a month before I came along. When the tracks stop, I can still see the animal, how it paused, how it rested its body, where it put its paws. The animal is there before me almost real enough to touch, fixed in time

by the impression of its track. I see from the track the motion of his feet, the motion of his body; I see the animal itself laying down the mystery of its coming and going. . . .

I was in awe of Stalking Wolf from the beginning. He was of medium 3 height and lean, like his grandson Rick, but his features were classically Indian. There were centuries of dead civilization in his face, and his eyes seemed to be looking at things very far away that distracted him. He seemed to be watching some complex totality that absorbed most of his attention.

It was years before I realized how far his perceptions extended, 4 how much he saw in a glance, how much he heard, how incredibly much he *knew.* But it was clear from the instant I first met him that he knew more of what was worth knowing than anyone I would ever meet. Rick idolized him, and the longer I knew Stalking Wolf, the more I understood why.

Stalking Wolf was very old, and he drifted into reveries that made 5 him seem as if he might be senile when I first met him. But I realized later, when I had seen with amazement how keen his senses were, that he had simply gone inside of himself for a moment to check his perceptions against the pattern of the world. Only after he had taught me how to be silent did I realize that he was stopping his own motion so he could tell the disturbances around him from his own.

It is a silence out of which the tracker listens for the scolding of 6 birds deeper in the woods, or the sound that crackles the branches against the rustle of the wind. Only by silence and rapt attention can anyone hope to feel the ripples in the flow of life in the woods, which spread outward from an intrusion or a disturbance. The scolding of a jay will put every bird within earshot on edge. . . .

We lived on a mixture of what Stalking Wolf had told us and per- 7 sonal conjecture, which we believed to be the True Indian Way of Life. We worked toward this ideal in everything we did. Indian braves were always fit. We rowed, a heavy rowboat, against the tide in the Toms River and cut wood every day. Indian braves were trained as warriors. We took Kung Fu with a neighbor and practiced our kicks continually in front of the cabin we built in the Pines. The life we led kept us fit. Walking, running, crawling all day long, or sitting motionless as a tree for hours at a time waiting to see something miraculous toned us better than any planned system of exercises could have. And we tracked constantly once Stalking Wolf showed us how to learn the secrets. Before that, we watched.

We watched *Everything:* animals, birds, plants, insects, weather, 8 sunlight, stars, fossils, people, hundreds of things. We watched the animals at first. We sat in swamps, in the woods, near lakes, by streams, along the river bank, any place an animal might live. And we waited. And waited. When we were lucky, we saw something special. When we didn't, we saw something else.

And then we learned about tracking. We tracked everything that 9
moved and some things that didn't. We tracked ourselves. We tracked
other people. We tracked animals, cars, snails. We no longer had to wait
for nature to come to us. Before we learned to track, our wandering had
been guided only by the range of our memory. We went places we were
familiar with. But once we could track, we could always backtrack ourselves if we got lost, and year by year our range increased.

From my literal back yard, we went deeper and deeper into the 10
woods until, by the time we were sixteen, there was not a place in the
Pine Barrens where I could be lost. We stayed away for longer and
longer periods of time as our parents got used to our spending every
spare moment studying nature. We kept up our schoolwork for the most
part, and we stayed out of trouble, except for being continually late
and forever out of reach. We were, if you don't count lies of necessity,
model boys for that time and place.

With every track, Stalking Wolf would tell us about the animal that 11
made it, the family it belonged to, and why its track was the way it was.
Why the Indians walked like the fox with one foot in front of the other
in a straight line. Why the groundhog with its broad chest could never
make the in-line tracks of a fox. This did not occur overnight, but over
months and often years. Tracking became a preoccupation with us. We
tracked everywhere we went. Whenever we watched anything, we always went back later and looked at its tracks to match them up with
what we had seen the animal do.

Rick liked to track, and he was a good tracker, but tracking came to 12
me with amazing ease. I worked at it, but it was always a joy to do. I
never tired of it. Rick was into stalking and watching nature more than
tracks themselves. I wanted to be able to do what Stalking Wolf had
done, to be able to look at the tracks and recreate what happened as
surely as if I was looking back in time.

It took a long time of constant effort to learn to do that. We tracked 13
everywhere. On the two-lane macadam road that was the biggest highway short of the Parkway, there was a butcher store where the owner
smoked his own meat. Rick and I used to go there and learn his techniques after we got involved in taxidermy, but we liked this place especially because it had a bare spot of soft ground near the doorway that
never completely dried out. The sets of tracks put down there were
endless.

We would sit off to the side and watch someone walk in, and then 14
we would rush over and follow his tracks marking where he stopped
or turned or tied his shoes. We would draw the print and mark it with
comments like, "Limp from hurt foot, two weeks later," and "Fat men
toe out."

When we had fixed the track and the person in our minds, we would 15
smooth out the dirt and wait for the next person to come along. When a

woman went storming in with a complaint and came back out mollified, the difference in her tracks was obvious when we ran over to look. The long wedging plumes of dirt in front of the pointed toes going in and the firm even stride with clearly defined prints coming back out could not have contrasted more.

It took us years before we could do it with great precision, but we were improving and we were weaving everything we learned into everything else we did. When we watched the animals, we went over and tracked what we had just watched. When we walked back along our own trail, we followed our incoming tracks and watched how much they had deteriorated. Sometimes we would stop at every change in the steady walking pace of the tracks and go over what we did at that point on the way in and why.

We intentionally made footprints when we came to a new kind of soil and put little sticks in them to measure their deterioration. We checked our past footprints every time we passed them to see what changes the weather and time had brought about in them. We would spend a whole day or so watching a track deteriorate, just putting a footprint in the ground and sitting there watching it dry out and go grain by grain into the oblivion of the wind. Sometimes we put sticks and string around the tracks to keep the animals off them, and watched the way they changed over a period of months.

We did this over a period of years, track by track, in every kind of soil we could find, and in each soil we watched for a change in the tracks associated with every change in weather. When we were waiting for some creature to show itself, getting ourselves into position so we were part of the landscape for a long time before the creature came out of his burrow, we would make a print in the ground with a deer foot we carried with us and watch how it deteriorated over an hour or two.

We put another print down near it every few minutes to see how much difference there was between the two and if they went through the same changes. We did that kind of thing constantly. Wherever we were, if there was nothing else worth watching, we watched the tracks change until we could see some of the minute variations that Stalking Wolf could see.

We learned to track and stalk, we learned to live in the wilderness and then learned to survive in it. We learned, by living, how to live. We became men and brothers in the woods. We came of age in the woods, and we came alive. Old Stalking Wolf guided us. This book is the story of how we did it and how I have applied what Stalking Wolf taught me.

From Tom Brown, Jr. and William Jon Watkins, *The Tracker*. New York: Berkley Books, 1978. Used with permission of Connie Clausen Associates, agent for Tom Brown, Jr.

STUDY QUESTIONS

1. Explain what Stalking Wolf taught the author about the role of silence in observing.

2. Explain the kind of "seeing" that the author claims he could obtain from a track.

3. Brown describes the days he spent with his friend Rick as times of *watching* everything and keeping as physically fit as Indian braves. Do these activities reinforce one another? Why or why not?

4. Why did the boys take such interest in the ground near the doorway of the butcher store?

5. Comment on the concluding statement: "We learned, by living, how to live. . . . We came of age in the woods, and we came alive."

BUS SERVICE

Carl Franz

Travel in unfamiliar regions can heighten our perceptions, enabling us to see and feel things freshly and intensely. Franz's guide to Mexico has long been a popular informal guide for shoestring travelers. He writes for those who want contact with the country on its own terms rather than travel insulated by a jet plane in and out of Acapulco. As you read, notice how your senses are affected by his description.

"Boy, when you cross that Rio Grande, *you are in a different country!*"—Texas Border Patrolman

1   Travelers who use buses often will find that they become totally immersed in Mexico. There is no other method, short of walking through the country, to establish such close and continual contact with the people.

2   The cost of traveling by bus is remarkably low. The expense of operating your car will buy an incredible number of bus tickets. . . .

3   There are two types of bus service: second class and first class. Second class buses vary from relatively comfortable to positively backbreaking, depending on where you're going and the age of the bus. In recent years, many companies have begun to replace their old second class buses with newer models and first class retirees. Once a bus becomes too funky for first class passengers to tolerate, it is sent into sec-

ond class service. (From there the only place for it to go is into the junkyard or over a cliff.)

As the ancient wrecks are gradually replaced, some of the color and 4 excitement has gone out of second class bus travel, but enough remains to overwhelm most tourists when they ride one of these mobile adventures.

The initial shock of being crammed into a rusty tin box with 50 5 other people, a variety of market goods and domestic animals, soon moderates to a feeling of warm camaraderie.

You smilingly agree to a woman's request that you hold her baby 6 while she whips up a few *tacos* from ingredients extracted from a greasy piece of newspaper. When she's managed to assemble her lunch she takes the baby back and offers you a rag for the mess on your lap.

Beads of sweat are breaking out on your upper lip but the window 7 is frozen shut by years of rust. You take a deep breath or two and find a *taco* under your nose. You've been invited to eat.

You want to decline the invitation, but from the thrusting motions 8 she is making with the *taco*, it is clear that it would be grossly impolite to refuse. No matter, it turns out to be your favorite: steamed goat head with lots of chili pepper. The air you suck in through tightly pursed lips sounds like ripping cloth and you attempt to cover your embarrassment at reacting to the pepper by staring out the window.

Through tear-filled eyes, you gaze over a thousand foot precipice, 9 but the *taco*, stuck halfway down your throat, blocks a scream of fear.

The lurching of the bus is considerable, very similar to that of a 10 boat foundering on a storm-tossed sea. The ringing in your ears almost drowns out the voice behind the hand that is holding a crude pottery mug under your nose. You look up, eyes filled with a plea for mercy, but the smiling face insists. You tip the mug back, determined to do a chug-a-lug and have done with it. It is *pulque*, the fermented sap of the *maguey* plant, and it is distinctly slimy. It hits your stomach like warm mustard water.

Your apparently experienced manner of tossing down the *pulque* 11 brings admiring remarks from other people jammed in nearby. They appreciate the fact that you're trying to be sociable and to show this appreciation, they contribute little delicacies they're bringing home from market. A piece of deep-fried pig skin, a cactus fruit, some incredibly sour berries and two old *tortillas* with something brown smeared on them are offered up for your enjoyment.

You are just about to go under when the bus lurches to a stop. 12 Everyone piles out to see what's gone wrong and you gratefully stagger into the fresh mountain air.

A front tire has blown, the second flat of the trip, and there doesn't 13 seem to be another spare. After a quick look at the other tires, the driver decides to remove one of the rear duals and put it on the front.

As he does this, his assistants, a motley collection of boys about eight years old, fill the leaking radiator with water from a nearby ditch. They're using one beer bottle and a leaky oil can so they have to make several trips.

When the repairs are finished, everyone crowds back into the bus   14 and in the confusion you lose your seat. You're grateful, however, because you can now assume a position in the aisle near the front door. The body of the bus is so low that you have to stand with your neck slightly bent. Every really bad bump gets you a crack on the back of your skull. At least there is air to breath—since half of the windshield and the entire door are missing.

When you've settled into a more or less tolerable slouch, you begin   15 to take a new interest in the driver and the road ahead. Before entering the mountains, the road had been reasonable. Now, however, with occasional boulders to dodge, half filled washouts, and vertical drops of hundreds of feet just scant inches from the edge of the road, you wonder seriously if the bus will make it.

The driver is shifting like a madman; something is wrong with the   16 clutch and he's having trouble on the steeper grades. You notice anxiously that the brake pedal goes very close to the floor when he throws his weight on it. You wonder then about the motto painted on the front bumper, the one you and your friends had laughed about before you left: "Guide Me God, For I Am Blind."

It's anyone's guess just how much is getting through those opaque   17 sunglasses and the heavily decorated windshield to the driver's eyes. The garlands of plastic flowers, intertwined with blinking Christmas tree lights, have sagged so low that he has to lean forward to peer over them on particularly tight corners.

A large crucifix is mounted between the two front windshields and   18 each point of the cross lights up to correspond with a particular gear. As he shifts, you follow the lights: white . . . green . . . red . . . red . . . green . . . white. The ceiling is plastered with an unlikely assortment of faded pictures. The Virgin Mary peers from between an old Marilyn Monroe magazine photo and a rather obscene playing card.

In addition, a variety of dangling objects, evidently amulets and   19 charms, swing in crazily distracting patterns in front of the driver, occasionally whacking him on the forehead. Between shifts he idly fondles the gearshift knob, a blindly staring doll baby head that winks conspiratorially at each bump. Before you can determine the significance of this macabre object, the bus arrives at your destination and you gratefully jump off.

Because second class bus rides that last more than a few minutes   20 invariably become social affairs, it's nice to have something to offer people who offer something to you. This can be nothing more than a piece of candy, a cigarette or a turn with a newspaper.

It is not customary to offer your seat to anyone standing unless they 21
are ill or very old. This conflicts with what most of us had drummed
into our heads as children, but standing for hours in a bouncing hot bus
can do a great deal of attitude changing. In most cases, you'll find that
after you've offered a lady your seat, she takes it gratefully and then
gets off within the next mile. You then continue standing as some guy
elbows past you and drops into the vacant spot with a big sigh of relief.

If you don't feel like giving up your seat, it is polite to offer to hold 22
something for people who are standing. Children seem to be the most
common bundle, though you may be given a chicken or a bag of groceries.

Should the cozy atmosphere get to be too much for your stomach, 23
ask the driver or his accomplice for permission to ride on the roof or
rear bumper. The roof is not only much safer than the bumper but offers
a better view with less chance of fume poisoning. The only time I've
ever driven a fast car in Mexico, I was passed by a second class bus
traveling at over 80 mph. This wasn't unusual, nor were the three young
men on the rear bumper. The one reading a comic book, however, *without
holding on*, seemed abnormally *blasé*.

Whenever a bus slows down, someone will be there selling cake, 24
tacos, sandwiches, pop, beer and fruit. Vendors will often board the bus
and sell their wares between stops.

Most of this food is relatively good, but it is wise to be especially 25
cautious of greasy food while bus riding. We have found that almost
every problem we have had with diarrhea or upset stomach occurred
after eating something greasy. If you get sick on a bus, it is a real hassle.
I always carry a handy supply of emergency medicines, at the very minimum some type of pills or liquid . . . to prevent uncontrollable diarrhea.

If you absolutely must request an unscheduled stop, the bus driver will oblige, though perhaps with a ribald comment.

In addition to regular vendors, bus passengers are the favorite tar- 26 gets for a variety of enterprising hucksters, offering everything from Salvation to Kleenex. They often work in cooperation with the driver, who allows them aboard during regular stops or picks them up along the way, giving them a long enough ride to reel off their pitch.

The best are groups of musicians; they pile onto the bus with beat- 27 up guitars, accordions and flutes and bang out a few discordant tunes as a hat or tin can is passed for donations. . . .

Deaf mutes selling miniature key chain screwdrivers and sign lan- 28 guage cards are also common. They have it down to a profitable science: they prefer buses that are making five minute stops as most of the passengers stay aboard. The deaf mute hustles down the aisle, dropping the item for sale in each person's hand or lap. The card invariably translates as "Give generously." Once he's reached the rear of the bus he starts back, collecting donations. If you don't want a pot metal miniature screwdriver or are just tired of all the deaf mutes, hand it back or put it on the seat beside you. They seldom argue.

In addition to musicians and mutes you'll often see men selling 29 books on medicinal herbs (some are good). Other people may give short impassioned speeches, recite epic poems or gasp out a heart-rending tale of woe that ends with the inevitable open palm.

You may be offered merchandise rather than an appeal for charity. 30 Regional variations can be very interesting: homemade molasses in *tequila* bottles, honey, bottles of *rompope* (like alcoholic eggnog), bags of trimmed sugar cane, live iguanas and armadillos, birds, beadwork, guitars, Huichol Indian God's Eyes and other irresistibles. It's a far cry from the Greyhound and "Please do not speak to the operator while the coach is in motion."

From Carl Franz, *The People's Guide to Mexico.* Santa Fe, N.M.: John Muir Publications, 1986. Used with permission of John Muir Publications.

STUDY QUESTIONS

1. Does the idea of traveling by bus through Mexico interest you, or would you rather drive in your own car or go first class? Defend your answer.

2. Notice how the author describes intense or startling sensory experiences. Beginning with the sense of taste, describe what details affect you and how.

3. One critic of this excerpt said the author stereotypes Mexicans and is condescending, almost racist, in his attitude. What details

of the story might have led him to this conclusion? Explain whether you agree or disagree with this criticism.

4. U.S. visitors to third world countries often notice a different attitude toward time. Delays and inconveniences are not causes for anger and frustration, as they are with us. Life just goes on with as much interest for everyone regardless of what happens. How do you see this different time sense influencing the events in this story? How does this different time attitude affect the senses?

5. Have you ever suffered hardships on a journey that later turned into a good travel story? Write down this story in one paragraph to share with a small class group. Emphasize your senses in your description.

For Further Reading

The following works deal with the training and exercise of observation skills:

Castaneda, Carlos. *The Teachings of Don Juan: A Yaqui Way of Knowledge.* Berkeley: University of California Press, 1968.

———. *A Separate Reality: Further Conversations with Don Juan.* New York: Simon & Schuster, 1971.

Darwin, Charles. *The Voyage of The Beagle.* New York: New American Library, 1972.

Fossey, Dian. *Gorillas in the Mist.* Boston: Houghton Mifflin, 1983.

Mowat, Farley. *Never Cry Wolf.* New York: Bantam, 1963.

Schneider, Meir. *Self-Healing: My Life and Vision.* New York and London: Routledge & Kegan Paul, 1987.

Shah, Idries. *Tales of the Dervishes.* New York: E. P. Dutton, 1970.

Suzuki, Shunryu. *Zen Mind, Beginner's Mind.* New York: Weatherhill, 1980.

CHAPTER

Word Skills

"I liked it because you can read it with both the TV and the
radio on."

Used with permission of Richard Guindon.

Word skills go together with observation skills. Observations must be communicated through words, and finding the right words takes considerable thinking—as you search through memory, consult a dictionary, and interpret and apply dictionary information. This chapter combines observation, word skills, and thinking, and it should be studied in close conjunction with Chapter 1.

This chapter cannot tell you everything there is to know about word skills, but when you have finished it you should feel more aware of the thinking process involved in word selection and comprehension, be more alert to word confusion, and better understand how definition study can clarify thinking. You will also see how all these skills are basic to developing critical thinking, and especially to the study of this book.

Discovery Exercises

A COLLABORATIVE LEARNING OPPORTUNITY

A Definition of *Word*

Word comes from the Indo-European root *wer,* meaning to speak. A *word* is therefore a sound or symbol that communicates meaning. Explain, with examples, how words convey meaning. What is your definition of *meaning?*

Words Matching Senses

This exercise requires reading, then discussion and writing. You will be working on this assignment with four people. Take turns reading this selection aloud. Then answer the study questions with one student taking notes to report back to the whole class in a general discussion.

THE HOT SPRING

Barry Lopez

*This reading is the second chapter in a short book of lyric prose that is the first of a trilogy. (*River Notes *was the second, and the third is yet to be published.) Barry Lopez is best known for his book* Arctic Dreams *(1986) for which he received the National Book Award.*

I.

The man would set off late in the spring, after the dogwood had 1
bloomed, in the blue '58 Chevy pickup with the broken taillight and the
cracked Expando mirrors. He would take a thin green sleeping bag and
a blue tarpaulin, a few dishes and a one-burner stove. He would take his
spoon and only cereal to eat and tea to drink. He would take no books,
no piece of paper to write on.

He would stop only for gas and would pick up no hitchhikers. He 2
would drive straight through on the two-lane, blacktop roads, cracked
and broken with the freeze of last winter, without turning the radio on.
He would lift his damp buttocks from the hot naugahyde seat and let
the wind, coming in through the window that was stuck halfway down,
cool him.

It would take seven hours to drive the 278 miles. First, over the 3
mountains, past the great lava flows at the ridge, past the slopes of
black obsidian glass, down into the sweet swamp of thick air in the pon-
derosa forest.

He would drive out then into the great basin over arroyos and 4
across sage flats dotted with juniper and rabbit brush, past the fenced
squares marked Experimental Station where the government was trying to grow crested wheat grass, trying to turn the high desert into
grassy fields for bony Herefords with vacant eyes. He would see few
cows. He would see, on a long stretch of road, a golden eagle sitting on
a fence post.

There would be more space between the towns and more until 5
there were no towns at all, only empty shacks, their roof ridges bowed,
their doors and windows gone.

He would come around the base of another range of mountains, slip 6
down on the southeastern side and drive on a one-lane dirt road along
the edge of the alkaline desert for twenty miles until he came to the hot
spring. There he would stop. He would stop the truck, but he would
leave the motor running to keep the engine cool. He would always arrive by one in the afternoon.

II.

He inhaled the tart, sulphurous fumes rising up from the green 7
reeds, the only bit of green for miles. He watched the spiders spinning
webs in the wire grass and the water bugs riding the clots of yellow
bubbles. He stared at the bullet-riddled walls of tin that surrounded the
sandy basin where the water collected.

When he had seen these things, that they had weathered the winter, 8
the man put the truck in gear and rolled down over the sagebrush and
onto the desert floor. He drove out over the dry, bleached soil for a mile

before he put the truck in neutral and let it coast to a stop. He was careful with the silence. He could hear his fingers slide over the plastic steering wheel. He could feel the curve of his lips tightening in the dryness.

He took off his clothes, all of them, and put them in a zippered airlines bag on the floor of the truck. Then he put his sneakers back on and went naked across the desert back to the hot spring with a pair of linen socks in his hand. The cool breeze from the mountains raised his flesh into a lattice of pin-pricked hills. 9

He removed his shoes. He lay on his back in the hot water, his toes grazing the shallow, sandy bottom of the pool. He could hear the water lapping at the entrance to his ears, the weight of water pulling on his hair; he could feel the particles of dust falling off his flesh, floating down, settling on the bottom of the pool; he could feel the water prying at the layers of dried sweat. He concentrated and tried to hear the dirt and sweat breaking away from his body. The tips of his fingers wrinkled, and he stared at the water pooling in the cavity of his chest and falling away as he breathed. 10

He wanted to stay until the sun set but he couldn't: he could feel himself sinking. He climbed out of the pool and walked out of the roofless tin shelter onto the floor of the desert. The wind began to evaporate the water and his pores closed like frightened mussels and trapped the warmth beneath his skin. 11

When his feet were dry he put on only the linen socks and left. He could feel the wind eddying up around him like a cloak and his feet barely touched the ground. His eyes felt smoother in their sockets and he could tell, without looking, how his fingers were curled; he could see the muscles of his legs tied beneath his kneecaps, feel the patella gliding over the knot. He felt the muscles anchored on the broad, flat plate of his hipbones and the wind soft deep in the roots of his hair. He felt the pressure of his parting the air as he walked. 12

When he got back to the truck he poured a cup of water and placed a handful of cereal into an earthen bowl. He ate and looked out across the desert and imagined that he had come to life again. 13

From Barry Lopez, *Desert Notes: Reflections in the Eye of a Raven.* New York: Avon Books, 1976. Reprinted with permission of Andrews and McMeel and Barry Lopez.

STUDY QUESTIONS

1. What is simple about this writing? What is complex about it?

2. How does this reading affect your body and feelings? Do you identify with the protagonist? If so, how did the author manage to get you to feel you were inside the man?

3. Read paragraphs 7, 8, and 9 and notice how the verbs, nouns, and adjectives convey sensory information. Make a list of these sense-conveying words under columns headed *verbs, nouns,* and *adjectives.*

4. Notice the use of the verb *would* in the first paragraphs conveying a habitual action. Why do you think this man would regularly take such a long drive to a desert location?

5. Explain his last statement: "He ate and looked out across the desert and imagined that he had come to life again."

6. Do you think the author chose a boring subject? What makes a subject boring?

7. Working on your own or with a partner, choose any *two paragraphs* of "The Hot Spring" to analyze. Make column headings for word categories that convey different kinds of sensory information. Use the format given in the example below, which covers the first two sentences. Put parentheses around sensations that are associatory or implied.

Images	*Texture*	*Kinesthetic*	*Color*	*Time*	*Size*	*Sound*
dogwood	(soft)	bloomed	blue	late	thin	cracked
Chevy pickup	(slick, dirty)	broken	green	spring	Expando	
taillight	(shiny)					
tarpaulin	(rough)					
dishes	(smooth)					
one-burner stove	(fire)					

Create other word categories to match sensations as you find them.

ON FINDING THE RIGHT WORD

You have just analyzed the writing of a skilled professional author, who, like you, began with conscious observations. Looking back at your descriptive writing in the last chapter, you may explain putting this experience into words in stages. When you were immersed in observing your fruit, shoe, or household tool, your first stage was one of silent absorption. If words came to you at that time, you might have had to struggle to keep them from interfering prematurely with your sensing process. Nevertheless, once this stage was finished—when you were ready to write down your experiences—you may have been surprised to find

CONSCIOUS PROBLEM SOLVING THROUGH FINDING THE RIGHT WORD

"Is your name Caspar?" asked the Queen.

"No."

"Is your name Hans?"

"No. Now or never, woman! I've been patient long enough! If you don't guess my name right—I'll give you just one more time—then your baby is mine!"

"I wonder . . . I wonder . . . Could your name be . . . Could it be . . . *Rumplestiltskin?*"

"The Devil told you that! The Devil told you that!" shrieked the ugly little man.

And in a fury, he flew out the window on his cooking spoon.

And he was never heard from again.

Question: Have you ever been disturbed for a long time by a feeling, symptom, or event that you could not quite identify? What happened when you found there was a right word to describe it? Did the word rob the problem of its power?

yourself at a loss for words. You knew what you had seen or touched or felt, but you also realized that any word choices would only result in *translations* into another medium that would never fully duplicate your silent experience. And it took a lot of thinking to try to convey that experience in translation.

If you were working with an orange, you might have found yourself in a mental struggle to describe its taste. If you wrote, "It tastes like an orange," you knew that that did not convey your actual sensations, but was only a mental summary or categorization of them. To say "It had a citrus flavor" would have sounded even more abstract. Perhaps you needed to go back and mentally relive your experience, or taste your orange again, which might have summoned up such words as *sticky-sweet, tangy-flesh, spicy-warm.* If these words did not seem to offer you the equivalent you wanted, you might have longed for the help of a friend with a wider vocabulary for sensations.

Perhaps you used reference books, such as a thesaurus, or encyclopedia, or even cookbooks. Keeping an experience in mind as a constant, while searching both the memory and other sources for word correspondences, is a very complex mental operation. Writing challenges you to stretch your abilities to use the words you know, to find new ones, and through this process to move in time toward more and more word mastery.

An additional reward of word mastery is that when you know the words for things, you actually *see* them better. If you recognize by name a Washington navel orange and a Valencia orange, this also means that you know how to look for their distinguishing characteristics, such as their navel formations, the rinds' different textures and thicknesses, and their different shades of color. When someone gives you an orange, you will actually look closer in order to appreciate its specifics rather than to dismiss it in a perceptual blur as "just another orange." *The advantage of experience combined with a precise vocabulary is that it enables you to observe better, to see more, and to take a greater interest in what you see.* And the more words you know for what you see, the more you do see, and the more you have to communicate to yourself and others.

Discovery Exercises

Sorting Out Confusion About Dictionaries

Rate each of the following statements as *true* or *false*. Be prepared to defend your answers in writing or in a class discussion.

_____ 1. Dictionaries are like phone books; basically, they all offer the same information.

_____ 2. If a dictionary is named Webster's, that means it is one of the best.

_____ 3. Dictionaries are written by experts who decide how we should speak English.

_____ 4. Small pocket dictionaries are the best kind to use for an in-depth study of words, because they eliminate unnecessary, confusing information and make understanding easier.

_____ 5. Since a dictionary can confuse us with so many definitions for any single word, it is better to try to figure out a word's meaning from its context or ask someone else.

_____ 6. Dictionaries are like cookbooks; a family only needs to buy one for the family's lifetime.

_____ 7. Dictionaries give us information about spelling and definitions, but that is about all they offer.

_____ 8. Dictionaries list word definitions in the order of most frequent use. Therefore, it is usually best to choose the first definition given.

Here is a discussion of the correct answers. Read this only *after* you've completed the quiz.

1. False. A comparative study of several dictionaries—for instance, *The American Heritage Dictionary, Webster's New Collegiate Dictionary,* and *Webster's New World Dictionary*—will make this apparent.

2. False. Noah Webster was a nineteenth-century American lexicographer. The rights to his book were purchased by the Merriam Company, which has continued, under the name Merriam-Webster, to publish and revise the large *Webster's New International Dictionary.* However, since the name Webster's is not protected by a copyright, many other companies have used it to put out both excellent and inferior products. In any case, the most prestigious and scientifically researched dictionary is the *Oxford English Dictionary,* bound in versions that range from two to twenty volumes.

3. False. Dictionaries serve as authoritative reference sources; however, they are not authoritative in the sense of being infallible, but in the sense of offering reliable historical information about words and their use. In the case of *The American Heritage Dictionary,* this information is based on the opinions of a panel of lexicographers, linguists, writers, and scientists. Dictionaries are not written to dictate dogma but only to reflect agreements and standards about how people use their language both in popular speech and formal writing.

4. False. Pocket dictionaries may be more convenient to carry and use for understanding simpler words or spellings, but they are too condensed for use in the more serious study of word ideas, concepts, and usage. Moreover, their definitions can sometimes be oversimplified to the point of being misleading. Finally, and more obviously, a pocket dictionary containing 30,000 words cannot offer you as much as an unabridged dictionary with 600,000 words or a college desk-sized one with 60,000 words.

5. False. Although most study skills texts suggest this, and most English composition-reading texts select out the vocabulary for you, a guess based on your view of the context may be mistaken, and your friend may be even more confused than you. The result may be having to "unlearn" a misunderstood word later. If you are skilled in dictionary use, it is not a chore to confirm a guess or a friend's definition by consulting the dictionary. Furthermore, having certainty about a word's meaning can enable you to cement it more confidently into your memory.

6. False. If your dictionary is more than fifteen years old, it is time to buy a new one. The English language acquires or invents thousands of new words each year, and our customs about word usage change also.

7. False. It's worth spending a little time just browsing through your dictionary to find out all it has to offer. You'll find a concise history of the English language, for one thing.

8. False. This is true of *The American Heritage Dictionary,* but not of *Webster's Collegiate Dictionary, Webster's New World Dictionary,* or the *Oxford English Dictionary.* These dictionaries begin with the oldest meaning of the word, which, in some cases, has already become obsolete. Thus, if you choose the first definition regardless of the type of dictionary you are using, you might not be able to make yourself understood. It is important, therefore, to make sure you know which system is being used in your dictionary.

A COLLABORATIVE LEARNING OPPORTUNITY

How Skillfully Do You Use Your Dictionary?

Bring to class a college desk-sized dictionary. If you need to buy one, the following are recommended:

The American Heritage Dictionary of the English Language (Houghton Mifflin Company, 1982).

Webster's New World Dictionary of the American Language, third college edition (Simon & Schuster, 1988).

Working with a partner, take turns finding three random entries to discuss. Explain to your partner, who will be writing all this down, every piece of information that you find there, including every symbol and every abbreviation. If you do not understand something, take the time to look it up. (If, for instance, you do not understand what is meant by the abbreviation *OF,* find out where your dictionary explains its abbreviations.) Work together to understand *all* the information given and do not let one another off the hook until you sense everything interpreted is fully understood.

Using the same sheet of paper upon which your partner wrote your explanations of the three entries, answer the following questions:

1. State the name of the dictionary you own and its date of publication. How many pages does it have? How many entries? Is it a desk-sized dictionary?

2. Do you feel you have had sufficient instruction in school to know how to make use of an unabridged or a desk-sized dictionary?

3. Test your knowledge of the history of the English language by explaining what your dictionary means when it refers to a word

as *Anglo Saxon* or *Middle English, Late Latin,* and *Indo-European.*

4. Look up *Pago Pago.* Write down how it is pronounced. Pronounce it to your partner. Was this easy or difficult for you?

5. Have you ever discovered that you had misunderstood a familiar word and were misusing it? Give an example and explain how you found out.

6. How does the word *plan* differ from the words *design, project,* and *scheme?* The *Webster's New World Dictionary* will explain how they differ in connotation. What are word connotations and why are they important to consider when you make your selection?

7. Describe the mental signals that show you, in dictionary study, that you have fully understood a new word. Do you usually persist in word study until you have these signals?

8. If you can't find a word or clear definition of a word in one dictionary, do you usually think to consult another dictionary? Explain why or why not.

9. When do you use a thesaurus? Is it helpful when you do not know the word for something?

CLEAR THINKING DEPENDS
ON CLEAR WORD DEFINITIONS

In order to think and communicate well, we have to clearly understand the words we use. Yet, as obvious as this statement may seem, this is not a common habit, although it is a basic one for critical thinking. For one thing, it means recognizing in oneself the type of mental confusion that is caused by word confusion. And more than that, it means taking the time to isolate an unknown word and then to look it up and study it in the dictionary. And this applies not only to *new* words, but to *familiar* ones as well, although confusion about the latter may not be as easy to recognize. It is more obvious, for instance, to confront the blank felt on hearing the word *libertarian* for the first time than to sort out confusion about a word heard as often as *liberal.*

Words that describe the thinking process fall in this latter category of being familiar, but nevertheless not always clearly understood and defined. Such words are given special attention in this text, as you have seen in the previous chapter's discussion of perceiving, sensing, and thinking. And just as you can see more of an orange when you can name its different parts, knowing the names and definitions of the elements of thinking enables you to make closer observations of them as they occur.

This identification also allows you to make finer adjustments in their functions.

Although dictionaries can give readers the power of fully understanding words, few readers are in the habit of using them as often as they should. This is understandable, because it usually is annoying to interrupt conversation or reading in order to look up a word. Yet word confusion creates the same kind of mental discomfort or disequilibrium that an unsolved problem causes. And discomfort is usually something all want to escape from, rather than continue through, as is necessary to reach understanding of a word's meaning. To persist in this process can require a lot of discipline, but the disequilibrium connected with that word will stay stored until the necessary action is taken to clear up its meaning.

This phenomenon is even more apparent in reading. If you come across a word that you do not understand, you might tell yourself that if you keep going, you might understand it from the context. Indeed, textbooks on reading often advise that. However, if you do not get the meaning from the context, you will actually find yourself soon *losing consciousness,* better known as becoming drowsy or falling asleep. The knack here is to become alert to the early inner signs of word confusion before unconsciousness takes over, and to exert sufficient will power to pause and clear up misunderstanding through dictionary study. If you do this, you will find yourself more alert, with a renewed energy for the continuation of work. To reach this stage of renewal, however, you must persist in dictionary study until you reach full comprehension; this may mean referring to several dictionaries, diagramming the word, and using it in several sentences. If you find that you have difficulty understanding a word in one dictionary, it is also a good practice to compare the word's definition in one or two other dictionaries before making your own synthesis of the word's meaning. Later in this chapter you will learn a method for doing this.

The word definitions offered in every chapter of this text are designed to lay the foundation for the development of better word-understanding habits. However, you will also find many words that are unfamiliar to you while reading this textbook. *It will remain your responsibility to use the dictionary to understand any unfamiliar words that you may find in this book, and thus to reinforce this important critical thinking skill.*

WHAT MAKES A DEFINITION?

The *etymology,* or history, of the word *definition* shows us something interesting; it comes from the Latin roots *de,* meaning off or away from, and *finis,* meaning end or boundary; the Latin word *definire* means to

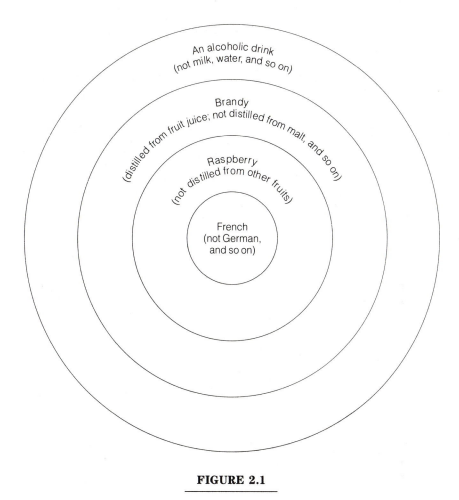

FIGURE 2.1

set bounds to. So when we *define* something, we discover or establish its boundaries. When we learn a new word, the definition shows us what boundaries separate it from every other word. For example, the definition of the word *framboise* establishes four distinct boundaries (see also Figure 2.1):

Framboise: A French raspberry brandy; an alcoholic drink
Brandy: alcoholic liquor distilled from fermented fruit juice
Raspberry: edible berry of the plant *Rubus*
French: pertaining to France, a republic of western Europe

In a definition, the word to be defined is called a *term.* Every term can be included in a *class,* or the largest family to which it is related; thus, the term *framboise* belongs in the *class* of alcoholic drinks whose boundaries exclude all nonalcoholic drinks. Within this class, the distinguishing *characteristics* of *framboise* are brandy, raspberry, and French, each of which forms further boundaries. Thus when we *define* a word, we methodically separate what the word represents from everything else. And when we are able to make clear differentiations, we have the necessary certainty to think more clearly about the subject at hand.

Writing Application

Word Boundaries

Set up a piece of paper with three columns headed Term, Class, and Characteristics. For each of the words below, list the class and characteristics, and diagram the boundaries as we did for *framboise*.

EXAMPLE

Term	*Class*	*Characteristics*
Scissors	are a cutting tool	with two blades, each with a loop handle joined by a swivel pin.

1. mailbag
2. moppet
3. November
4. pneumonia
5. cat

KINDS OF DEFINITIONS

When you looked up the word *cat,* you probably found it described as a mammal of the family felidae, or of the genus and species *Felis catus.* This taxonomic description indicates the boundaries that differentiate cats from all other animals. The cat family includes lions and tigers as well as house cats, while a particular breed name distinguishes a Siamese from a Persian cat. The rules that govern this system of classification are based on a science called *taxonomy.* This science, established by an international commission, enables us to know what *agreements* have been made to identify all plants and animals so that no two can be confused. Just as taxonomy helps us distinguish one living thing from another, *logical definitions* in dictionaries describe terms according to the boundaries established by shared and separate characteristics. Both taxonomy and logical definitions owe their value to the fact that they are based on general agreements that can be referred to by everyone.

There are also definitions that are not based on general agreements: these might be called *personal definitions*. Based on individual experiences, they can be whimsical, like "Happiness is a commute before the rush hour," or philosophical, like "Death is the invisible companion of life." Sometimes misunderstandings occur when people confuse personal with logical definitions. Imagine the following conversation:

"You don't make me *happy*."

"Yes, I do. Didn't I just give you a new car?"

"You just don't understand what happiness is!"

In this dialogue, one person has a personal definition of happiness (to receive things wanted), while the second person seems to have a different definition. Yet, both could be assuming that they are talking about the kind of logical definition found in a dictionary.

A classic dialogue related to this subject takes place between Alice and Humpty Dumpty (from Lewis Carroll's *Through the Looking Glass*).

"I don't know what you mean by 'glory,'" Alice said.

Humpty Dumpty smiled contemptuously. "Of course you don't—till I tell you. I meant 'there's a nice knock-down argument for you!'"

"But 'glory' doesn't mean 'a nice knock-down argument," Alice objected.

"When *I* use a word," Humpty Dumpty said in rather a scornful tone, "it means just what I choose it to mean—neither more nor less."

"The question is," said Alice, "whether you *can* make words mean so many different things."

"The question is," said Humpty Dumpty, "which is to be master—that's all."

Clearly, Humpty Dumpty is making a personal definition here. Alice's objection is that without agreement about what a word means, communication becomes difficult.

Another category of definitions might be called *persuasive definitions*. These are definitions formulated for the purpose of praising or condemning something. Examples of these would be such statements as the following:

"A state lottery is a form of voluntary taxation."

"A state lottery is a disease in the body politic."

"To be anti-abortion is to be pro-life."

"To be for abortions is to be pro-choice."

All these are personal equations expressed as though they were given truths in order to win others over to the same view. Obviously, they should not be confused with dictionary definitions.

THE CONNOTATIONS OF WORDS

An important aspect of definitions are the *connotations* of words or the *associations* that they suggest to us. These associations can evoke reactions, images, emotions, or thoughts. For instance, let's take the word *snake*. The *denotation* of this word, or its literal meaning, is a reptile without legs. There it is: simply a "thing," nothing to get excited about. But for most people the word *snake* carries many negative *connotations,* such as being slimy, treacherous, poisonous, or evil. These common reactions can nevertheless be overcome through conscious familiarity with snakes.

Do dictionaries define connotations? Not so in the case of the snake, where such connotations are universally understood. But in some cases, dictionaries can help. Imagine you are a Cambodian student who wonders why your American friend John got so upset when you said he was *lying.* You consult the *Oxford English Dictionary* to find ". . . in modern use, the word *lie* is normally a violent expression of moral reprobation, which in polite conversation is to be avoided . . ." You wonder, what word should I have used? You find some help in the *Webster's New World Dictionary of the American Language, Second Edition,* which offers synonym and antonym discussions for most items. Here a paragraph explains the connotative differences among *lie, prevaricate, equivocate,* and *fib.*

Feeling enlightened, you look for John and find him in the cafeteria. You say to him, "Excuse me, I only meant you were *fibbing!*" And magically, that word turns him into your friend again. The denotation was the same—his past action remained the same—but you used a word with a more acceptable connotation.

In later chapters of this book we will look at how connotations show our judgments of things and how they can be used for manipulation. But for now you should become sensitive to possible connotations in your word choices and in your reading; persist with questions or dictionary study until you understand them.

CLASS DISCUSSION

1. Explain the meaning and connotative differences among *disinformation, misspeaking,* and *falsifying.*
2. Make a list of the synonyms for *cheating* and rank their connotations as either negative, positive, neutral, or phony neutral (meaning a euphemism that hides a true negative meaning).
3. Repeat the procedure for the word *stealing.*

THE IMPORTANCE OF DEFINING KEY IDEAS

The French philosopher Voltaire once said, "If you would argue with me, first define your terms." What he was talking about was not arguing in the sense of quarreling, but in the sense of persuasive reasoning. He did not say *how* terms should be defined, but that one should be very clear about what one has decided that key ideas mean. For example, if you wanted to argue in defense of the unregulated use of drugs, you should first define what you mean by *drugs.* Do you mean aspirin, or heroin, or both? How you define the term affects not only what you include within your boundaries to consider, but also what remains outside to ignore. Undefined words have to be confronted sooner or later, and that is better done by you than by your opponent, because an argument based on undefined words will simply crumble when challenged.

Clear definitions are an essential part of all fields of learning. For example, in law, definitions help juries decide the difference between crimes and misdemeanors, between sanity and insanity. In public affairs, definitions often lead to considerable debate, as, for instance, is the case with the meaning of the expression "comparable worth." So formulating and understanding definitions comprise a large part of any subject of learning. If you want to study thinking, you have to spend some time just studying the word *thinking.* If you study political science, you have to begin by asking what the word *political* really means. The study of any subject requires attention to its vocabulary of both familiar and unfamiliar terms.

DEFINING REALITY

Reality comes from the Latin word *res*, which means thing, property, possession; and from *itas*, which means state or quality. Related to *res* is *reri*, which means to consider, confirm, think, reason; and from which we derive our words *reason, ratio, realize*. The past participle of *reri* is *ratus*, which means fixed by calculation, established, firm, for certain, sure, valid. The ideas etymologically involved in the word *reality* are therefore:

1. That which is thought of
2. That which belongs to the thing itself
3. That which belongs to you
4. Something ascertained by counting and thoughtful consideration: a calculation
5. Something established as certain

The Sanskrit word for *truth* and *reality* that appears in the Vedas is *satya*, or "this which IS." This comes from the word *sat*, which is the present participle of the verb root *as*, which means to be. This root word, which comes from *es* in Indo-European, is also the root for our forms of the verb *to be*, which can be most clearly seen in our word *is*. Quite possibly, the Latin word *res* for thing is also related to the word *es* = to be. According to William L. Reese's *Dictionary of Philosophy and Religion: Eastern and Western Thought*, the term *reality* (in the form of the Latin word *realitas*) was first introduced into philosophy in the thirteenth century by Duns Scotus, who used the word as a synonym for *being*. Reese then says that no distinction between *reality* and *being* has been drawn by any philosopher.

Here is what other noted thinkers have said about reality:

Everything flows.
Heraclitus, Greek philosopher

The world was created by the word of God so that what is seen was made out of things which do not appear.
St. Paul

Yet, to thoroughly understand the vocabulary of a given field of study, you need to go beyond memorizing dictionary definitions. You also need to become familiar with the etymology of key words. As we noted earlier, a word's etymology is its history. A study of a word's etymology can help us trace a word back to its earliest root idea. Sometimes this idea gives us an image that conveys a more concrete sense of the word's logic and that helps us remember the word and recognize its relationship to other words with the same root meanings. Maybe you've noticed by

Reality is what we bump against.
William James, American psychologist

Reality is something as it actually is, independent of our thoughts about how it is.
Mortimer J. Adler, American philosopher

Reality is an unknown and undefinable totality of flux that is the ground of all things and of the process of thought itself, as well as the movement of intelligent perception.
David Bohm, philosopher and physicist

And about the difficulty of defining reality:

As far as the laws of mathematics refer to reality, they are not certain; and as far as they are certain, they do not refer to reality.
Albert Einstein

The Eastern mystics are well aware of the fact that all verbal descriptions of reality are inaccurate and incomplete. . . . The direct experience of reality transcends the realm of thought and language, and since all mysticism is based on such a direct experience, everything that is said about it can only be partially true.
Fritjof Capra, physicist

Reality is process. . . . Not only is everything changing, but all is flux. That is to say, what is is the process of becoming itself, while all objects, events, entities, conditions, structures, etc., are forms that can be abstracted from this process.
David Bohm

There is no reality until that reality is perceived. Our perceptions of reality will, consequently, appear somewhat contradictory, dualistic, and paradoxical. The instantaneous experience of the reality of Now will not appear paradoxical at all. It is only when we observers attempt to construct a history of our perceptions that reality seems paradoxical.
Fred Alan Wolf, physicist

now that when we introduce a new word in this book, we often provide the word's etymology as an aid to understanding. Other aids to understanding key ideas in a field are knowing the definitions formulated by leading thinkers in the field and studying the implications of common usage of key words.

You might be interested in using these skills as we look at two key concepts in the field of critical thinking: *truth* and *reality*. The purpose of critical thinking is to discern what is true and what is real, as sug-

DEFINING TRUTH

The word *true* comes from the Old English form of *troewe*, which means loyal, trustworthy, which in turn comes from the Indo-European base *deru*, meaning firm, solid, steadfast. Related to the base word *deru* is *dru*, meaning firm as a tree, hard as wood. This etymology suggests that *truth* is something as hard and firm and as steadfast as a tree or its wood.

The following definitions have been given for truth:

Truth suggests conformity with the facts or with reality, either as an idealized abstraction ("What is truth?" said jesting Pilate) or in actual application to statements, ideas, acts, etc. ("There is no truth in that rumor").
The American Heritage Dictionary

Truth is a correspondence or agreement between our minds and reality.
Mortimer J. Adler

The ordinary mode of language is very unsuitable for discussing questions of truth and falsity, because it tends to treat each truth as a separate fragment that is essentially fixed and static in its nature. . . . However, truth and falsity have to be seen from moment to moment, in an act of perception of a very high order.
David Bohm

gested by the Discovery Exercise you did in the Introduction. If this is our goal, we need to understand the definitions of these key concepts. We can start by defining *concept*. *Conceive* comes from the Latin *concipere*, derived from the root words *com*, meaning comprehensively or together, and *capere*, meaning to take. *Concept* comes from the Latin *conceptus*, a thing conceived. A *concept* is therefore a general idea or understanding of something formed by mentally combining all its characteristics or particulars.

WHAT IS CRITICAL READING?

Whether you are reading a dictionary entry, a textbook, or a novel, the first stage of critical reading is *accurate comprehension*. Challenging or questioning comes later; first you must accurately duplicate the information in your mind. Indeed, in this first stage, debates or judgments can distort content or interfere with the concentration needed to correctly decipher the letters, words, and meaning. And sometimes this process of accurate comprehension takes many rereadings to achieve. In addition, active thinking is needed to make the inferences that the author intended and keep them separate from our own inferences, a procedure that we will be discussing in a later chapter.

Although it is beyond the scope of this text to teach reading comprehension skills, it is helpful for you to recognize when you are in a state of *mental receptivity* so that you can sustain that in your first stage of reading. When we do not remain open (as we learned in the chapter on observation skills), we tend to alter or distort whatever appears before us. *Receptive reading* does not substitute different words or ideas, but faithfully and accurately records the message, regardless of whether or not it agrees with personal values, experiences, or expectations.

Critical reading is the second stage of reading. The definition of *critical* traces the root ideas of this term back to the words *sift* and *separate*. When one reads critically, one sifts out words and ideas, separates content from structure, questions, and reflects. In critical reading the reader interacts with the material, is involved with what is said, and questions and evaluates the information. Above all, a critical reader knows *which* questions to ask.

In this chapter, you have been considering three questions:

Is this the most accurate word choice?

What is the connotation of this word?

Does this word need defining?

The reading selections in this text are followed by study questions intended to provoke critical reading. You are encouraged to read each selection at least twice—once for comprehension and once for critical interaction. If it is helpful, think of your first reading as a sponge reading and your second as a sifting. Consult your dictionary regularly as you read, and write down the questions you need to ask—whether for clarification or in challenge of the material. Make your reading an active thinking endeavor.

CHAPTER SUMMARY

1. Words help us think better. They give forms to our thoughts so that we can make use of them. Words enable us to communicate with ourselves and others. Knowing the words for things and experiences helps us see and perceive more.

2.   Writing helps us learn more about words and how to use them. When we struggle to select words that will describe our experiences, we realize that words are only *translations* of experience and not the experience itself.

3.   Clear thinking depends on a clear understanding of the words we use. Word confusion leads to less consciousness, or disequilibrium, which can only be restored through dictionary word study.

4.   We need to understand what dictionaries can and cannot offer us and how to use them skillfully and frequently.

5.   The thesaurus helps us when we are writing and translating nonverbal experiences and ideas into words; the dictionary helps us when we are reading and interpreting the words of others.

6.   Definitions set boundaries for word ideas and show us their specific and general characteristics and how they are related to or distinguished from one another.

7.   Logical definitions show us the agreements that society has made about a word's meaning. But we may also compose our own personal definitions of experiences, or compose persuasive definitions to sway the opinions of others. In critical thinking it is important not to confuse these different kinds of definitions, or to believe that personal or persuasive definitions carry the same agreements as those to be found in a dictionary.

8.   The test of our understanding of a word is our ability to define it. This ability is particularly important for words representing key ideas that we wish to explain or defend. Taking the time to define the words we use is an essential preliminary to genuine communication.

9.   A study of a word's etymology can help us trace a word back to its earliest root idea and can give us an image that conveys a more concrete sense of the word's logic. Learning a word's etymology can also help us recognize its relationship to other words with the same root meanings.

10.   The connotations of a word are its associative meanings, which can be positive, negative, or neutral. These associations can take the form of feelings, ideas, images, or thoughts. Thus, although a politician would never admit to *lying* or being *confused*, it is quite acceptable for him to admit he *misspoke*.

11.   The first stage of critical reading is objective receptivity to the material; this means having both the technical ability as well as the willingness to accurately reproduce its content without alterations or distortions. If we question and interact with material

that we have not accurately interpreted, our criticisms will not be fair or worthwhile.

Chapter Quiz

Rate each of the following statements as *true* or *false*. To answer some of these questions, you will need to consult your dictionary.

_____ 1. The word *etymology* comes from the Greek *etymon,* meaning true, and *logos,* meaning word—"true word."

_____ 2. Words can be used to do a better or worse job of describing experiences but can never be more than translations of the experiences themselves.

_____ 3. A dictionary can help us think better when we use it to clear up word confusion.

_____ 4. Definitions of a word show the word's boundaries.

_____ 5. Knowing the words for things helps us see them better.

_____ 6. We do not fully understand a word unless we can define it.

_____ 7. It is rude to ask people to define the words they use.

_____ 8. Etymology gives us word histories.

_____ 9. Pocket dictionaries are sufficient guides for a critical study of word meanings.

_____ 10. The word *ohm* comes from the Sanskrit language and means the sound of creation.

_____ 11. According to most dictionaries, there is more than one acceptable spelling of the word *cooperate.*

_____ 12. The term *French leave* means to say goodbye with a big kiss.

_____ 13. The prefix *in* in the words *insignificant* and *inflammable* means *not* in Latin.

_____ 14. The following words all contain the sound called a schwa: *mass, polite, placement, bogus, visible.*

_____ 15. The word *nausea* can be pronounced at least three different ways.

_____ 16. The word *round* can function as six different parts of speech: adjective, noun, transitive and intransitive verb, adverb, and preposition.

_____ 17. *Egregious* comes from a Latin word meaning standing out from the herd.

_____ 18. The word *nadir* in the phrase "the nadir of politics" means the highest point.

_____ 19. A *cogent* argument is a convincing one.

_____ 20. The word *decimate* means to dice something up into pieces.

Writing Application

An Essay of Definition

Write an essay based on an extended definition, or full discussion, of a word or phrase, with the support of examples. It should also be an essay of exposition, which is a form of writing that explains something. In this case you will want to *explain your definition* as fully as you can through stories, examples, or specific information. The thinking tasks of making definitions followed by explanations play a frequent part in our daily conversations. If you are having a conversation with a friend and say, "She just isn't *mature*," your friend may reply, "What do you mean by *mature*?" Thus, you are challenged to respond with a definition together with an explanation of how you use that term.

The directions for this assignment, and for all the other writing assignments in this book, are designed to make you conscious of the thinking elements involved in solving it as a given problem, much as you would solve a problem in mathematics. In order to solve the problem, however, you must follow the instructions exactly. To help you grasp the details of each assignment, the instructions are set up in terms of parameters.

A parameter is a fixed limit or boundary (*para* = alongside, *meter* = measure); it is also a variable or a fixed constant. In the case of this assignment, you will be asked to observe the four parameters listed below. These parameters are intended to provide you with both *guidelines* for solving the problem and *standards* for evaluating your work. In order to succeed in this assignment, therefore, be careful not to ignore or neglect any of these specified parameters.

1. *Objective:* To give your own definition of a word, and to explain that word's meaning through your own experience.

2. *Form and length:* Do this in one paragraph or one typed page.

3. *Structure:* Begin with a topic sentence and end with a conclusion.

4. *Suggested topics:*

    (a) What is an adult?

    (b) A word that I came to understand through experience

(c) A word I misunderstood

(d) A word that I had trouble understanding

(e) A word that interests me

Suppose you choose the first topic—defining *adult.* Think of all the word's uses in the world you live in. Look up its definition in at least three dictionaries. Now turn back to the diagram of the word *framboise.* Draw and define the boundaries for the word *adult* using dictionary definitions and whatever you can add in terms of street knowledge or common sense.

Now try *clustering* with the word *adult.* This warm-up technique was first introduced as a tool for writing in a book by Gabriele Rico (*Writing the Natural Way*). It allows you to discover what conscious and unconscious ideas, images, symbols, and feelings you associate with any key word. Place the word in an oval or circle in the center of a page. Then draw lines and more ovals radiating from that key word to enclose whatever words, ideas, images, or memories that may come to you. This method works best when done without censorship, allowing discoveries and surprises at the results.

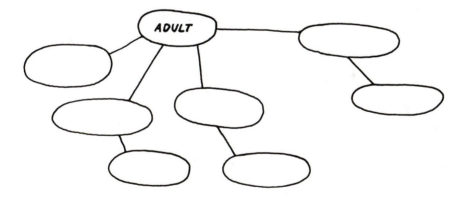

Next, sit down and create a good paragraph about the various meanings and boundaries of the word *adult.* Contrast what you feel to be the true meaning of the word with some false meanings.

Bring together your findings into one sentence that announces all you want to say about the definitions and boundaries of *adult.* This is a *topic sentence,* which generalizes your findings into a kind of conclusion. The rest of the sentences in the paragraph should support, or provide examples that support, the topic sentence.

In this paragraph you can see how well you think about words while also working on the college level in expository writing.

Peer Review

In class read your essays of definition to one another in small groups. For each paper, write a critique that answers these questions:

1. Was each of the parameters observed?
2. Did you understand all that was said? Did anything need to be explained more?
3. Did you honestly find the writing interesting?

STUDENT WRITING EXAMPLE

SUCCESS
Bill Eubanks

Although *success* is a word that is most commonly used to denote wealth and affluence, my personal definition revolves around a state of mind. Success, as defined by U.S. societal standards, is monetary gain. That is to say, most Americans define success in terms of real and personal property: a mansion and its surrounding grounds, the most expensive or fastest car, a high-yielding investment portfolio, and so on through countless possessions. Yet the true power of success is the drive and positive attitudes that lead to such acquisitions. It seems logical that the investment of hard work and long hours should pay off in cash and its benefits. But it appears just as logical that the attitude should pay off as well. This emotional payoff is the very heart of success for me, a payoff that is not received by everyone who is wealthy. Unhappy wealthy people searching for a deeper meaning to their lives is the subject of many a film and novel. This is a romantic ideal born of human nature, nurtured by life itself, but one that can be crushed by the material values of the corporate-controlled world of today. In my own lower middle-class life working in the garment industry, I have made many acquaintances of very wealthy people. Most of them had to undergo some kind of therapy to feel good about themselves. I have yet to see an example of money or possessions bringing about emotional happiness and peace of mind to these people. If we look inside ourselves for the answer in our own feelings, we are headed in the right direction. If we work to achieve inner peace and tranquility as a definition of success, then the resulting effect on ourselves and all we touch shall be positive and fruitful.

Used with permission of Bill Eubanks.

Readings

ADDICTION

Anne Wilson Schaef

In this book, Anne Wilson Schaef, a therapist, begins with an original definition of addiction. Notice as you read how her definition gives her an advantage over authors who assume that everyone already knows what addiction is.

An addiction is any process over which we are powerless. It takes 1
control of us, causing us to do and think things that are inconsistent with our personal values and leading us to become progressively more compulsive and obsessive. A sure sign of an addiction is the sudden need to deceive ourselves and others—to lie, deny, and cover up. An addiction is anything we feel *tempted* to lie about. An addiction is anything we are not *willing* to give up (we may not *have* to give it up *and* we must be *willing to* do so to be free of addiction).

Like any serious disease, an addiction is progressive, and it will 2
lead to death unless we actively recover from it. I shall give some examples of how addiction affects individuals and also what it does at a cultural level.

An addiction keeps us unaware of what is going on inside us. We do 3
not have to deal with our anger, pain, depression, confusion, or even our joy and love, because we do not feel them, or we feel them only vaguely. We stop relying on our knowledge and our senses and start relying on our confused perceptions to tell us what we know and sense. In time, this lack of internal awareness deadens our internal processes, which in turn allows us to remain addicted. At some point we must choose to recover—to arrest the progress of the addiction—or we will die. This dying process does not happen only at a personal level: it is also systemic to our culture.

As we lose contact with ourselves, we also lose contact with other 4
people and the world around us. An addiction dulls and distorts our sensory input. We do not receive information clearly; we do not process it accurately; and we do not feed it back or respond to it with precision. Since we are not in touch with ourselves, we present a distorted self to the world—in AA terms, we "con" people—and eventually lose the ability to become intimate with others, even those we are closest to and love the most.

We are aware that something is very wrong, but the addictive think- 5
ing tells us that it could not possibly be our fault. This kind of thinking also tells us that we cannot make things right, that someone else will have to do it for us.

When they cannot (of course), we blame them for what is happen-   6
ing. (On a system level, we believe we are not causing the unrest in the
world. If others would only behave, we would not *have to* retaliate.)
An addiction absolves us from having to take responsibility for our
lives. We assume that someone—or something—outside ourselves will
swoop down to make things better or help us to deal with what we are
going through. Since addicts tend to be dependent and to feel increasingly powerless and bad about themselves, the notion that they can
take responsibility for their lives is inconceivable to them.

The longer we wait to be rescued, the worse our addiction be-   7
comes. Regardless of what we are addicted to, it takes more and more
to create the desired effect, and no amount is ever enough.

Addictions can be divided into two major categories: substance ad-   8
dictions and process addictions. Both function in essentially the same
way and produce essentially the same results. Although I shall describe
each separately, it is important to remember that addictions are quite
common in our culture and that most addicts have multiple addictions.
Although not all addictions are of equal severity, all eventually exhibit
similar behavioral dynamics and processes and lead to death.

Substance Addictions

Substance addictions—I also call these "ingestive addictions"—   9
are addictions to substances, usually artificially refined or produced,
that are deliberately taken into the body. These substances are almost
always mood-altering and lead to increased physical dependence.

Alcohol

Alcohol addiction may be the most common chemical dependency;   10
it is certainly the best documented and understood. Treatment professionals call it a "primary addiction," a disease that will sooner or later
lead to death if it is allowed to progress unchecked.

How and when does alcoholism begin? No one knows for certain,   11
although some people in AA maintain that alcoholics are alcoholics
long before they take their first drink. What is known is that alcoholics
at some point start abusing alcohol—drinking for the specific purpose
of altering a mood and/or staying out of touch with their feelings and
thoughts. What may at one time have been casual use moves into abuse,
and abuse moves into addiction.

Drugs

In our drug-happy society a person can start taking drugs for any   12
number of reasons: to relieve pain or anxiety, to stifle fear, or to put
reality in a better light.

Any mood-altering drug has the potential for being addictive. Many   13
people believe that only the illegal ones—heroin, marijuana, cocaine,
and street drugs, uppers and downers—are dangerous; in fact, prescription drugs such as Valium, Librium, and Empirin with codeine can
be just as addictive. There can come a point at which use moves into
abuse.

Any drug taken for the specific purpose of altering a mood and/or   14
avoiding one's inner feelings can become an addictive substance no
matter what its original purpose may have been.

Nicotine and Caffeine

Nicotine and caffeine are not as deadly (at least initially) as alcohol   15
and drugs, but they can be just as addictive, both physically and
emotionally.

Nicotine and caffeine can be used for essentially the same purpose   16
as any other ingested chemical substance: to "take the edge off," to
"push things down," to "give a lift," in other words, to alter moods and
mask feelings. Since they kill less quickly and lead to less obvious self-
destructive and interpersonally destructive behavior, they have not received as much attention, although public awareness is changing.

Alcohol, drugs, nicotine, and caffeine may be the best-known addic-   17
tive substances, but they are not the *only* addictive substances. There
are plenty of other things we ingest that function much the same as
mood-altering chemicals. Sugar can be a "fix"; so can salt. Even food
can be a problem; food addictions are gaining more recognition and
present more difficulties for recovery.

Food

When use moves into abuse, food becomes an addictive substance   18
and eating becomes compulsive and out of control, a way of avoiding
taking responsibility for oneself.

Treating food addictions can be especially difficult, since food is es-   19
sential to life and the addict cannot withdraw from it completely in
order to recover.

To complicate matters further, there are various types of food-   20
related addictions. Overeating may be the most widespread, but two
other conditions are becoming more prevalent: anorexia (self-starva-
tion) and bulimia (binging and purging). One can be addicted to eating,
to *not* eating, or to eating a huge quantity of food and then desperately
trying to get rid of it.

People with food-related addictions talk in terms of "burying" what   21
is going on inside of them and "stuffing" their feelings. Food (or the
avoidance of food) is perceived as a "cure" for anger, depression, fear,
anxiety, and other unpleasant feelings—and for pleasant feelings as

well. Many compulsive eaters head for the refrigerator whenever they feel too good or "alive."

Process Addictions

In a process addiction one becomes hooked on a process—a spe- 22
cific series of actions or interactions. Almost any process can be an addictive agent; those described here are merely examples.

Accumulating Money

In our culture the process of accumulating money often becomes 23
addictive. Like any other addiction it is progressive; it takes more and more to achieve a fix, and eventually no amount is enough.

People caught up in this process use it to avoid dealing with being 24
human and confronting human feelings. They look outside for a solution rather than face the feelings inside. Often they do not care about money in and of itself; what drives them is the series of actions and interactions involved in accumulating it.

Gambling

Much the same can be said for a gambling addiction. The process 25
becomes more important than the winning or the money.

Like all addicts, compulsive gamblers use their addiction to keep 26
them unaware of their internal feelings. Their lives become progressively more unmanageable. Gambling can be just as addictive as alcohol; although it does not destroy the body, as alcohol does, it is equally capable of destroying a life and of wreaking havoc with relationships.

Sex

Sex has been increasingly identified as an addictive process. More 27
and more people seem to be using sex not as a means of relating but as a way of getting a fix.

For many of the couples I work with in therapy, "getting enough 28
sex" translates into avoiding tensions and feelings. They use sex (and each other) to keep from having to deal with themselves. In some cases the partners believe that sex is something they "deserve" and that their partner "owes" them. When a sex addict gets a fix, it serves the same purpose as a drink or a drug, and the personality dynamics that develop are essentially the same.

Work

Much has been written about workaholics, and we are becoming 29
aware that working—which can be one of the important ways we express ourselves—can also become a negative process.

When work becomes an obsession, compulsive behaviors develop 30
that can be harmful and even death-producing. As in accumulating
money, gambling, sex, or any other process addiction, the act itself
(working) loses its intrinsic meaning. Although the line between simple
overwork and an unhealthy addiction to work is tenuous, it is fairly
easy to tell when one has crossed it. The workaholic uses work to avoid
dealing with inner and interpersonal life.

Religion

Religion can also be a process addiction. I am not talking here 31
about *being* religious or *being* spiritual. Rather, my concern is with
"quick-fix" religions, those that avoid thoughtful prayer, meditation,
and dialogue and claim to have all the answers.

The religion addict is very different, inside and out, from the person 32
who is involved in spiritual growth. The religion addict loses touch with
personal values and develops behaviors that are the same as those of
the alcoholic or drug addict—judgmentalism, dishonesty, and control.
Use moves into abuse.

Worry

One of my clients introduced me to the idea that worry could be a 33
process addiction. As we worked together, it became evident that she
was completely devoted to worrying.

We made up a "worry list," and over time it grew longer and longer. 34
Every angle of every issue provided new and fertile possibilities. She
worried when she felt bad and when she felt good (the good feelings
might go away!). She worried about not having enough money (she had
plenty) and felt guilty about the money she had (other people were
starving!).

One of her biggest worries was that no one would ever love her and 35
she would always be alone. Yet whenever someone tried to get close to
her, she became fearful of too much intimacy (she would be swallowed
up!). Then she started worrying about whether she was loving the other
person "right" and being loved "right" in return. If she made herself vul-
nerable, the love might go away—or maybe it wouldn't, and then what?
Would she be able to handle it?

When she didn't have anything specific to worry about, she felt lost 36
and started looking for a "worry fix." When I asked her what would happen if she stopped worrying, she voiced concern over the possible loss
of an "old friend." We both became aware that worry had become an
addictive process for her, taking on a life of its own and exhibiting all
the signs of an addiction. The content—the reason behind a particular
bout of worrying—was far less important than the act of worrying
itself.

It should be obvious by now that almost everything, substance or   37
process, *can* become addictive. Television or running also can be addictions. On the other hand, it is equally true that there is nothing that
must become addictive; it may even be that the whole system that develops in conjunction with a specific addiction is more important than
the specific addiction itself.

Because we live in an addictive society, temptation is all around us.   38
The society in which we live needs addictions in order to perpetuate
itself. We do have other choices, however (and I hope this book will
make them more obvious), but first we must understand our present
situation.

From Anne Wilson Shaef, *When Society Becomes an Addict*. New York: Harper &
Row, 1987. Copyright © 1987 by the author. Reprinted with permission of Harper &
Row, Publishers, Inc.

STUDY QUESTIONS

1. What is the author's definition of *addiction?* How effective is
   her placement of it in the first line of the first paragraph?

2. How does she distinguish between substance and process
   addictions?

3. Explain, question, and discuss the following quotations. Provide
   examples from your own experience.

   (a) "An addiction is anything we feel *tempted* to lie about. An
       addiction is anything we are not *willing* to give up."

   (b) "Like any serious disease, an addiction is progressive, and it
       will lead to death unless we actively recover from it."

   (c) "An addiction keeps us unaware of what is going on inside
       us."

   (d) "Since addicts tend to be dependent and to feel increas-
       ingly powerless and bad about themselves, the notion that
       they can take responsibility for their lives is inconceivable
       to them."

4. The author says that addicts do not receive information clearly
   or process it accurately, and, moreover, that we live in an addictive society. Assuming that this is true, how would unclear reception and inaccurate processing affect a person's thinking?

5. Do you feel her definition is convincing? Too broad? Defend your
   answer.

LYING, LEAKAGE,
AND CLUES TO DECEIT

Paul Ekman

This excerpt, which defines lying and deceit, is taken from the second chapter of the book Telling Lies. *Ekman is a professor of psychology who has consulted with the Department of Defense and the FBI. Read first for understanding, and then a second time following your study questions.* *

Eight years after beginning as president, Richard Nixon denied 1 *lying* but acknowledged that he, like other politicians, had *dissembled.* It is necessary to win and retain public office, he said. "You can't say what you think about this individual or that individual because you may have to use him. . . . you can't indicate your opinions about world leaders because you may have to deal with them in the future." Nixon is not alone in avoiding the term *lie* when not telling the truth can be justified. As the *Oxford English Dictionary* tells us: "in modern use, the word [lie] is normally a violent expression of moral reprobation, which in polite conversation tends to be avoided, the synonyms *falsehood* and *untruth* being often substituted as relatively euphemistic." It is easy to call an untruthful person a liar if he is disliked, but very hard to use that term, despite his untruthfulness, if he is liked or admired. Many years before Watergate, Nixon epitomized the liar to his Democratic opponents—"would you buy a used car from this man?"—while his abilities to conceal and disguise were praised by his Republican admirers as evidence of political savvy. . . .

In my definition of a lie or deceit, then, one person intends to mis- 2 lead another, doing so deliberately, without prior notification of this purpose, and without having been explicitly asked to do so by the target. There are two primary ways to lie: to *conceal* and to *falsify.* In concealing, the liar withholds some information without actually saying anything untrue. In falsifying, an additional step is taken. Not only does the liar withhold true information, but he presents false information as if it were true. Often it is necessary to combine concealing and falsifying to pull off the deceit, but sometimes a liar can get away just with concealment.

Not everyone considers concealment to be lying; some people re- 3 serve that word only for the bolder act of falsification. If the doctor

*Notes to the original reading have not been included here.

does not tell the patient that the illness is terminal, if the husband does not mention that he spent his lunch hour at a motel with his wife's best friend, if the policeman doesn't tell the suspect that a "bug" is recording the conversation with his lawyer, no false information has been transmitted, yet each of these examples meets my definition of lying. The targets did not ask to be misled, and the concealers acted deliberately without giving prior notification of their intent to mislead. Information was withheld wittingly, with intent, not by accident. There are exceptions, times when concealment is not lying because prior notification was given or consent to be misled was obtained. If the husband and wife agree to have an open marriage in which each will conceal affairs unless directly asked, concealing the assignation at the motel will not be a lie. If the patient asks the doctor not to be told if the news is bad, concealing that information is not a lie. By legal definition, however, a suspect and attorney have the right to private conversation; concealing the violation of that right will always be a lie.

When there is a choice about *how* to lie, liars usually prefer concealing to falsifying. There are many advantages. For one thing, concealing usually is easier than falsifying. Nothing has to be made up. There is no chance of getting caught without having the whole story worked out in advance. Abraham Lincoln is reported to have said that he didn't have a good enough memory to be a liar. If a doctor gives a false explanation of a patient's symptoms in order to conceal that the illness is terminal, the doctor will have to remember his false account in order not to be inconsistent when asked again a few days later.

Concealment may also be preferred because it seems less reprehensible than falsifying. It is passive, not active. Even though the target may be equally harmed, liars may feel less guilt about concealing than falsifying. The liar can maintain the reassuring thought that the target really knows the truth but does not want to confront it. Such a liar could think, "My husband must know I am playing around, because he never asks me where I spend my afternoons. My discretion is a kindness; I certainly am not lying to him about what I am doing. I am choosing not to humiliate him, not forcing him to acknowledge my affairs."

Concealment lies are also much easier to cover afterward if discovered. The liar does not go as far out on a limb. There are many available excuses—ignorance, the intent to reveal it later, memory failure, and so on. The person testifying under oath who says "to the best of my recollection" provides an out if later faced with something he has concealed. The claim not to remember what the liar does remember and is deliberately withholding is intermediate between concealment and falsification. It happens when the liar can no longer simply not say anything; a question has been raised, a challenge made. By falsifying only a failure to remember, the liar avoids having to remember a false story; all that needs to be remembered is the untrue claim to a poor memory. And, if the truth later comes out, the liar can always claim not to have lied about it, that it was just a memory problem.

An incident from the Watergate scandal that led to President 7 Nixon's resignation illustrates the memory failure strategy. As evidence grows of their involvement in the break-in and cover-up, presidential assistants H. R. Haldeman and John Ehrlichman are forced to resign. Alexander Haig takes Haldeman's place as the pressure on Nixon mounts. "Haig had been back in the White House for less than a month when, on June 4, 1973, he and Nixon discussed how to respond to serious allegations being made by John W. Dean, the former White House counsel. According to a tape recording of the Nixon-Haig discussion that became public during the impeachment investigation, Haig advised Nixon to duck questions about the allegations by saying 'you just can't recall.'"

A memory failure is credible only in limited circumstances. The 8 doctor asked if the tests were negative can't claim not to remember, nor can the policeman if asked by the suspect whether the room is bugged. A memory loss can be claimed only for insignificant matters, or something that happened some time ago. Even the passage of time may not justify a failure to remember extraordinary events, which anyone would be expected to recall no matter when they happened.

A liar loses the choice whether to conceal or falsify once chal- 9 lenged by the victim. If the wife asks her husband why she couldn't reach him at lunch, the husband has to falsify to maintain his secret affair. One could argue that even the usual dinner table question—"How was your day?"—is a request for information, but it can be dodged. The husband can mention other matters concealing the assignation unless a directed inquiry forces him to choose between falsifying or telling the truth. . . .

From Paul Ekman, *Telling Lies.* New York: W. W. Norton, 1985. Copyright © 1985 by Paul Ekman. Reprinted with permission of W. W. Norton & Company, Inc.

STUDY QUESTIONS

1. Do you think that politicians should always be truthful?

2. Before and since the time of Richard Nixon, many other political figures have been accused of lies and cover-ups. Discuss a case that you can remember and how you judged it.

3. What is the author's definition of lying? Do you find this to be concisely or awkwardly worded? Why?

4. Would something be a lie if someone gives you permission to lie? Discuss circumstances where this might occur.

5. What does the author say is the difference between concealing and falsifying?

6. How does lying affect a person's thinking, feelings, and choice of words?

7. If you suspect people are lying to you, do you feel it is better to confront them or not?

8. As a rule, do you feel that it is better to speak the truth regardless of the consequences?

Facts

© Jared Lee 1985. Reprinted with permission of Jared Lee.

Why is it funny to find "fresh milk" confirmed as fact through observation? Is it because we are embarrassed by cows' udders? Or does it remind us that the fresh milk claims we usually accept may not be factual?

This is an easy problem compared to some of the difficulties we run into when trying to establish facts. Because facts are judged on the basis of truth and reality, establishing them can be a tricky business. But we *can* learn to recognize pitfalls and to apply standards in gathering them. These are the skills that this chapter aims to teach.

We begin by considering what a fact is and proceed to unravel some common confusion about the relationship of facts to reality. We then practice discovering and describing facts accurately, which should bring more clarity to both our thinking about and communication of facts.

Discovery Exercises

A COLLABORATIVE LEARNING OPPORTUNITY

The following three discovery exercises can be done on an individual or collaborative basis; they can be done outside class in preparation for discussion, or in class itself.

Beginning with the Word *Fact*

After consulting at least two dictionaries, write down your own definitions of the following words:

1. know	6. existence
2. certain	7. agree
3. experience	8. real
4. objective	9. actual
5. verified	10. fact

Then read your definitions of *fact* aloud in class. Which definitions seem to cover all kinds of facts?

Does your definition of *fact* contain the following elements?

1. *Fact* comes from the Latin *factum,* meaning a deed, something done.

2. A fact is something known with certainty through experience, observation, or measurement.

3. A fact is something that can be objectively demonstrated and verified.

4. A fact becomes a fact when we can get another source or person to *agree* that it corresponds to a reality.

Learning to Recognize Facts

Answer the following questions in writing, in preparation for a class discussion.

1. List five facts about the room you are in right now. Do not just name objects or events (such as window, door, breeze), but make statements describing exactly what you see in a full context. For instance, do not say "Four windows" but "There are four open windows without blinds or curtains in this room."

2. Write an example of how each of the five senses gives us factual information; for instance, "An ear hears the sound of a telephone ringing."

3. Why do you think the chapter on observation skills preceded this one on facts?

4. Which of the following are statements of fact?

   (a) Water freezes at 0 degrees Celsius and 32 degrees Fahrenheit at sea level or under standard pressure.

   (b) The major religion in Mexico is Roman Catholicism.

   (c) The food is awful in the cafeteria.

   (d) No volcanoes are located in North America.

   (e) Everybody should jog every day.

   (f) She must have forgotten her lunch; it is still on the table.

   (g) Advertisement: "Johnson's Music offers you the best buys in records and tapes."

5. Explain why items 4c through 4g are not facts.

Verifying Facts

One characteristic of facts is that they can be objectively verified—that is, proven to be true through the testimony of witnesses, through agreed-upon observations, or through records or documentation. Read the facts listed below. Select three to study. How would you go about verifying that each is indeed a fact?

1. Jan Vermeer was a Dutch painter who lived from 1632 to 1675.
2. Captain James Cook arrived in Hawaii in 1778.
3. The interest rate on Americans' personal savings in 1980 was 4.7 percent.
4. The largest industrial corporation in the United States in 1979 in terms of sales and assets was Exxon.
5. The mean height and weight for children between one and three years old in the United States are 35 inches and 29 pounds.
6. Tallahassee is the capital of Florida.
7. A normal temperature for the human body is 98.6 degrees Fahrenheit or 37 degrees Celsius.
8. William and Mary College is located in Williamsburg, Virginia.
9. Gravity is a force that tends to draw all bodies in the earth's sphere toward the center of the earth.
10. Water is wet.
11. The word *bible* comes from the Greek word *biblia,* meaning a collection of writings.

FACTS AND REALITY

A search for facts can raise many questions for us, but the basic question is what the correspondence between facts and reality is. In the history of human thought, *reality* has been considered by some to be relative and by others to be absolute. That is, some say the observer determines what reality is, and others say that reality is what it is regardless of what people may think about it. This lack of agreement shows how elusive reality is for us; even what we call "facts" may not always correspond to reality. At one time in history it was agreed that the atom could *not* be split. In the 1940s it was demonstrated that the atom *could* be split. In this case, reality itself did not change, only our perception of reality. And so we discovered the fact we had considered true was false.

The trouble really begins when we are convinced, or try to convince others, that a fact corresponds to an absolute reality. Viewpoints defined as absolute reality have often been used to justify bigoted, fanatical behavior. In human history, religious, political, and social ideas have gained acceptance, each self-righteously proclaiming that it represents the reality, only to be exposed later as ignorant and misguided. Consider these examples:

"Witches and heretics exist. They can be identified by some of us who have the right to punish or execute them."

"We are the Master Race with the right to eliminate inferior races."

These ideas were based on social agreements enforced through political power. Those who challenged or denied them suffered persecution and death. Yet, in these instances, the ideas of those who disagreed eventually won out because the truth was on their side. Disagreements about facts are therefore important events; a free and healthy society is one that maintains the freedom necessary for the expression of conflicting ideas. Indeed, the right to investigate and disagree with ideas is essential for critical thinking to flourish. In politics, in the sciences, and in all aspects of life, we need to be able to challenge the "facts" in order to find our way to truth.

So facts are not necessarily always the same as the truth or reality, although confusion about this is common. We are also susceptible to confusing fact with fiction; we may believe that facts and feelings are two different things; and we may believe that facts are absolute. These are all common confusions. Let's look more closely at these areas of confusion about facts.

DISCERNING FACT FROM FICTION

In the Introduction to this book you met the Thomas family. The majority of people who take the quiz in that Discovery Exercise never realize that they are making not one but two assumptions when they accept the statement "This is graduation day for the Thomas family." In their preoccupation with whether the photo really depicts a graduation day for one or all family members, they overlook assumptions they have made about whether the family's last name is actually Thomas and whether they are a real family. Yet, if they go along with either assumption, they fall into believing that most of the following statements are true as well. This easy willingness to accept a contrived situation as real may be based on film and television viewing habits. The enjoyment of watching a fictional narrative depends upon the magic of our forgetting that we are pretending. Indeed, we call a film bad when this illusion is shattered by clumsiness or poor actors and sets.

Commercial advertising exploits this psychological principle. Actors in commercials have to convince us that they are not actors: they should look ordinary—like one of us. They persuade us that it is natural for two housewives doing aerobics together to share advice on soap detergents. When recognized celebrities appear to make product testimonials, their acting needs to convince us that they are sincere. We are accustomed to pretense, to being kept in the hypnotic trance of fiction while watching advertisements. *We forget we have only made an agreement to accept the fictional as real.*

The new trend in media of mixing fact and fiction can add further confusion. We watch documentaries that alternate between actual news footage and reenactments. We watch adventure stories that use actual news footage with pseudo-newsreels. Consider these instances of fact becoming mixed up with fiction:

1. A soap opera magazine that keeps its readers informed on plot developments is so popular that it can be bought at the checkout stands in grocery stores. Since the 1930s, when the soaps first appeared on radio, audiences have become so immersed in their plots that they regularly send the stars wedding gifts and sympathy and birthday cards in accordance with plot situations.

2. In a newspaper cartoon a father is changing a flat tire in the rain while his two children complain from the car window. The father says, "Don't you understand? This is *life,* this is what is happening. We *can't* switch to another channel."

3. Some TV stations regularly reenact true local crime events for the news, using actors to play the parts on the exact locations. They claim this is done as a public service.

4. A film star who regularly played the surgeon Colonel Potter on the TV series "M*A*S*H" appeared, wearing a doctor's white coat, in an aspirin commercial to endorse the product.

5. Carlos Castaneda's popular series of books written in the style of an anthropologist's notes were at first widely accepted as factual accounts. Controversy still reigns about what in his works is fact and what is fiction, while the author himself refrains from comment.

6. In the summer of 1985 the House Democratic Task Force on Agriculture brought in three Academy Award–winning actresses— Jessica Lange, star of the movie *Country,* Sissy Spacek, who portrayed a farm wife in *The River,* and Jane Fonda, who played the part of a rural woman in the movie *The Dollmaker*—to testify about the problems facing American agriculture.

7. In 1990 both the Mexican government and some U.S. Drug Enforcement Administration agents protested gross factual inaccuracies in the NBC mini-series "Drug Wars: The Camarena Story." In defense, a DEA spokesperson said: "We're not going to go through it all with a fine-tooth comb. In our view, it captures the spirit of events."

For all of us, *discerning the distinction between fiction and fact* is beginning to require more and more alertness, although at times we can be deluded into thinking the difference doesn't really matter.

FEELINGS CAN BE FACTS

Is it important to discern feelings from facts, as it is to discern facts from fiction? It is often said that we should be objective and not subjective in order to determine facts. To be subjective is to be swayed by irrational feelings to distort data; it is to have prejudices or preconceived ideas. To be objective, on the other hand, is to be willing to seek the truth no matter what our feelings may say.

These are traditional guidelines, but in some situations, our feelings *do* provide relevant information for us to consider. Look at the picture on page 9. If you described it to someone else without indicating that it gave you a summertime laid-back feeling, wouldn't that be omitting an important piece of information? And if you showed the photograph to several other people and found that they felt the same way, that reaction could become an agreed-upon fact for all of you. On the other hand, if they disagreed, you could still say these feelings were a fact for you.

Still, there are some situations in which feelings are inappropriate or irrelevant as data. A scientist who felt disgust while dissecting a worm, a frog, or a human body would not consider the facts of these personal feelings as relevant information. A chemist would not enter a statement on a lab report that the smell of sulphur resulted in personal nausea. Each would consider this information too subjective, and therefore inappropriate for the purposes of his or her work—mere reactions based on personal frailties. After all, neither sulphur nor dead bodies are disgusting in themselves.

So when are feelings appropriate as data, and under what conditions? When we are studying art, a conscious awareness of subjective reactions provides important clues that might lead us to an understanding of a work's meaning. An artist never states purpose directly, but manipulates the viewer to experience the work, and through that experience, to understand it. An artist who paints dissected frogs in clouds of sulphur may want to evoke your reaction of repulsion. Indeed, you cannot receive the message unless you can consciously identify your aversion as a fact. In music a joyful waltz entices us to dance. The joy we feel and the desire to express that joy in movement are facts, and quite appropriate, not irrelevant, reactions. To disregard that fact because it is a feeling is to miss the whole point of the art.

In the arts, a feeling response is a reality that can be shared by many people, and its stimulation and transmission is the communication. All of

Photo by John Pearson. Used with permission of the photographer.

us have experienced this while in movie theaters with a group of strangers all laughing or crying together. In this context, feeling is not irrational or irrelevant. The important distinction here is not between objectivity (rational and good) and feelings (subjective and bad) but whether or not one can be *objective about feelings*. When you can both clearly experience and observe your feelings at the same time, you have a very useful skill for recording, evaluating, and learning. To be *subjective about feelings*, on the other hand, is to be unaware of the influence of your feelings on your thoughts and decisions.

CLASS DISCUSSION

1. If you were asked to list five facts about yourself that anyone could verify, what would you say?

2. Could you list five personal facts about yourself—such as feelings, pains, sensations—that would be difficult if not impossible for others to verify? Would these still be facts?

3. Analyze the statements given below. Are they factual?

   (a) Today I feel blue and depressed.

   (b) This view always cheers me up.

   (c) I have pains in my legs when I walk.

(d) I was bored while he was talking, but I pretended to be interested.

(e) This painting conveys a mood of festivity.

(f) Pink elephants were dancing on my bed last night.

FACTS ARE NOT ABSOLUTES

In order to obtain facts, we need verification from many sources and from repeated tests. But often the most we can say is that a fact has a higher or lower probability of being certain. Whether or not a fact is *absolutely* a reality or truth, or a certainty, may not be something that any of us either alone or together can establish, contrary to the convictions of those who have used force in an effort to prove otherwise.

In the sciences, many statements that most people consider facts are actually *probability* statements. In taking a person's temperature, for instance, if the thermometer shows 98.6 degrees, a scientist would say that there is a 90 percent chance that the temperature is between 98.3 and 98.9 degrees. This would take into account any possible inaccuracies of the instrument as well as any variables in the individual. Certainty in science usually means probability that approaches certainty.

Why are facts not absolutes? For one thing, facts are based on social agreements, which can and do change, and on human knowledge, which evolves. New discoveries reveal that some "facts" were never true. The earth was long considered to be the center of the universe. This belief had the authoritative sanction of both scholars and clergy. As the case of Galileo shows, anyone who openly questioned this "fact" could be forced to recant. History offers us many such examples of mistaken ideas accepted in their time as absolute truths, ranging from the idea that women are inferior to the belief that drawing blood reduces fever. And mistaken ideas do not reside solely in the past: ideas taken for truths today may be found mistaken in another time.

This happens because facts are human products. Facts are based on human senses and perceptions, which are limited. The designation of something as factual or not factual is a decision people make; people base their decisions on perceptions and judgments that range from the least skilled to the most highly developed. Unconscious factors also affect all skill levels. Facts are based only on how people *interpret* the way things are, and their interpretations may or may not be in accordance with reality. For this reason, a scientific approach to any field of knowledge has to be continually open to what reality has to say, or to a constant reexamination of accepted facts.

FACTS AND SOCIAL PRESSURE

Our senses and our perceptions are what we use to determine the correspondence between facts and reality. To test the accuracy of our perceptions, we need confirmation from other sources. For instance, if we feel warm and dizzy, we might ask a friend to put a hand on our forehead and tell us if our forehead feels feverish. If we have a thermometer, we can verify our temperature more certainly by a reading over 98.6. Often verifications cannot be done with the objectivity of instruments, yet we need them for psychological certainty or for what might be called social agreements. In the following exchanges consider how confirmations of perceptions are requested and needed to establish something's factuality.

1. JOHN: "Tell me, am I asleep or awake?"
    MARY: "You are awake."

2. BILL: "Did that woman make a pass at me or did I imagine it?"
    JANE: "She made a pass, all right."

3. EMILY: "I think this suit is too large for me. What do you think?"
    MAY: "Much too large."

4. VERNA: "My checking account balances."
    NORMA: "My figures show you are correct."

5. JOSE: "I was hurt by what you said."
    WANDA: "I can see that on your face."

To understand how the principle works, ask yourself how you feel after someone verifies your experience. And how do you feel when they do not?

6. JOSE: "I didn't have too much to drink last night."
    WANDA: "Yes, you did! You were drunk!"

7. CHILD: "I don't want to eat my carrots. They taste icky."
    PARENT: "Yes, you do want to eat them. You are just imagining things."

As these examples illustrate, a fact becomes a fact when we can get another source or person to agree that our perception corresponds to a reality. This dependency on confirmation involves some complex social factors that can sometimes obstruct the way to truth. This was demonstrated by American psychologist Solomon Asch, who conducted some simple experiments to test how a group could affect the perceptions of an individual. He found that in a small group, people are willing to deny the evidence of their own senses if the other members of the group interpret reality differently.

Standard   Comparison

FIGURE 3.1

Standard and Comparison Lines in the Asch Experiment

In the experiment, Asch assembled groups of seven to nine college students in what was described as a test of visual judgment. In each group, only one of the students was actually a subject in the experiment; the others were the researcher's secret accomplices. The researcher informed the students that they would be comparing the length of lines. He showed them two white cards. On the first was a single vertical black line—the standard whose length was to be matched. On the second white card were vertical lines of various lengths. The subjects were to choose the one line of the same length as the standard line (see Figure 3.1).

A series of eighteen trials was conducted. When the first pair of cards was presented, the group gave a unanimous judgment. The same thing happened on the second trial. In twelve of the remaining sixteen trials, however, all of Asch's accomplices agreed on what was clearly an incorrect answer. The real subject of the experiment was left to react.

In about a third of the cases, the subject yielded to the majority and conformed to its decision. In separate experiments with a control group consisting only of genuine subjects, Asch found that people made mistakes less than 1 percent of the time. Subsequent interviews with those who yielded to the majority revealed that only a few of them had actually believed that the majority choice was correct. They admitted that they thought they had judged the length of the lines correctly but did not want to "rock the boat" or "spoil the results" by giving the right answer. And then there were also those who had doubted their own perceptions and had concluded that they had better hide this from the others.

In the final analysis, the test made a significant demonstration of the power of consensus to bring about conformity and to make a person invalidate his or her own perception.*

---

*Figure and text adapted from Solomon Asch, "Effects of Group Pressure upon Modification and Distortion of Judgments," in H. Proshansky and B. Seidenberg (eds.), *Basic Studies in Social Psychology* (New York: Holt, Rinehart and Winston, 1965), pp. 393–401. Used with permission of CBS College Publishing.

FACTS AND CONSCIOUS PROBLEM SOLVING

Norman Cousins had what his doctors called an incurable illness; he decided to apply to himself the old saying "Laughter is the best medicine." He rented some old Charlie Chaplin movies and found that ten minutes of solid belly laughter could give him two hours of sleep free of pain from severe spine and joint inflammation.

In 1976, after he was healed, he wrote a book about his experience called *Anatomy of an Illness.* In 1989 Cousins was informed by the American Medical Association that his discovery that laughter helps combat serious illness was indeed a fact. Intervening research has confirmed his findings. Laughter therapy is now used in cancer wards in Houston, Texas, and Durham, North Carolina.

From "Proving the Power of Laughter," *Psychology Today,* October 1989.

CLASS DISCUSSION

1. Why did a third of the subjects in Asch's experiments conform to the incorrect majority even when their perceptions told them they were correct?

2. Did these subjects have any other means of judging the correctness of their perceptions outside of the confirmation of others in the group?

3. If group pressure can affect us this much in such a simple problem as determining the relative length of a line, what do you think are the implications in more complex problems such as public opinion on controversial issues?

4. If you are familiar with the story "The Emperor's New Clothes," what parallels do you see between its theme and Asch's experiment?

FACTS AND OUR LIMITED SENSES

We have seen how consensus and conformity influence perception and thus limit our ability to know the facts. But even aside from the influence of social pressure, we are limited in our ability to know the facts because our human senses are limited. We now know that dogs can hear levels of pitch that we cannot and that butterflies can see colors invisible to us. If we look at a chart of the electromagnetic spectrum, the portion visible

to us is only a tiny slit in the whole band. We have to use instruments—
X rays, radar, the seismograph, smoke detectors—to compensate for our
sense limitations.

But aside from all this, our senses are affected by many other variables such as mental preoccupations, distractions, or our varying degrees of alertness in different circumstances. How much do you actually
see on your commute route? How much attention do you pay to background sounds when you live in the city? Has a friend ever complained
you didn't notice when he shaved off his beard?

All these problems and more were once succinctly illustrated in a
short tale told by the Buddha called "The Blind Men and the Elephant."

THE BLIND MEN AND THE ELEPHANT

Once upon a time a king gathered some blind men about an elephant and asked them to tell him what an elephant was like. The first
man felt a tusk and said an elephant was like a giant carrot; another
happened to touch an ear and said it was like a big fan; another touched
its trunk and said it was like a pestle; still another, who happened to
feel its leg, said it was like a mortar; and another, who grasped its tail,
said it was like a rope. Not one of them was able to tell the king the
elephant's real form.

STATEMENTS OF FACT

As the preceding sections have demonstrated, we cannot be absolutely
certain about what we call facts. For this reason, we need to be careful in
discerning and communicating facts. Language can be shaped to convey
degrees of certainty and uncertainty, depending on the context and degree of precision appropriate for the occasion. When we are describing a
figure in a photograph wearing a wedding dress and veil and not offering
any clues that might contradict her being female, we can say, "This is a
woman dressed as a bride." However, if we see someone with shoulder-
length hair who could be either a male or a female dressed in a man's
bulky business suit, then we might say, "This is an *individual* dressed in
man's clothing."

Yet, when we are communicating, either in writing or speaking, with
conscious awareness of our facts, we do not have to be tentative about

Photo by John Pearson. Used with permission of the photographer.

our every statement. If we are sitting on an ordinary chair that we can touch and feel, we do not have to say, "This mass of particles on which I am now sitting appears to be a chair." If someone motioned for us to sit on a pile of clothes, perhaps we would be more careful to say, "This *appears* to be my chair."

Study the photograph on page 96. Then read the following statements, and notice how those in italics differ from those in regular type.

1. *This is a lone football player.*

   In the center of this black-and-white photograph is a rear view of an individual dressed in light, knee-length pants and a dark jersey shirt. On his shoulders he wears a stiff, light-colored leather or plastic shoulder brace, on top of a darker shaded padding that covers his shoulder blades and fans over the tops of his shoulders in beetle-wing flaps. Padding also bulges from the inside of his pants over his rear. The back of his head is completely covered with a light-colored moplike wig that hangs in long, straight strands down his back to the length of his shoulder-blade brace; two parts bring it forward to cover each side of his face.

2. *He is roller skating down a city street.*

   He is wearing high-top white socks above high-top leather roller skating shoes. His left foot is suspended while the right foot seems to be gliding on a hard pavement surface. The surface on which he moves extends on his left to some building fronts, which are cropped by the top of the photograph. There is a white line down the center of this pavement, over which the bus seems to be moving. No other traffic is visible.

3. *He is carrying an umbrella and a flipper.*

   His left arm is extended, his hand grasping by a strap a long, dark, triangular shape that could be a purse or a flipper. In his right arm, which is bent closer to his waist at the elbow, he holds an opened umbrella. Inside the umbrella, metal supports are visible crisscrossing one another in a flowerlike pattern. On its surface we can see the reverse side of some painted letters, such as *A, T,* and *O.* The pavement appears dry with no signs of moisture.

4. *He is following a bus.*

   We can see the rear of a large white vehicle about fifteen feet before him that has the rounded curves often found in old school buses. In the rear are three top windows; the middle one is rectangular while the two side ones wrap around the bus. Written in decorative script across the back of the vehicle is the word *Partners,* with flourishes that encircle the whole word.

5. *He is in a city parade.*

   The pavement around the central individual is littered with pieces of paper in two sizes: some, which are of the same whiteness as the line down the road, have the thickness of cards and are about three by five inches in size, while the other pieces seem to be confetti size. To the left of this figure, facing him at a distance of about twelve yards, are seven individuals. Five appear underneath a prominent white number 7000 on a black background. All but one are sitting or leaning on wooden or metal railings. Their attention seems to be directed toward the skating figure. The far adjoining building covering the top right center of the picture has two sides, six stories, and about one hundred windows visible.

As you may have guessed, the statements in regular type are statements of fact, while the italicized sentences are conclusions that interpret these facts. The factual statements have the following characteristics:

1. Factual statements show an awareness of the limitations of the data under consideration. If a photo is being described, the writer does not forget that it is *just* a photograph, rather than a life situation where one can inspect and ask questions.

   "The far building that covers the top right center of the picture has two sides, six stories, and about one hundred windows visible."

2. Factual statements assume an outsider's viewpoint, offering clues that orient the reader in space and time.

   "In the center . . . is a rear view of an individual dressed in light knee-length pants. . . ."

3. A factual statement uses appropriate qualifiers to indicate uncertainties and does not mistake assumptions for facts.

   ". . . it appears to be that of a city street."

4. A factual statement states the obvious.

   "In this black-and-white photograph . . ."

5. A factual statement shows a disciplined effort to describe precisely what is present.

   "On his shoulders he wears a stiff, light-colored leather or plastic shoulder brace on top of a darker shaded padding. . . ."

6. A factual statement is not inappropriately cautious, like this statement is:

   "This individual *appears* to have arms and legs."

7. A factual statement does not state guesses, like this one does:

   "He is in a parade in New York City."

8. A factual statement provides specific evidence that others can verify.

    "To the left of this figure, facing him . . . are seven individuals . . ."

9. A factual statement is willing to be dull in the name of accuracy rather than exciting in the name of possibility.

    "His left foot is suspended while the right foot seems to be gliding on a hard pavement surface."

CLASS DISCUSSION

1. Do the detailed statements resemble police reports? Why are police taught to write like this?

2. If you were on a jury, how could it be useful to know the difference between factual and nonfactual statements?

3. Why would it be important to know the difference if you were an attorney or judge, a witness, a defendant?

4. Why would a reporter be concerned with the difference between factual and nonfactual statements?

5. Why would the difference matter to (a) a doctor, (b) a car mechanic, (c) a biologist, (d) a pharmacist?

6. How could the difference matter if a police officer or doctor were not skilled in formulating statements of fact about you?

Writing Application

A COLLABORATIVE LEARNING OPPORTUNITY

★ **Finding Facts in Photographs**

This exercise asks you to list all the facts you can determine about a photograph. Three students should work together on the same photograph either in class or outside of class.

1. Choose one picture from this book to study. First work individually, without discussion, so that you are not influenced by any thinking but your own. Your task is to list *in complete sentences* all the facts you can about your mutually chosen photograph.

2. Arrange your information in logical order, describing one element of the picture at a time. (Don't jump around from the details about one individual, to the background, then to another

Photo by John Pearson. Used with permission of the photographer.

Photo by John Pearson. Used with permission of the photographer.

figure, then back again to the original figure.) Have a spatial or thematic system for organizing your information.

3. Be precise and specific in describing exactly what you see. Restrain the tendency to jump to conclusions or interpretations. Confine yourself to simply describing what is there. (This discipline may help you to see that your initial impressions were mistaken.)

4. Write to enable the reader to confirm what you have seen.

5. When you are working with these photographs, take your feelings into account as evidence for consideration. These photographs are the works of art photographers—not illustrations for news stories. Each was composed by a photographer who had an idea—or a meaning—that he or she wanted to convey to you, just as a painter or a musician conveys ideas, meanings, and feelings.

6. When you have finished your individual list of factual statements, compare your paper with the others in your group. How do you agree or differ? Star the facts you agree on.

STANDARDS WE USE TO DETERMINE FACTS

A fundamental task of critical thinking is determining the facts in a given situation. Such a situation may involve practical problems like proving you have paid a bill, or it may involve intricate forms of investigation in a field like business, science, or politics. In the course of time, standards have been developed to help us determine the facts and how reliable they might be. When we think critically, we know and use these traditional standards, many of which have already been mentioned in this chapter. In review, let's look at four of them: verifiability, reliability, plausibility, and probability.

Verifiability means the data can be confirmed by another source. This source can be a reference source, like a dictionary, a record, like a marriage license, or a standard, like Greenwich mean time. Another source could be the testimony of a witness, or of an expert. Data can be verified by the senses, by agreements, by measurements, or by documentation.

A second standard for determining facts is *reliability*. When we obtain agreements or disagreements about facts, we have to consider their degree of dependability. To do this we have to ask some critical questions. Is the witness biased? Do we need a larger survey? Were the senses used carefully and consciously? Were they adequate to the task? Were the measurements accurate? Were the documents genuine?

Another standard used to determine reliability is the test of time and repetition (probability). If the weather pattern in one region alters radically over a period of several years, then this phenomenon of change becomes a fact. If things always drop when they fall on this planet, gravity remains a fact. Still another standard test for reliability is to consider whether a given fact confirms or contradicts other known facts (plausibility). If a person claims to be over twenty-one, whereas his ID and birth certificate show he is now eighteen, this contradiction calls into question his statement. The same can be said of a senator who claims to support a particular issue but whose voting record demonstrates no support at all.

The standards of *plausibility* and *probability* are familiar ones that we all use but may not always recognize as standards. It does not seem plausible or probable that a person is actually twenty-one if he offers up an ID that says he is eighteen. For facts to be accepted, they have to make sense to us or seem to be the most likely possibility.

CHAPTER SUMMARY

1. By definition, a fact is something known with certainty through experience, observation, or measurement. A fact can be objectively demonstrated and verified. A fact depends on other sources to agree that it corresponds to reality.

2. Nevertheless, facts do not always correspond to reality. They depend on our socially agreed-upon interpretation of reality.

3. We need to be alert to discern facts from fiction.

4. Feelings can be facts. Feelings about art can offer us clues to the artist's intentions.

5. Facts are not absolutes, but statements of probability.

6. Because we are dependent on confirmation from others in our search for facts, we are susceptible to distorting our perceptions as a result of social pressure.

7. Our senses are limited both in range and capacity and are affected by many factors, such as selective focus and mental preoccupations.

8. Facts must be expressed in carefully formulated statements that have the following characteristics:

(a) They define their own limitations.

(b) They are objectively stated.

(c) They use appropriate qualifiers.

(d) They state the obvious.

(e) They are not inappropriately cautious.

(f) They do not include guesses or inferences.

(g) They are specific and offer their evidence for others to verify.

9. The standards traditionally used to determine facts are verifiability, reliability, plausibility, and probability. Facts have to undergo the test of time and repetition and not contradict other known facts.

Chapter Quiz

Rate each of the following statements as *true* or *false*. In class discussion or in writing, give an example to substantiate your answer in each case.

_____ 1. Some facts can be determined by measurements.

_____ 2. Some facts can be confirmed by the senses, others by records.

_____ 3. The most reliable facts are those that have been repeatedly confirmed by tests over time.

_____ 4. Facts often consist of obvious details that are seen but not consciously recognized.

_____ 5. Sometimes what we claim to be facts are untrue because the human perceptions used to determine them are limited and fallible.

_____ 6. A person educated in critical thinking qualifies statements to reflect any uncertainties, using such phrases as "it appears that . . ."

_____ 7. Often it is hard to make a decision because we do not have enough facts.

_____ 8. The study of many subjects consists of memorizing facts, because they are the nearest thing we have to certainties.

_____ 9. All newspapers can be depended upon as reliable sources of facts about world events.

_____ 10. An atmosphere that permits disagreements about widely accepted perceptions and beliefs helps critical thinking to flourish.

Writing Application

Writing a Fact-Finding Report

FIRST OPTION

Select a topic—such as choosing a college or choosing a car—for a fact-finding report. Imagine that you have narrowed your choice to two candidates. Make a list of the most essential needs you have to consider. Then make a list of the facts you have, or what verified information you have, about each candidate. For instance:

Needs	*Facts: Ravenwood*	*Facts: Greenspan*
a college in my hometown	in town	in suburbs
low tuition	free	free
evening classes	yes	yes
accreditation	don't know (need to see catalogue)	yes

Put all this information into a composition of one coherent paragraph (*coherent* means clear, logically connected, and consistent in a manner that is easy for the reader to follow). Begin with a sentence that sums up the decision you made (or didn't make). This is known as your topic sentence. Everything that follows in your paragraph should support that statement with the information you discovered through your research and your comparisons. Your last sentence or sentences in this paragraph should make a summary statement that brings all this information together.

Here is a summary of the parameters:

1. *Objective:* To write a simple report about using facts to make a personal decision between two choices.

2. *Form and length:* The equivalent of one typed page.

3. *Structure:* Begin with a topic sentence and end with a summary statement. On another sheet of paper, attach your list of essential needs and your list of facts regarding each candidate for your choice.

4. *Suggested topics:*

(a) Choosing a college

(b) Choosing a car

(c) Choosing a friend

(d) Choosing a computer

(e) Choosing a job

(f) Choosing a career

SECOND OPTION

Think of a problem that was solved through an investigation and verification of the facts. This could be a case of injustice, a mysterious illness affecting a community, an unexpected business loss, a miscommunication between people or nations, or an investment decision. Find a problem that interests you for the writing of a simple report on the subject.

1. Describe the problem.

2. Describe each stage of the investigation and verification of the facts involved.

3. Describe the final outcome—how an ascertainment or application of the facts helped solve the problem.

4. Follow the parameters for form, length, and structure listed under First Option.

STUDENT WRITING EXAMPLE

A PROBLEM SOLVED BY FACTS

Anthony Choy

I am an auto mechanic; a large part of my job requires skills in observing, investigating, and determining facts. Often people bring in cars with problems they can't identify, much less repair. In such cases, they hire me to get the facts. And the final test of whether or not I got the facts right is a car that runs right. Let me illustrate this with a story.

One day a customer brought in a 1977 Ford Pinto. His complaint was about the awful noise in his V-6 engine, which was louder when it revved high and quieter when it revved low. I began my inspection by locating the noise at the front of the engine area. I checked the alternator, water pump, valve adjustment, cam gears. Nothing was out of the ordinary. I was stumped.

I then removed the timing chain cover. I noticed there was a gear-to-gear system that is known to make a racket, but nothing comparable to the sound this engine was producing. Again the gears checked out okay. I was stumped again.

Then I started looking at the obvious. I retraced my diagnosing steps to study the engine some more. I noticed an excessive amount of silicone on the oil pan gasket where the bottom of the timing chain cover meets the oil pan. I noticed some broken gears inside the oil pan. I wondered: "Why didn't the last mechanic take care of this?"

I examined the gears again and noticed how hard it was to remove the crank gear. The only way to remove that gear would be to remove the oil pan by lifting the engine off its mounts first. I realized then that the last mechanic who replaced the cam and crank gears did not do the job correctly: if the mechanic had removed the gears, there would not have been an excessive amount of silicone on the oil pan gasket. The gasket had not been replaced, otherwise the broken pieces in the oil pan would have been cleaned out. Why did the mechanic omit doing this? I realized it was probably because he or she could not figure out how to remove the oil pan.

Well, I replaced the parts and proceeded to repair the vehicle the way I was taught. I started up the engine, checked for leaks, and there were none. Then I revved the engine high for a moment and left it at idle, and the noise was completely gone. It purred like a kitten. I felt good to have corrected the problem. When my customer returned, he shook my hand and gave me a bonus.

Used with permission of Anthony Choy.

Readings

THE ACCIDENT AND AFTERMATH

Hayden Herrera

"I made two terrible mistakes in my life: the one was a bus accident and the other was Diego Rivera." Thus did Frida Kahlo, a Mexican artist of great charismatic beauty, sum up her life. Her writing and paintings had a lot to say about these two events: the first was a disaster suffered at age eighteen that left her crippled, and the second was her stormy marriage to Diego Rivera, the most famous Mexican muralist of this century. This reading selection describes her first "mistake"—the bus accident. Although the trauma would seem to have been so terrible as to be unconfrontable, through its telling and retelling, Kahlo achieved a measure of transcendence over its impact. In

*the years that followed, she managed to lead a highly creative life. Her
own healing seemed to have begun with simply confronting the reality
of the facts.*

It was one of those accidents that make a person, even one sepa- 1
rated by years from the actual fact, wince with horror. It involved a trolley car that plowed into a flimsy wooden bus, and it transformed Frida
Kahlo's life.

Far from being a unique piece of bad luck, such accidents were 2
common enough in those days in Mexico City to be depicted in numerous *retablos*. (Small votive paintings offering thanks to a holy being,
usually the Virgin, for misfortunes escaped.) Buses were relatively new
to the city, and because of their novelty they were jammed with people
while trolley cars went empty. Then, as now, they were driven with to-
reador bravado, as if the image of the Virgin of Guadalupe dangling near
the front window made the driver invincible. The bus in which Frida
was riding was new, and its fresh coat of paint made it look especially
jaunty.

The accident occurred late in the afternoon on September 17, 1925, 3
the day after Mexico had celebrated the anniversary of its independence from Spain. A light rain had just stopped; the grand gray government buildings that border the Zócalo looked even grayer and more severe than usual. The bus to Coyoacán was nearly full, but Alejandro and
Frida found seats together in the back. When they reached the corner of
Cuahutemotzín and 5 de Mayo and were about to turn onto Calzada de
Tlalpan, a trolley from Xochimilco approached. It was moving slowly
but kept coming as if it had no brakes, as if it were purposely aiming at
a crash. Frida remembered:

> A little while after we got on the bus the collision began. Before that we had
> taken another bus, but since I had lost a little parasol, we got off to look for
> it and that was how we happened to get on the bus that destroyed me. The
> accident took place on a corner in front of the San Juan market, exactly in
> front. The streetcar went slowly, but our bus driver was a very nervous
> young man. When the trolley car went around the corner the bus was
> pushed against the wall.
>
> I was an intelligent young girl, but impractical, in spite of all the free-
> dom I had won. Perhaps for this reason, I did not assess the situation nor
> did I guess the kind of wounds I had. The first thing I thought of was a *bal-
> ero* [Mexican toy] with pretty colors that I had bought that day and that I
> was carrying with me. I tried to look for it, thinking that what had happened
> would not have major consequences.
>
> It is a lie that one is aware of the crash, a lie that one cries. In me there
> were no tears. The crash bounced us forward and a handrail pierced me the
> way a sword pierces a bull. A man saw me having a tremendous hemor-
> rhage. He carried me and put me on a billiard table until the Red Cross came
> for me.

When Alejandro Gómez Arias describes the accident, his voice constricts to an almost inaudible monotone, as if he could avoid reliving the memory by speaking of it quietly: 4

"The electric train with two cars approached the bus slowly. It hit 5 the bus in the middle. Slowly the train pushed the bus. The bus had a strange elasticity. It bent more and more, but for a time it did not break. It was a bus with long benches on either side. I remember that at one moment my knees touched the knees of the person sitting opposite me, I was sitting next to Frida. When the bus reached its maximal flexibility it burst into a thousand pieces, and the train kept moving. It ran over many people.

"I remained under the train. Not Frida. But among the iron rods of 6 the train, the handrail broke and went through Frida from one side to the other at the level of the pelvis. When I was able to stand up I got out from under the train. I had no lesions, only contusions. Naturally the first thing that I did was to look for Frida.

"Something strange had happened. Frida was totally nude. The collision had unfastened her clothes. Someone in the bus, probably a house painter, had been carrying a packet of powdered gold. This package broke, and the gold fell all over the bleeding body of Frida. When people saw her they cried, '*La bailarina, la bailarina!*' With the gold on her red, bloody body, they thought she was a dancer.

"I picked her up—in those days I was a strong boy—and then I no- 8 ticed with horror that Frida had a piece of iron in her body. A man said, 'We have to take it out!' He put his knee on Frida's body, and said, 'Let's take it out.' When he pulled it out, Frida screamed so loud that when the ambulance from the Red Cross arrived, her screaming was louder than the siren. Before the ambulance came, I picked up Frida and put her in the display window of a billiard room. I took off my coat and put it over her. I thought she was going to die. Two or three people did die at the scene of the accident, others died later.

"The ambulance came and took her to the Red Cross Hospital, 9 which in those days was on San Jeronimo Street, a few blocks from where the accident took place. Frida's condition was so grave that the doctors did not think they could save her. They thought she would die on the operating table.

"Frida was operated on for the first time. During the first month it 10 was not certain that she would live."

The girl whose wild dash through school corridors resembled a 11 bird's flight, who jumped on and off streetcars and buses, preferably when they were moving, was now immobilized and enclosed in a series of plaster casts and other contraptions. "It was a strange collision," Frida said. "It was not violent but rather silent, slow, and it harmed everybody. And me most of all."

Her spinal column was broken in three places in the lumbar region. 12
Her collarbone was broken, and her third and fourth ribs. Her right leg
had eleven fractures and her right foot was dislocated and crushed. Her
left shoulder was out of joint, her pelvis broken in three places. The
steel handrail had literally skewered her body at the level of the ab-
domen; entering on the left side, it had come out through the vagina. "I
lost my virginity," she said.

STUDY QUESTION

1. This excerpt gives two observers' accounts of the bus acci-
    dent—its impact and aftermath. Compare and contrast the de-
    tails given from the two viewpoints. How do you account for
    their different assessment of the most important facts?

SHADOWS ON THE WALL

Donna Woolfolk Cross

*This reading is taken from the last chapter in a book about the way
television affects our minds. Donna Woolfolk Cross is a professor of
English in upstate New York.**

I see no virtue in having a public that cannot distinguish fact from
fantasy. When you start thinking fantasy is reality you have a serious
problem. People can be stampeded into all kinds of fanaticism, folly
and warfare.
—Isaac Asimov

Why sometimes I've believed as many as six impossible things before
breakfast.
—Queen to Alice in Lewis Carroll's *Through the Looking Glass*

In Book Four of *The Republic,* Plato tells a story about four pris- 1
oners who since birth have been chained inside a cave, totally isolated
from the world outside. They face a wall on which shadows flicker, cast

*Notes to the original reading have not been included here.

by the light of the fire. The flickering shadows are the only reality they know. Finally, one of the prisoners is released and permitted to leave the cave. Once outside, he realizes that the shadows he has watched for so long are only pale, distorted reflections of a much brighter, better world. He returns to tell the others about the world outside the cave. They listen in disbelief, then in anger, for what he says contradicts all they have known. Unable to accept the truth, they cast him out as a heretic.

Today, our picture of the world is formed in great part from television's flickering shadows. Sometimes that picture is a fairly accurate reflection of the real world; sometimes it is not. But either way, we accept it as real and we act upon it as if it were reality itself. "And that's the way it is," Walter Cronkite assured us every evening for over nineteen years, and most of us did not doubt it.   2

A generation of Americans has grown up so dependent on television that its images appear as real to them as life itself. On a recent trip to a widely advertised amusement park, my husband, daughter, and I rode a "white-water" raft through manufactured "rapids." As we spun and screamed and got thoroughly soaked, I noticed that the two young boys who shared our raft appeared rather glum. When the ride ended, I heard one remark to the other, "It's more fun on television."   3

As an experiment, Jerzy Kosinski gathered a group of children, aged seven to ten years, into a room to show them some televised film. Before the show began, he announced, "Those who want to stay inside and watch the films are free to remain in the classroom, but there's something fascinating happening in the corridor, and those who want to see it are free to leave the room." Kosinski describes what happened next: 4

> No more than 10 percent of the children left. I repeated, "You know, what's outside is really fantastic. You have never seen it before. Why don't you just step out and take a look?"
>
> And they always said, "No, no, no, we prefer to stay here and watch the film." I'd say, "But you don't know what's outside." "Well, what is it?" they'd ask. "You have to go find out." And they'd say, "Why don't we just sit here and see the film first?" . . . They were already too corrupted to take a chance on the outside.

In another experiment, Kosinski brought a group of children into a room with two giant video screens mounted on the side walls. He stood in the front of the room and began to tell them a story. Suddenly, as part of a prearranged plan, a man entered and pretended to attack Kosinski, yelling at him and hitting him. The entire episode was shown on the two video screens as it happened. The children did not respond, but merely watched the episode unfold on the video screens. They rarely glanced at the two men struggling in the front of the room. Later, in an interview with Kosinski, they explained that the video screens captured the event   5 much more satisfactorily, providing close-ups of the participants, their expressions, and such details as the attacker's hand on Kosinski's face.

Some children can become so preoccupied with television that they 6 are oblivious to the real world around them. UPI filed a report on a burglar who broke into a home and killed the father of three children, aged nine, eleven, and twelve. The crime went unnoticed until ten hours later, when police entered the apartment after being called by neighbors and found the three children watching television just a few feet away from the bloody corpse of their father.

Shortly after this report was released, the University of Nebraska 7 conducted a national survey in which children were asked which they would keep if they had to choose—their fathers or their television sets. *Over half* chose the television sets!

Evidence of this confusion between reality and illusion grows daily. 8 Trial lawyers, for example, complain that juries have become conditioned to the formulas of televised courtroom dramas.

Former Bronx District Attorney Mario Merola says, "All they want 9 is drama, suspense—a confession. Never in all my years as a prosecutor have I seen someone cry from the witness stand, 'I did it! I did it—I confess!' But that's what happens on prime-time TV—and that's what the jurors think the court system is all about." He adds, "Such misconceptions make the work of a district attorney's office much harder than it needs to be." Robert Daley describes one actual courtroom scene in which the defendant was subjected to harsh and unrelenting cross-examination: "I watched the jury," he says. "It seemed to me that I had seen this scene before, and indeed I had dozens of times—on television. On television the murderer always cracks eventually and says something like 'I can't take it any more.' He suddenly breaks down blubbering and admits his guilt. But this defendant did not break down, he did not admit his guilt. He did not blubber. It seemed to me I could see the jury conclude before my eyes: ergo, he cannot be guilty—and indeed the trial ended in a hung jury . . . Later I lay in bed in the dark and brooded about the trial . . . If [television courtroom dramas] had never existed, would the jury have found the defendant guilty even though he did not crack?" . . .

From Donna Woolfolk Cross, *Media-Speak: How Television Makes Up Your Mind.* New York: A Mentor Book, 1983. Copyright © 1983 by Donna Woolfolk Cross. Reprinted with permission of The Putnam Publishing Group.

STUDY QUESTIONS

1. This reading begins with an analogy. What is it?

2. What does the author seek to prove in the examples describing the behavior of the children, both in Kosinski's experiments as well as in the two other reports?

3. How do the customary expectations about jury trials derived from watching television dramas seem to affect actual jurors?

For Further Reading

Andersen, Hans Christian. "The Emperor's New Clothes."

Cousins, Norman, "The Computer and the Poet," *Present Tense: An American Editor's Odyssey.* New York: McGraw-Hill, 1967.

Crane, Stephen. "An Illusion in Black and White." *The Complete Short Stories and Sketches of Stephen Crane.* New York: Doubleday, 1963.

Inferences

"Dump all my shares of Peabody and Fenner!"

From *I Paint What I See*. Copyright © 1971 by Gahan Wilson. Used with permission of Simon & Schuster, Inc.

Maybe the man on the phone in this cartoon is right in inferring that news of financial ruin is causing everyone at Peabody and Fenner to jump out of the windows. And maybe his second inference is also correct, that he had better dump all his stock there. But what if it's a fire?

We can be excellent observers, we can have a set of facts plainly before us, and we can still err in our judgment about a situation if we're not careful about our inferences. For inferences are shakier ground than facts when it comes to building a solid structure of critical thinking. Still, inferences can be useful tools in the thinking process if we learn to wield them skillfully. This chapter is dedicated to helping you do just that.

We begin by learning to distinguish inferences from facts, and then consider how inferences can be used skillfully. We then practice drawing inferences from facts. We conclude by learning to combine facts, inferences, and generalizations to create an effective piece of descriptive writing.

Discovery Exercises

Recognizing Inferential Thinking

Study the cartoons on pages 115–116. What kind of thinking is going on in the cartoons? How does the humor relate to this kind of thinking? What kind of thinking did you have to do in order to understand the cartoons?

Defining *Infer*

After consulting at least two dictionaries, write down your own definitions of the following words:

1. reasoning
2. conclusion
3. guess
4. explanation
5. imagine
6. infer
7. inference
8. interpret

"Does this mean it's all over between us, Harvey?"

From *I Paint What I See.* Copyright © 1971 by Gahan Wilson. Used with permission of Simon & Schuster, Inc.

"If I'm right in my guess that this is the Atlantic, then we're the biggest fish in the world."

Used with permission of Richard Guindon.

From *I Paint What I See.* Copyright © 1971 by Gahan Wilson. Used with permission of
Simon & Schuster, Inc.

UNDERSTANDING THE WORDS
INFER AND *INFERENCE*

Did your definition of *infer* mention that it comes from the Latin root
inferre, meaning to bring in or to carry? When we infer, we *bring in*
imagined or reasoned explanations that try to link known facts with
missing facts *to carry* us to more facts and conclusions. When we infer,
we bring in our imagination or reasoning power to explain something. To
infer is to draw a conclusion on the basis of available facts or on the basis
of other inferences. *When we infer, we make a guess in order to find
explanations that can put the known and the unknown together.*

When we make an inference, we draw a conclusion by reasoning
from *evidence:* "They inferred she was upset when she left the room."
An inference can also be a conclusion drawn from *premises,* or from a

logical progression of statements that lead to a conclusion: "All foreign guests in this country are required to have passports. He is a foreign guest. Therefore he must have a passport."

We can also use the word *infer* as a synonym for the word *conclude,* as in this example: "After he had dozed off at the wheel once, he inferred he shouldn't travel any more that day without more sleep." The word *infer* is also used as a synonym for *guess, speculate, surmise:* "I inferred he liked me when he asked me to dance."

Sometimes the word *infer* is used incorrectly to mean imply, hint, or suggest: "He inferred that I didn't have to wait in line if I wanted to tip him." This use of *infer* for *imply* is what linguists call a *solecism,* or a use of the word that is nonstandard. In this text the word *infer* is *never* used in the sense of imply, hint, or suggest.

Discovery Exercises

Drawing Inferences from Evidence

Read the following scenarios and think of three inferences you could make to explain each situation.

1. Your neighbors have regular habits and spend a lot of time at home. One day you notice that there have been no lights on in their house in the evenings for at least a week.

2. In an airport waiting room, you sit down next to a nun wearing a dark blue dress, starched white collar, and starched white head-dress. You notice she is reading *Playboy* magazine.

3. Your child, age four, who usually has a good appetite, says no this morning when you offer her a dish of applesauce.

4. You are on a Greyhound bus. A man gets on and sits beside you. He is carrying an expensive briefcase although he is shabbily dressed, unshaven, and perspiring heavily. When you suggest he place his briefcase on the rack overhead, he refuses, saying he doesn't mind holding it in his lap.

5. You are looking in your wife's closet for your missing shoe and you notice a new and expensive man's sports jacket hanging there.

6. After a class you go to see your professor about an error in addition on your test score. You explain to him respectfully that 100 minus 18 is 82, not 79. He tells you to get the hell out of his office.

7. You are driving through a valley on a spring morning in a heavy rainstorm. You are on a two-lane highway and you notice that

only about half of the cars that pass you head-on have their lights on.

Drawing Inferences from Facts

When we interpret the meaning of facts, we draw inferences about them. How many inferences can you draw from the following facts?

1. **Births to unmarried women in the United States (in thousands)**

Age	1981	1975	1965	1955	1940
Under 15	8.6	11.0	6.1	3.9	2.1
15–19	259.2	222.5	123.1	68.9	40.5
20–24	246.9	134.0	90.7	55.7	27.2
25–29	109.2	99.6	36.8	28.0	10.5
30–34	45.3	19.8	19.6	16.1	5.2

2. **Twenty Fastest Growing Occupations by 1995**

Occupation	Percent Growth
Computer service technicians	96.8
Legal assistants	94.3
Computer systems analysts	85.3
Computer programmers	76.9
Computer operators	75.8
Office machine repairers	71.7
Physical therapy assistants	67.8
Electrical engineers	65.3
Civil engineering technicians	63.9
Peripheral EDP equipment operators	63.5
Insurance clerks, medical	62.2
Electrical technicians	60.7
Occupational therapists	59.8
Surveyor helpers	58.6
Credit clerks	54.1
Physical therapists	53.6
Employment interviewers	52.5
Mechanical engineers	52.1
Mechanical engineering technicians	51.6
Compression and injection mold machine operators, plastics	50.3

3. **Twenty Most Rapidly Declining Occupations by 1995**

Occupation	Percent Decline
Railroad conductor	−32.0
Shoemaking machine operatives	−30.2
Aircraft structure assemblers	−21.0
Central telephone office operators	−20.0
Taxi drivers	−18.9
Postal clerks	−17.9
Private household workers	−16.9
Farm laborers	−15.9
College faculty	−15.0
Roustabouts	−14.4
Postmasters and mail superintendents	−13.8
Rotary drill operator helpers	−11.6
Graduate assistants	−11.2
Data entry operators	−10.6
Railroad brake operators	− 9.8
Fallers and buckers	− 8.7
Stenographers	− 7.4
Typesetters and compositors	− 7.3
Farm owners and tenants	− 7.3
Butchers and meatcutters	− 6.3

From *Almanac of the American People.* New York: Facts on File, 1988.

Do you know how it feels when you are making an inference now? Can you describe how this is done mentally?

DISTINGUISHING INFERENCES FROM FACTS

Inferences are very often confused with facts, as you may well have discovered from taking the quiz on the mythical Thomas family in the Introduction.

1. This is graduation day for the Thomas family.
2. The father is proud of his son.
3. The sister looks up to her brother.
4. This is a prosperous family.
5. The son has just graduated from law school.

If you said *true* to any of these assertions, you were confusing inferences with facts. And if you had recognized this, you would have realized that you had no facts, but were basing your answers on a guess about missing details. The only right response in each case is *can't answer* because all five statements are inferences.

As you learned when you described a photograph in the last chapter, the work of identifying the facts by stating details instead of substituting inferences made *about* these details is the primary challenge of descriptive writing. Usually, specific details are the most conspicuous and obvious information we can see; indeed, they can be so obvious that we do not even realize that we are seeing them. One of the most difficult things about learning how to write descriptive reports is to remember to give the details and let them speak for themselves as much as possible instead of substituting our inferences or interpretations of what they mean.

To review the difference between statements of fact and inferences, suppose for example that a number of individuals were asked to describe what they saw when they looked at a photograph of a man wearing overalls, lying with eyes closed under a tree. One person might say, "This is a picture of a man who is dead drunk"; another might say, "This is a farmer resting during his lunch hour"; or another: "This is a picture of a man who just had a car wreck." Such statements are inferences or *interpretations;* though they all may be plausible, they cannot all be factual. The only statements of fact that can be made describe the basis for these interpretations. So in order to describe accurately, *we have to state the obvious.*

The practice of stating the obvious also helps the writer think through what can be said. When we articulate the details that led to our inferences, we often discover that our interpretations were hasty. Thus, descriptive writing is a process that cannot be rushed; it takes time to find the right words to describe details and to distinguish facts from inferences. Nevertheless, the results are worth it, for a responsible statement is also an *interesting* statement. When we observe carefully and clearly describe what we observe, our work always becomes more alive and interesting to ourselves and to others.

You may have the impression now that you should avoid inferences or not use them at all in your writing. You might feel you should take on the personality of a police detective who says, "Just give me the facts, please!" Although to restrict yourself in this way might be appropriate for writing some kinds of objective reports, it is *not* appropriate for descriptive writing. If you are describing a hospital ward and you mention only that you see men and women in beds, you might leave the reader with a misleading impression of the circumstances. To withhold a reasonable inference that seems to tie all the facts together is an unnecessary restraint, as well as a denial to the reader of useful information.

Both facts and inferences are needed to discover and convey information: *the important thing to remember is not to confuse inferences with facts.* Beyond that, we can learn to use inferences skillfully in our writing and thinking, through practice and awareness.

USING INFERENCES SKILLFULLY

We do not need to make inferences when we have all the facts about a situation or a satisfactory explanation of its meaning. We make inferences when some important facts and a fully satisfying explanation are missing. Some questions exist that may take years or a lifetime or many generations to answer. In our generation, these might include how to cure AIDS, how to safely and reliably prevent unwanted pregnancy, or how to communicate about conflicts in a way that makes war obsolete. Yet, in order to solve these problems, all we can do is to continue asking questions, gathering facts, making inferences from them, and then letting these inferences suggest strategies for finding new facts, which in turn lead to new inferences, until the objective is reached. When we use inferences consciously and imaginatively, they help us reach the certainties we need to solve life's problems.

Therefore, inferences are not something to be avoided, either in thinking or in writing—they are *essential* mental operations in the search for knowledge. The important thing to remember is that inferences are imaginative constructs and should not be confused with facts or acted upon as though they were facts. When we use inferences with conscious skill, they lead us to knowledge. When we use them without conscious awareness, they lead us to confusion and illusion.

Let us consider examples of both skillful and careless use of inferences. For an example of the former, we turn to that master of inference, Sherlock Holmes. Holmes gained fame for his ability to examine facts and make the best inferences from them.

A STUDY IN SCARLET

Sir Arthur Conan Doyle

"I wonder what that fellow is looking for?" I asked, pointing to a stalwart, plainly dressed individual who was walking slowly down the other side of the street, looking anxiously at the numbers. He had a large blue envelope in his hand, and was evidently the bearer of a message.

"You mean the retired sergeant of Marines," said Sherlock Holmes.   2

"Brag and bounce?" thought I to myself. "He knows that I cannot   3
verify his guess."

The thought had hardly passed through my mind when the man   4
whom we were watching caught sight of the number of our door, and
ran rapidly across the roadway. We heard a loud knock, a deep voice
below, and heavy steps ascending the stair.

"For Mr. Sherlock Holmes," he said, stepping into the room and   5
handing my friend the letter.

Here was an opportunity of taking the conceit out of him. He little   6
thought of this when he made that random shot. "May I ask, my lad," I
said in the blandest voice, "what your trade may be?"

"Commissionaire, sir," he said, gruffly. "Uniform away for repairs."   7

"And you were?" I asked, with a slightly malicious glance at my   8
companion.

"A sergeant, sir, Royal Marine Light Infantry, sir. No answer? Right,   9
sir."

He clicked his heels together, raised his hand in salute, and was   10
gone. . . .

"How in the world did you deduce that?" I asked.   11

"Deduce what?" said he, petulantly.   12

"Why, that he was a retired sergeant of Marines."   13

"It was easier to know it than to explain why I know it. If you were   14
asked to prove that two and two made four, you might find some difficulty, and yet you are quite sure of the fact. Even across the street I
could see a great blue anchor tattooed on the back of the fellow's hand.
That smacked of the sea. He had a military carriage, however, and regulation side whiskers. There we have the marine. He was a man with
some amount of self-importance and a certain air of command. You
must have observed the way in which he held his head and swung his
cane. A steady, respectable, middle-aged man, too, on the face of him—
all facts which led me to believe he had been a sergeant."

"Wonderful!"   15

From Sir Arthur Conan Doyle, *A Study in Scarlet.* New York: Penguin Books, 1982.
(Originally published in 1887.)

CLASS DISCUSSION

1. Where in the story does Sherlock Holmes make an inference
   about the profession of the man seen walking down the street?

2. On what observations does he base this inference?

3. Describe a situation in which one of the following individuals
   would be required to make skillful inferences.

(a) A physician

(b) A salesperson

(c) A car mechanic

(d) A cook

MORE ON USING INFERENCES SKILLFULLY

In contrast to Holmes, many people fall into the trap of building inference on top of inference without ever stopping to check inferences against facts. Inferences, as you may have discovered in your writing and thinking, are not isolated explanations or conclusions. One inference can lead to another and another and another, with each new inference built on the one suggested by those that came before. This can lead different people to entirely different conclusions based on the same set of facts. In this situation, the conscious person is alert to check each inference

---

CONSCIOUS PROBLEM SOLVING THROUGH SKILLED USE OF INFERENCES

Archimedes, a Greek mathematician, was a friend of King Hieron of Syracuse. The king had a problem: he had his doubts about the purity of the gold in his crown. He had given his goldsmith a cube of pure gold with which to make the crown, but now he was wondering if the goldsmith could have substituted some silver or copper alloy and kept the rest of the gold for himself.

The king asked Archimedes to solve the problem for him. Archimedes knew that if he could figure out the volume of the crown and compare that to the original volume of the golden cube, they would have to be the same. While thinking over how it would be possible to measure the volume of an irregular shape like a crown, he went down to the public baths. As he stepped into his tub, he noticed something he had seen countless times before: how the water ran over the top. Then he shouted "Eureka!"

Archimedes had realized that the volume of the water overflow was equal to the bulk of his body under water. When Archimedes measured the volume of the water displaced by the king's crown, he found it to be far greater than that of the original cube of gold. Subsequently Archimedes was rewarded, but the poor goldsmith was executed.

From Royston M. Roberts, *Serendipity: Accidental Discoveries in Science.* New York: John Wiley, 1989.

against available evidence, while the unconscious person sinks deeper into illusion at each step. Let's look at an example of two different chains of inference drawn by two different neighbors from the same set of facts.

Neighbor #1	*Neighbor #2*

Facts:

1. I see my neighbor sitting on the front steps of his house.
2. It is Monday morning. He usually is at work at this time.

Chain of inferences:

1. He must be taking the day off.
2. He probably called work to say he was sick.
3. If he were really sick, he'd be in bed.

Conclusion:

He's pretending to be sick.

Chain of inferences:

4. If he's pretending, he's a loafer.

Conclusion:

He is a loafer.

Chain of inferences:

5. If this keeps up, he'll lose his job.
6. If he's unemployed, his property will deteriorate and that will affect the value of my property.
7. Maybe he's unemployed already.

Conclusion:

I had better sell my house now.

Facts:

1. I see my neighbor sitting on the front steps of his house
2. It is Monday morning. He usually is at work at this time.

Chain of inferences:

1. Either he is sick or on vacation or he's lost his job.
2. In any case, I don't think he'd mind talking to me.

Conclusion:

I'll go over and ask him what's up.

CLASS DISCUSSION

1. Why do the inferences drawn by Neighbor #1 and Neighbor #2 go in such different directions?

Photo by Arthur Rothstein, "Mrs. Thaxton's Daughters," from *The Depression Years*,
Dover Publications, 1978. Courtesy Library of Congress.

2. What is the difference between the way Neighbor #1 and Neighbor #2 work with their facts and inferences?

3. Is it all right to build inferences on inferences?

4. Read the following story, which describes the photo above. What happens here in terms of inferences, and at what point does this description begin to go wrong?

   It is a special day for the little girls since they are wearing their best dresses and holding new dolls. They don't like their gifts, since they are frowning. They are also unhappy because they are orphans. Their parents have just died. The little sisters are having their last picture taken before they leave their home for an orphanage. Their neighbors brought them the dolls to cheer them up on their trip, but they did not succeed. The girls would prefer to have their parents and their home back again the way it used to be.

5. Write your own example of a story in which the inferences take off, leading someone astray.

DRAWING INFERENCES
FROM CAREFUL OBSERVATION

Though we may not have all the facts about a photograph, we can learn a lot from it by observing carefully and drawing inferences skillfully. It's easier to show than describe how this is done, so we'll examine how one person used observation and inference to describe the photo on page 127. As you read this description of the reading woman, notice these features:

1. The facts appear first, followed by the inferences that can reasonably be drawn from them.
2. More than one inference can be drawn from each set of facts.
3. The factual information groups together the details of one segment or feature of the photograph at a time. (For instance, it does not describe the person's hair, then the background, then her posture.)
4. The conclusion draws together the facts and the possible inferences into a plausible explanation of the message, purpose, and meaning of the photograph.

Facts

A fair-skinned individual wearing a woman's dress sits flat on the floor to the right of this photograph: both legs, having the smooth sheen of stockings, are extended before her. Her feet, covered by dark flat-heeled shoes point outward at a 170 degree angle. Her head and shoulders are bent forward over a stack of three hardbound books that rest on her knees and thighs.

Inferences

1. This is a woman reading one book and preparing to read two others.
2. Although she does not have a chair to sit on, she does not seem to mind; her reading completely absorbs her interest.

Facts

She wears an unspotted, unwrinkled, short-sleeved dress that appears to have the weight and texture of cotton; its pattern of horizontal stripes forms bands of white flowerlike shapes alternating with stripes of two darker colors. Her chest is covered by wide lapels cut in two segments of the same fabric whose stripes intersect the dress's horizontal stripes.

Photo by John Pearson. Used with permission of the photographer.

Her hair is wavy and cut short to the nape of her neck; its color could be gray, with some white showing over her ear.

Inferences

1. She is middle-aged. Her sensible dress, hairstyle, shoes, and stockings reflect middle-class values of neatness, conservatism, practicality, modesty, and thrift that were typical in America through the 1960s.

2. She could be a schoolteacher, nun, or librarian, or perhaps a rural or small-town housewife.

3. Nothing in her appearance suggests nonconformity.

4. She is an eccentric university professor who has long lost her interest in clothing styles.

Facts

Only one corner of one eye can be seen behind her plastic-rimmed glasses; her lips are pressed close together. Her visible left arm, wearing a dial watch, is held close to the side of her body in order to support the hand that rests on the bottom of a page. Her small finger is pressed on the first billowing pages of the book, while her thumb and index finger are grasping the bottom of the page where her gaze is directed.

Inferences

1. She finds her reading so interesting that she does not feel or care how awkward this position is for her body; she does not even notice that the floor may be dirty or cold. She reads rapidly and can hardly wait to turn the next page.

2. She is tired from standing up or walking all day; the floor feels better to her than her feet.

3. She cannot sit in a cross-legged position because she is wearing a skirt and stockings.

Facts

Above her on her right is a tall shelf with seven full rows of paperback-sized books. The covers of a few of the books face forward, revealing the name of one mystery author, Agatha Christie. Above her feet, a display stand offers popular magazines such as *People* and *Harper's*.

Inferences

1. This is a public place but not a library. It is a magazine and newspaper store that also carries books, or a bookstore that also sells magazines.

2. The store offers no chairs in order to keep its patrons moving.

3. She is a mystery fan.

4. She is reading the books so that she will not have to pay for them.

5. She wants to buy one of these books, but has to do some reading in order to make her selection.

6. She doesn't care what people think.

Facts

The floor upon which the woman is seated shows the lines of tile squares decorated with a speckled paint pattern and spattered with some larger dark spots and streaks. About three feet away from the woman's feet lies a dark shell-shaped crumpled object of two contrasting textures and shades of color. No other people are visible in this scene.

Inferences

1. It is a linoleum floor, and dirty. Perhaps it is just before cleaning time; or perhaps the store has such constant traffic that it does not attempt to keep the floor spotless.
2. The crumpled object is her coat; she was so excited to get on with her reading that she forgot that she had dropped it there.
3. On the other hand, she appears to be too tidy a person to have scattered her belongings in public; perhaps it belongs to a second reader out of the camera's view.
4. If other people are in the store, this woman is not inhibited by what they may think, or whether or not she is taking up too much space and blocking other customers from the shelves. She is lost in her books.

Facts

To the left of the seated figure and on the right margin of the photograph are rows of small posters covering a dark surface serving as a multisided bulletin board. One can read "James Mason," "People of the Wind," and "Nyingma Institute." On the floor at the base of this structure are stacks of printed materials the size of small newspapers.

Inferences

1. This store also serves as a kind of community center, offering up-to-date information about cultural and educational events.
2. The nature of these events is intellectual and would seem to appeal to a college community.

Conclusion

This photograph plays with some incongruities of public and private, formality and informality. Here a conventionally dressed woman is behaving unconventionally in a public bookstore. Although one would expect her to seek to remain clean and inconspicuous, here she is sitting legs stretched out on a dirty floor, blocking access to at least part of the store. Moreover, although one might expect her to browse standing up, later taking her books home to read, she seems to be absorbed by a stack of books that she may not even pay for. The photographer makes us uncomfortable as he pokes fun at the discomfort some social rules can cause us.

Writing Application

A COLLABORATIVE LEARNING OPPORTUNITY

★ Using Facts and Inferences to Describe a Photograph

Choose one of the photographs in this book to describe. Using the preceding description of the reading woman as a model, write a series of factual paragraphs, each followed by a list of possible inferences. Work alone, and take time and care with this assignment because it is meant to help you integrate what you have learned so far about facts and inferences and work with them more skillfully.

Here is a summary of the parameters:

1. Write about a photograph in this book that has not already been described by you or the author.

2. State a short series of related facts about your subject in one paragraph. (This means organizing your description into some sequence that is easy for the reader to follow. Notice in the example that the reading woman was described first, and then the background, and then the foreground.) Choose an organization that best suits your subject.

3. Follow each group of stated facts with a paragraph listing the inferences you might draw from them.

4. Continue in the same manner until you have covered all the information you can discern.

5. Finally, and this is very important, state a *conclusion* that draws all your facts and inferences together into the most likely explanation of the photograph. This conclusion should follow logically from the information given and not introduce additional facts or inferences. Do not overlook this important thinking experience of synthesizing and interpreting. (If you are uncertain about how

Photo by John Pearson. Used with permission of the photographer.

Solomon D. Butcher Collection. Nebraska State Historical Society. Used with
permission of the society.

to do this, study the "Conclusion" given in the example of the reading woman.)

6. Length should be about two typed pages.

Peer Review

When you have finished, share your writing with a partner. Check one another's work to see if:

1. The inferences follow in logical parallel from the facts given; for instance, in the model of the reading woman, facts given about her hair did not lead to inferences about her reading.

2. The facts support the inferences drawn, or provide reasonable

Photo by John Pearson. Used with permission of the photographer.

evidence for them; for instance, no facts support the inference that the reading woman is a famous author of mystery stories.

3. Inferences are not confused with facts; for instance, one could not say with factual support that the reading woman is a librarian.

Next, see if you can suggest other equally plausible inferences that could be drawn from the facts described by the writer. Finally, decide whether you agree with the conclusion. Is it consistent with the facts and inferences offered, or does it introduce new and unprovable information (such as "This is a photograph of a woman who always reads the ends of mystery stories before she buys them")?

Working together, see if you can interpret the photographs you have chosen in an entirely new and different way, given the same facts and inferences. For instance, perhaps the reading woman is a store cleaning woman who always comes in to work early to catch up on her reading before sweeping the floors and straightening the shelves. Let your imagination run free here, letting go of the track of inferences already made.

GENERALIZING FROM
FACTS AND INFERENCES

Samuel Scudder, whose encounter with a fish was described in Chapter 1, stated that ". . . Agassiz's training in the method of observing facts and their orderly arrangement was ever accompanied by the urgent exhortation not to be content with them. 'Facts are stupid things,' he would say, 'until brought into connection with some general law.'" We can apply this statement to our concerns about thinking and writing by paraphrasing it to say that it is not enough just to collect and state facts and inferences alone; these necessary building blocks have no meaning in themselves until they are collected and organized under general laws.

In science, laws are generalizations that are based on observations and that deal with recurrence, order, and relationships. Generalizations, in turn, relate individual members of a class or category to a whole. To arrive at laws or generalizations, we must first collect information, then analyze patterns or configurations, and finally draw conclusions about the relationships, recurrences, and order of the gathered data. These were the mental actions you followed when drawing conclusions in the last exercise.

The human tendency to generalize too soon, before evidence has been observed very carefully, was illustrated by the way Scudder began his studies. After Scudder had trained himself in the art of observing, he was reminded by his teacher that his collection of facts should lead to inferences and conclusions and a formulation of general laws. After having become an astute observer, he was in a position to draw responsible conclusions about his evidence.

When you first listed facts about the photographs you chose for the exercise, you may have experienced the sense of the "stupidity" of facts that Agassiz referred to. Perhaps you had a sense of not knowing where to stop or how to separate the relevant details from the irrelevant. However, this first stage of simpleminded observing and collecting is important.

In the second stage of writing and of thinking, we begin to separate, compare, categorize, and organize our information. In photograph description we may be led by a feeling, an idea, or an intuition that seems to put everything together. Eventually we are able to formulate all this into a generalization that is a summary statement. In paragraph writing, this statement becomes our topic sentence. This (usually first) sentence states in a general way the main idea to be proven or explained. What then follows is the evidence—the facts and inferences that support the main idea. So we present our topic sentence, which is actually our conclusion, *first* in our writing, although we arrived at it *last* in our thinking. This is exactly what you did in the exercise where you first wrote down your facts and inferences in columns and then drew a conclusion at the end that summarized all your information.

The topic sentence becomes a kind of commitment as well as a guide, aiding us in sorting out our facts for their significance or insignificance as supportive evidence. Some may turn out to be entirely irrelevant. Some may even contradict the topic sentence. This discovery could lead us to reexamine our facts, or search for new ones. A topic sentence can serve as a magnet to pick up supporting details, leaving all the rest behind. It also *tests* our facts and our inferences about them. We may even discover that we really can't support our topic sentence very well at all. In such cases, we can simply discard it and begin again.

The willingness to do this comes from a resolve to arrive at truth as best we can. Such a process may be familiar to you from your own writing experience, although you may never have looked at what you were doing in this conscious way before. The final exercise is designed to have you write with this conscious awareness in mind.

Writing Application

Writing a Paragraph from Facts, Inferences, and Generalizations

Choose a photograph from this chapter that you have not described before. Working alone, observe your photograph for a while, noticing what is plainly visible. Make notes by listing your facts and seeing what inferences you can draw from them.

Putting this information together, draw a conclusion about the photograph as a whole. What message, what statement about life do you think is being conveyed by the photographer here? What does the photographer say to you through the work? Write this conclusion at the top of your page. Use this sentence as a *topic sentence* for a paragraph to follow that makes a general statement or conclusion about your evidence.

Now write the rest of the paragraph in sentences. Describe the photograph using all the facts you can to support your topic sentence. Link these facts to your inferences appropriately throughout. At the end,

Doonesbury ©1985, G. B. Trudeau. Reprinted with permission of Universal Press Syndicate. All rights reserved.

Questions:

1. What is the professor trying to teach his students?
2. What inferences does he expect them to make?
3. What inferences do they make?
4. What clues led you to your own conclusions about this cartoon?
5. How would you describe the professor's teaching style?

bring everything together into a second conclusion, or a summary of what you have demonstrated.

Read your paragraph aloud to one to three other students who selected the same photo. Do you find that you supported your topic sentence adequately?

CHAPTER SUMMARY

1. The word *infer* means (a) to derive by reasoning; (b) to conclude; (c) to guess. When we infer, we use imagination or reasoning to provide explanations for situations where all the facts are either not available or not yet determined.

2. Responsible report writing or descriptive writing lets the facts speak for themselves as much as possible. This often means taking the time to find the right words to describe the obvious and abandoning inferences drawn too hastily that cannot be supported.

3. Writing that offers specific detailed support for its conclusions makes interesting writing. When we perceive and think clearly, we interest both ourselves and others.

4. Reasonable inferences can be used in descriptive writing to tie facts together. Care must be taken to distinguish facts from inferences, though.

5. In solving problems, inferences can be used as a strategy in planning and choosing alternatives. When we think well, we assess all facts, derive as many inferences as we can, and devise strategies for confirming or obtaining more information.

6. Detectives and consultants of all kinds are valued for their ability to examine facts and make the best inferences from them.

7. Inferences can build on inferences in chains of association. Unless each inference is tested for its support of evidence, a series of inferences can mislead us into flights of imagination, away from reliable knowledge.

8. Facts and inferences are linked together through generalizations. Facts have little significance in themselves until generalizations or laws can be derived from them. Generalizing too soon, before we have gathered a sufficient number of facts, is hazardous; but this does not mean that we should not generalize at all. It simply means that we should learn how to draw generalizations that can be supported.

9. The topic sentence of a paragraph is a generalization that summarizes the main idea to be demonstrated in that paragraph. When we think, we usually arrive at this generalization last, after we have examined all our facts and inferences; nevertheless, we state it first, at the beginning of the paragraph. The topic sentence is a kind of conclusion, which is repeated again in another form at the end of the paragraph.

10. By the time you have finished this chapter, you should understand more about the thinking operations involved in the construction of a paragraph or descriptive writing: how it requires observation to determine facts, and imagination and reasoning to link the facts with explanations, and how a generalization ties all this information together into a meaningful whole.

Chapter Quiz

Write two inferences to explain each of the following events:

1. An elderly woman is being pushed down Main Street in a large baby carriage by a little girl.

2. Your best friend leaves you a note saying she has joined the Marines.

3. You have received no mail for the past two weeks.

4. A recent study found that men between fifty and seventy-nine years old married to women one to twenty-four years younger tended to live longer or had a mortality rate 13 percent below the norm.

5. The same study found that men married to older women died sooner or had a death rate that was 20 percent higher than the norm.

Rate each of the following statements as *true* or *false*. Explain your choice in each case or give an example to defend your choice.

_____ 6. To state that "the total U.S. sales of VCRs in 1984 was more than eight million—just about double the number of VCRs sold in 1983" is to make a generalization without facts.

_____ 7. To state the obvious is to state the sensory details of what is actually seen, as opposed to what is *thought* or interpreted about what is seen.

_____ 8. Good thinking does not continue to build inferences on top of inferences, but stops whenever possible to check these inferences out against the original facts, or to find new ones.

_____ 9. One should always avoid making inferences in every kind of writing.

_____ 10. Strategies help us check out our inferences.

Writing Application

Analyzing the Use of Facts and Inferences in a Newspaper Article

Previous exercises in this chapter have helped you to understand inferences and to become more conscious of their occurrence in your own thinking and writing. In this assignment you will be extracting facts and inferences from the writing of others (in this case, a short newspaper article) and using them to form an analysis. You will be evaluating the journalist's use of facts and inferences. Your criteria for this evaluation will be (1) whether probable and reasonable inferences are offered to interpret the facts given; (2) whether the facts are sufficient to warrant the inferences offered; and (3) whether you are left wondering about any missing facts or supplying missing inferences. (Note that if you chose to analyze a *report* you would probably find few inferences supplied by the writer, whereas if you chose an *editorial,* there would be many.)

Photocopy your selected article to accompany your paper. In outline form, just as you did in "Using Facts and Inferences to Describe a Photograph," write down the facts as they appear, followed by the inferences drawn from them. Using this information, write a paragraph beginning with a topic sentence that states your evaluation about the article's use of facts and inferences. Proceed from that point to offer your evidence, illustrating with the facts and inferences you have extracted, together with the reasons you feel that the article either measures up to or does not measure up to the criteria listed earlier.

A summary of the assignment parameters follows:

1. *Objective:* To identify, extract, and evaluate use of facts and inferences in newspaper articles.

2. *Form:* (a) Outline of facts in article with accompanying inferences; (b) paragraph summary and evaluation of findings. (*Be sure you differentiate clearly between the inferences supplied by the writer and the inferences you yourself derived from reading this information.*)

3. *Length:* One-page outline and one-page paragraph; include photocopy of article summarized.

Readings

THE THREE PERCEPTIVES

Idries Shah

This is an old teaching story of the Sufis, a mystic Muslim sect that claims to be far older than Islam. Their stories are parables told to help people understand the nature of the mind and how to use it to gain wisdom. The term perceptives *might also be translated as wise men. This reading was translated by Idries Shah, one of the leading interpreters of Sufi philosophy in the West. As you read it, take note of how accurately the three men connect their inferences to their observation skills and their past experiences.*

There were once three Sufis, so observant and experienced in life 1
that they were known as The Three Perceptives.

One day during their travels they encountered a camelman, who 2
said, "Have you seen my camel? I have lost it."

"Was it blind in one eye?" asked the first Perceptive. 3

"Yes," said the cameldriver. 4

"Has it one tooth missing in front?" asked the second Perceptive. 5

"Yes, yes," said the cameldriver. 6

"Is it lame in one foot?" asked the third Perceptive. 7

"Yes, yes, yes," said the cameldriver. 8

The three Perceptives then told the man to go back along the way 9
they had come, and that he might hope to find it. Thinking that they had
seen it, the man hurried on his way.

But the man did not find his camel, and he hastened to catch up 10
with the Perceptives, hoping that they would tell him what to do.

He found them that evening, at a resting-place. 11

"Has your camel honey on one side and a load of corn on the 12
other?" asked the first Perceptive.

"Yes," said the man. 13

"Is there a pregnant woman mounted upon it?" asked the second 14
Perceptive.

"Yes, yes," said the man. 15

"We do not know where it is," said the third Perceptive. 16

The cameldriver was now convinced that the Perceptives had 17
stolen his camel, passenger and all, and he took them to the judge, accusing them of the theft.

The judge thought that he had made out a case, and detained the 18
three men in custody on suspicion of theft.

A little later, the man found his camel wandering in some fields, and   19
returning to the court, arranged for the Perceptives to be released.

The judge, who had not given them a chance to explain themselves   20
before, asked how it was that they knew so much about the camel,
since they had apparently not even seen it.

"We saw the footprints of a camel on the road," said the first   21
Perceptive.

"One of the tracks was faint; it must have been lame," said the sec-   22
ond Perceptive.

"It had stripped the bushes at only one side of the road, so it must   23
have been blind in one eye," said the third Perceptive.

"The leaves were shredded, which indicated the loss of a tooth,"   24
continued the first Perceptive.

"Bees and ants, on different sides of the road, were swarming over   25
something deposited; we saw that this was honey and corn," said the
second Perceptive.

"We found long human hair where someone had stopped and dis-   26
mounted, it was a woman's," said the third Perceptive.

"Where the person had sat down there were palm-prints, we   27
thought from the use of the hands that the woman was probably very
pregnant and had to stand up in that way," said the first Perceptive.

"Why did you not apply for your side of the case to be heard so that   28
you could explain yourselves?" asked the judge.

"Because we reckoned that the cameldriver would continue look-   29
ing for his camel and might find it soon," said the first Perceptive.

"He would feel generous in releasing us through his discovery,"   30
said the second Perceptive.

"The curiosity of the judge would prompt an enquiry," said the third   31
Perceptive.

"Discovering the truth by his own enquiries would be better for all   32
than for us to claim that we had been impatiently handled," said the
first Perceptive.

"It is our experience that it is generally better for people to arrive at   33
truth through what they take to be their own volition," said the second
Perceptive.

"It is time for us to move on, for there is work to be done," said the   34
third Perceptive.

And the Sufi thinkers went on their way. They are still to be found at   35
work on the highways of the earth.

From Idries Shah, *The Caravan of Dreams.* New York: Penguin Books, 1972. Author
and date of origin of "The Three Perceptives" unknown. Reprinted with permission
of The Octagon Press Ltd., London.

STUDY QUESTIONS

1. Make a list with two columns. On one side state the inferences made by the three men. On the other side show the facts to which they related these inferences.

2. Why were the men so restrained in defending themselves?

3. What do you think of their statement: "It is our experience that it is generally better for people to arrive at truth through what they take to be their own volition"? Can you apply this to learning and teaching?

4. What would you say is the most important value of the three Perceptives?

THE STONE BOY

Gina Berriault

This story was first published in Mademoiselle *magazine; it was then scripted by Berriault into a Hollywood film—with a happy ending—in 1984. The author has received many awards and has served on the faculty of San Francisco State University. In your first reading of this story, look at (1) how the plot of this story revolves around the inference making of its characters, and (2) how your own inference making enables you to "participate" in the story, thus achieving a deeper understanding of it.*

Arnold drew his overalls and raveling gray sweater over his naked 1
body. In the other narrow bed his brother Eugene went on sleeping, undisturbed by the alarm clock's rusty ring. Arnold, watching his brother sleeping, felt a peculiar dismay; he was nine, six years younger than Eugie, and in their waking hours it was he who was subordinate. To dispel emphatically his uneasy advantage over his sleeping brother, he threw himself on the hump of Eugie's body.

"Get up! Get up!" he cried. 2

Arnold felt his brother twist away and saw the blankets lifted in a 3
great wing, and, all in an instant, he was lying on his back under the covers with only his face showing, like a baby, and Eugie was sprawled on top of him.

"Whassa matter with you?" asked Eugie in sleepy anger, his face 4
hanging close.

"Get up," Arnold repeated. "You said you'd pick peas with me." 5

Stupidly, Eugie gazed around the room as if to see if morning had 6
come into it yet. Arnold began to laugh derisively, making soft, snorting
noises, and was thrown off the bed. He got up from the floor and went
down the stairs, the laughter continuing, like hiccups, against his will.
But when he opened the staircase door and entered the parlor, he
hunched up his shoulders and was quiet because his parents slept in the
bedroom downstairs.

Arnold lifted his .22-caliber rifle from the rack on the kitchen wall. 7
It was an old lever-action Winchester that his father had given him because nobody else used it any more. On their way down to the garden
he and Eugie would go by the lake, and if there were any ducks on it
he'd take a shot at them. Standing on the stool before the cupboard, he
searched on the top shelf in the confusion of medicines and ointments
for man and beast and found a small yellow box of .22 cartridges. Then
he sat down on the stool and began to load his gun.

It was cold in the kitchen so early, but later in the day, when his 8
mother canned the peas, the heat from the wood stove would be almost
unbearable. Yesterday she had finished preserving the huckleberries
that the family had picked along the mountain, and before that she had
canned all the cherries his father had brought from the warehouse in
Corinth. Sometimes, on these summer days, Arnold would deliberately
come out from the shade where he was playing and make himself as
uncomfortable as his mother was in the kitchen by standing in the sun
until the sweat ran down his body.

Eugie came clomping down the stairs and into the kitchen, his head 9
drooping with sleepiness. From his perch on the stool, Arnold watched
Eugie slip on his green knit cap. Eugie didn't really need a cap; he hadn't
had a haircut in a long time and his brown curls grew thick and matted,
close around his ears and down his neck, tapering there to a small
whorl. Eugie passed his left hand through his hair before he set his cap
down with his right. The very way he slipped his cap on was an announcement of his status; almost everything he did was a reminder that
he was eldest—first he, then Nora, then Arnold—and called attention
to how tall he was (almost as tall as his father), how long his legs were,
how small he was in the hips, and what a neat dip above his buttocks
his thick-soled logger's boots gave him. Arnold never tired of watching Eugie offer silent praise unto himself. He wondered, as he sat en-
thralled, if when he got to be Eugie's age he would still be undersized
and his hair still straight.

Eugie eyed the gun. "Don't you know this ain't duck-season?" he 10
asked gruffly, as if he were the sheriff.

"No, I don't know," Arnold said with a snigger. 11

Eugie picked up the tin washtub for the peas, unbolted the door 12
with his free hand and kicked it open. Then, lifting the tub to his head,

he went clomping down the back steps. Arnold followed, closing the door behind him.

The sky was faintly gray, almost white. The mountains behind the 13 farm made the sun climb a long way to show itself. Several miles to the south, where the range opened up, hung an orange mist, but the valley in which the farm lay was still cold and colorless.

Eugie opened the gate to the yard and the boys passed between the 14 barn and the row of chicken houses, their feet stirring up the carpet of brown feathers dropped by the molting chickens. They paused before going down the slope to the lake. A fluky morning wind ran among the shocks of wheat that covered the slope. It sent a shimmer northward across the lake, gently moving the rushes that formed an island in the center. Killdeer, their white markings flashing, skimmed the water, crying their shrill, sweet cry. And there at the south end of the lake were four wild ducks, swimming out from the willows into open water.

Arnold followed Eugie down the slope, stealing, as his brother did, 15 from one shock of wheat to another. Eugie paused before climbing through the wire fence that divided the wheatfield from the marshy pasture around the lake. They were screened from the ducks by the willows along the lake's edge.

"If you hit your duck, you want me to go in after it?" Eugie said.   16

"If you want," Arnold said.   17

Eugie lowered his eyelids, leaving slits of mocking blue. "You'd 18 drown 'fore you got to it, them legs of yours are so puny," he said.

He shoved the tub under the fence and, pressing down the center 19 wire, climbed through into the pasture.

Arnold pressed down the bottom wire, thrust a leg through and 20 leaned forward to bring the other leg after. His rifle caught on the wire and he jerked at it. The air was rocked by the sound of the shot. Feeling foolish, he lifted his face, baring it to an expected shower of derision from his brother. But Eugie did not turn around. Instead, from his crouching position, he fell to his knees and then pitched forward onto his face. The ducks rose up crying from the lake, cleared the mountain background and beat away northward across the pale sky.

Arnold squatted beside his brother. Eugie seemed to be climbing 21 the earth, as if the earth ran up and down, and when he found he couldn't scale it he lay still.

"Eugie?"   22

Then Arnold saw it, under the tendril of hair at the nape of the 23 neck—a slow rising of bright blood. It had an obnoxious movement, like that of a parasite.

"Hey, Eugie," he said again. He was feeling the same discomfort he 24 had felt when he had watched Eugie sleeping; his brother didn't know that he was lying face down in the pasture.

Again he said, "Hey, Eugie," an anxious nudge in his voice. But Eu- 25
gie was as still as the morning about them.

Arnold set his rifle on the ground and stood up. He picked up the 26
tub and, dragging it behind him, walked along by the willows to the garden fence and climbed through. He went down on his knees among the
tangled vines. The pods were cold with the night, but his hands were
strange to him, and not until some time had passed did he realize that
the pods were numbing his fingers. He picked from the top of the vine
first, then lifted the vine to look underneath for pods and then moved
on to the next.

It was a warmth on his back, like a large hand laid firmly there, that 27
made him raise his head. Way up the slope the gray farmhouse was
struck by the sun. While his head had been bent the land had grown
bright around him.

When he got up his legs were so stiff that he had to go down on his 28
knees again to ease the pain. Then, walking sideways, he dragged the
tub, half full of peas, up the slope.

The kitchen was warm now; a fire was roaring in the stove with a 29
closed-up, rushing sound. His mother was spooning eggs from a pot of
boiling water and putting them into a bowl. Her short brown hair was
uncombed and fell forward across her eyes as she bent her head. Nora
was lifting a frying pan full of trout from the stove, holding the handle
with a dish towel. His father had just come in from bringing the cows
from the north pasture to the barn, and was sitting on the stool, unbut-
toning his red plaid Mackinaw.

"Did you boys fill the tub?" his mother asked. 30

"They ought of by now," his father said. "They went out of the 31
house an hour ago. Eugie woke me up comin' downstairs. I heard you
shootin'—did you get a duck?"

"No," Arnold said. They would want to know why Eugie wasn't 32
coming in for breakfast, he thought. "Eugie's dead," he told them.

They stared at him. The pitch cracked in the stove. 33

"You kids playin' a joke?" his father asked. 34

"Where's Eugene?" his mother asked scoldingly. She wanted, Ar- 35
nold knew, to see his eyes, and when he had glanced at her she put the
bowl and spoon down on the stove and walked past him. His father
stood up and went out the door after her. Nora followed them with little
skipping steps, as if afraid to be left alone.

Arnold went into the barn, down along the foddering passage past 36
the cows waiting to be milked, and climbed into the loft. After a few
minutes he heard a terrifying sound coming toward the house. His parents and Nora were returning from the willows, and sounds sharp as
knives were rising from his mother's breast and carrying over the slop-

ing fields. In a short while he heard his father go down the back steps, slam the car door and drive away.

Arnold lay still as a fugitive, listening to the cows eating close by. If his parents never called him, he thought, he would stay up in the loft forever, out of the way. In the night he would sneak down for a drink of water from the faucet over the trough and for whatever food they left for him by the barn.   37

The rattle of his father's car as it turned down the lane recalled him to the present. He heard voices of his Uncle Andy and Aunt Alice as they and his father went past the barn to the lake. He could feel the morning growing heavier with sun. Someone, probably Nora, had let the chickens out of their coops and they were cackling in the yard.   38

After a while another car turned down the road off the highway. The car drew to a stop and he heard the voices of strange men. The men also went past the barn and down to the lake. The undertakers, whom his father must have phoned from Uncle Andy's house, had arrived from Corinth. Then he heard everybody come back and heard the car turn around and leave.   39

"Arnold!" It was his father calling him from the yard.   40

He climbed down the ladder and went out into the sun, picking wisps of hay from his overalls.   41

Corinth, nine miles away, was the county seat. Arnold sat in the front seat of the old Ford between his father, who was driving, and Uncle Andy; no one spoke. Uncle Andy was his mother's brother, and he had been fond of Eugie because Eugie had resembled him. Andy had taken Eugie hunting and had given him a knife and a lot of things, and now Andy, his eyes narrowed, sat tall and stiff beside Arnold.   42

Arnold's father parked the car before the courthouse. It was a two-story brick building with a lamp on each side of the bottom step. They went up the wide stone steps, Arnold and his father going first, and entered the darkly paneled hallway. The shirt-sleeved man in the sheriff's office said that the sheriff was at Carlson's Parlor examining the Curwing boy.   43

Andy went off to get the sheriff while Arnold and his father waited on a bench in the corridor. Arnold felt his father watching him, and he lifted his eyes with painful casualness to the announcement, on the opposite wall, of the Corinth County Annual Rodeo, and then to the clock with its loudly clucking pendulum. After he had come down from the loft his father and Uncle Andy had stood in the yard with him and asked him to tell them everything, and he had explained to them how the gun had caught on the wire. But when they had asked him why he hadn't run back to the house to tell his parents, he had had no answer—all he could say was that he had gone down into the garden to pick the peas.   44

His father had stared at him in a pale, puzzled way, and it was then that he had felt his father and the others set their cold, turbulent silence against him. Arnold shifted on the bench, his only feeling a small one of compunction imposed by his father's eyes.

At a quarter past nine, Andy and the sheriff came in. They all went into the sheriff's private office, and Arnold was sent forward to sit in the chair by the sheriff's desk; his father and Andy sat down on the bench against the wall. 45

The sheriff lumped down into his swivel chair and swung toward Arnold. He was an old man with white hair like wheat stubble. His restless green eyes made him seem not to be in his office but to be hurrying and bobbing around somewhere else. 46

"What did you say your name was?" the sheriff asked. 47

"Arnold," he replied; but he could not remember telling the sheriff his name before. 48

"Curwing?" 49

"Yes." 50

"What were you doing with a .22, Arnold?" 51

"It's mine," he said. 52

"Okay. What were you going to shoot?" 53

"Some ducks," he replied. 54

"Out of season?" 55

He nodded. 56

"That's bad," said the sheriff. "Were you and your brother good friends?" 57

What did he mean—good friends? Eugie was his brother. That was different from a friend, Arnold thought. A best friend was your own age, but Eugie was almost a man. Eugie had had a way of looking at him, slyly and mockingly and yet confidentially, that had summed up how they both felt about being brothers. Arnold had wanted to be with Eugie more than with anybody else but he couldn't say they had been good friends. 58

"Did they ever quarrel?" the sheriff asked his father. 59

"Not that I know," his father replied. "It seemed to me that Arnold cared a lot for Eugie." 60

"Did you?" the sheriff asked Arnold. 61

If it seemed so to his father, then it was so. Arnold nodded. 62

"Were you mad at him this morning?" 63

"No." 64

"How did you happen to shoot him?" 65

"We was crawlin' through the fence." 66

"Yes?" 67

"An' the gun got caught on the wire." 68

"Seems the hammer must of caught," his father put in. 69

"All right, that's what happened," said the sheriff. "But what I want 70 you to tell me is this. Why didn't you go back to the house and tell your father right away? Why did you go and pick peas for an hour?"

Arnold gazed over his shoulder at his father, expecting his father to 71 have an answer for this also. But his father's eyes, larger and even lighter blue than usual, were fixed upon him curiously. Arnold picked at a callus in his right palm. It seemed odd now that he had not run back to the house and wakened his father, but he could not remember why he had not. They were all waiting for him to answer.

"I come down to pick peas," he said. 72

"Didn't you think," asked the sheriff, stepping carefully from word 73 to word, "that it was more important for you to go tell your parents what had happened?"

"The sun was gonna come up," Arnold said. 74

"What's that got to do with it?" 75

"It's better to pick peas while they're cool." 76

The sheriff swung away from him, laid both hands flat on his desk. 77 "Well, all I can say is," he said across to Arnold's father and Uncle Andy, "he's either a moron or he's so reasonable that he's way ahead of us." He gave a challenging snort. "It's come to my notice that the most reasonable guys are mean ones. They don't feel nothing."

For a moment the three men sat still. Then the sheriff lifted his hand 78 like a man taking an oath. "Take him home," he said.

Andy uncrossed his legs. "You don't want him?" 79

"Not now," replied the sheriff. "Maybe in a few years." 80

Arnold's father stood up. He held his hat against his chest. "The gun 81 ain't his no more," he said wanly.

Arnold went first through the hallway, hearing behind him the heels 82 of his father and Uncle Andy striking the floor boards. He went down the steps ahead of them and climbed into the back seat of the car. Andy paused as he was getting into the front seat and gazed back at Arnold, and Arnold saw that his uncle's eyes had absorbed the knowingness from the sheriff's eyes. Andy and his father and the sheriff had discovered what made him go down into the garden. It was because he was cruel, the sheriff had said, and didn't care about his brother. Was that the reason? Arnold lowered his eyelids meekly against his uncle's stare.

The rest of the day he did his tasks around the farm, keeping apart 83 from the family. At evening, when he saw his father stomp tiredly into the house, Arnold did not put down his hammer and leave the chicken coop he was repairing. He was afraid that they did not want him to eat supper with them. But in a few minutes another fear that they would go to the trouble of calling him and that he would be made conspicuous by his tardiness made him follow his father into the house. As he went through the kitchen he saw the jars of peas standing in rows on the workbench, a reproach to him.

No one spoke at supper, and his mother, who sat next to him, 84
leaned her head in her hand all through the meal, curving her fingers
over her eyes so as not to see him. They were finishing their small, silent supper when the visitors began to arrive, knocking hard on the
back door. The men were coming from their farms now that it was
growing dark and they could not work any more.

Old Man Matthews, gray and stocky, came first, with his two sons, 85
Orion, the elder, and Clint, who was Eugie's age. As the callers entered
the parlor, where the family ate, Arnold sat down in a rocking chair.
Even as he had been undecided before supper whether to remain outside or take his place at the table, he now thought that he should go
upstairs, and yet he stayed to avoid being conspicuous by his absence.
If he stayed, he thought, as he always stayed and listened when visitors
came, they would see that he was only Arnold and not the person the
sheriff thought he was. He sat with his arms crossed and his hands
tucked into his armpits and did not lift his eyes.

The Matthews men had hardly settled down around the table, after 86
Arnold's mother and Nora had cleared away the dishes, when another
car rattled down the road and someone else rapped on the back door.
This time it was Sullivan, a spare and sandy man, so nimble of gesture
and expression that Arnold had never been able to catch more than a
few of his meanings. Sullivan, in dusty jeans, sat down in the other
rocker, shot out his skinny legs and began to talk in his fast way, recall-
ing everything that Eugene had ever said to him. The other men interrupted to tell of occasions they remembered, and after a time Clint's
young voice, hoarse like Eugene's had been, broke in to tell about the
time Eugene had beat him in a wrestling match.

Out in the kitchen the voices of Orion's wife and of Mrs. Sullivan 87
mingled with Nora's voice but not, Arnold noticed, his mother's. Then
dry little Mr. Cram came, leaving large Mrs. Cram in the kitchen, and
there was no chair left for Mr. Cram to sit in. No one asked Arnold to get
up and he was unable to rise. He knew that the story had got around to
them during the day about how he had gone and picked peas after he
had shot his brother, and he knew that although they were talking only
about Eugie they were thinking about him and if he got up, if he moved
even his foot, they would all be alerted. Then Uncle Andy arrived and
leaned his tall, lanky body against the doorjamb and there were two
men standing.

Presently Arnold was aware that the talk had stopped. He knew 88
without looking up that the men were watching him.

"Not a tear in his eye," said Andy, and Arnold knew that it was his 89
uncle who had gestured the men to attention.

"He don't give a hoot, is that how it goes?" asked Sullivan, 90
trippingly.

"He's a reasonable fellow," Andy explained. "That's what the sheriff 91 said. It's us who ain't reasonable. If we'd of shot our brother, we'd of come runnin' back to the house, cryin' like a baby. Well, we'd of been unreasonable. What would of been the use of actin' like that? If your brother is shot dead, he's shot dead. What's the use of gettin' emotional about it? The thing to do is go down to the garden and pick peas. Am I right?"

The men around the room shifted their heavy, satisfying weight of unreasonableness. 92

Matthews' son Orion said: "If I'd of done what he done, Pa would've hung my pelt by the side of that big coyote's in the barn." 93

Arnold sat in the rocker until the last man had filed out. While his family was out in the kitchen bidding the callers good night and the cars were driving away down the dirt lane to the highway, he picked up one of the kerosene lamps and slipped quickly up the stairs. In his room he undressed by lamplight, although he and Eugie had always undressed in the dark, and not until he was lying in his bed did he blow out the flame. He felt nothing, not any grief. There was only the same immense silence and crawling inside of him; it was the way the house and fields felt under a merciless sun. 94

He awoke suddenly. He knew that his father was out in the yard, closing the doors of the chicken houses so that the chickens could not roam out too early and fall prey to the coyotes that came down from the mountains at daybreak. The sound that had wakened him was the step of his father as he got up from the rocker and went down the back steps. And he knew that his mother was awake in her bed. 95

Throwing off the covers, he rose swiftly, went down the stairs and across the dark parlor to his parents' room. He rapped on the door. 96

"Mother?" 97

From the closed room her voice rose to him, a seeking and retreating voice. "Yes?" 98

"Mother?" he asked insistently. He had expected her to realize that he wanted to go down on his knees by her bed and tell her that Eugie was dead. She did not know it yet, nobody knew it, and yet she was sitting up in bed, waiting to be told, waiting for him to confirm her dread. He had expected her to tell him to come in, to allow him to dig his head into her blankets and tell her about the terror he had felt when he had knelt beside Eugie. He had come to clasp her in his arms and, in his terror, to pommel her breasts with his head. He put his hand upon the knob. 99

"Go back to bed, Arnold," she called sharply. 100

But he waited. 101

"Go back! Is night when you get afraid?" 102

At first he did not understand. Then, silently, he left the door and for a stricken moment stood by the rocker. Outside everything was still. The fences, the shocks of wheat seen through the window before him 103 were so still it was as if they moved and breathed in the daytime and had fallen silent with the lateness of the hour. It was a silence that seemed to observe his father, a figure moving alone around the yard, his lantern casting a circle of light by his feet. In a few minutes his father would enter the dark house, the lantern still lighting his way.

Arnold was suddenly aware that he was naked. He had thrown off 104 his blankets and come down the stairs to tell his mother how he felt about Eugie, but she had refused to listen to him and his nakedness had become unpardonable. At once he went back up the stairs, fleeing from his father's lantern.

At breakfast he kept his eyelids lowered as if to deny the humiliat- 105 ing night. Nora, sitting at his left, did not pass the pitcher of milk to him and he did not ask for it. He would never again, he vowed, ask them for anything, and he ate his fried eggs and potatoes only because every-body ate meals—the cattle ate, and the cats; it was customary for everybody to eat.

"Nora, you gonna keep that pitcher for yourself?" his father asked. 106

Nora lowered her head unsurely. 107

"Pass it on to Arnold," his father said. 108

Nora put her hands in her lap. 109

His father picked up the metal pitcher and set it down at Arnold's 110 plate.

Arnold, pretending to be deaf to the discord, did not glance up but 111 relief rained over his shoulders at the thought that his parents recog-nized him again. They must have lain awake after his father had come in from the yard: had they realized together why he had come down the stairs and knocked at their door?

"Bessie's missin' this morning," his father called out to his mother, 112 who had gone into the kitchen. "She went up the mountain last night and had her calf, most likely. Somebody's got to go up and find her 'fore the coyotes get the calf."

That had been Eugie's job, Arnold thought. Eugie would climb the 113 cattle trails in search of a newborn calf and come down the mountain carrying the calf across his back, with the cow running down along be-hind him, mooing in alarm.

Arnold ate the few more forkfuls of his breakfast, put his hands on 114 the edge of the table and pushed back his chair. If he went for the calf he'd be away from the farm all morning. He could switch the cow down the mountain slowly, and the calf would run along at its mother's side.

When he passed through the kitchen his mother was setting a kettle 115 of water on the stove. "Where you going?" she asked awkwardly.

"Up to get the calf," he replied, averting his face. 116

"Arnold?" 117

At the door he paused reluctantly, his back to her, knowing that she 118 was seeking him out, as his father was doing, and he called upon his pride to protect him from them.

"Was you knocking at my door last night?"   119

He looked over his shoulder at her, his eyes narrow and dry.   120

"What'd you want?" she asked humbly.   121

"I didn't want nothing," he said flatly.   122

Then he went out the door and down the back steps, his legs trem-   123
bling from the fright his answer gave him.

From Gina Berriault, "The Stone Boy," *Mademoiselle*, 1957. Copyright © 1957 by The Condé Nast Publications, Inc. Reprinted courtesy *Mademoiselle*.

STUDY QUESTIONS

1. What inferences do you make, before the tragic incident, about the relationship between Arnold and Eugie? What evidence do you base your inferences on?

2. What does Arnold do immediately after the shooting? What inferences do you make about that?

3. What inferences do his parents and the sheriff and the family's friends make about Arnold's behavior?

4. What information does the author give you about how well Arnold understands his own feelings and behavior?

5. What inferences do you make by the end of the story about Arnold's needs? Explain your evidence.

6. What inferences do you make by the end of the story about Arnold's future?

The first three chapters of this part are about some potentially problematic forms of inferences known as assumptions, opinions, and evaluations. When used consciously, these are modes of thinking that can serve as valuable vehicles for problem solving. When used unconsciously, they deceive us into believing that we are thinking when we are not. These chapters talk about the differences between examined and unexamined assumptions, opinions, and evaluations.

Chapter 8 shows how viewpoint shapes both the content and style of any communication. Again, the polarities of conscious and unconscious use exist here, and again, some knowledge and awareness are required to recognize the distinction. When we think critically we remember to ask, Who wrote this? What perspective and values underlie this message?

The final chapter in Part Two, Chapter 9, examines research skills and discusses how to recognize and overcome the challenges of writing a research paper.

Because an understanding of this new section depends on a clear assimilation of Part One, take time out now, if you have any uncertainties, for a quick review of the past chapter summaries.

5

Assumptions

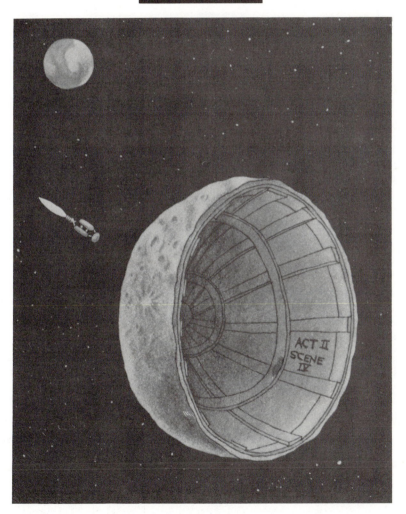

"... Only a minute or so more and man will have his first view of
the other side of the moon!"

From *I Paint What I See.* Copyright © 1971 by Gahan Wilson. Used with permission of
Simon & Schuster, Inc.

It's always a shock, and not necessarily a funny one, to discover that we have made a basic wrong assumption. Perhaps these astronauts might have been less astonished to find the moon to be a hunk of cheese.

Yet learning that assumptions and reality don't match is an everyday occurrence. In this chapter we will study types of assumptions and how they operate in our thinking. We will learn how to recognize, expose, and articulate hidden assumptions, thereby developing skills essential to critical thinking.

Discovery Exercises

A COLLABORATIVE LEARNING OPPORTUNITY

The following three exercises can be done with a partner or alone, depending on your instructor's directions.

What Is an Assumption?

Using at least two dictionaries, write your own definitions of the following words:

1. accepted
2. supposed
3. taken for granted
4. presumption
5. assumption

Finding Assumptions in Cartoons

For each cartoon on pages 157–158 decide what assumption was made—either by a character in the cartoon or by you—that resulted in a humorous situation.

Finding Assumptions in Stories

As you read the stories recounted in each of the paragraphs below, think how each depends on an assumption. Write your answers to the questions that follow each paragraph, in preparation for a class discussion.

1. You are a prisoner in Alcatraz. You get the idea that you could dig your way out through the floor if you only had a pickax or

"We can't afford to send you to college, but we can give you bus fare so you can join the Moonies."

Used with permission of Richard Guindon.

Reprinted with permission of Chronicle Features, San Francisco.

Used with permission of Richard Guindon.

spade. However, because the guards have had the same idea, no such tools are available on the premises. One day you realize that your escape plan is flawed because you have made two assumptions. What are they?

2. You are a guard at a station on the border next to the country of Mesamania. Your duty is to inspect for smuggled goods. Every day some notorious smugglers pass through carrying heavy loads of goods on donkeys. You always examine their loads carefully for contraband but never find anything. What are the smugglers smuggling?

3. You have a dinner guest from a foreign country who belches loudly all through the meal. You find him disgusting and want to get rid of him. But he insists that he be allowed to return your hospitality. So you go to his house for dinner. There everyone but you belches loudly all through the meal. Before you leave, your host says, "I am sorry you did not like my dinner, but you didn't have to be so rude about it." What was the assumption of the foreign guest?

4. George Bernard Shaw was once approached by a woman who proposed marriage. "Imagine a child," she said, "with my body and your brains." "Yes," he said, "but what if the child has my body and your brains?" What was his assumption?

5. In his struggles to receive backing for the voyage of his ships to the Far East by sailing west, Christopher Columbus once spent some hours trying to persuade a nobleman to lend his support.

The nobleman maintained that he was trying to do the impossible, like making an egg stand on end. Then the nobleman called for an egg and handed it to Columbus, who was sitting across from him at a table. Taking up the challenge, Columbus tried wobbling the egg on one end, and then the other, while the nobleman laughed in derision. Then, picking up the egg, Columbus gently smashed its end on the table, allowing it to stand firmly in position, while its contents oozed out between them. What assumption did the nobleman make about the problem that Columbus did not?

6. In California, a bank holdup was staged by a man wearing a levi jacket and pants, a beard, and hair in a "dreadlock" style. He waved a hand grenade and pointed to some sticks of "dynamite" strapped to his waist, which were actually road flares. After leaving the bank he ran into a warehouse next door where he shed his wig, beard, the flares, and clothing and changed into a blue, pin-striped suit. Stopped by a police officer outside, he insisted, "I'm not the one!" And because he didn't look the same as the robber, the police officer let him go. What assumptions did the robber count on in his strategy?

UNDERSTANDING ASSUMPTIONS

Looking at the etymology of the word *assume* is a good way to begin to understand what an assumption is. *Assume* comes from the Latin *assumere,* to take, to adopt, to accept; and from the Indo-European root *em,* to obtain, to buy. To assume is to take for granted; the word *grant* comes from the Latin *cedere,* meaning believe. When we make an assumption, we *believe* in something, and, as we say colloquially, we "buy" it. But before we literally buy things, we are supposed to check them out carefully. An assumption is something bought that is not carefully checked out beforehand.

How does an assumption differ from an inference? As you learned in the last chapter, an inference is arrived at by a process of reasoning from what is known. By contrast, an assumption is taken as a given, without necessarily having any basis in fact or conscious reasoning.

An inference can be based on an assumption, just as an assumption can be based on an inference. For example, most out-of-state visitors who go to San Francisco in foggy July are conspicuous on the streets because they are shivering in their light summer clothing. Based on the summer temperatures where they live, they have inferred that summer in northern California means warm weather. When they take this inference for granted, it becomes an assumption; based on their assumption, they infer that they should pack lightweight clothing for their trip.

Often, as in the preceding example, assumptions are only recognized in retrospect because of the problems they cause. Sometimes we can recognize our assumptions before making decisions based on them that we might regret later. If we are taking out a loan on a car, we need to ask before we sign if that widely advertised loan at no interest is as good as it sounds. If a single woman meets an attractive man who is friendly and flirtatious at a party, she might feel reluctant to ask if he is married; but unless she does, the assumption that he is single may lead to some unwanted complications.

There are different *types* of assumptions, and not all types of assumptions cause problems. What is important in critical thinking is to learn the difference between conscious and unconscious and between warranted and unwarranted assumptions.

TYPES OF ASSUMPTIONS

Making assumptions can be a pitfall in the thinking process, but it can also be a tool—it all depends on the type of assumption you are making. Assumptions can be conscious or unconscious, warranted or unwarranted.

If you take something for granted, you have an *unconscious assumption.* If you sit at the counter of a restaurant that promises home cooking, only to have your food dished out of a saucepan by a motherly figure dressed in a houserobe and hair curlers, you might realize that you had taken it for granted that home cooking would not be this informal. Unconscious assumptions are beliefs, values, or ideas that are not consciously recognized or expressed.

A *conscious assumption,* on the other hand, can be defined as a kind of creative strategy. Sometimes we can make a conscious assumption and use it to guide us to new information. This is also known as a working assumption. Imagine a person looking for a house in an isolated rural area. He comes to a fork in the road and does not know which way to go. He decides to *assume* for the time being that the house is to the left and to proceed for two miles. If at the end of that distance, he still has not found the house, he will return to the fork and proceed to the right. He has not *believed* in his assumption, or bought it—he has only borrowed it. When assumptions are used consciously, they can be helpful as temporary guides to action. When assumptions are unconscious, choices based on them may lead to surprising and undesirable consequences.

As another example, suppose your family has to make an investment decision. Finally it decides to invest in real estate, *assuming* that property values will continue to rise in the years to come. In this case, the assumption is made consciously; nothing is taken for granted. To make a decision, a conscious assumption is made to work with the best possible interpretation of the unknown factors. The assumption may turn out to be incorrect, but as a conscious assumption, it will not lead to the shock or surprise of discovering the wrongness of an unconscious one.

In mathematics, conscious assumptions are essential. For example, $2 + 2 = 4$ is not a fact, but a conclusion or theorem based on axioms that are *assumed* to be fundamental. An axiom is defined as a statement assumed as a basis for the development of a subject. Usually axioms are very acceptable assumptions—not outlandish ones—that can be applied to the real world. Sometimes, as in this case, they are said to be self-evident, but basically they are labeled "assumptions." We will return in Chapter 10 to the topic of creating working assumptions—or hypotheses.

A distinction can also be made between warranted and unwarranted assumptions, or those that are reasonable to make and those that are not. If you buy a carton of milk at your neighborhood grocery dated for use within a week, you can make a *warranted assumption* that it will not be sour when you open it. The same can be said of assumptions that the city buses will arrive and leave on schedule, that the post office will be open on weekdays but not holidays, and that gas and electricity will be available at the flick of a switch. Routine matters like these offer us convenience because they are based on an agreed-upon code of warranted assumptions.

Unwarranted assumptions are those based on ignorance of or lack of awareness of unwritten codes or agreements. If a friend offers you a ride to school one day, or even two days in a row, it would be an *unwarranted assumption* to expect her to provide the same service for you regularly. If a friend breaks a promise, you discover that your assumption that this person was dependable was unwarranted.

Unconscious and unwarranted assumptions have no place in critical thinking. They lead to faulty reasoning and undermine arguments, as we will see.

IDENTIFYING HIDDEN
ASSUMPTIONS IN REASONING

When unconscious assumptions form the basis for reasoning that leads to a particular conclusion, we call them hidden assumptions. The ability to identify hidden assumptions is an important critical thinking skill.

Critical thinking articulates hidden assumptions to expose the fundamental but unexamined thoughts that form the basis for reasoning. It exposes what was taken for granted that should not have been, and thus what made the reasoning unsound. We can learn to identify hidden assumptions in reasoning through practice and through awareness of some of the most common forms of hidden assumptions.

Stereotypes are one form of hidden assumption that crops up often in reasoning. Stereotypes might be described as automatic mental filing systems for classifying new data in old and familiar categories. For instance, consider the statement "All cocker spaniels are friendly dogs; this dog looks mean; therefore it's not a cocker spaniel." The obvious hidden assumption here is that all cocker spaniels fit into one category of friendly dogs. Consider the stereotypes behind the reasoning offered in these sentences:

1. Don't you have a girlfriend to sew on that button?
2. If your friend is Japanese, he must be moody.
3. He must be intelligent if he has a college degree.

Some hidden assumptions are based on belief in the superiority of a particular race, nationality, religion, gender, or individual viewpoint. For instance, someone who says, "Indians do not eat cows because they are superstitious" is judging Indians according to Judeo-Christian or white Anglo-Saxon Protestant beliefs. The speaker shows an ignorance of the philosophy, logic, and culture of the Hindu tradition. Such a viewpoint is both ethnocentric and religiocentric. Belief in the superiority of males is called androcentrism; of humankind over other living things is called anthropocentrism; and of one's individual viewpoint is called egocentrism. We will examine these *isms* in more detail in Chapter 8, "Viewpoints." For now, it's important to recognize when any of these beliefs take the form of hidden assumptions in reasoning.

Still another kind of hidden assumption, related to the others we've mentioned, is based on value judgments. These are called value assumptions. For instance, the statement "Anyone with a million dollars would be happy" is based on the hidden assumption that happiness depends on money, perhaps beginning with a $1 million minimum. Moreover, an additional assumption is that this is a commonly shared value.

Any of these forms of hidden assumptions leads to faulty reasoning. We need to learn to recognize when hidden assumptions creep into our reasoning or someone else's.

CLASS DISCUSSION

Identify and express the hidden assumptions behind each of the following statements:

1. What's a nice girl like you doing in a place like this?

2. I couldn't visit a Buddhist temple because they worship idols there.

3. How can that marriage counselor help people if he himself is divorced?

4. Interviewer to couple on TV show: "What would your parents say if they knew you both belonged to a swingers' club?"

5. You shouldn't be critical of corporations. Aren't you in favor of free enterprise?

6. I can't understand why I haven't met my soul mate this year. My astrologer said I would.

7. Native Americans need to learn the importance of competition for success.

8. People in the Fiji Islands live in poverty and hardship, lacking running water, baths, and toilets in their homes.

9. In a cartoon two men are sitting on the edge of a river polluted with floating oil cans, syringes, industrial wastes, and dead fish. Smoke billows over them from a factory smokestack and diesel trucks in the background. One man says to the other, "Can you imagine what would happen if some irresponsible nut got hold of chemical weapons?"

10. In a television program about earthquake preparedness, an expert demonstrated his gas-driven generator. "In the event of a major disaster," he said, "this generator would run our children's television set so that they would have something to do."

ARGUMENTS AND VALUE ASSUMPTIONS

Arguments, as defined in critical thinking, are not fights or disagreements, but the use of reasoning to defend an idea. Arguments may also seek to persuade others to agree to that idea. When you write or read an argument you need to stop frequently to see if you have made any assumptions in the course of your reasoning. This is an essential attitude in critical thinking: to take nothing for granted. An entire argument can be demolished if it contains a basic hidden and unexamined assumption. A standard for critical thinking is that *an argument should be made as conscious a mental construction as possible.*

In arguments, hidden assumptions appear most often in the underlying values that a person has adopted and taken for granted. Consider the following examples.

Statement: "Children should be taught in school to believe in the Bible."

Hidden assumptions:

1. All public school children are either Christians or Jews or they should be.
2. Maintaining the separation of church and state is not important.
3. The Bible is something to "believe in" rather than to study with critical understanding.
4. Any indoctrination program should begin at an early age. Public schools offer to us children ready for indoctrination.

Value assumption: Teaching "belief in the Bible" is the only right way to develop moral behavior.

Statement of a public official on hearing twelve million Americans were unemployed: "If you ladies would stay at home, maybe we could solve America's unemployment problem."

Hidden assumptions:

1. Women are working while men are unemployed.
2. Women are taking jobs away from men.
3. Women do not really need jobs.
4. All working women are middle-class "ladies" with husbands who indulge women's working like they indulge their hobbies.
5. All women could have someone else support them if they really wanted that.
6. Men want and will take women's jobs (and pay).
7. It is unpatriotic for women to insist on indulging themselves in this way.

Value assumption: Women belong in the home.

Statement: "Hospitals shun the poor and suffering. John Andrews, who was severely beaten, was brought to a private hospital by a friend. He was suffering from a collapsed lung, concussion, and broken rib. Because he couldn't prove he had insurance, he was turned away and dumped on a county hospital."

Hidden assumptions:

1. He was poor and a victim in this beating.
2. His friend brought him to the nearest hospital.
3. The hospital mistreated him by insisting on proof of insurance.
4. The private hospital should be willing to treat anyone who is critically injured, whether they can pay for their services or not.
5. His life was endangered by being sent away to a county hospital.
6. County hospitals suffer from dumping by private hospitals.

Value assumption: The poor and victimized cannot be held responsible for their condition and deserve charity.

Writing Exercise

★ **Articulating Hidden Assumptions Behind Arguments**

Write down the hidden assumptions you find in the following quotations, to share in a later class discussion.

1. "The $280 million special revenue bond earmarked for construction of new county jails is a misguided, expensive attempt to solve a very real problem: overcrowded, inhumane conditions in our jails.

    "But that very problem is rooted in our current criminal justice system and the existence of oppressive laws which create a whole category of victimless 'crimes.'

    "Over 50 percent of those arrested in California are victimized by the existence of these laws—which regulate drug use, voluntary sexual activities, gambling, and other aspects of personal life. Most of those convicted and serving time are sent to our county jails. While violent criminals roam our streets, our extensive county jail system is filled to overflowing with people who have injured no one else." (*California Voters' Pamphlet* [Libertarian party view], November 1982)

2. "The federal government is doing a great many things for which there is no warrant in the Constitution. Among these are collecting taxes for Social Security, providing Medicare and Medicaid, imposing a *graduated* income tax, prohibiting child labor, and granting low-cost loans to students." (*Your Heritage News* [a Far-Right publication], November 1983)

3. "In 1921, Mongolia was just being liberated [by the Communists]. Centuries of feudalism and Lamaist [Buddhist] theocracy had put a stranglehold on the land. Out of a population of 650,000, almost a third of the able-bodied males were lamas [monks] in the Buddhist monasteries, living a life of idleness." (*World Magazine* [a communist publication], March 19, 1983)

4. "I'm nothing," he said. "You understand that, nothing. I earn $250,000 a year, but it's nothing, and I'm nobody. My expenses range from maintaining an apartment on Park Avenue for $20,400 a year to $30,000 a year for private schools for my children. My total expenses come to over $300,000 a year, leaving nothing left over for dinner parties, paintings, furniture, a mistress, psychiatrists, or even a week in Europe." (From Lewis

Lapham, "The Gilded Cage," *Money and Class in America*. New York: Random House, 1988)

5. "As the federal judge I rule that schools violate the Constitution by requiring fundamentalist Christian children to use textbooks that offend their religious beliefs. I hereby order the Hawkins County Tennessee public schools to excuse fundamentalist children from reading class to avoid books that their parents say promote feminism, pacifism, and other themes that they regard as anti-Christian."

6. *Radio Interviewer:* "The U.S. government released figures yesterday to show that rural highways that had increased their speed limits from 55 to 65 mph also had an increase of 20,000 more fatalities per year. What do you, as a representative of the Society for Sane Speed Limits, think of this?"

Spokesperson: "Well, first of all, it has not been proven that the increase in the speed limit was the cause of the increase of fatalities. However, even if it were, our organization feels this statistic is within acceptable limits as needed for speed, accessibility, and for our greater economic growth and welfare." (Interview on National Public Radio, Washington, D.C., October 1989)

ASSUMPTIONS, INCONGRUITIES, AND THINKING

When we see a picture of a mannequin in a bathing suit in a church tower window, it challenges our assumptions of how a church is supposed to be: concerned with spiritual, not commercial matters. An image that is so *incongruous* (from the Latin *in* = not, *congruere* = meet together) does not *meet together with* our memories and assumptions; it makes us uncomfortable. Yet, despite this discomfort, it is good for us to have our assumptions challenged, because this is the way we learn and grow.

Recall from Chapter 1 that according to Jean Piaget, we are required to think, or reorganize what we know, when we have experiences that we cannot easily assimilate. This process, which Piaget calls accommodation, is provoked by an inner sense of disequilibrium between ourselves and our environment. This is what happens when our assumptions are challenged by something we observe. For instance, seeing a woman in a hardhat pounding nails at a construction site may challenge our assumptions about what women can do. Only when we successfully accomplish a

Photo by John Pearson. Used with permission of the photographer.

reorganization of our mental categories to accommodate this new experience do we restore our sense of equilibrium.

While describing many of the photographs in this book so far, you may have felt especially uncomfortable. This is because all of them, whether you realized it while viewing them or not, are *based on incongruities*. In studying the photographs, you have had the choice of either denying, suppressing, or avoiding the disequilibrium they aroused, or of staying with the task long enough to reach equilibrium by finding a satisfactory explanation for their incongruities.

To return to the picture of the mannequin in the church window, you might find your explanation by inferring (1) the church has a liberal pastor concerned with fund raising; (2) the church has been sold and turned into a boutique; or (3) an architect designed a commercial building with a bell tower. To find a satisfactory explanation that *reconciles* all our facts sometimes means tolerating a period of doubt and confusion; we have to experience and mentally contain incongruity until we can bring our information into another pattern of order. And although we may never be able to confirm the final truth of our explanation, we at least have the satisfaction of having reconciled all the available information. Persistence in this process of moving from disequilibrium to equilibrium is what Piaget says develops our thinking skills.

Thinking comes about in life through provocation: when we meet situations that do not fit a familiar pattern, that do not fall into familiar stereotypes, that do not meet expectations. In such cases, we have the personal choice to deny or ignore—or to think, to learn, and to grow. When we were toddlers, if we touched a hot stove, the experience of being burned was an unpleasant encounter with reality. And yet, even then, if we had not stopped to analyze even in a simple way what caused the pain, we would have had to suffer the same pain over and over again. Even if we decided to always depend on someone else to think for us and protect us, we would eventually have found such a solution to be impractical. We survive best when we can think for ourselves. And the more we think, the more willing, open, and able we are to accept life's challenges of our assumptions.

CLASS DISCUSSION

1. Give an example of an incongruity that you have experienced that has challenged one of your assumptions.

2. Can you describe the disequilibrium you felt when you saw this incongruity?

3. How did you restore your equilibrium?

4. Have you experienced disequilibrium at times while studying this textbook? How was your equilibrium restored?

THE DECISION TREE

	Start-Up Costs	Average Yearly Expenses	Average Yearly Income	Expected Value
San Antonio	$100,000	$125,000	$270,000	$45,000
Houston	$140,000	$140,000	$375,000	$95,000
Dallas	$130,000	$120,000	$350,000	$100,000

A Vietnamese family living in San Antonio, Texas, decided to open up their own restaurant. They learned from a bank what the start-up costs would be in three cities. They learned that it would cost less in San Antonio than in Houston or Dallas. However, their eldest son, who was a business major at Trinity University, suggested that they get more information before making their final decision and analyze their options through a decision tree. He explained to his parents that to use this method, it would be necessary to take the average annual income and subtract the average yearly expenses and start-up costs to find the expected value. After obtaining more figures from the chambers of commerce involved, he was able to make the diagram above.

Questions:

1. What choice do you think they made?
2. What assumptions did the decision tree keep them from making?

Used with permission of Mark Frey.

SOLVING PROBLEMS
BY UNCOVERING ASSUMPTIONS

People who are good at solving problems will tell you that the first thing they do is check for any unexamined assumptions. This technique was illustrated earlier in the story of Columbus and the egg. His challenger, who assumed, but did not stipulate, that the egg should remain whole, was left surprised by Columbus's creative solution. And Columbus sized up the situation by recognizing that smashing the egg could make a mess, but after all, he had been challenged to make the egg stand on end, not to preserve it.

Here Columbus was using what Edward de Bono calls *lateral thinking,* or the ability to solve problems in an innovative manner by breaking through the restraints of unnecessary assumptions. Lateral thinking, de Bono says, differs from its opposite, *vertical thinking,* in that vertical thinking uses logic in sequential steps to prove or develop patterns. When we think vertically, we tend to stay on the same track, rather than to think the situation through from a different angle. Both vertical and lateral thinking are necessary for problem solving, but only lateral thinking can restructure thought patterns or provoke new ones. If you wish to read more about this interesting distinction, see Edward de Bono's book *Lateral Thinking: Creativity Step by Step* (New York: Harper Colophon Books, 1970).

An excerpt from de Bono's book is a reading selection in this chapter. The study questions that follow it will give you some mental exercise in lateral thinking.

CHAPTER SUMMARY

1. An assumption is something we take for granted, something we buy before checking it out carefully. Often, we do not recognize that we have made an assumption until it causes a problem for us.

2. Assumptions can be conscious or unconscious, warranted or unwarranted. Unconscious and unwarranted assumptions can lead to faulty reasoning, whereas conscious and warranted assumptions can be useful tools for problem solving. We need to recognize the difference.

3. Hidden assumptions are unconscious assumptions that form the basis for reasoning that leads to a particular conclusion. Common forms of hidden assumptions are stereotypes, where we file new experiences in old categories; belief in the superiority of a particular race, nationality, religion, gender, or individual viewpoint; and assumptions based on value judgments, known as value assumptions.

4. Arguments are the use of reasoning to defend an idea or to persuade someone else to believe in the idea. Arguments that contain assumptions are easily demolished, so it is important to make an argument as conscious a mental construction as possible.

5. Incongruities are things we observe that do not meet our expectations or assumptions. When our assumptions are challenged by incongruities, we can choose to reexamine our assumptions and adjust them to regain our equilibrium. This is the process of growth and learning.

6. Someone who brings a fresh perspective to a problem that has stumped others is often able to find a solution because he or she

does not buy the unexamined assumptions that restrain others. As a conscious tool, we can look for unnecessary assumptions when we are confronted with a problem to solve.

Chapter Quiz

Rate each of the following statements as *true* or *false*. Justify your answer with an example or explanation.

_____ 1. When we articulate hidden assumptions, we simply read what we find in print before us.

_____ 2. A good argument invariably contains a few hidden assumptions.

_____ 3. To make a value assumption is to offer a line of reasoning based on a value or belief assumed to be shared by everyone.

_____ 4. "Can you believe it? She is twenty-three years old and not even thinking of getting married." This statement, made by a Puerto Rican, contains no value assumption.

_____ 5. Assumptions are often only recognized in retrospect because of the problems they cause.

_____ 6. In mathematics, conscious assumptions are called *axioms.*

_____ 7. A *conscious* assumption can be used as a strategy to lead us to new information. If a child does not come home from school at the usual time, we might first decide to call the homes of the child's friends; then if that turns up no information, we might call the police.

_____ 8. Stereotypes contain no assumptions.

_____ 9. To be uncomfortable is to be in disequilibrium. Thinking through a problem restores the comfort of our mental equilibrium.

_____ 10. Incongruities can provoke us into thinking in order to resolve their conflict with our assumptions and expectations.

Writing Application

Essay on Solving a Problem by Uncovering Assumptions

Think of a major problem you know about from your own life (or someone else's) that was solved by the discovery of one or more hidden assumptions. If you prefer to use historical examples from the lives of explorers, artists, or scientists, do some research on the kinds of problems they succeeded in solving. (Besides using ordinary encyclopedias, you might also look for some special science encyclopedias in the library.)

Write in sketch form your basic findings, searching for the following elements to develop and emphasize:

1. What particular problem concerned your subject?
2. What assumptions were embedded in the problem?
3. How were these assumptions discovered?
4. What restraints did these assumptions impose?
5. What, if any, wrong assumptions were made?

Prepare a working outline for an essay of about three typewritten pages. Then begin your essay with a thesis statement that explains what you concluded from your research and analysis.

The *thesis statement,* also called the *thesis,* has some similarity to the topic sentence in that it states a generalization. However, it may be introduced and stated through several sentences instead of one, and it proposes an idea that will be developed, explained, and illustrated over many pages and many paragraphs. By definition, the thesis is the idea that the essay intends to prove. Again, in the process of thinking, the thesis, like the topic sentence, may only come after some study of the subject. However, in the academic essay, it is stated in the first paragraph. A thesis is also called the *controlling idea* because everything written in the essay is based on the dictates of its objective. We can visualize the thesis as a frame, like a picture frame: everything that will appear in that picture—the essay—is contained in and limited by the thesis (see Figure 5.1).

The act of stating the thesis also assists us in organizing our thoughts around one main purpose; it enables us to decide what information would be relevant to this subject and what would not be. If we are writing about assumptions, for instance, we do not need to cover opinions as well. Every statement and every fact appearing in the essay should either support or develop the thesis.

Let's look at the anatomy of a thesis. Suppose you decided to write a personal narrative essay about a problem you solved at work through the discovery of a hidden assumption. Your thesis might begin like this:

(1) All of us have heard fables about villages that suffered long and hard from a particular problem, like a famine or a wayward dragon. (2) Then one day a stranger appeared and solved the problem simply, quickly, and miraculously. (3) In such stories, what seems to be a miracle to the villagers was only a matter of a newcomer's bringing a fresh perspective unbiased by any past assumptions. (4) My own life had a parallel situation several years ago when I came to work for the municipal utilities district. (5) And although I did not

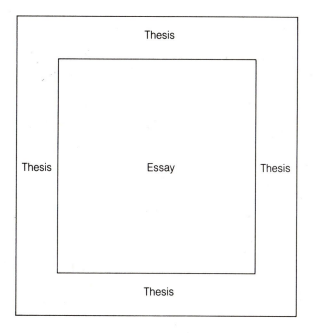

FIGURE 5.1

The Thesis Frames the Essay

arrive on a horse or in a suit of armor, I did bring a fresh perspective that solved an "insoluble problem."

These five sentences comprise the thesis statement. The first two introduce the topic and invite interest. The third states a principle and a limitation of focus. The fourth makes the transition to a personal incident that will illustrate this principle. And the fifth sentence states the actual thesis that the narrative will prove.

Here is a summary of the parameters for this assignment:

1. *Topic:* How one creative individual challenged the restraints of some mistaken assumptions in solving a problem.

2. *Objective:* To isolate a component in the creative thinking process of an individual and to explain how its manifestations, whether conscious or unconscious, correct or incorrect, affected the outcome.

3. *Form:* Essay using personal or researched information for illustration and exposition to support the thesis statement.

4. *Length:* Three to four typed pages.

Submit your working outline with your paper if your instructor requests that you do so. To follow up in class, read your essays to one another in pairs or small groups. Check over one another's work to see if the parameters were followed. Critique each essay with these questions in mind:

1. Does the writer state the thesis clearly and develop it well?
2. Does the essay really stay with the topic of illustrating how an individual solved one major problem through working with some mistaken assumptions?

STUDENT WRITING EXAMPLE

A MISPLACED ASSUMPTION

Terry Ruscoe

All of us have heard fables about villages that suffered long and hard from a particular problem, like a famine or a wayward dragon. Then one day a stranger appeared and solved the problem simply, quickly, and miraculously. In such stories, what seemed to be a miracle to the villagers was only a matter of a newcomer's bringing a fresh perspective, unbiased by any past assumptions. My own life had a parallel situation several years ago when I went to work for the municipal utilities district. And although I did not arrive on a horse or in a suit of armor, I did bring a fresh perspective that solved an "insoluble problem."

My work as a storekeeper was to receive and distribute merchandise, such as plumbing supplies, to our work crews. Here was the problem: after our trucks rolled out of the yard to make deliveries, we would often get calls asking for a modification in the order. But, we had no way of getting in touch with the trucks once they left. This could mean even more frustration for the frantic caller who needed just one more of those special pipeline fittings to complete the job and get traffic moving again.

"Radios, that's what we need," said the foreman as he burst into the office. He had just been chewed out by the Supervisor of Maintenance for a work delay of two hours because of some missing material. "The only problem is the budget. How can we afford eight hundred dollars right away to put a radio in each of the trucks?" Carl, the receiving clerk, who was instructing me on the proper manner of keeping stock records, looked up and quipped, "Yeah, not only is that too much money, but say the driver is out of his truck unloading . . . he may not even hear the thing."

Later that day at lunch, several of us were in the break room. We began tossing the problem around. One of the guys came up with a good idea, suggesting that we augment the radios with an attachment to automatically sound the horn of the truck when it was called. But this would be even more expensive and still be useless if the driver was out of range or was out in a pool vehicle.

Another problem that arose was the lack of firsthand communication; every message would have to be channeled through the base station operator unless we bought our own base station transmitter, which would cost even more money. And then there was the question of privacy: what if we wanted the driver to stop on the way back to pick up some doughnuts? We didn't need the whole district to know about it. "It's the same old problem," moaned one driver. "Face it, we're just going to have to pop for the whole deal, base station and all, and be done with it. Consider it a long-term investment into our sanity."

I had been listening, just listening, for about twenty minutes when I realized that what we had here were two misplaced assumptions: the first was that we had to reach the *truck;* and the second was that we had only *one* way of communicating. It's the driver we need to reach, I reasoned. And what else was there besides radios? Telephones? He couldn't carry a phone around with him but . . . what about a beeper? That way, when he got our message, he could go to any nearby phone and call us. (Remember that this was back in the times when only doctors carried beepers.) "Okay," I said, "why not supply each driver with a remote controlled beeper, so that when he gets our message he can go directly to a phone and call us. As they say, 'phoning is the next best thing to being there.'" And guess what? It worked. If we wanted to contact a driver we simply beeped him. It was far less expensive, and we were able to rent the beepers immediately. Above all, the troops could now get what they wanted without any of those old-fashioned glazed or chocolate mix-ups.

Used with permission of Terry Ruscoe.

Readings

THE GIFT OF THE MAGI

O. Henry

William Sidney Porter, who wrote under the name O. Henry, was a prolific short-story writer. He was widely read and beloved by Americans for about fifty years. As you read, you may feel you are looking into a faded brown turn-of-the-century photograph, but the work is a classic about assumptions.

One dollar and eighty-seven cents. That was all. And sixty cents of it was in pennies. Pennies saved one and two at a time by bulldozing the grocer and the vegetable man and the butcher until one's cheeks burned with the silent imputation of parsimony that such close dealing implied. Three times Della counted it. One dollar and eighty-seven cents. And the next day would be Christmas.

Della finished her cry and attended to her cheeks with the powder rag. She stood by the window and looked out dully at a gray cat walking a gray fence in a gray backyard. Tomorrow would be Christmas Day, and she had only $1.87 with which to buy Jim a present. She had been saving every penny she could for months, with this result. Twenty dollars a week doesn't go far. Expenses had been greater than she had calculated. They always are. Only $1.87 to buy a present for Jim. Her Jim. Many a happy hour she had spent planning for something nice for him. Something fine and rare and sterling—something just a little bit near to being worthy of the honor of being owned by Jim. . . . 2

Suddenly she whirled from the window and stood before the glass. Her eyes were shining brilliantly, but her face had lost its color within twenty seconds. Rapidly she pulled down her hair and let it fall to its full length. 3

Now, there were two possessions of the James Dillingham Youngs in which they both took a mighty pride. One was Jim's gold watch that had been his father's and his grandfather's. The other was Della's hair. Had the Queen of Sheba lived in the flat across the airshaft, Della would have let her hair hang out the window some day to dry just to depreciate Her Majesty's jewels and gifts. Had King Solomon been the janitor, with all his treasures piled up in the basement, Jim would have pulled out his watch every time he passed, just to see him pluck at his beard from envy. 4

So now Della's beautiful hair fell about her rippling and shining like a cascade of brown waters. It reached below her knee and made itself almost a garment for her. And then she did it up again nervously and quickly. Once she faltered for a minute and stood still while a tear or two splashed on the worn red carpet. 5

On went her old brown jacket; on went her old brown hat. With a whirl of skirts and with the brilliant sparkle still in her eyes, she fluttered out the door and down the stairs to the street. 6

Where she stopped the sign read: "Mme. Sofronie. Hair Goods of All Kinds." One flight up Della ran, and collected herself, panting. Madame, large, too white, chilly, hardly looked the "Sofronie." 7

"Will you buy my hair?" asked Della. 8

"I buy hair," said Madame. "Take yer hat off and let's have a sight at the looks of it." 9

Down rippled the brown cascade. 10

"Twenty dollars," said Madame, lifting the mass with a practised hand. 11

"Give it to me quick," said Della. 12

Oh, and the next two hours tripped by on rosy wings. Forget the hashed metaphor. She was ransacking the stores for Jim's present. 13

She found it at last. It surely had been made for Jim and no one else. 14
There was no other like it in any of the stores, and she had turned all of
them inside out. It was a platinum fob chain simple and chaste in design, properly proclaiming its value by substance alone and not by mer-
etricious ornamentation—as all good things should do. It was even
worthy of The Watch. As soon as she saw it she knew that it must be
Jim's. It was like him. Quietness and value—the description applied to
both. Twenty-one dollars they took from her for it, and she hurried
home with the 87 cents. With that chain on his watch Jim might be properly anxious about the time in any company. Grand as the watch was, he
sometimes looked at it on the sly on account of the old leather strap
that he used in place of a chain.

When Della reached home her intoxication gave way a little to pru- 15
dence and reason. She got out her curling irons and lighted the gas and
went to work repairing the ravages made by generosity added to love.
Which is always a tremendous task, dear friends—a mammoth task.

Within forty minutes her head was covered with tiny, close-lying 16
curls that made her look wonderfully like a truant schoolboy. She
looked at her reflection in the mirror long, carefully, and critically.

"If Jim doesn't kill me," she said to herself, before he takes a sec- 17
ond look at me, he'll say I look like a Coney Island chorus girl. But what
could I do—oh! what could I do with a dollar and eighty-seven cents?"

At 7 o'clock the coffee was made and the frying-pan was on the 18
back of the stove hot and ready to cook the chops.

Jim was never late. Della doubled the fob chain in her hand and sat 19
on the corner of the table near the door that he always entered. Then
she heard his step on the stair away down on the first flight, and she
turned white for just a moment. She had a habit of saying little silent
prayers about the simplest everyday things, and now she whispered:
"Please God, make him think I am still pretty."

The door opened and Jim stepped in and closed it. He looked thin 20
and very serious. Poor fellow, he was only twenty-two—and to be bur-
dened with a family! He needed a new overcoat and he was without
gloves.

Jim stopped inside the door, as immovable as a setter at the scent 21
of quail. His eyes were fixed upon Della, and there was an expression in
them that she could not read, and it terrified her. It was not anger, nor
surprise, nor disapproval, nor horror, nor any of the sentiments that she
had been prepared for. He simply stared at her fixedly with that peculiar expression on his face.

Della wriggled off the table and went for him. 22

"Jim, darling," she cried, "don't look at me that way. I had my hair 23 ·
cut off and sold it because I couldn't have lived through Christmas without giving you a present. It'll grow out again—you won't mind, will you?
I just had to do it. My hair grows awfully fast. Say 'Merry Christmas!'

Jim, and let's be happy. You don't know what a nice—what a beautiful, nice gift I've got for you."

"You've cut off your hair?" asked Jim, laboriously, as if he had not arrived at that patent fact yet even after the hardest mental labor.   24

"Cut it off and sold it," said Della. "Don't you like me just as well, anyhow? I'm me without my hair, ain't I?"   25

Jim looked about the room curiously.   26

"You say your hair is gone?" he said, with an air almost of idiocy.   27

"You needn't look for it," said Della. "It's sold, I tell you—sold and gone, too. It's Christmas Eve, boy. Be good to me, for it went for you. Maybe the hairs of my head were numbered," she went on with a sudden serious sweetness, "but nobody could ever count my love for you. Shall I put the chops on, Jim?"   28

Out of his trance Jim seemed quickly to wake. He enfolded his Della. For ten seconds let us regard with discreet scrutiny some inconsequential object in the other direction. Eight dollars a week or a million a year—what is the difference? A mathematician or a wit would give you the wrong answer. The magi brought valuable gifts, but that was not among them. This dark assertion will be illuminated later on.   29

Jim drew a package from his overcoat pocket and threw it upon the table.   30

"Don't make any mistake, Dell," he said, "about me. I don't think there's anything in the way of a haircut or a shave or a shampoo that could make me like my girl any less. But if you'll unwrap that package you may see why you had me going a while at first."   31

White fingers and nimble tore at the string and paper. And then an ecstatic scream of joy; and then, alas! a quick feminine change to hysterical tears and wails, necessitating the immediate employment of all the comforting powers of the lord of the flat.   32

For there lay The Combs—the set of combs, side and back, that Della had worshipped for long in a Broadway window. Beautiful combs, pure tortoise shell, with jewelled rims—just the shade to wear in the beautiful vanished hair. They were expensive combs, she knew, and her heart had simply craved and yearned over them without the least hope of possession. And now, they were hers, but the tresses that should have adorned the coveted adornments were gone.   33

But she hugged them to her bosom, and at length she was able to look up with dim eyes and a smile and say: "My hair grows so fast, Jim!"   34

And then Della leaped up like a little singed cat and cried, "Oh, oh!"   35

Jim had not yet seen his beautiful present. She held it out to him eagerly upon her open palm. The dull precious metal seemed to flash with a reflection of her bright and ardent spirit.   36

"Isn't it a dandy, Jim? I hunted all over town to find it. You'll have to look at the time a hundred times a day now. Give me your watch. I want to see how it looks on it."   37

Instead of obeying, Jim tumbled down on the couch and put his 38
hands under the back of his head and smiled.

"Dell," said he, "let's put our Christmas presents away and keep 'em 39
a while. They're too nice to use just at present. I sold the watch to get
the money to buy your combs. And now suppose you put the chops on."

The magi, as you know, were wise men—wonderfully wise men— 40
who brought gifts to the Babe in the manger. They invented the art of
giving Christmas presents. Being wise, their gifts were no doubt wise
ones, possibly bearing the privilege of exchange in case of duplication.
And here I have lamely related to you the uneventful chronicle of two
foolish children in a flat who most unwisely sacrificed for each other
the greatest treasures of their house. But in a last word to the wise of
these days let it be said that of all who give gifts these two were the
wisest. Of all who give and receive gifts, such as they are wisest. Everywhere they are wisest. They are the magi.

From O. Henry, *The Complete O. Henry.* New York: Doubleday, 1953. "The Gift of the
Magi" was originally published in 1899.

STUDY QUESTIONS

1. Around what major assumptions does this plot revolve?

2. Did your assumptions about this reading begin to change at
   about the time the husband arrives home?

3. Why did you first assume the husband had so much trouble
   grasping the fact that his wife had actually cut off her hair?

4. What details in the story suggest sexist attitudes prevalent in
   this era?

5. How does the story define the word *magi?*

6. Do you rate this as just a sentimental story, or does it convey a
   deeper meaning to you?

DIFFERENCES BETWEEN
LATERAL AND VERTICAL THINKING

Edward de Bono

*Edward de Bono, who first developed the idea of a distinction be-
tween lateral and vertical thinking, contrasts their differences here.
A former professor at Cambridge, Oxford, and Harvard, de Bono has
written many innovative books about thinking, maintaining that it is*

a learnable and teachable skill. He has also conducted a successful BBC television series on the subject.

Vertical thinking is selective, lateral thinking is generative.

Rightness is what matters in vertical thinking. Richness is what 1
matters in lateral thinking. Vertical thinking selects a pathway by ex-
cluding other pathways. Lateral thinking does not select but seeks to
open up other pathways. With vertical thinking one selects the most
promising approach to a problem, the best way of looking at a situation.
With lateral thinking one generates as many alternative approaches as
one can. With vertical thinking one may look for different approaches
until one finds a promising one. With lateral thinking one goes on generating as many approaches as one can even *after* one has found a promising one. With vertical thinking one is trying to select the best approach but with lateral thinking one is generating different approaches
for the sake of generating them.

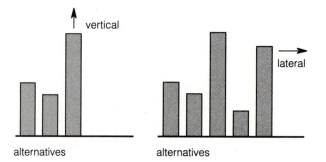

*Vertical thinking moves only if there is a direction in which to move,
lateral thinking moves in order to generate a direction.*

With vertical thinking one moves in a clearly defined direction to- 2
wards the solution of a problem. One uses some definite approach or
some definite technique. With lateral thinking one moves for the sake of
moving.

One does not have to be moving towards something, one may be 3
moving away from something. It is the movement or change that matters. With lateral thinking one does not move in order to follow a direction but in order to generate one. With vertical thinking one designs an
experiment to show some effect. With lateral thinking one designs an
experiment in order to provide an opportunity to change one's ideas.
With vertical thinking one must always be moving usefully in some direction. With lateral thinking one may play around without any purpose
or direction. One may play around with experiments, with models, with
notation, with ideas.

The movement and change of lateral thinking is not an end in itself 4
but a way of bringing about repatterning. Once there is movement and
change then the maximizing properties of the mind will see to it that
something useful happens. The vertical thinker says: 'I know what I am
looking for.' The lateral thinker says: 'I am looking but I won't know
what I am looking for until I have found it.' . . .

Vertical thinking is sequential, lateral thinking can make jumps.

With vertical thinking one moves forward one step at a time. Each 5
step arises directly from the preceding step to which it is firmly connected. Once one has reached a conclusion the soundness of that conclusion is proved by the soundness of the steps by which it has been
reached.

With lateral thinking the steps do not have to be sequential. One 6
may jump ahead to a new point and then fill in the gaps afterwards. In
the diagram below vertical thinking proceeds steadily from A to B to C
to D. With lateral thinking one may reach D via G and then having got
there may work back to A.

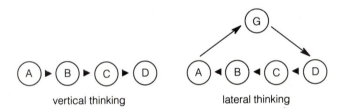

vertical thinking   lateral thinking

When one jumps right to the solution then the soundness of that 7
solution obviously cannot depend on the soundness of the path by
which it was reached. Nevertheless the solution may still make sense in
its own right without having to depend on the pathway by which it was
reached. As with trial-and-error a successful trial is still successful
even if there was no good reason for trying it. It may also happen that
once one has reached a particular point it becomes possible to construct a sound logical pathway back to the starting point. Once such a
pathway has been constructed then it cannot possibly matter from
which end it was constructed—and yet it may only have been possible
to construct it from the wrong end. It may be necessary to be on the top
of a mountain in order to find the best way up.

*With vertical thinking one has to be correct at every step, with lateral
thinking one does not have to be.*

The very essence of vertical thinking is that one must be right at 8
each step. This is absolutely fundamental to the nature of vertical thinking. Logical thinking and mathematics would not function at all without

this necessity. In lateral thinking however one does not have to be right at each step provided the conclusion is right. It is like building a bridge. The parts do not have to be self-supporting at every stage but when the last part is fitted into place the bridge suddenly becomes self-supporting.

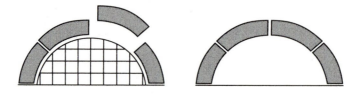

With vertical thinking one uses the negative in order to block off certain pathways. With lateral thinking there is no negative.

There are times when it may be necessary to be wrong in order to 9 be right in the end. This can happen when one is judged wrong according to the current frame of reference and then is found to be right when the frame of reference itself gets changed. Even if the frame of reference is not changed it may still be useful to go through a wrong area in order to reach a position from which the right pathway can be seen. This is shown diagrammatically below. The final pathway cannot of course pass through the wrong area but having gone through this area [left] one may more easily discover the correct pathway [right]. . . .

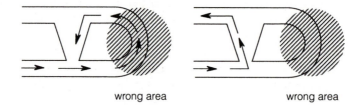

wrong area   wrong area

Summary

The differences between lateral and vertical thinking are very fun- 10 damental. The processes are quite distinct. It is not a matter of one process being more effective than the other for both are necessary. It is a matter of realizing the differences in order to be able to use both effectively.

With vertical thinking one uses information for its own sake in 11 order to move forward to a solution.

With lateral thinking one uses information not for its own sake but ₁₂ provocatively in order to bring about repatterning.

From Edward de Bono, *Lateral Thinking: Creativity Step by Step*. New York: Harper Colophon Books, 1970. Copyright 1970 by the author; reprinted with permission of Harper & Row Publishers, Inc.

STUDY QUESTIONS

1. Working solely on the basis of the first paragraph, create two columns with the traits of vertical thinking in one and those of lateral thinking in the other:

Vertical Thinking	Lateral Thinking
selective	generative

2. Is de Bono saying that lateral thinking should replace vertical thinking?

3. At election time, which politicians tend to be more popular: those that demonstrate vertical thinking or those that demonstrate lateral thinking? Give examples to back your answer.

4. Give an example to explain what the author means in paragraph 3 where he states: "With vertical thinking one must always be moving usefully in some direction. With lateral thinking one may play around without any purpose or direction."

5. What does the author say about the importance of taking sequential steps in vertical thinking?

6. The author defines lateral thinking as "having no negative" or as welcoming mistakes to learn from. Do you think we tend to imagine alternatives more freely when we stop labeling them as either right or wrong?

7. Every year many states in the United States face bond issues to build more prisons, and every year the prisons remain overcrowded. If we look at prison building as a vertical solution, it does not seem to have been successful. Exactly what is the problem that prisons are trying to solve? What might be some lateral solutions?

8. Another persistent U.S. problem is ever-growing illegal drug use. A recent solution has been the "war on drugs." Do you think this is a vertical or lateral solution? If you feel it is vertical, suggest some lateral solutions. If you claim it is lateral, then describe some vertical solutions.

Opinions

"This is Prentiss J. Parmenter recording. It's eight o'clock, the morning of August 24th. The air is crisp and the sky is clear as I leave for my office. On the way, I shall record my thoughts on business, politics, the parlous state of humanity, and perhaps, should the spirit move me, a word or two of philosophical commentary."

Drawing by Stan Hunt; © 1981 The New Yorker Magazine, Inc.
Used with permission of *The New Yorker*.

Prentiss J. Parmenter seems so enamored of his own opinions that he can't wait to get to his office before putting them on tape. Parmenter is a caricature of an *opinionated* person; with all seriousness, he saves and records for posterity whatever passes through his mind. The irony is that, for most of us, what he has to say is probably trite, conventional, and boring.

This is a chapter about the nature of opinions and how they affect our ability to think critically. Opinions might be defined as personal inferences drawn from observations and experiences that we have chosen to keep on mental record. We keep them filed in memory; we communicate them to others. Sometimes they are generalizations and preferences, sometimes judgments and beliefs, sometimes advice to others. They may be based on a careful study of the evidence, or they may not. Like inferences, their function is to fill in the space between the known and the unknown. However, the problem with opinions is that when they are kept and stored in the mind for some years, they get further and further away from the original facts or impressions that gave birth to them in the first place. And although some may bear up under the test of time, others in the form of fixed opinions remain in our minds like fossils, unrecognized and ossified. In this chapter, we'll consider all of these characteristics and problems of opinions.

Discovery Exercises

A COLLABORATIVE LEARNING OPPORTUNITY

The following four discovery exercises can be done either alone or with a partner in preparation for class discussion of this chapter.

Comparing a Sample of Opinions

Study the following statements of opinion.

1. "It's a proven fact that capital punishment is a known detergent [sic] to crime." (Archie Bunker, in the TV series "All in the Family")

2. "Those who indulge in sex for sheer excitement and physical pleasure get exactly what they bargained for and nothing more. After the fleeting moments of pleasure, they are spent and empty." (*Ann Landers Talks to Teen-Agers About Sex*, Crest Books, 1963)

3. "I need to meet a new woman. I need to have an affair. I may not look the part, but I'm a man who needs romance. I need softness.

I need flirtation. I'm not getting any younger, so before it's too late I want to make love in Venice . . . and exchange coy glances over red wine and candlelight. You see what I am saying?"

Dr. Mandel shifted in his chair and said, "An affair will solve nothing. You're so unrealistic. Your problems run much deeper." (From "The Kugelmass Episode," by Woody Allen, *Woody Allen Side Effects,* Random House, 1980)

4. "Chinese Communists have this view that only after the liberation of the whole world can one liberate oneself. But I believe that if each person would liberate himself first, then the world could liberate itself." (Shen Tong, Chinese student leader at Tiananmen Square)

5. Any person on welfare is a bum.

6. "All this . . . persuades us that the word 'person' as used in the Fourteenth Amendment does not include the unborn. . . . We need not resolve the difficult question of when life begins. When those trained in the respective disciplines of medicine, philosophy, and theology are unable to arrive at any consensus, the judiciary, at this point in the development of man's knowledge, is not in a position to speculate as to the answer." (U.S. Supreme Court, *Roe* v. *Wade,* 1973)

In writing or class discussion, answer these questions about the statements:

1. What do these opinions have in common?
2. How are they different?
3. Do they all have equal weight and value?

Why Do We Get Confused by the Word *Opinion?*

Comparing two dictionaries, find at least three different meanings for the word *opinion.* (Be sure to look at the word's etymology.) Write down each definition and give a sentence that clearly expresses each meaning. Do you find that some of these meanings of *opinion* seem to be contradictory to one another? Explain exactly how.

After you have finished, compare your different meanings to those given below.

1. No one can say if our weather has changed permanently for the worse or not, but it's my *opinion* that it has. (a judgment that, though open to dispute, seems probable to the speaker)

2. There'll always be an England. (a belief held with confidence but not substantiated by proof)

"Young man, it's high time you accepted gravity as a fact of life!"

From *I Paint What I See*. Copyright © 1971 by Gahan Wilson.
Used with permission of Simon & Schuster, Inc.

3. This editor is of the *opinion* that the community colleges' enrollment of students would not be seriously affected by charging tuition if this estimate is not based on initial enrollments but final enrollments. A payment of tuition implies a commitment that may make even more students stay with their courses who might drop out casually otherwise. (a statement backed by rational arguments presented with the realization that its truth is open to dispute)

4. As your doctor of long standing, it is my *opinion* that you should not have surgery at this time. (a judgment formed by an expert)

5. Public opinion supports arms talks. (prevailing sentiment)

6. It is the *opinion* of the court that the defendant is guilty. (a formal statement of a judgment drawn after a legal hearing)

SHARING OPINIONS WITH ANN LANDERS

Dear Ann:

After reading your column on how college students "parrot information" and the amusing comment by Dr. Hanna Gray, president of the University of Chicago, I thought you might be interested in what Ben Franklin said in his discourse on higher education.

This is from Franklin's autobiography: "I reflected in my mind on the extreme folly of those parents who, blind to their children's dullness and insensible of the solidity of their skulls, because their purses can afford it, will send their offspring to a temple of higher learning where they learn little more than how to carry themselves handsomely and enter a room genteelly. (The same could be acquired at a dancing school for a fraction of the price.) They return, after an abundance of trouble and money spent, more blockheaded than ever and a great deal more conceited."—A Reader, Not a Typist

Dear Reader:

Just keep reading and passing on those gems. There are plenty of people around who can type.

Dear Ann:

I've read some dandies in your column, but that letter from Baton Rouge topped them all. The man complained that his 40-year-old wife is beautiful, college-educated, cultivated, and a wonderful mother, but he is turned off by her sexually because she secretly imbibes alcohol every Friday, Saturday, and Sunday night. He said her drunkenness disgusts him.

Rating Opinions

Rate the following opinions as:
A. An opinion I would accept and act on.
B. Worthy of consideration.
C. I'd want another opinion.
D. Forget it!

_____ 1. Your doctor says you need surgery immediately to remove your _____.

_____ 2. A psychiatrist testifies in court that the defendant is not guilty by reason of insanity.

_____ 3. The weather forecaster says it will rain tomorrow.

_____ 4. Your attorney says you should sue your neighbor for damages.

Maybe the reason the poor thing gets sloshed on weekends is because her husband doesn't pay any attention to her on Monday, Tuesday, Wednesday, or Thursday. If he was half the man he would have you believe he is, he would wear her out those evenings during the week when she is sober. Perhaps then she wouldn't be getting into the hootch on weekends.—An Experienced Lover from Fla.

Dear Lover:

You may have something there. I hope that fellow from Baton Rouge sees your letter and gives it a try. If he's up to it.

Questions:

1. To what would you attribute the popularity of this column, which has been running for about thirty years?
2. What opinions do you find expressed here? Do they tend to be well substantiated?
3. In the case of the man from Baton Rouge, do Ann Landers and the "Experienced Lover" have enough information to give this man sound advice?
4. Is advice the same thing as opinion?
5. Are irresponsible (unsubstantiated) opinions more entertaining than well-supported conclusions?

_____ 5. You want to rent an apartment but the neighbor next door says the landlord is a weirdo.

_____ 6. Your best friend tells you your fiance is tacky.

_____ 7. Your English instructor says you don't know how to think and should see a psychiatrist.

_____ 8. Your astrologer tells you not to go on any long trips in May.

_____ 9. Your biorhythm advisor tells you to stay home February 13.

_____ 10. The judge says you are guilty of driving under the influence of alcohol.

_____ 11. An engineer says you can prevent your basement from flooding by blasting holes for drainage in your foundation.

_____ 12. Your utility energy advisor says you can conserve energy by having your floors insulated.

_____ 13.   Ann Landers says you should see a psychiatrist.

_____ 14.   You are an investigator for the FBI getting information about a government employee. His secretary says she thinks he is a security risk because he subscribes to *Mother Jones.*

_____ 15.   The General advised that we should invade North Korea.

TYPES OF OPINIONS

Let's review what you may have discovered so far by categorizing opinions into types. First, there are the *judgments:* this is *good,* this is *bad;* this is *right,* this is *wrong;* this *should be,* this *should not be.* Look at the two following examples and provide a third one of your own.

1.   Men and women should not share college dorms.
2.   That car you bought was a lemon.
3.   _____

Judgments are based on personal or collective codes of values. They are conclusions, arrived at through a long chain of reasoning. Judgments can also be simple *evaluations* of good and bad, desirable and undesirable. These are all discussed fully in the next chapter, on evaluations. At root, all forms of judgments are based on values or belief systems not necessarily shared by everyone. However, a person can state a judgment as an opinion without having to offer substantiation.

A second type of opinion could be seen in the *advice* category: *you should do this; you should not do this.* Examples of such opinions are as follows:

1.   I wouldn't advertise for a roommate if I were you.
2.   You need a new car.
3.   _____

As you must have concluded from the earlier rating exercise, whether or not one chooses to accept advice is an individual matter depending on how one evaluates the circumstances.

A third category of opinions includes simple *generalizations,* typically preceded by the words *all, no,* or *some.* In this manner, the opinion is housed in a generalization to suggest that it represents a general truth.

1.   All of today's adolescents are taking longer to grow up.
2.   Nothing comes without a price.
3.   _____

Here again, support for the opinion may be either offered or not. Those who take more responsibility for their opinions do offer their reasons and might defer expressing an opinion at all until all possible evidence has been considered. A person trained in critical thinking always takes the time to gather and evaluate evidence before generalizing and, in turn, examines all generalizations for their basis in evidence.

A final category of opinions is *personal taste* or *sentiments: I like this; I don't like that.* Examples of such opinions would be:

1. Movies aren't much fun without popcorn.
2. Backpacking is the best kind of vacation.
3. _____

DISTINGUISHING BETWEEN RESPONSIBLE AND IRRESPONSIBLE OPINIONS

As you have probably gathered by now, the fact that there are so many different types of opinions can lead to some confusion. And indeed, when we study the definition of the word *opinion,* we find many contradictory meanings. The word is used to mean (1) an expert's judgment, *as well as* an unsubstantiated belief or conclusion; (2) a well-reasoned argument presented in an openness to challenge and dispute, *as well as* a final legal judgment; and (3) the prevailing sentiment (feeling) on a topic. When we study critical thinking, we understand the contradictions in a word used for feelings without reasons, on the one hand, and reasoned judgment, on the other; for arguments based on proof, as well as arguments based on no proof; and finally, for final judgments as well as no judgments.

Given the contradictions in the meaning of the word *opinion,* there is even more confusion when it becomes linked with the popular truism "Everyone is entitled to an opinion." To some of us this expression means anything goes: people are entitled to be heard on any subject that they have strong convictions about; the only important thing is that they speak from strong feelings. For others, "Everyone is entitled to an opinion" merely means that all have a right to free speech; however, every opinion is not equal in its significance to every other opinion, nor is strong conviction a criterion for truth.

Reverence for opinion involves many problems when it does not discriminate between those expressed responsibly and those expressed irresponsibly. If you wanted to decide how to vote on a safe drinking water bond issue, whose opinion would you respect the most? That of the League of Women Voters? Of your assembly representative? Of the Save-Us-from-More-Taxes Association? Of your Uncle George?

Actually, your Uncle George might be the most knowledgeable person in the world on this subject. To determine the value of his contribution, you would need to know how well he had studied the subject, how much inside knowledge he had, what sources he had consulted, to what extent his viewpoint was independent of bias or vested interests, how much evidence he had to offer, how sound his reasoning appeared. We should apply these same standards to any opinion offered to influence us. On the other hand, opinions that merely reflect personal tastes or beliefs are of a different category; they do not require evidence or substantiation. In critical thinking, the essential thing is to make a distinction between the two kinds of opinions: between those for which we should expect responsible support and those that we need not take that seriously.

Yet, the objective study of opinions is not always that easy, especially when an opinion is accompanied by a lot of emotion. Well-supported opinions can also carry conviction that will move us from its basis in feelings that are truly justified. On the other hand, strong emotional expression can camouflage a lack of evidence or logic. This is well illustrated by the old country joke about a preacher who wrote in the margin of his sermon, "Argument weak here, shout like hell!" Therefore, when you find an opinion loaded with emotional language, look carefully for its supporting evidence.

To sum up, well-founded, carefully weighed opinions can be very valuable, and they are necessary when decisions must be made without all the facts available. Expert opinions are—and should be—highly esteemed and well paid for. But to be a specialist or expert in any field means to know exactly which facts are available and which are missing, what the variables are, and how much risk is involved in judging and predicting the odds. The ability to form a useful opinion lies not only in the ability to gather and evaluate data, but also in the recognition of the unknowns and uncertainties the opinion must bridge. If we mistake our opinions for truths or facts, we are headed for trouble.

LOOKING AT PUBLIC OPINION POLLS

Some congressional representatives and senators regularly poll their constituents by sending questionnaires with questions like the following:

Of every dollar now spent by state government, how much do you feel is wasted?
1. None
2. 0–10 cents
3. 10–20 cents

4.   20–40 cents
5.   40–50 cents
6.   Over 50 cents

On the whole, do you consider the following institutions and people to be trustworthy and credible?

1.	Major industry and corporations	Yes	No
2.	Small businesses	Yes	No
3.	Labor unions	Yes	No
4.	Government bureaus and agencies	Yes	No
5.	Elected officials	Yes	No
6.	Judges	Yes	No
7.	Newspaper journalists	Yes	No
8.	TV journalists	Yes	No

Here, the constituent is asked to give opinions without the assistance of any facts. Moreover, judgments are requested on the basis of general impressions or feelings. The government representative who formulated this poll appears to have abdicated the idea that an electorate should give informed consent, and by responding to this poll his constituents could get the same message. In tabulating the poll's results, legitimacy and weight will be given equally to conclusions based on vague impressions and to those based on study and knowledge.

Unfortunately, such polling practices are becoming more common in the United States. Indeed, with citizens voting less and less, polls provide at least some kind of feedback for representatives, but nevertheless, polls carry none of the legal safeguards of a public vote or election. Poll results can also be influenced by many factors that do not affect voting, such as how the question was phrased, how the sampling was taken, and how the poll was interpreted. Finally, although election results must be released, the release of poll results depends upon the discretion of individuals. Poll results can be published for the calculated purpose of *creating* public opinion. (Remember what Solomon Asch taught us?) Thus their purpose need not necessarily simply reflect public sentiment. In sum, polls are not equivalent to public elections in terms of legal safeguards, the extent of their representation, or even the measure of responsibility assumed for them by either pollsters or the public.

CLASS DISCUSSION

1.   If the President announced that a recent poll has shown that three out of every five Americans favor invading Canada, do you think this should give the President a mandate to go ahead?

2.   Do you think it is becoming too complex for most Americans to be well informed on public issues, and that this is why many tend fall back on sentiments and feelings?

CONSCIOUS PROBLEM SOLVING THROUGH A REEXAMINATION OF OLD OPINIONS

"We have changed our attitude on some matters, such as religion, for example, which admittedly we used to treat in a simplistic manner. Now we not only proceed from the assumption that no one should interfere in matters of the individual's conscience, we also say that the moral values which religion generated and embodied for centuries can help in the work of renewal in our country.

"We no longer think that we are the best and that we are always right, that those who disagree with us are our enemies. We have now decided, firmly and irrevocably, to base our policy on the freedom of choice, to build our economy on the principle of mutual advantage, and to develop our culture and ideology through dialogue."

Questions:

1. Was this rhetoric, or did Gorbachev really mean it?

2. How difficult is it to reverse an opinion that has shaped a nation and its history for over seventy years?

3. Can you think of any parallel negative opinions that have shaped U.S. history and were later reversed?

Mikhail Gorbachev in a conversation with Pope John Paul II. As reported in the *New York Times*, December 1, 1989.

CHAPTER SUMMARY

1. Opinions can be well substantiated or not. They can either be based on reasons or solely on whim, feelings, emotions, or prejudice.

2. Critical thinking requires that we recognize the difference between responsible and irresponsible opinion, and that we distinguish statements based on evidence from statements based on feelings.

3. People enjoy expressing and reading opinions.

4. Fixed opinions can prevent us from thinking clearly and restrict our growth toward more understanding.

5. Expert opinion is based on an understanding of evidence and risks in a situation and is important and highly valued.

6. Public opinion polls can be used to *determine* public sentiment on social and political issues as well as to *manipulate* public sentiment. This occurs when we forget that sentiment is not the same as informed opinion and that opinion polls are not subject to the same safeguards as public elections.

Chapter Quiz

Rate each of the following statements as *true* or *false*. Justify each answer.

_____ 1. Expert opinion calculates the risk involved in spacing the gap between the known and the unknown for a particular situation.

_____ 2. People enjoy expressing their opinions.

_____ 3. The results of public opinion polls are equivalent to votes in elections.

_____ 4. Opinions in the form of judgments state what is right and wrong, bad and good.

_____ 5. Some opinions are based on generalizations, such as stereotypes, as in the statement "All Chinese look alike."

_____ 6. Opinions can be treasured but become obsolete when they are too far abstracted from the original experiences upon which they were based.

_____ 7. Responsible opinions are based on a careful examination of the evidence.

_____ 8. Opinions are the same as facts.

_____ 9. Gossip is a kind of recreation because it permits opinion-sharing without any requirement for substantiation.

_____ 10. Everyone is entitled to his or her own opinion because all opinions carry equal value.

Writing Application

First Option: Analyzing an Opinion Piece

Study your local newspaper editorial pages to find some editorials and letters to the editor that interest you. Select three to analyze, and photocopy them. For each, paste your photocopy at the top of a page and then analyze the piece of writing by answering these questions:

1. Is the opinion a judgment, advice, an expression of taste or sentiment, a belief, or a generalization? Support your answer in each case, providing an example and explaining it fully in these terms.

2. Is this opinion just a personal expression of taste or sentiment, or is it offered in an attempt to influence others? Explain fully.

3. Does the person giving this opinion show any special expertise regarding the subject or have any special qualifications? Explain what information you have and what is lacking.

4. Is the opinion backed up by evidence and sound reasoning? Show why or why not.

5. Does this opinion appear to be based on an objective study of the facts, or does it seem to be motivated by vested interests or a profit motive? Explain your judgment.

6. Would you call this a responsible opinion? Why or why not?

Second Option: An Essay About an Opinion

Write a short essay describing an opinion of your own. Follow these steps:

1. *What:* State an opinion.

2. *Source:* Was this opinion based on your own experience or something you heard or read? Be specific about the circumstances around which you formulated it.

3. *Reasons:* Why is it a good opinion or a poor one? What tests of life and time has it survived? Have any experiences suggested that you need to alter this opinion?

The length of your essay should be two to three typed pages. It should take the form of an essay with a thesis. The first paragraph should cover step 1. The second or next two paragraphs should cover step 2. The main part of your essay (two to three paragraphs) should offer the support of reasons requested in step 3. The final paragraph should sum up the whole.

Peer Review

To follow up in class, form groups of two or more and read your papers aloud. Check one another's work to see if all the given parameters were observed. Evaluate the amount and strength of support given for the argument. Did you notice that your thesis was your opinion about an opinion? Is a thesis always an opinion?

Reading

A MODEST PROPOSAL

Jonathan Swift

Long acknowledged as a classic of English literature, this eighteenth-century essay has delighted many a generation of college students. Swift, who was Irish, was writing about his country at a time when it was suffering from both famine and British rule. As you read, ask yourself what exactly is this author's opinion?

It is a melancholy object to those who walk through this great town 1 or travel in the country, when they see the streets, the roads, and cabin doors, crowded with beggars of the female sex, followed by three, four, or six children, all in rags and importuning every passenger for an alms. These mothers, instead of being able to work for their honest livelihood, are forced to employ all their time strolling to beg sustenance for their helpless infants, who, as they grow up, either turn thieves for want of work, or leave their dear native country to fight for the Pretender in Spain, or sell themselves to the Barbados.

I think it is agreed by all parties that this prodigious number of chil- 2 dren in the arms, or on the backs, or at the heels of their mothers, and frequently of their fathers, is in the present deplorable state of the kingdom a very great additional grievance; and therefore whoever could find out a fair, cheap, and easy method of making these children sound, useful members of the commonwealth would deserve so well of the public as to have his statue set up for a preserver of the nation.

But my intention is very far from being confined to provide only for 3 the children of professed beggars; it is of a much greater extent, and shall take in the whole number of infants at a certain age who are born of parents in effect as little able to support them as those who demand our charity in the streets.

As to my own part, having turned my thoughts for many years upon 4 this important subject, and maturely weighed the several schemes of other projectors, I have always found them grossly mistaken in their computation. It is true, a child just dropped from its dam may be supported by her milk for a solar year, with little other nourishment; at most not above the value of two shillings, which the mother may certainly get, or the value in scraps, by her lawful occupation of begging; and it is exactly at one year that I propose to provide for them in such a manner as instead of being a charge upon their parents or the parish, or wanting food and raiment for the rest of their lives, they shall on the contrary contribute to the feeding, and partly to the clothing, of many thousands.

There is likewise another great advantage in my scheme, that it will 5 prevent those voluntary abortions, and that horrid practice of women murdering their bastard children, alas, too frequent among us, sacrificing the poor innocent babes, I doubt, more to avoid the expense than the shame, which would move tears and pity in the most savage and inhuman breast.

The number of souls in this kingdom being usually reckoned one 6 million and a half, of these I calculate there may be about two hundred thousand couples whose wives are breeders; from which number I subtract thirty thousand couples who are able to maintain their own children, although I apprehend there cannot be so many under the present distress of the kingdom; but this being granted, there will remain an hundred and seventy thousand breeders. I again subtract fifty thousand for those women who miscarry, or whose children die by accident or disease within the year. There only remain an hundred and twenty thousand children of poor parents annually born. The question therefore is, how this number shall be reared and provided for, which, as I have already said, under the present situation of affairs, is utterly impossible by all the methods hitherto proposed. For we can neither employ them in handicraft or agriculture; we neither build houses (I mean in the country) nor cultivate land. They can very seldom pick up a livelihood by stealing till they arrive at six years old, except where they are of towardly parts; although I confess they learn the rudiments much earlier, during which time they can however be looked upon only as probationers, as I have been informed by a principal gentleman in the country of Cavan, who protested to me that he never knew above one or two instances under the age of six, even in a part of the kingdom so renowned for the quickest proficiency in that art.

I am assured by our merchants that a boy or a girl before twelve 7 years old is no salable commodity; and even when they come to this age they will not yield above three pounds, or three pounds and half a crown at most on the Exchange; which cannot turn to account either to the parents or the kingdom, the charge of nutriment and rags having been at least four times that value.

I shall now therefore humbly propose my own thoughts, which I 8 hope will not be liable to the least objection.

I have assured by a very knowing American of my acquaintance in 9 London, that a young healthy child well nursed is at a year old a most delicious, nourishing, and wholesome food, whether stewed, roasted, baked, or boiled; and I make no doubt that it will equally serve in a fricassee or a ragout.

I do therefore humbly offer it to public consideration that of the 10 hundred and twenty thousand children, already computed, twenty thousand may be reserved for breed, whereof only one-fourth part to be males, which is more than we allow to sheep, black cattle, or swine; and my reason is that these children are seldom the fruits of marriage, a circumstance not much regarded by our savages, therefore one male will be sufficient to serve four females. That the remaining hundred thousand may at a year old be offered in sale to the persons of quality and fortune through the kingdom, always advising the mother to let them suck plentifully in the last month, so as to render them plump and fat for a good table. A child will make two dishes at an entertainment for friends; and when the family dines alone, the fore or hind quarter will make a reasonable dish and seasoned with a little pepper or salt will be very good boiled on the fourth day, especially in winter.

I have reckoned upon a medium that a child just born will weigh 11 twelve pounds, and in a solar year if tolerably nursed increaseth to twenty-eight pounds.

I grant this food will be somewhat dear, and therefore very proper 12 for landlords, who, as they have already devoured most of the parents, seem to have the best title to the children.

Infant's flesh will be in season throughout the year, but more plen- 13 tiful in March, and a little before and after. For we are told by a grave author, an eminent French physician, that fish being a prolific diet, there are more children born in Roman Catholic countries about nine months after Lent than at any other season; therefore, reckoning a year after Lent, the markets will be more glutted than usual, because the number of popish infants is at least three to one in this kingdom; and therefore it will have other collateral advantage, by lessening the number of Papists among us.

I have already computed the charge of nursing a beggar's child (in 14 which list I reckon all cottagers, laborers, and four-fifths of the farmers) to be about two shillings per annum, rags included; and I believe no gentleman would repine to give ten shillings for the carcass of a good fat child, which, as I have said, will make four dishes of excellent nutritive meat, when he hath only some particular friend or his own family to dine with him. Thus the squire will learn to be a good landlord, and grow popular among the tenants; the mother will have eight shillings net profit, and be fit for work until she produces another child.

Those who are more thrifty (as I must confess the times require) 15 may flay the carcass; the skin of which artificially dressed will make admirable gloves for ladies, and summer boots for fine gentlemen.

As to our city of Dublin, shambles may be appointed for this pur- 16 pose in the most convenient parts of it, and butchers we may be assured will not be wanting; although I rather recommend buying the children alive, and dressing them hot from the knife as we do roasting pigs. . . .

I can think of no one objection that will possibly be raised against   17 this proposal, unless it should be urged that the number of people will be thereby much lessened in the kingdom. This I freely own, and it was indeed one principal design in offering it to the world. I desire the reader will observe, that I calculate my remedy for this one individual kingdom of Ireland and for no other that ever was, is, or I think ever can be upon earth. Therefore let no man talk to me of other expedients: of taxing our absentees at five shillings a pound: of using neither clothes nor household furniture except what is of our own growth and manufacture: of utterly rejecting the materials and instruments that promote foreign luxury: of curing the expensiveness of pride, vanity, idleness, and gaming in our women: of introducing a vein of parsimony, prudence, and temperance: of learning to love our country, in the want of which we differ even from Laplanders and the inhabitants of Topinamboo: of quitting our animosities and factions, nor acting any longer like the Jews, who were murdering one another at the very moment their city was taken: of being a little cautious not to sell our country and conscience for nothing: of teaching landlords to have at least one degree of mercy toward their tenants: lastly, of putting a spirit of honesty, industry, and skill into our shopkeepers; who, if a resolution could now be taken to buy only our native goods, would immediately unite to cheat and exact upon us in the price, the measure, and the goodness, nor could ever yet be brought to make one fair proposal of just dealing, though often and earnestly invited to it.

Therefore I repeat, let no man talk to me of these and the like expe-   18 dients, till he hath at least some glimpse of hope that there will ever be some hearty and sincere attempt to put them in practice.

But as to myself, having been wearied out for many years with   19 offering vain, idle, visionary thoughts, and at length utterly despairing of success, I fortunately fell upon this proposal, which, as it is wholly new, so it hath something solid and real, of no expense and little trouble, full in our own power, and whereby we can incur no danger in disobliging England. For this kind of commodity will not bear exportation, the flesh being of too tender a consistence to admit a long continuance in salt, although perhaps I could name a country which would be glad to eat up our whole nation without it.

After all, I am not so violently bent upon my own opinion as to re-   20 ject any offer proposed by wise men, which shall be found equally innocent, cheap, easy, and effectual. But before something of that kind shall be advanced in contradiction to my scheme, and offering a better, I desire the author or authors will be pleased maturely to consider two points. First, as things now stand, how they will be able to find food and raiment for an hundred thousand useless mouths and backs. And secondly, there being a round million of creatures in human figure throughout this kingdom, whose sole subsistence put into a common stock would leave them in debt two millions of pounds sterling, adding those who are beggars by profession to the bulk of farmers, cottagers, and laborers, with their wives and children who are beggars in effect; I desire those politicians who dislike my overture, and may perhaps be so bold to attempt an answer, that they will first ask the parents of these mortals whether they would not at this day think it a great happiness to have been sold for food at a year old in this manner I prescribe, and thereby have avoided such a perpetual scene of misfortunes as they have since gone through by the oppression of landlords, the impossibility of paying rent without money or trade, the want of common sustenance, with neither house nor clothes to cover them from the inclemencies of the weather, and the most inevitable prospect of entailing the like or greater miseries upon their breed forever.

I profess, in the sincerity of my heart, that I have not the least personal interest in endeavoring to promote this necessary work, having no other motive than the public good of my country, by advancing our trade, providing for infants, relieving the poor, and giving some pleasure to the rich. I have no children by which I can propose to get a single penny; the youngest being nine years old, and my wife past childbearing. 21

From Jonathan Swift, "A Modest Proposal," *The Portable Swift.* New York: Penguin, 1977. Originally published in 1729.

STUDY QUESTIONS

1. Satire is a literary form that uses irony or parody to expose or criticize an idea or custom considered objectionable. At what point in this essay did you realize that Swift was writing satire?

2. In thinking terms, a satirical essay may be defined as one that states one opinion while actually conveying a very different one. Put into your own words Swift's thesis as stated and then the thesis you can read between the lines.

3. One definition of *irony* is an incongruity between what might be expected and what actually occurs. How does Swift's incongruous proposal highlight the existing incongruities in the treatment of the Irish poor?

4. De Bono describes a lateral thinker as provocative, generative, and unjudging in his or her ideas. What part does lateral thinking play in Swift's style and purpose?

5. Do you think Swift is prejudiced against Catholics (Papists) and Jews or is he using irony? What about his attitude toward absen-

tee British landlords? (If you need to familiarize yourself with British history during this period, see an encyclopedia for a quick review.)

6. "Let no man talk to me of other expedients. . . ." What are the proposals that Swift claims not to be proposing? If taken seriously, do you think they could have improved the situation?

7. Describe any parallels you might see between this situation and that of the poor and the homeless in the United States today.

7

Evaluations

"This is not the mood we're trying to get across out here, Parker!"

Why is Parker getting into trouble? *Senseless,* in this instance, is what we call an *evaluative word.* And one evaluative word can change the whole nature of a communication. Evaluations also come in the form of ideas or opinions that judge something as bad or good, desirable or undesirable. They can be applied consciously, skillfully, and fairly, or used carelessly and dishonestly. This is a chapter that teaches both recognition and detachment from that variety of opinion called evaluations.

Discovery Exercises

A COLLABORATIVE LEARNING OPPORTUNITY

Both of these Discovery Exercises can be studied alone or with a partner in preparation for class discussion of this chapter.

Defining *Evaluate*

First, study the etymology of the word *evaluate.* What do its prefix and root mean?

Then, write out definitions of the following words:

1. judge
2. appraise
3. estimate
4. value
5. evaluate

Based on your work, answer these questions either in writing or in class:

1. What does *evaluate* mean?
2. Is an evaluation an inference?
3. Is an evaluation an opinion?
4. Can an evaluation be based on an assumption?

Recognizing Evaluations

Evaluations can appear in the form of single words as well as ideas that judge something as positive or negative. Circle the words in the following passages that state or suggest evaluations. Note whether any evidence or reasons are given to support the evaluations made.

A reminder about Discovery Exercises: these are not tests in which you are expected to know all the answers; they are meant only to help you acknowledge what you already know and to inspire your curiosity to learn what you do not know.

1. "I think contraception is disgusting—people using each other for pleasure." (Director, Pro-Life Action League)

2. "The harsh truth is that sub-Saharan Africa today faces a crisis of unprecedented proportions. The physical environment is deteriorating. Per-capita production of food grains is falling. Population growth rates are the highest in the world and rising. National economies are in disarray. And international assistance in real terms is moving sharply downward." (Robert S. McNamara, 1986.)

3. *"The Gods Must Be Crazy:* This peculiar comedy, from South Africa's premier filmmaker, Jamie Uys, is whimsically amusing and probably well-meant—but the racial undertones are bothersome." (Review by N.W. in *Express,* November 1, 1985)

4. FRIENDS ARE WORTH SMEAROFF. When the friends are close and the mood is right, the party starts in the kitchen. And, of course, Smearoff vodka is there. Because nothing but Smearoff makes drinks that are as light and friendly as the conversation. Crisp, clean, incomparable Smearoff. FRIENDS ARE WORTH IT.

Discuss the following questions in writing or in class:

1. Look at your circled words. What can you generalize about how they work as evaluations?

2. Did you find differences here between evaluations that were directly stated and those that were suggested or implied?

3. Were any passages more indirect than others in their use of evaluations?

4. In the cases where the evaluations were unsupported, should they have been supported?

ON EVALUATIONS

Evaluate comes from the Latin *ex* = from, and *valere* = to be strong, to be of value. To evaluate, then, is (1) to determine or fix the value or worth of something or (2) to examine and judge, appraise, estimate. To

"Oh hey! I just love these things! . . . Crunchy on the outside
and a chewy center!"

Used with permission of Chronicle Features, San Francisco.

evaluate, appraise, and estimate the value of something according to a
standard is a thinking operation that involves comparisons and measurements. These comparisons are made according to ideals that may be either conscious or unconscious, or both. We may value watching TV football more than any other pastime both for reasons we can explain and for
those we cannot.

Without evaluations, we would not be able to make decisions: what
car to buy, what school to go to, what friends to spend our time with. To
determine the value of something, we have to decide what exchange we
would be willing to offer in terms of time, energy, and money. But this
exchange value depends on the individual and the situation—not on the
items or ideas themselves. Today I might feel a $20,000 car is a bargain in
value to me because it gives me prestige and power in the eyes of myself,
my friends, and my customers. Five years ago I might have felt that a
$2,000 used car was a bargain for me because it gave me a sense of pride
in my economy and left my assets free for other priorities. Here needs
and standards have to be measured against price—or the exchange of
energy, time, and money required.

To evaluate wisely, we first have to observe and compare, as well as
clarify our standards. We have to gather information to measure against
our needs, priorities, and assets. After this process is completed, then we
can make our final evaluation or decision.

THE PROBLEM OF PREMATURE EVALUATIONS

Premature evaluations are evaluations (decisions about "good" or "bad") made before we have taken sufficient time to explore and think about a situation. The word *premature* means literally before ripe—or before something has finished its natural process. Premature evaluations are snap judgments made hurriedly before the necessary preliminaries of fact-gathering are completed: "I knew before I spoke to him that he was too young for the job."

Premature evaluations may deceive us into thinking that they are based on our accumulated wisdom and experience, but actually they bypass the observing and thinking process, substituting prejudice or vague impressions for giving immediate study to what is present. Yet, when premature evaluations are recognized as such, they can be reexamined in the light of present circumstances and lead us back into experience and learning.

> COREY: "How do you know he is too young for the job?"
>
> ALEX: "OK, I'll interview him and see."

Premature evaluations also let us avoid thinking when they substitute or simply *reassert* a judgment as though it were a fact, instead of offering the evidence or considerations that led to that judgment.

> ALICE: "He looks like a turkey to me."
>
> RUTH: "What do you mean by a *turkey?*"
>
> ALICE: "You know—a TURKEY!"

The use of evaluations in this manner is also called the *fallacy of begging the question,* which means repeating and insisting on a judgment instead of offering evidence or valid argument in its support. (We will discuss this fallacy in Chapter 11.)

In daily life, evaluations are not usually made after careful study, but more often initially as instinctive or feeling reactions. True, an instinctive evaluation can have its own wisdom, and may, in some situations, help us survive. We can often sense when a place is unsafe or a person untrustworthy. The difficult problem is one of knowing the difference between intuitive intelligence and a hasty conclusion. What we usually have to do, *after* we make an evaluation, is to backtrack to our data and see if we covered everything relevant to the evaluation.

An honest examination of our feelings is an important part of the process of making sound evaluations. If the feelings are highly emotional, they are especially important to review for their measure of rationality or irrationality. Feelings can be blind and misguided at times, or they can be carriers of highly intelligent information. We all have to learn the skill of sorting feelings out. This requires development of the kind of sensitivity that is so helpful to many artists and scientists.

On the basis of feelings, a choreographer chooses the "right" dancers, and offers the "right" kind of coaching to get them to execute the movements he or she has in mind. Staying true to that sense of "rightness" is a matter of calibrating inner feelings in relationship to outer events. Likewise, a scientist has to make many decisions on the basis of feelings: a test may show good results, and yet, the scientist may have a feeling that something essential has been neglected that needs further pursuit. The soundness of evaluations depends on the clarity of perceptions, including the perception of personal feelings. To evaluate well, we must first observe well.

CLASS DISCUSSION

Premature evaluations bypass close observing and thinking. What observing and thinking could alter the following evaluations?

1. That's a hillbilly country band. You don't want to go hear them.
2. He's dressed like a hippy. Don't rent your house to him.
3. A couple is driving down a road early one morning when they pass a Cadillac parked on the curb. A man is standing bent forward in front of the car with one hand on the hood. He is swaying slightly and violently ill. The woman in the car remarks, "Look at that drunk."
4. You buy a new computer and the printer runs paper through it backward. Your brother says, "That printer is no good. You should ask for your money back." You go to the store to demand a refund.

EVALUATIONS ARE NOT FACTS

In making premature evaluations, we sometimes confuse evaluations with facts. Read the following dialogue.

CONSTANCE: "This steak is good. That's a fact!"

JOHN: "What do you mean, 'That's a fact'? I am a vegetarian and no steak tastes good to me. It's not a fact as far as I am concerned."

CONSTANCE: "Well, actually, it's just what I feel to be true. But I am absolutely certain."

JOHN: "Well, how did you come to that conclusion?"

CONSTANCE: "Well, it happened so fast I wasn't aware of my thinking. Let's see, it went something like this: when I took the steak out of the refrigerator it looked bright red, not purplish, and it smelled fine. These were my facts. Therefore I concluded it *was* still fresh. After I cooked and tasted the steak, it was clean and tender; it was also seasoned with the herbs and spices I like. These were also facts. I also have pleasant associations with steaks and eat them often."

JOHN: "All facts, I agree!"

CONSTANCE: "And so I concluded 'This steak is good.' So that was the *evaluation* I made on the basis of my facts, my memory associations, and my standards."

Substitution of evaluations for evidence, or even for objective description, is often based on confusion about the difference between the two. Constance was no doubt convinced that her personal evaluation of the steak *was* objective factual information. Until John questioned her, she was not consciously aware of what her standards were, or that her standards were just personal ones that others might not share.

The same situation occurs for all of us when we evaluate others with the self-righteous conviction that we are offering the last word in truth:

"You are just lazy!"

"You're a drip!"

"She's a bitch! And her brother's a wimp!"

Critical thinking teaches us to avoid stating evaluations as if they were facts.

EXPECTATIONS INFLUENCE EVALUATIONS

Premature evaluations are often based on expectations we hold. This is illustrated by the following story, told by psychologist Dr. John Enright. Read it aloud and then, in a class discussion, answer the questions that follow.

This morning I had a longing for some orange juice. I knew there must be some in the freezer, since my roommate went shopping yesterday. I took an orange-labeled can out of the freezer, and made myself a glass; as I did so, I noticed that it was a little darker than usual, but I concluded that it must just be another variety of orange or a different mix of rind and juice. Then when I tasted it, it was just *awful*. I spit it out in the sink and really made a mess of things, but I was sure it was spoiled, and I didn't want to make myself sick. Then I decided that I might as well take it back to the grocer's and get our money back. I fished the can out of the garbage and looked at the label. To my surprise it said "Tangerine Juice." I couldn't believe it. I tasted some of the juice left in the glass and . . . it was *good tangerine juice!*

CLASS DISCUSSION

1. Why did the evaluation change?
2. The liquid did not change, nor the taste buds of the person. How can you explain what happened?
3. What information was missing in the first evaluation?
4. What can you conclude from this story about the effect expectations have on our perceptions and evaluations?
5. Can you think of instances where new information made you backtrack and reconsider an earlier evaluation?

This story demonstrates that expectations and standards can influence perceptions and the evaluations made from them. In this case, when the person's expectations changed from orange to tangerine juice, so did his acceptance of its actual taste. Under the influence of expectations, evaluations of the same stimuli can switch from one extreme to another. All of us might have experienced this on our good days and bad days, when the same situation is seen in a radically contrasting light. One day the Safeway can be seen as a neon nightmare—and on another as an opportunity for a feast.

All this suggests that if we want to think critically, we should recognize evaluations for what they are and not accept them as final judgments about the truth of things. This is not meant to imply that we should *never* evaluate, or that we are not entitled to evaluations in matters of personal taste and pleasure. It only means that we should remember that evaluations are not facts, and that, under different circumstances, they might change.

SKILLED USE OF EVALUATIONS

Once we learn to avoid making premature evaluations, confusing evaluations with facts, and having our evaluations distorted by expectations, we're well on the way to using evaluations skillfully. And when we can use them skillfully, we can begin to evaluate others' evaluations. We can discern the difference between evaluations that are used responsibly and openly and those that seek covertly to slant or persuade.

In the writing or study of argumentation, it is important to consider how evaluations are used to sway opinion, whether fairly, expertly, or clumsily. When we evaluate according to critical thinking standards of objectivity and fairness, we are *direct* about what we are doing, and we *state our evidence.* This is what we look for when we evaluate others' evaluations. And we are careful to distinguish between forms of writing that are *not* expected to evaluate, such as news reports, and those that *are,* such as reviews. Indeed, film, theater, book, and music reviews are prized for their evaluations, which entertain the reader at the same time that they offer recommendations.

Experts in any field can function as skilled evaluators, and indeed, this is often why they are highly paid. Those who evaluate well provide important services for others. Offered here are two examples of skillful evaluations. One is written by a professional film reviewer, the second by a famous paleoanthropologist.

THE MALTESE FALCON

Humphrey Bogart at his most cynical, director John Huston at his nastiest, and the detective genre at its most hard-boiled and case-hardened (faithfully adapted from Dashiell Hammett's novel). Bogart's Sam Spade is the original Looking Out for Number One carrying on an affair with his partner's wife, shedding not a tear when his partner is murdered, and selling his private eye skills to the highest bidder in the search for the jewel-studded Maltese Falcon. Everything Bogart does in this film is galvanizing—from the casual way he wraps the priceless bird in newspaper and deposits it with an old man in a checkroom, to the magnificent rage he throws for Sydney Greenstreet (archvillain) and Peter Lorre, a rage which evaporates the instant he slams the door on them and steps into the corridor with a self-satisfied grin on his face, the satisfaction of a job well-done, a rage well-acted. With Mary Astor as the love interest Bogart sends to Death Row (1941).—M.C.

From *Express*, September 7, 1984, p. 2. Used with permission of the publisher.

DISCARDING THE CONCEPT OF MAN AS "KILLER APE"

Richard Leakey

Richard Leakey, a world-renowned paleoanthropologist, serves as director of the National Museums of Kenya. He is founder of the Foundation for Research Into the Origin of Man. His newest book is The Making of Mankind.

"Evidence for Aggression Does Not Exist"

I am concerned about the widespread belief that humans are in- 1
nately aggressive. Many people think that there is good anthropological
evidence for this. But when you actually look at the past, the evidence
for aggression and violence does not exist.

The only evidence of what people did in that primitive period is 2
what they left behind, and no weapons of death and destruction—no
clubs—have been found. The archeological record tells us what people
used to eat and to gather things, but there is no evidence of their behavior. Behavior doesn't fossilize. So where does the view of violent and
aggressive man come from? It's obviously created to explain present-
day problems.

The popularity of the concept of man as "killer ape" and macho 3
male was needed to explain the terrible atrocities that occurred in
World War II. Even before that, there was a feeling in Western culture
that Neanderthal man was primitive and brutish. Many people grew up
with images drawn from comics of the cave man as the hairy brute with
a club who used to beat fellow brutes on the head in the course of stealing women and dragging away victims.

These developments have created psychological acceptance of vio- 4
lence and aggression rooted in a primitive past. It's a dangerous perspective that leads to the conclusion that such behavior is inevitable.
But I would argue very strongly that violence and its acceptance are
purely cultural.

Today, given what we know about the working of the mind and 5
about techniques of education, we could take an infant from any family
anywhere in the world and by involvement in a particular cultural environment make the child *this* or *that*. The child's attitudes are not innate; they are learned. We could just as easily insist that everybody be
taught from childhood that everyone is beautiful and that everybody
should love everyone else as that people should hate each other.

I'm not necessarily taking a moral position on these matters. I'm 6
simply saying that what happens to this world is within our power to
determine.

"Even Warfare Requires Cooperation"

If there is any one thing that makes humans human, it is coopera- 7
tion, *not* aggression. If you tell people that if anything is innate it is their
ability to cooperate, then psychologically you are creating a much more
positive atmosphere. The underlying psychology is changed. Conflict
and violence are no longer viewed as inevitable.

Warfare, for example, is simply a response by man to the environ- 8
ment he has created—and it is possible to create an environment in
which warfare would have no place. And even warfare requires cooper-

---

CONSCIOUS PROBLEM SOLVING
THROUGH AN EVALUATION

"There's part of me that I didn't even know I had until recently—instinct, intuition, whatever. It helps me and protects me. It's perceptive and astute. I just listen to the inside of me and I know what to do."
—Inez, thirty-year-old mother of three

> From Mary Belenky, Blythe Clinchy, Nancy Goldberger, and Jill Tarule, "Women's Ways of Knowing," *The Development of Self, Voice, and Mind.* New York: Basic Books, 1986.

---

ation. An individual can't wage war; you have to get people to do things together. In fact, the most extreme form of cooperation is putting an army together for battle: Everybody works together knowing that the consequence may well be death. . . .

> From *U.S. News & World Report,* February 15, 1982. Copyright © 1982 U.S. News & World Report, Inc. Used with permission of the publisher.

CLASS DISCUSSION

1. In his article Leakey is correcting a mistaken evaluation. How does he say it came about? How has it affected us?

2. For what different purpose are evaluations used in the review of *The Maltese Falcon?*

RECOGNIZING EVALUATIONS
CONVEYED BY CONNOTATIVE WORDS

Some evaluations we read or hear present us with evidence or state straightforwardly that they are opinions. These are the kind that stimulate our own thinking. Others seek to manipulate our feelings and thoughts without our being aware of what's going on, and thus seek to discourage independent thought. Arguments of the latter type often use connotative words for this purpose.

In Chapter 2, "Word Skills," we looked at definitions and examples of word connotations. At that time we were considering how to select words with connotations that accurately convey our intentions. At this point, we are concerned with how connotations can carry *evaluations* that may be used to convey or influence opinions.

Evaluations may be made directly or covertly. If we say about a woman, "I don't like her sexual behavior," we are clearly recognizing our feelings and separating them from the woman herself. If we say instead, "She is a tramp," we show our disapproval indirectly through the use of a word with a negative connotation. With the choice of this word, however, we move one step away from openly stating our feelings about a person's behavior, to making an assertion about his or her identity. All of this becomes even more complicated should we begin to mistake labels for reality.

CLASS DISCUSSION

Show how the connotations of each of the following words differ, by writing a plus or minus beside each word that carries either a positive or a negative connotation. Then share your evaluations in class.

1. girl   doll   lady
2. undependable person   flake   carefree spirit
3. to cheat   ripoff   defraud
4. drinker   wino   alcoholic
5. soldier   terrorist   military advisor

You may have found some differences in your evaluations of these words, even for those that most people would consider to be neutral. What is a neutral word for one person may be highly charged for another. Our concern in critical thinking is with calculated choices of words with connotations that are not easily detected, yet that are powerful enough to arouse the feelings of most people toward a bias. It is one thing to state judgments directly and openly, and another to cloak them in words that seek to persuade through hidden emotional appeals. Such appeals seek to covertly *transfuse* evaluations rather than to invite *choice* through thinking.

Exercise

Recognizing Evaluative Words' Persuasive Powers

Underline the words in the following passages that carry feeling connotations. How do they persuade either for or against an issue? Do any make a charged issue seem more neutral?

1. "I listen to the feminists and all these radical gals—most of them are failures. They've blown it. Some of them have been married,

but they married some Caspar Milquetoast who asked permission to go to the bathroom. These women just need a man in the house. That's all they need. Most of these feminists need a man to tell them what time of day it is and to lead them home. And they blew it and they're mad at men. Feminists hate men. They're sexist. They hate men—that's their problem." (Rev. Jerry Falwell)

2. "We saved these helpless pets from being butchered for 'gourmet' food in South Korea. You can help us save thousands more from the cruel 'Cages of Despair.'" (International Fund for Animal Welfare)

3. (Photograph of a happy white middle-class family walking into the arms of a grandfatherly figure) "*All these years we've been protecting you.* When you walk into our insurance office, you'll learn how we can protect the lives of a husband and wife. Your children. Or even the lives of your business associates."

4. "Glasnost Makes It Easier for UFO's to Touch Down"
   According to the official press agency TASS, towering extraterrestrial creatures with little knobby heads have landed in the Russian city of Voronezh. . . . The press agency has seemed to undergo a bizarre metamorphosis in the past year or so as the spirit of glasnost, or openness, has taken hold." (*San Francisco Chronicle* from the *New York Times,* October 10, 1989)

HOW PROPAGANDA USES HIDDEN EVALUATIONS

Usually the word *propaganda* bears a negative connotation, meaning the manipulation of public opinion for purposes not necessarily in the public's best interest. The benefit of the propaganda goes to the propagandist.

There are many tools of propaganda. One is the use of hidden evaluations that bypass the reader's awareness to embed reactions. The use of propaganda in this manner is not as distant as a World War II airplane dropping pamphlets on the enemy, but as close as the checkout stand in your neighborhood Safeway. During that boring wait for your turn in line, you can soak up hidden evaluations through such popular magazines as *Time* and *The National Enquirer*. Evaluations can spice things up for the reader, and journalists and advertising copywriters know well how to exploit their appeal. On social and political issues, writers and editors of many publications are quite willing to do all the thinking for you; with the pretense of offering objective news reports, they serve up their own conclusions for your digestion with all the convenience of fast-food service.

Advertisers also find it advantageous to do the thinking for you, through a calculated and generous offering of the evaluations they want you to absorb about their products. This technique has the additional advantage of not requiring evidence. It is only necessary to get "good, good, good" identified with their product in the time it takes to turn a page or glance at a TV commercial.

> These are times when only the BEST will do! Fine Distinction Whiskey is the BEST. Fine Distinction Whiskey—"The BEST in the House."

To discern objective reports demands painstaking attention from readers. For those whose only reading time is while commuting or when the children are in bed, careful attention is not always an easy attitude to muster. A person considering purchasing some expensive equipment might be willing to do careful research and thus might appreciate wordy ads, such as those for computers, but generally speaking, ads are most effective when they are both simple and entertaining. The approach most frequently used is to offer some images surrounded by a few repeated words or phrases. The additional advantage of this formula is that it can imprint itself directly on the unconscious memory before the viewer or reader is aware that it has happened. Thus, resistance can be warded off as well as a thinking choice. Before they know it, shopping consumers find themselves reaching automatically for the advertised products on the shelves—never fully aware that a mental imprint of images and evaluative phrases is instructing them to do so. Simple messages filed under the category of "good" make a purchasing decision easy.

Evaluations are especially powerful if they are transmitted while the viewer or reader is in a form of trance. Trance reception, also called hypnotism, is a routine event, if hypnotism is defined as altering a person's state of consciousness and making the person prone to suggestion. Hypnotism is not, as commonly believed, something performed only by a magician on stage or by a psychiatrist. Receptivity to hypnotism can be accomplished in personal contact by establishing rapport with someone, through imitation of his or her breathing patterns, and through subtle imitation of gestures.

Television, according to the book *The Plug-In Drug* (by Marie Winn, Bantam, 1978), induces an immediate trance state in viewers, regardless of the subject matter. The induction into an altered state is achieved by the television projection itself, by the manner in which it affects our eyes and consciousness. Perhaps you have become aware of this phenomenon yourself when you have found it requires an extreme effort to get up out of your chair and turn the television off. And if that were not enough, commercials themselves use all the techniques standardly associated with hypnotic induction: an object waved in front of the eyes and a pleasant, comforting, slow-speaking voice repeating evaluations over and over again. "Reach for aspirin for relief, aspirin for relief, for relief. Reach for aspirin for relief whenever you have those awful headaches, those awful headaches again. Aspirin."

Thinking critically requires that we simply *wake up*. It means watching television and studying magazine and billboard advertisements from the perspective of their method as well as their content. It means maintaining an attitude of analysis rather than passive absorption of those ads that encourage consumption of addictive products such as sugar, liquor, caffeine, and cigarettes. It means observing, instead of soaking up, the appeals made to our less conscious needs for status, recognition, sex appeal, potency, or escape. Staying awake also means taking an interest in the contradictions: the cigarette ads that promise you beauty with an athletic, strong, sexy body; the beer ads that assure you beer will make you into a cowboy or football athlete. Advertisers use extremely sophisticated psychology to make you associate desirable qualities with their products. And it is only when you remain alert to their strategies that you can retain the power of making your own choices. In short, all of us have to continuously reclaim the right to think for ourselves.

CLASS DISCUSSION

Read the following advertisements and notice how much actual information they offer you about products.

1. Ask for the cigarette with the *smooth* taste.

2. First class. For you, first class is a way of life. For you, there is CADMON's finest . . . "THE MONTE CARLO." Elegant. Dependable. Distinctive. Supremely comfortable. Superbly engineered. A car for those who seek the better things in life. Drive CADMON'S finest . . . an American model of luxury.

3. ORAL GRAT COOKIES. When you gotta have one, you gotta have two!

CHAPTER SUMMARY

1. Making evaluations is a complex thinking task that requires making judgments according to standards that are both conscious and unconscious.

2. Premature evaluations are prejudicial and bypass observing and thinking.

3. Evaluations appear sometimes as instinctive reactions that can help us survive. The problem is to distinguish sound instinct

from hasty conclusion. The feelings invoked in evaluations have to be sorted out carefully.

4. Evaluations are not facts. Factual reports keep the distinction clear between facts and evaluations.

5. Expectations affect our perceptions and evaluations. We need to guard against making premature evaluations based on expectations.

6. We need not completely avoid making evaluations. Evaluations make descriptive writing interesting and colorful. Used skillfully by experts, evaluations provide a service for us.

7. Connotative words convey evaluations that can be used to sway us toward a bias. When we think critically, we recognize their hidden emotional appeals.

8. Evaluations are used in advertising and journalism to persuade us, sometimes hypnotically, to make positive associations with products.

9. Critical thinking requires that we stay alert to manipulative advertising techniques, which are most effective when we are not alert—or when we are in a trance state.

10. Propaganda is an art with many sophisticated techniques for manipulation that may or may not be ethical. One of these is the use of hidden evaluations. A critical thinker detects propaganda and evaluates its true objectives.

Chapter Quiz

Rate the following statements as *true* or *false*. Give an example to substantiate your answer in each case.

_____ 1. Evaluations are not facts, but judgments based on conscious as well as unconscious standards.

_____ 2. Premature evaluations bypass observing and thinking.

_____ 3. The use of highly connotative words to influence opinion can be a form of hidden evaluation.

_____ 4. Evaluations should never be used in writing reviews, such as of films and books.

_____ 5. Repeating evaluations, as is done in advertising, is a way of hypnotizing and swaying opinion.

_____ 6. A critical thinking skill is the ability to detect when evaluations are substituted for evidence in an argument.

_____ 7. Prior expectations influence perceptions and our evaluation of these perceptions.

_____ 8. Our first reactions, when we evaluate experiences before we have the facts, are usually the best.

_____ 9. To evaluate wisely, we first have to observe and then compare, and then be clear about our standards.

_____ 10. Words that carry a lot of feelings or connotations for us need not be universally considered negative or positive. If you were once trampled on by a cow, for you the word _cow_ might always have a negative connotation.

Writing Application

First Option: Analyzing Evaluations in Ads

Select two printed advertisements of the same product or type of product, and circle all the evaluative words used. Photocopy them to hand in with your paper, or save the originals to hand in. Write at least a one-page analysis of each advertisement; then compare the ads to one another in a final page. Make a summation at the end that states your thesis. Try to decide which ad uses evaluations least responsibly, with distortions or confusing language that might mislead or trick the reader. Which ad is the most honest? Which is the most _effective_ as an advertisement?

In your one-page analysis of each, go over every major evaluative word you have circled, and thoroughly discuss both its literal and connotative (associative) meanings. Notice what appeals they carry to make you want to buy the product. Do the words make a pattern of evaluation that conveys a subliminal message? Is one key or primary evaluation repeated a lot, reinforced by secondary or lesser evaluations?

In review, the parameters are:

1. _Topic:_ Comparison of the use of evaluative language in two advertisements of the same or related products.

2. _Method:_ Descriptive analysis using exposition, comparison, and evaluation.

3. _Length:_ Three typed pages.

4. Summation at the end can state your thesis.

Second Option: Writing a Critical Review

Write a review that evaluates a film, music album, or concert. Be conscious of your standards for evaluation. Try working with just three criteria, such as _exciting, entertaining,_ and _instructive._ Be sure to define each. Describe strengths as well as weaknesses. Make this into a one-page paragraph, like the review of *The Maltese Falcon* that you read in this chapter. Let your topic sentence be your recommendation for (or against) consumption.

In review, the parameters are:

1. *Topic:* A review of a film, music album, or concert.

2. *Method:* A summary and evaluation of an event or product on the basis of three criteria. The topic sentence states your recommendation as a reviewer.

3. *Length:* One-page paragraph.

Readings

THE INHERENT NEED TO CREATE NEED

Jerry Mander

Jerry Mander holds degrees in economics and spent fifteen years in the advertising business. His book title, Four Arguments for the Elimination of Television, *is provocative, and he means it. In this excerpt Mander evaluates the value of products advertised on television.*

Advertising exists only to purvey what people don't need. Whatever 1 people do need they will find without advertising if it is available. This is so obvious and simple that it continues to stagger my mind that the ad industry has succeeded in muddying the point.

No single issue gets advertisers screaming louder than this one. 2 They speak about how they are only fulfilling the needs of people by providing an information service about where and how people can achieve satisfaction for their needs. Advertising is only a public service, they insist.

Speaking privately, however, and to corporate clients, advertisers 3 sell their services on the basis of how well they are able to create needs where there were none before.

I have never met an advertising person who sincerely believes that 4 there is a need connected to, say, 99 percent of the commodities which fill the airwaves and the print media. Nor can I recall a single street demonstration demanding one single product in all of American history. If there were such a demonstration for, let's say, nonreturnable bottles, which were launched through tens of millions of dollars of ads, or chemically processed foods, similarly dependent upon ads, there would surely have been no need to advertise these products. The only need that is expressed by advertising is the need of advertisers to accelerate the process of conversion of raw materials with no intrinsic value into commodities that people will buy.

If we take the word "need" to mean something basic to human 5 survival—food, shelter, clothing—or basic to human contentment— peace, love, safety, companionship, intimacy, a sense of fulfillment— these will be sought and found by people whether or not there is advertising. In fact, advertising intervenes between people and their needs, *separates* them from direct fulfillment and urges them to believe that satisfaction can be obtained only through commodities. It is through this intervention and separation that advertising can create value, thereby justifying its existence.

Consider the list of the top twenty-five advertisers in the United 6 States. They sell the following products: soaps, detergents, cosmetics, drugs, chemicals, processed foods, tobacco, alcohol, cars, and sodas, all of which exist in a realm beyond need. If they were needed, they would not be advertised.

People do need to eat, but the food which is advertised is *processed* 7 food: processed meat, sodas, sugary cereals, candies. A food in its natural state, unprocessed, does not need to be advertised. Hungry people will find the food if it is available. To persuade people to buy the processed version is another matter because it is more expensive, less naturally appealing, less nourishing, and often harmful. The need must be created.

Perhaps there is a need for cleanliness. But that is not what adver- 8 tisers sell. Cleanliness can be obtained with water and a little bit of natural fiber, or solidified natural fat. Major world civilizations kept clean that way for millennia. What is advertised is *whiteness*, a value beyond cleanliness; *sterility*, the avoidance of all germs; *sudsiness*, a cosmetic factor; and *brand*, a surrogate community loyalty.

There is need for tranquility and a sense of contentment. But these 9 are the last qualities drug advertisers would like you to obtain; not on your own anyway.

A drug ad denies your ability to cope with internal processes: feel- 10 ings, moods, anxieties. It encourages the belief that personal or traditional ways of dealing with these matters—friends, family, community, or patiently awaiting the next turn in life's cycle—will not succeed in your case. It suggests that a chemical solution is better so that you will choose the chemical rather than your own resources. The result is that you become further separated from yourself and less able to cope. Your ability dies for lack of practice and faith in its efficacy.

A deodorant ad never speaks about the inherent value of applying 11 imitation-lemon fragrance to your body; it has no inherent value. Mainly the ad wishes to intervene in any notion you may have that there is something pleasant or positive in your own human odor. Once the intervention takes place, and self-doubt and anxiety are created, the situation can be satisfied with artificial smells. Only through this process of intervention and substitution is there the prospect of value added and commercial profit.

The goal of all advertising is discontent or, to put it another way, an internal scarcity of contentment. This must be continually created, even at the moment when one has finally bought something. In that event, advertising has the task of *creating* discontent with what has just been bought, since once that act is completed, the purchase has no further benefit to the market system. The newly purchased commodity must be gotten rid of and replaced by the "need" for a new commodity as soon as possible. The ideal world for advertisers would be one in which whatever is bought is used only once and then tossed aside. Many new products have been designed to fit such a world. 12

From Jerry Mander, *Four Arguments for the Elimination of Televison.* New York: William Morrow, 1978. © 1977, 1978 by Jerry Mander. Used with permission of William Morrow & Company.

STUDY QUESTIONS

1. What is the thesis of this essay and where is it stated?
2. List the examples Mander uses to illustrate his thesis.
3. How does the author define *need?* How does he say advertising separates us from our needs and creates new needs?
4. According to Mander, what do drug ads do?
5. Explain the process of intervention and substitution.
6. Give examples to support the author's statement that "the goal of all advertising is discontent."
7. How does television advertising evaluate for us and thus affect our behavior and values?

THE USE OF FORCE

William Carlos Williams

William Carlos Williams had an unusual career: he was a New Jersey family doctor, a story writer, and a great American poet. In this short story a doctor is called in as a specialist to make an evaluation or diagnosis of the little girl's illness. In his struggle to obtain the facts he needs, he finds himself involved in an interchange of personal evaluations between himself and the family. Read and reread this story to trace these evaluations and see how they create its plot.

They were new patients to me, all I had was the name, Olson. Please come down as soon as you can, my daughter is very sick. 1

When I arrived I was met by the mother, a big startled looking woman, very clean and apologetic who merely said, Is this the doctor? and let me in. In the back, she added. You must excuse us, doctor, we have her in the kitchen where it is warm. It is very damp here sometimes. 2

The child was fully dressed and sitting on her father's lap near the kitchen table. He tried to get up, but I motioned for him not to bother, took off my overcoat and started to look things over. I could see that they were all very nervous, eyeing me up and down distrustfully. As often, in such cases, they weren't telling me more than they had to, it was up to me to tell them; that's why they were spending three dollars on me. 3

The child was fairly eating me up with her cold, steady eyes, and no expression to her face whatever. She did not move and seemed, inwardly, quiet; an unusually attractive little thing, and as strong as a heifer in appearance. But her face was flushed, she was breathing rapidly, and I realized that she had a high fever. She had magnificent blonde hair, in profusion. One of those picture children often reproduced in advertising leaflets and the photogravure sections of the Sunday papers. 4

She had a fever for three days, began the father and we don't know what it comes from. My wife has given her things, you know, like people do, but it don't do no good. And there's been a lot of sickness around. So we tho't you'd better look her over and tell us what is the matter. 5

As doctors often do I took a trial shot at it as a point of departure. Has she had a sore throat? 6

Both parents answered me together, No . . . No, she says her throat don't hurt her. 7

Does your throat hurt you? added the mother to the child. But the little girl's expression didn't change nor did she move her eyes from my face. 8

Have you looked? 9

I tried to, said the mother, but I couldn't see. 10

As it happens we had been having a number of cases of diphtheria in the school to which this child went during that month and we were all, quite apparently, thinking of that, though no one had as yet spoken of the thing. 11

Well, I said, suppose we take a look at the throat first. I smiled in my best professional manner and asking for the child's first name, I said, come on, Mathilda, open your mouth and let's take a look at your throat. 12

Nothing doing. 13

Aw, come on, I coaxed, just open your mouth wide and let me take a 14
look. Look, I said opening both hands wide, I haven't anything in my
hands. Just open up and let me see.

Such a nice man, put in the mother. Look how kind he is to you. 15
Come on, do what he tells you to. He won't hurt you.

At that I ground my teeth in disgust. If only they wouldn't use the 16
word "hurt" I might be able to get somewhere. But I did not allow myself to be hurried or disturbed but speaking quietly and slowly I approached the child again.

As I moved my chair a little nearer suddenly with one cat-like move- 17
ment both her hands clawed instinctively for my eyes and she almost
reached them too. In fact she knocked my glasses flying and they fell,
though unbroken, several feet away from me on the kitchen floor.

Both the mother and father almost turned themselves inside out in 18
embarrassment and apology. You bad girl, said the mother, taking her
and shaking her by one arm. Look what you've done. The nice man. . . .

For heaven's sake, I broke in. Don't call me a nice man to her. I'm 19
here to look at her throat on the chance that she might have diphtheria
and possibly die of it. But that's nothing to her. Look here, I said to the
child, we're going to look at your throat. You're old enough to understand what I'm saying. Will you open it now by yourself or shall we have
to open it for you?

Not a move. Even her expression hadn't changed. Her breaths how- 20
ever were coming faster and faster. Then the battle began. I had to do it.
I had to have a throat culture for her own protection. But first I told the
parents that it was entirely up to them. I explained the danger but said
that I would not insist on a throat examination so long as they would
take the responsibility.

If you don't do what the doctor says you'll have to go to the hospi- 21
tal, the mother admonished her severely.

Oh yeah? I had to smile to myself. After all, I had already fallen in 22
love with the savage brat, the parents were contemptible to me. In the
ensuing struggle they grew more and more abject, crushed, exhausted
while she surely rose to magnificent heights of insane fury of effort
bred of her terror of me.

The father tried his best, and he was a big man but the fact that she 23
was his daughter, his shame at her behavior and his dread of hurting her
made him release her just at the critical moment several times when I
had almost achieved success, till I wanted to kill him. But his dread also
that she might have diphtheria made him tell me to go on, go on though
he himself was almost fainting, while the mother moved back and forth
behind us raising and lowering her hands in an agony of apprehension.

Put her in front of you on your lap, I ordered, and hold both her 24
wrists.

But as soon as he did the child let out a scream. Don't, you're hurt- 25 ing me. Let go of my hands. Let them go I tell you. Then she shrieked terrifyingly, hysterically. Stop it! Stop it! You're killing me!

Do you think she can stand it, doctor! said the mother. 26

You get out, said the husband to his wife. Do you want her to die of 27 diphtheria?

Come on now, hold her, I said. 28

Then I grasped the child's head with my left hand and tried to get 29 the wooden tongue depressor between her teeth. She fought, with clenched teeth, desperately! But now I also had grown furious—at a child. I tried to hold myself down but I couldn't. I know how to expose a throat for inspection. And I did my best. When finally I got the wooden spatula behind the last teeth and just the point of it into the mouth cavity, she opened up for an instant but before I could see anything she came down again and gripping the wooden blade between her molars she reduced it to splinters before I could get it out again.

Aren't you ashamed, the mother yelled at her. Aren't you ashamed 30 to act like that in front of the doctor?

Get me a smooth-handled spoon of some sort, I told the mother. 31 We're going through with this. The child's mouth was already bleeding. Her tongue was cut, and she was screaming in wild hysterical shrieks. Perhaps I should have desisted and come back in an hour or more. No doubt it would have been better. But I have seen at least two children lying dead in bed of neglect in such cases, and feeling that I must get a diagnosis now or never I went at it again. But the worst of it was that I too had got beyond reason. I could have torn the child apart in my own fury and enjoyed it. It was a pleasure to attack her. My face was burning with it.

The damned little brat must be protected against her own idiocy, 32 one says to one's self at such times. Others must be protected against her. It is social necessity. And all these things are true. But a blind fury, a feeling of adult shame, bred of a longing for muscular release are the operatives. One goes on to the end.

In a final unreasoning assault I overpowered the child's neck and 33 jaws. I forced the heavy silver spoon back of her teeth and down her throat till she gagged. And there it was—both tonsils covered with membrane. She had fought valiantly to keep me from knowing her secret. She had been hiding that sore throat for three days at least and lying to her parents in order to escape just such an outcome as this.

Now truly she *was* furious. She had been on the defensive before 34 but now she attacked. Tried to get off her father's lap and fly at me while tears of defeat blinded her eyes.

STUDY QUESTIONS

1. When the doctor first arrives, how does he size up the family's attitude toward him?

2. What observations does he make about the little girl, and what conclusions does he draw from them?

3. Why does the doctor want to look at her throat?

4. How do the little girl and the doctor react to the mother's use of the evaluative words *nice man, hurt,* and *bad girl?*

5. At the midpoint of the story the doctor says "I had already fallen in love with the savage brat, the parents were contemptible to me." What leads him to make these evaluations and how do they influence his subsequent actions?

6. Why does the doctor get increasingly forceful even though the little girl is hysterical and bleeding?

7. Notice the point at which he views her as "the damned little brat." How does this judgment affect his behavior?

8. What conclusion does he reach upon finally seeing her tonsils?

9. Who felt shame in this story?

10. Would you evaluate him as a good doctor?

For Further Reading

Bagdikian, Ben H. *The Media Monopoly.* Boston: Beacon Press, 1983. See "Democracy and the Media," pp. 176–194.

Huxley, Aldous. *Brave New World Revisited.* New York: Harper & Row, 1960. See especially "Propaganda in a Democratic Society," "Propaganda Under Dictatorship," "The Arts of Selling," "Brainwashing," "Subconscious Persuasion."

Jacobson, Michael, and George Hacker. *Booze Merchants: Inebriating America.* Center for Science in the Public Interest, 1983.

Key, Wilson Bryan. *The Clam-Plate Orgy and Other Subliminal Techniques for Manipulating Your Behavior.* New York: Signet, 1980.

Mander, Jerry. *Four Arguments for the Elimination of Television.* New York: William Morrow, 1978.

Winn, Marie. *The Plug-In Drug.* New York: Bantam, 1978.

Viewpoints

"That was incredible. No fur, claws, horns, antlers, or nothin' . . .
Just soft and pink."

Used with permission of Chronicle Features, San Francisco.

From the point of view of the crocodile, the meal of a human being is certainly a delicacy without any problems, "just soft and pink." The humor in this cartoon results from the shift to an unaccustomed viewpoint, which nevertheless has its own reality and logic.

The ability to step out of one's point of view and to assume another's is an important critical thinking skill. When we are "stuck" in our own viewpoints, we have difficulty in either understanding or evaluating what others tell us. If we forget that content is shaped by point of view, we tend to confuse information with reality. This also makes us more susceptible to propaganda. A person trained in critical thinking does not passively absorb information but asks, Who said this? Where is this coming from? What do they want of me? This chapter is about how to ask these questions and get some answers.

Discovery Exercises

A COLLABORATIVE LEARNING OPPORTUNITY

These exercises may be done alone or with a partner in preparation for class discussion of the chapter.

Understanding Point of View

Using at least two dictionaries, formulate your own definition of *point of view*. Then answer these questions either in writing or in a class discussion.

1. Name some different kinds of points of view.
2. What do we call some of the points of view that writers assume in telling stories?
3. If you were a professional writer for *Reader's Digest*, do you think its readers would be interested in your article entitled "Where and How to Pick Up Safe Prostitutes Abroad"? Why or why not?
4. If you were writing for *Esquire*, do you think your article "Living on Social Security Through Farming Communes" would be accepted by its editors? Why or why not?
5. How do we go about assuming another person's point of view?

Studying One Man's Viewpoint

Read the following excerpt and then answer in writing the questions that follow, in preparation for a class discussion.

THIS IS MY LIVING ROOM

Tom McAfee

My Living Room

it ain't big but big enough for me and my family—my wife Rosie   1
setting over there reading recipes in the Birmingham *News* and my two
girls Ellen Jean and Martha Kay watching the TV. I am setting here holding
Life magazine in my lap. I get *Life*, the *News*, and *Christian Living*. I
read a lots, the newspaper everyday from cover to cover. I don't just look
at the pictures in *Life*. I read what's under them and the stories. I consider myself a smart man and I ain't bragging. A man can learn a lots
from just watching the TV, if he knows what to watch for and if he listens close. I do. There ain't many that can say that and be truthful.
Maybe nobody else in this whole town, which is Pine Springs.

Yonder in the corner, to the other side of the Coca-Cola calendar, is   2
my 12 gauge. When I go in to bed, I take it with me, set it against the
wall, loaded, ready to use, so I can use it if I need to. I've used it before
and maybe will again. The only one to protect you is yourself and if you
don't you're a fool. I got me a pistol and a .22 locked up in the back
room. I could use them too.

Rosie can shoot, I taught her how, but she's afraid. The noise scares   3
her. She said, Don't make me shoot that thing one more time. We was in
the forest. The girls was waiting for us in the car. Don't make me shoot
that thing again, she said, and started to cry. I slapped her face and told
her to shoot the rifle. She did. Then I took it and told her to go back to
the car with the girls. She started to cry again, but I stayed a long
time—till it was dark—and shot the rifle and pistol and shotgun.

You can't tell what people are going to do in a town like this. They   4
want your money and they're jealous of you. They talk about you in
front of the courthouse and plan up schemes. You can't trust the police
or sheriff. You got to watch out for yourself.

My Two Girls

are fourteen and sixteen years old. Both of them want to go on   5
dates but I won't let them. I know what the boys will do, what they want
to get out of a girl.

Ellen Jean, the oldest, is a right good-looking girl but sassy and you   6
can't hardly do anything with her. She started to paint her face at
school, so I took her out. I've got her working at my store.

I seen her passing notes to Elbert. I seen her get out of his car one   7
night. She said she was going to the picture show by herself. She's a
born liar and sassy. Like as not he's had her. Like as not she's got a baby

starting in her belly right now. She's a sassy bitch-girl and don't take after her ma or me. Sometimes I wonder if she's mine.

Martha Kay is like her ma. She cries all the time, minds good. I let 8
her stay in high school and will keep on letting her as long as she can act right. The first time I see lipstick, out she comes. She can work at the store too. I could use her to dust and sweep up. You can always use somebody to keep things clean.

I ask Martha Kay, Why're you late gettin' in from school? Where you 9
been? Off in the woods with some boy? She starts to cry. She's like her ma.

Martha Kay helps at the store on Saturdays but can't add up figures 10
good.

Ellen Jean is watching that man on TV make a fool of hisself and 11
she's laughing. She'll end up a Birmingham whore. Her sister is laughing too and they look like a bunch of fools.

People

in this town are like they are in any other town on earth. I was in the 12
World War I and seen a good many places. Since then I've stayed here most of the time. What's the good of moving? People are as mean one place as they are another and they're always out to get you. They won't get me because I won't let them.

Take Sam Coates who owed me twenty dollars for that fencing. 13
Sam wouldn't pay. I said to him pay up by first of the month or I'll make you pay. He says how will I make him. Sue him for twenty dollars? Won't no lawyer in town take it anyway, he says, because they're all looking out for election. You pay, I told him.

When first of the month come I got in my car and rode out in the 14
country to his front door. Where is your husband? I said to his wife. Milking, she said, and I went around to the barn with my .22, stuck it in his face, and told him to pay me or I'd blow the hell out of him. Sam turned as white as that bucket of milk. Him and his wife counted me out the money.

There ain't a one on earth that wouldn't try to cheat you if they 15
could.

I use to think that women was worse than men but now I think just 16
the opposite. Women are easier to handle. About the worst they can do is talk and what does that matter?

Niggers are better than anybody because you can handle them. 17
They don't hardly ever give you any trouble. Except that one time with Ezmo. I didn't have no trouble handling him. . . .

Old Ezmo

was what you'd call a low class of nigger. He'd come into the store 18
and say, Give me a pound of sugar and I'll pay you Saturday evening. I

wouldn't do it. I'd say, You give me the money, I give you the best prices in town. You give me the money.

One time Ellen Jean let him have a loaf of bread on credit. I 19 smacked her for it and told her she was a fool, which she is. On Saturday Ezmo come in and wanted some side meat for cooking greens. Pay me off, I told him, for that loaf of bread. What loaf? he wanted to know.

Ellen Jean, didn't you charge this nigger a loaf of bread? She said 20 yes and he said she didn't. You ain't calling my girl a liar, are you? Naw, he said, but he didn't get no loaf of bread. Somebody's a liar, I told him, and it ain't my girl.

He said he wouldn't pay me. You're a crooked, low-down nigger, I 21 told him, and they ain't nothing much worse than that. You ain't fit for making side meat out of. I told him if he had any younguns he better watch out. I didn't wants lots of black bastards like him growing up in my town. You get out of here right now.

That night I was setting in this chair where I am right now—this 22 same chair. The girls was watching TV. Rosie was shelling peas.

I heard somebody outdoors and I knew right off who it was. I got 23 better ears than most people. Any time somebody sets foot in this yard, I know it. Even if I'm asleep.

That's Ezmo, I said to myself. I got up, picked up my 12 gauge over 24 in the corner and said I was gonna clean it, went through the house without turning any lights on, then eased out the back door.

There wasn't much moon but I spotted Ezmo right off, standing be- 25 hind some hedge bushes over by my bedroom window. I got just this side of him without him hearing. EZMO! I hollered, and up he comes with a knife about eight inches long. I was ready for him. I triggered my 12 gauge and got him square in the face.

Rosie and the girls come running to the back door. Get me a flash- 26 light, I told them. I never seen such a blowed-up face. The girls started getting sick and Rosie started crying. I want you to take a good look, I told Rosie, and see what this world is coming to. You see that knife he had. I held Rosie's arm and made her stand there till Ellen Jean could get Sheriff Claine.

Rosie

ain't exactly good-looking. She's got to be dried-up but once was on 27 the fat side. She makes a good wife. I've been married to her for going on thirty years. Sometimes I get fed up with her and go to my woman in South Town. I take her a couple of cans of beans and some hose or a pair of bloomers. There ain't nothing much a woman won't do for food or clothes.

Rosie knows about her, all about her. I talk about it sometimes 28 when we're in bed. I wouldn't trade Rosie for her but Rosie don't know that.

Tomorrow's Saturday and I got to get some sleep.   29

"Turn off the TV, girls. Get in yonder to bed. Tomorrow's Saturday."   30

I stand in front of Rosie. "Go in yonder and get in bed." She starts to   31
cry and that's all right. It wouldn't be a bit like her if she didn't.

From Tom McAfee, *Poems and Stories*. Used with permission of Jeanie K. McAfee
and the Department of English at the University of Missouri–Columbia on behalf of
the Thomas McAfee Memorial Fund.

STUDY QUESTIONS

1. Why is this story entitled "This Is My Living Room"?

2. What kind of mental living room does the storyteller live in? How
   does he see his world and himself in it?

3. How does he justify his sexist and racist behavior?

4. How well does he understand his wife, daughters, and "Old
   Ezmo"? Does he observe or stereotype them?

5. What clichés do you find in his speech? What does this suggest
   about his capacity to perceive life freshly and clearly?

6. Why isn't he capable of compassion or sympathy for others?

ON UNCONSCIOUS VIEWPOINTS

So far in Part Two, "Problems of Critical Thinking," we have been careful
to distinguish between the conscious and unconscious uses of assumptions, opinions, and evaluations. To recognize assumptions, we have to
know that an assumption can be unconscious. To appreciate well-supported opinions, we need to distinguish them from superficial sentiment
or fixed opinions immune to conscious reexamination. To make sound
evaluations, we need to guard against jumping to them prematurely. In
this chapter, as we work with viewpoints, we also have to consider the
distinction between conscious and unconscious use of them.

To return to the example of our storyteller in "This Is My Living
Room," a person can live in a viewpoint as narrow as one room and yet
believe this is the world. Another way of describing this level of consciousness is to say that this person is not even aware that *viewpoints
are just viewpoints*. He cannot step outside of himself and say, "Well, I
have a way of looking at things, but that does not mean that I am always
right. Other people also have viewpoints, which I could assume and even
learn from." Thus, his viewpoint remains unconscious. He confuses the

way he sees things with the way things are, and uses his "thinking" to rationalize feelings that others would identify as selfish, paranoid, racist, and sexist. He is what we call egocentric.

The word *egocentric* is used to describe individuals who believe that everyone in the world either has or should have the same viewpoint as they do. Egocentric individuals find it very difficult to put themselves in someone else's shoes. But egocentrism is not in itself negative. Psychologist Jean Piaget, who studied learning stages in children, theorized that egocentrism is typical for most young children before the age of seven. The ability to grow beyond this cognitive limitation varies from one individual to another, depending on the measure of intelligence, emotional stability, or cultural and educational factors. As we grow out of egocentrism, we also develop the ability to be *exterior* to our own viewpoint—to see and recognize it from the outside, objectively. We learn how to see the world through the eyes of others. Such a capacity enables us to respect ourselves and others more, to separate who we are as fellow human beings from how we sometimes think and behave. We learn the meaning of the word *compassion* and move from the unconsciousness of egocentrism to the consciousness of objectivity.

Other viewpoints that might be described as less conscious, that share this feature of self-identification or self-absorption, include ethnocentrism and religiocentrism, mentioned briefly in Chapter 5. Ethnocentrism, in its milder forms, is an attitude that judges other peoples by one's own cultural practices, values, and standards, as though these were the only reasonable norm. The relativity of ethnocentrism is well illustrated in the Gahan Wilson cartoon on page 234. To the caveman father, the child is deviant and obstinate, whereas for us, of course, it is the parents who are disgusting. This ethnocentric comedy of judging relative cultural mores in absolutes of right and wrong extends from nation to nation. Americans consider it barbaric that Asian Indians reserve the right hand for eating and the left for toilet details, while Indians are shocked by the immodesty of American women in their shorts and sleeveless dresses. And ethnocentrism can lead to tragedy, as is so clearly depicted in the novel *A Passage to India* by E. M. Forster.

In its most severe forms, ethnocentrism has provided a justification for extreme nationalism, imperialism, racism, and genocide.

> We are the chosen, we are the only true men. Our minds give off the true power of the spirit; the intelligence of the rest of the world is merely instinctive and animal. They can see, but they cannot foresee. . . . Does it not follow that nature herself has predestined us to dominate the whole world? . . .
>
> We shall paint the misdeeds of foreign governments in the most garish colors and create such ill-feeling towards them that the peoples would a thousand times rather bear a slavery which guarantees them peace and order than enjoy their much-touted freedom. The peoples will tolerate any servitude we may impose on them, if only to avoid a return to the horrors of wars

"What's wrong with that damned kid?"

From *I Paint What I See.* Copyright © by Gahan Wilson.
Used with permission of Simon & Schuster, Inc.

and insurrection. . . . (Alfred Rosenberg in *The Myth of the Twentieth Century,* Noontide, 1982)

The author of these lines provided some philosophical arguments that were later eagerly adopted by Hitler for the German Nazi party. These lines not only proclaim one race's superiority, but justify its right to domination.

It is easier to see ethnocentricity in other nations, especially if they have been our enemies, than in ourselves. Certainly, you can think of many quotations or popular sayings that express American ethnocentricity. It is the kind of thinking that Bob Dylan mocked in the ironic title and refrain of his song "With God on Our Side."

Religiocentrism is another form of ethnocentricity; in this case a total identification is made with a particular religious tradition or ideology. Again, the implicit assumption is that "we are right and everyone else is wrong; there is only one correct religious viewpoint and that is ours."

"All any couple needs to have a happy marriage is to be good Christians."

"In Islam we know that women are morally crooked because they came from Adam's rib. It is best for a girl not to come into existence, but being born she had better be married or buried."

CONSCIOUS PROBLEM SOLVING THROUGH UNDERSTANDING A VIEWPOINT

The film *The Killing Fields* was based on the experiences of *New York Times* correspondent Sidney Schanberg. It is an account of his friendship with Cambodian Dith Pran, who was his *Times* assistant at the time that Cambodia was invaded by the Khmer Rouge in 1975. Schanberg managed to escape, but Dith Pran had to stay behind in a country where two million people were to be massacred or die of starvation or disease.

Four years later Dith Pran walked to freedom over the border into Thailand. He remarkably survived by thoroughly understanding the viewpoint of the communist Khmer Rouge. Knowing that he would be killed immediately if they suspected his association with Westerners, he cut his hair, threw away the dollars Schanberg had given him, and disguised himself in the dress, manner, and language of a working-class taxi driver. He survived by pretending to be ignorant. "I did not care if they thought I was a fool," he said.

Question: In this case, Dith Pran had to lie and deceive in order to assume his oppressor's viewpoint. Can you think of an example in which a person survived or prospered by learning how to assume a viewpoint of greater compassion or understanding?

The first statement assumes that there are no viable religious alternatives to Christianity, or if so, then they should be abandoned for the only right one. This religiocentric observation appears rather innocent, however, compared to the second example, which adds to religiocentrism the elements of male chauvinism and a rationalization for genocide. Religiocentrism can be a prevalent feature in some religious sects that seem to take pride in repeatedly asserting that they have the only true path to salvation. However, no one particular religion lays exclusive claim to this kind of blinders mentality; religiocentrism is representative of an individual or collective level of consciousness that could make use of any religion for its expression.

Finally, in recent times two newer concepts describing self-centered viewpoints have come into being: androcentrism and anthropocentrism. The women's movement has drawn attention to the prevalence of androcentric (male-dominated) thinking, whereas the animal rights and deep ecology movements have pointed out our pervasive anthropocentrism (human centeredness).

Discovery Exercise

Identifying Political and Social Points of View

Read the following passages and notice how they express very different viewpoints. As you go, see if you can assign each quote one of the following political or social labels: radical left (communist), left liberal, feminist, gay, radical center (new age), right conservative, right-wing fundamentalist (reactionary).

Study each passage for clues that might already be familiar to you such as typical rhetoric, style, or attitudes on specific issues. One guideline is also to consider whether the viewpoint (1) wants to maintain the status quo (conservative) or return to the past (reactionary), or (2) criticizes the status quo (liberal) or wants radical changes in the status quo (radical left, radical center, libertarian).

1. "Now, even after he has won the presidency, friends keep asking me: Who is the real George Bush? What will his agenda be? The direction of a presidency is impossible to predict with any degree of certainty. But of one thing I am confident: George Bush is sincere in his desire to lead a kinder, gentler nation. Behind the combative campaign is a 'healing' candidate. Beneath the patina of leadership 'noblesse oblige' is a reflection of American common sense and common virtue." (Jim Leach, Iowa, Republican member of the House of Representatives)

2. "During World War II 'things began to make sense' to millions of Americans who had never thought about homosexuality before, particularly to isolated lesbians and gay men, who as a result of the war effort, found themselves in situations in which they could discover who they were and meet others like themselves. Our war mobilization, in fact, was the catalyst for a gay awakening in the U.S. that continues today." (Allen Berube, "Coming Out Under Fire," *Mother Jones*, February 1983)

3. *"What can we do about world hunger?* Our tasks are very clear: Work to halt U.S. military and countersurgency assistance to underdeveloped countries . . . Work to end all support for agribusiness penetration into food economies abroad . . . Work to end foreign assistance to governments working against the food security of their people . . . Work to limit U.S. foreign assistance only to those countries where a genuine redistribution of power over productive assets is underway . . . Work to build a democratically controlled and food self-reliant economy in America . . . Support the unionization of farm workers as well as worker-managed production units . . . Promote investigative research . . .

Educate yourself and others about the root causes of hunger . . . Counter despair." (Frances Moore Lappe & Joseph Collins, *World Hunger: 10 Myths,* 4th ed., Institute for Food and Development Policy, 1982. Used with permission of *Food First.*)

4. "By the year 2000 . . . there will be a demystification of medicine in society at large. That means no more doctors as Great White Father, whether kindly or stern—and no more patient as reluctant or willing child. The dashing Dr. Kildares, with their air of secret knowledge and special favor, will have gone for good." (Rony Cherry, "The End of the Medicine Man," *Woman in the Year 2000,* Dell, 1974)

5. "We are a party of struggle. A party of slaves who are determined not to be slaves any longer. It's the organized general staff and leadership of our class, to lead it in this historic battle, this historic mission of advancing human society to a completely new stage, to end wage slavery, and all the evils and suffering of this capitalist system. To end exploitation and to rip out for once and for all the weeds and roots of exploitation, so that they will never grow again. . . . We will free ourselves and all mankind." (Bob Avakian, *Bullets,* R.C.P. Publications, 1986)

6. "Although most presidential candidates and their running mates claim a Christian heritage, it's important to carefully examine their actual stand on the biblical issues—abortion, pro-life, pornography (literature decency), ERA/pro-family, voluntary school prayer, parental rights/child rights, homosexuality/lesbianism, marijuana legalization/drug law enforcement, prostitution, balanced budget/deficit spending, capital punishment, national defense. . . ." (David Balsinger, *The Presidential Biblical Scoreboard,* 1984)

7. "June 13th, 1989, was an extraordinary day in the history of relations between the United States and El Salvador. As a Salvadoran union leader was being brutally tortured by Salvadoran security forces, the Vice President of the United States was exchanging smiles and handshakes with Roberto d'Aubuisson, one of the most powerful and feared death squad leaders in the country." (Dennis Bernstein in "Legalizing Fascism," *KPFA Folio,* November 1989)

ANSWERS

1. Conservative (new right)
2. Gay
3. Radical center (progressive grassroots organizing)
4. Feminist

5.   Radical left (communist)
6.   Right-wing fundamentalist
7.   Left liberal

Discuss these questions in writing or in class.

1.   Which quotes were the most difficult for you to identify?
2.   How did you identify your choices?
3.   Do you feel confident of your ability to identify political points of view?
4.   If you disagree with any of these labels, explain why.

Writing Application

★ First Option: Observing Viewpoints in Magazines

Go to the library and pick out any two magazines or newspapers from the racks that never attracted your attention before. Study these publications, writing down your notes in the following order:

1.   *Magazine name.*
2.   *Cover page or front page:* What feelings, associations, impressions, direct and indirect message does it give you?
3.   *Table of contents or list of news articles:* Write them down and make inferences about the leading interests of this publication.
4.   *Advertisers:* Who are they? What inferences can you make about their reader appeal? What do you think they have concluded, from market research, about who their readers are and what they would want to buy?
5.   Can you categorize this publication as appealing to a particular political, social, ethnic, or special interest group? Or does it bridge two groups, like a men's sports magazine? See how much information you can deduce about its readers. Does it seem to be aimed at upper class, middle class, yuppies, or working class—or all of these?

Write out your notes into a report and attach either the publication or a photocopy of its cover or headline page together with the magazine's table of contents.

Second Option: Determining a Political Viewpoint and Its Shaping of Content

This library research assignment will give you more practice in determining political viewpoints. This assignment can be done individually or in pairs, depending on your instructor's directions. As an individual, choose *two* magazines, or with your partner, choose *four* magazines from the list that follows. Make your selection from different viewpoints on the political spectrum. You need not confine yourself or your partner to current issues displayed on the periodicals racks but should ask to see past issues from the stacks as well. (Back issues can be obtained in libraries for some of these periodicals that are no longer being published.)

RADICAL LEFT–COMMUNIST

The Daily World (American Communist Party), *Soviet Life* (Soviet propaganda), *Revolutionary Worker*

SOCIALIST TO FAR LEFT

People's World, Mother Jones, The Progressive, The Guardian, In These Times

LEFT LIBERAL

The Nation, The Village Voice, Commonweal (Catholic), *Black Scholar*

CENTER TO RIGHT LIBERAL

Ebony, Rolling Stone, Atlantic Monthly, Consumer Reports, Ms. (back issues), *Washington Monthly, Harper's, Esquire, New Republic*

RADICAL CENTER (NEW AGE)

The Utne Reader, New Age Journal, Co-Evolution Quarterly, Brain/ Mind Bulletin, East West Journal, World Policy

LIBERTARIAN

Reason, Policy Report, Libertarian Review, Inquiry (back issues)

CENTER CONSERVATIVE

Public Opinion, U.S. News & World Report, Time, Newsweek, Barron's

RIGHT CONSERVATIVE

National Review (William Buckley, editor), *Commentary* (American Jewish Committee sponsored), *Conservative Digest*

NEW RIGHT TO RADICAL RIGHT

Armed Forces Journal, American Opinion (John Birch Society), *Christian Crusade Weekly, Moral Majority Report, Christian Beacon, Plain Truth, Your Heritage News* (back issues), *The Citizen* (white supremacy), *Cross the the Flag, Freedom, White Power* (American Nazi Party) (back issues)

Examine each periodical by skimming through, noting its style, language, and topics of interest. Notice how its values are expressed in both style and content. Also decide whether you consider it to be labeled correctly.

If you find that you need further clarification about the definitions of these political labels, a discussion with some diagrams follows this assignment. Moreover, you are encouraged to study recent political science textbooks or the following reference sources:

Katz, Bill. *Magazines for Libraries*. New York: R. R. Bowker Co., 1978. (This is a reference used by librarians to assist their choice of a representative range of periodicals. Entries in this book describe the background and orientation of each periodical, and label them under such headings as *Conservative, Liberal, Libertarian, Radical Left, Radical Right*.)

Plano, Jack C., and Milton Greenberg, eds. *American Political Dictionary*, 4th ed. New York: Holt, Rinehart & Winston, 1976.

Safire, William. *Safire: Political Dictionary*. New York: Random House, 1978.

Select two of these periodicals to write a review of (or four altogether with your partner, depending on your instructor's directions). Write two pages on each magazine, following the guidelines given below.

Remember that the purpose of this exercise is to give you an experience of observing and describing the characteristics of a particular orientation and the manner in which this orientation shapes information. This is not meant to be an in-depth study of each periodical. You should make this a concise paper of only about two typed pages for each periodical selected.

1. At the top of the page list the name of the periodical and its orienation (for example, left conservative).

2. Describe the cover page and the tone it sets for the publication. Describe the way it affects you. Does it elicit any particular feelings such as anger, fear, greed, or humor? What does it promise you? What does it emphasize? What is its message? With what words and symbols is this all accomplished?

3. Study the table of contents. What are the subjects of the main feature articles?

4. Make a general statement about what kinds of advertisements appear, and specify some of their sponsors.

5. What inferences can you make—on the basis of the types of articles and advertising sponsors—about what interests could control or influence this magazine's policies?

6. Did you notice any special characteristics about the language used in this periodical? To what social or educational level does it seem to be addressed?

To follow up on this assignment in class, bring your periodicals to class with you if you own them or if you have checked out issues from the library. Read your work aloud to others in small groups. Work with a partner to see to what extent your work managed to succeed within the given guidelines.

When you have finished, recommend one paper from your group to be read aloud, in whole or in part, to the class by one of you or by the instructor. Discuss what you have observed and what you have learned from this assignment.*

STUDENT WRITING EXAMPLE

MS. MAGAZINE
NOVEMBER 1985 ISSUE
CENTER LIBERAL

Rachel Fitzgerald

"Working at what you love—and Getting Paid for It!" This notion jumps out enthusiastically from the cover of *Ms.* magazine, framed in tall black letters that portray an aura of novelty. A split second later, the eye is captured by the turquoise *Ms.* logo in the upper left-hand corner of the page. Obscuring the period following the "s" is a fuchsia-clothed arm, upraised in jubilation, capped by a loosely clenched fist. The arm belongs to the third most dominant feature: a woman stands almost the full eleven inches of glossy page, her toes chopped by the bottom edge, her upraised hands soaring toward the top. Her whole body expresses triumph, but with restraint, as though the sharp eyes of boss or secretary have not yet left her. She appears to be around thirty and is slightly incongruous in an oversized fuchsia V-neck hiding most of a canary tee shirt, only a demure black shirt saving her from the ranks of Esprit. Those happy fists lead the eye to stark black letters strung along a yellow border: "The Suppressed 'Doonesbury' Cartoons." This caption sets the tone for the whole cover, and presumably the magazine: serious issues served with snappy pizzazz and a dab of wry humor.

---

*The author is indebted to Donald Lazere's unpublished monograph *Composition for Critical Thinking* for the kernel ideas upon which this assignment was modeled and developed.

The Table of Contents bears this out. Spanning a full page, it presents article titles, authors, and page numbers in black on white background, but the department headings are in red print bordering on script style. The *Ms.* logo reigns boldly in black, center top. Drawn to this page like flypaper, I am struck by two qualities. First, the sheer number of articles ranging from "Working: for Love and Money" to "Stories for Free Children." Wondering how *Ms.* defines a "free" child, I notice that other titles are full of charged words and teasing phrases, using active verbs to hook the reader: "The Art Biz" for example. "Biz"? Woman, put down your briefcase and find your dictionary!

The advertisements are annoyingly plentiful, usually garish one-pagers. After the obligatory Kotex ad, I found one for Bombay gin with a "masculine" message "Play to Win!" in "feminine" colors: pink, lavender, and that hideous neon green. This was followed by Dodge appealing to the (tasteful) sports fan in all of us. Overall, the products appeal to the working woman adopting traditional male passions as part of her armor: booze, cars, and little gadgets.

The articles themselves read quickly, aided by those snappy phrases, but they are written with an intelligent, fairly educated, middle-class reader in mind. The sentences are crisp, polished, and often complex. Lurking behind the competent journalism, however, is the spirit of dogma, which crops up in the letters to the editor and the editorials. "Of all the changes in this country, perhaps the one with the most far-reaching impact is the revolution in the kinds of work done by women." Technically the sentence is good, hooking the reader with a beginning subordinate clause and using hard-hitting words like "impact" and "revolution." Stylistically it has the flavor of rhetoric. Terming changes in female work patterns "revolution" implies a sweeping, conscious overthrow of custom, overlooking the fact that the changes occurred over several decades and were spurred by economic necessity. Nor are the objects of "impact" made clear. Women? Everyone? Does *Ms.* address only hard-line feminists? The majority of articles suggest this is not so. On the whole, *Ms.* is a well-heeled feminist publication seeking a broad mainstream readership.

Used with permission of Rachel Fitzgerald.

CATEGORIZING TODAY'S
POLITICAL AND SOCIAL VIEWPOINTS

Today's students often find it both frustrating and confusing to understand, use, and apply the labels *left* and *right* to categorize shifting world patterns of political, social, economic, and religious values (see Figures 8.1 and 8.2). Perhaps this is because, as some political scientists maintain, the use of the left-to-right spectrum as a paradigm (model of

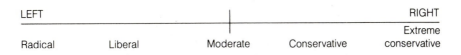

FIGURE 8.1

The Left-to-Right Political Spectrum

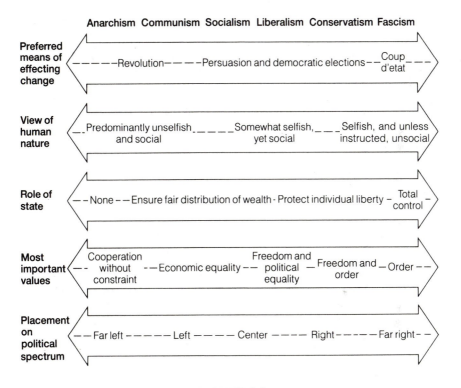

FIGURE 8.2

Traits of Political Systems on Left-to-Right Spectrum

Adapted from Kay Lawson, *The Human Polity: An Introduction to Political Science.*
Boston: Houghton Mifflin, 1985, p. 118. Used with permission of the publisher.

reality) to explain viable political positions is now obsolete. It was derived, they say, from the period of the French, American, and industrial revolutions, which conceived oppositions between monarchies and democracies, between more or less authoritarian control, and between open markets and free trade versus "social protection" from the market system's inequities.

Other models or viewpoints, besides the left-to-right spectrum, have been offered, such as the two-axis model depicted in Figure 8.3. This model has the advantage of including perspectives that do not fit on the single-axis left-to-right paradigm, such as anarchism, populism, agrarianism, libertarianism, and environmentalism. A horseshoe arrangement, shown in Figure 8.4, makes other relationships apparent, as for instance, some shared characteristics of the far right and far left.

In the United States, it is also not easy for us to determine any clear distinctions between the Democratic and Republican parties.

Unlike other developed democracies, the United States does not have a parliamentary political system in which voters cast their votes for parties. Parties in most countries have distinct commitments to differing national programs, differences easily discerned by voters. Citizens voting in those countries know that when they cast their ballots for a party's candidate they are voting for particular policies. In the United States, voters cast ballots for individual candidates who are not bound to any party program except rhe-

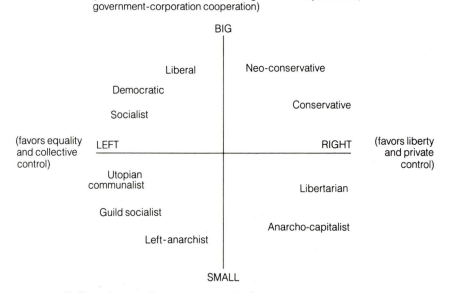

(Hamiltonian: favors nationalization, global interdependence, government-corporation cooperation)

BIG

Liberal   Neo-conservative

Democratic

Socialist   Conservative

(favors equality   LEFT   RIGHT   (favors liberty
and collective   and private
control)   control)

Utopian
communalist   Libertarian

Guild socialist

Anarcho-capitalist

Left-anarchist

SMALL

(Jeffersonian; populist, green perspective [peace and environmentalism]: favors liberty and equality, small cooperatives, community self-reliance)

FIGURE 8.3

The Two-Axis Model of Political Views

From Michael Marien, "The Two Post-Industrialisms and Higher Education," *World Future Society Bulletin,* May 1–June 1982, p. 20. Used with permission of World Future Society.

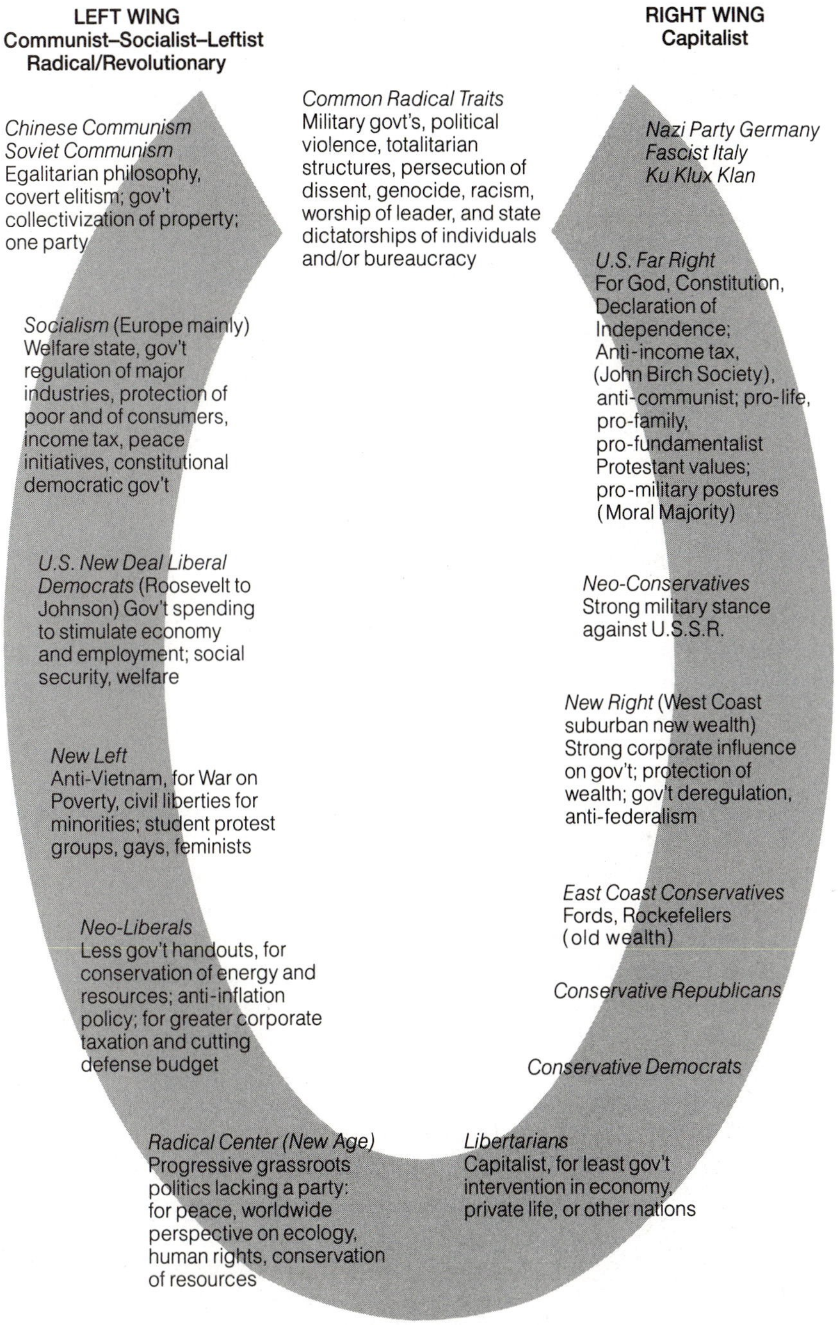

LEFT WING
Communist–Socialist–Leftist
Radical/Revolutionary

RIGHT WING
Capitalist

Common Radical Traits
Military govt's, political
violence, totalitarian
structures, persecution of
dissent, genocide, racism,
worship of leader, and state
dictatorships of individuals
and/or bureaucracy

Chinese Communism
Soviet Communism
Egalitarian philosophy,
covert elitism; gov't
collectivization of property;
one party

Nazi Party Germany
Fascist Italy
Ku Klux Klan

U.S. Far Right
For God, Constitution,
Declaration of
Independence;
Anti-income tax,
(John Birch Society),
anti-communist; pro-life,
pro-family,
pro-fundamentalist
Protestant values;
pro-military postures
(Moral Majority)

Socialism (Europe mainly)
Welfare state, gov't
regulation of major
industries, protection of
poor and of consumers,
income tax, peace
initiatives, constitutional
democratic gov't

U.S. New Deal Liberal
Democrats (Roosevelt to
Johnson) Gov't spending
to stimulate economy
and employment; social
security, welfare

Neo-Conservatives
Strong military stance
against U.S.S.R.

New Left
Anti-Vietnam, for War on
Poverty, civil liberties for
minorities; student protest
groups, gays, feminists

New Right (West Coast
suburban new wealth)
Strong corporate influence
on gov't; protection of
wealth; gov't deregulation,
anti-federalism

Neo-Liberals
Less gov't handouts, for
conservation of energy and
resources; anti-inflation
policy; for greater corporate
taxation and cutting
defense budget

East Coast Conservatives
Fords, Rockefellers
(old wealth)

Conservative Republicans

Conservative Democrats

Radical Center (New Age)
Progressive grassroots
politics lacking a party:
for peace, worldwide
perspective on ecology,
human rights, conservation
of resources

Libertarians
Capitalist, for least gov't
intervention in economy,
private life, or other nations

FIGURE 8.4

The Horseshoe Model of Political Views

torically, not always then. Some Republicans are more liberal than some Democrats, some libertarians are more radical than some socialists, and many local candidates run without any party identification. No American citizen can vote intelligently without knowledge of the ideas, political background, and commitments of each individual candidate.

Ben H. Bagdikian, *The Media Monopoly,* 1983, p. 176. Used with permission of the author.

And to make this even more complicated, we also have difficulty defining many of the terms used to describe the range of views within any one party. The meanings of the words *liberal, conservative, radical left,* and *radical right* can shift from one decade to another. In the 1930s, Franklin Roosevelt's New Deal proposal for social security was called radical Jewish socialism. Today social security is a conservative American institution. Since the late 1960s, views have shifted around so many new issues that we now have the new left, the neo-liberals, the new right, the neo-conservatives, and the far right. As for the more familiar terms *conservative* and *liberal,* their more traditional definitions seem to contain inconsistencies when applied to contemporary issues. For instance, if one defines a *conservative* as one who wants to conserve existing wealth, values, and traditions, one nevertheless finds conservatives wanting to minimize government responsibility for the conservation of natural resources, whereas liberals complain they must support many private environmental organizations in order to promote that priority. And if one defines a *liberal* as open to changes in the status quo, one finds liberals strongly objecting to the radical new economic policies and constitutional amendments proposed by conservatives. Finally, how one defines all these terms, whether *liberal, conservative, radical left,* or *radical right,* depends on one's own ideology and perspective within the whole political spectrum.

The professed neutrality of the American mass media is perhaps another reason why it is so difficult to categorize viewpoint today in America. Our largest city newspapers, national radio programs, and television networks generally claim to be objective and nonideological. This situation differs from European countries, where party newspapers, representative of individual parties, interpret the news and issues on the basis of their ideologies. In such countries a person might sit down to breakfast to read a dialogue on topical issues among newspapers with such titles as *Communist Express, The Socialist News, Christian-Democrats, The Catholic World, The Independent, Green Peace,* and *The Nazi Hope.* Here no reader could wonder about a viewpoint's source, its stands on issues, or its sponsors. Moreover, in comparing such papers, the reader is constantly reminded that reports of historical events and issues are *not* realities in themselves, but are *interpretations* from different viewpoints.

In the United States, our mainstream newspapers, radio shows, and television shows do not reflect this country's full diversity of opinion, or include much expression of extreme or minority views. Nevertheless, a trip to a neighborhood library can offer a very wide selection of non–mass media publications that are identified by their social, religious, or political affiliations. Reading these small newspapers and magazines can help you develop your own sense of what constitutes right-wing opinion or left-wing opinion or whatever. Moreover, for the purposes of critical thinking, it can be quite stimulating to become acquainted with a wide spectrum of views on contemporary social and political issues.

CHAPTER SUMMARY

1. Critical thinking means learning to recognize viewpoints and how they shape the content of any message.

2. Viewpoints, like assumptions, opinions, and evaluations, can be either consciously or unconsciously assumed.

3. We communicate best when we are aware of our own viewpoint (see it objectively as relative) and can understand and assume the viewpoints of others as well. For a writer, it is especially important to be able to anticipate the viewpoints of potential readers.

4. Unconscious viewpoints include the egocentric, ethnocentric, religiocentric, androcentric, and anthropocentric.

5. Political and social labels are based on the recognition of stable or predictable ideologies, values, and policies. At present our political and social differences are not easy to define in terms of a left-to-right spectrum.

6. In periodicals we find a wider range of viewpoints than in the mass media.

7. Periodicals can express viewpoints through symbols as well as words. Evidence of viewpoint can be seen in the selection of and emphasis on topics, and in advertising sponsors.

Chapter Quiz

Rate each of the following statements as *true* or *false*. Rewrite any false statements to make them true.

_____ 1. Viewpoints can be either consciously or unconsciously assumed.

_____ 2. To be exterior to one's own viewpoint is to see it objectively as just a viewpoint among many possible ones.

_____ 3. Ethnocentrism means being absorbed in one's own personal viewpoint without being able to put oneself in other people's shoes.

_____ 4. "The Jewish people are God's chosen race" could be interpreted as an example of religiocentrism.

_____ 5. In wartime, people tend to become more and more ethnocentric in their attitudes, expressing ideas that righteously affirm their own national superiority.

_____ 6. A _reactionary_ viewpoint is one that advocates major political, social, or economic changes in order to return to an earlier, more conservative system of the past.

_____ 7. A _conservative_ viewpoint believes it is often necessary to change the political, economic, or social status quo to foster the development and well-being of the individual.

_____ 8. A _liberal_ viewpoint defends the status quo against major changes in the political, economic, or social institutions of a society.

_____ 9. So-called _radical_ groups, whether right or left, want extreme, drastic, or fundamental changes in the status quo.

_____ 10. We communicate best when we can hear or anticipate the viewpoints of others and are objective about our own.

Writing Application

Essay Comparing and Contrasting Two Viewpoints

This essay will build on the research you did in the previous writing application. In that exercise you observed, recorded characteristics, and made inferences about information to determine viewpoint, values, and objectives. You also personally evaluated this information. Mentally, you classified, categorized, compared and contrasted, and inferred cause and effect.

In this essay you are to make your classifications, comparisons, and contrasts more explicit. Here are the parameters for your work:

1. _Form and length:_ Essay of four typed pages.

2. _Topic:_ Comparison of two viewpoints, their values and ideologies, as expressed in two magazines from the same month and year. Limit your topic by focusing on (a) the same issue or controversy (for instance, tax reform, the nuclear debate, or a public personality) as discussed in both periodicals; or (b) a report of the same event; or (c) the magazines' subjects of advertising and approach to advertising (one could limit this even more, for

instance, by comparing the liquor ads in *Ms.* to those in *Time* or *Esquire*); or (d) tone of the magazines, or their attitudes toward life: optimistic, paranoid, pessimistic, suffering and angry, conspiratorial, superficial, and so on.

3. *Thesis:* This should show the limitations of your coverage and the conclusion you reached from this comparative study.

4. *Evidence and support:* Give concrete examples from the materials you are using to show the sources of your inferences about the values and ideology of each viewpoint.

5. *Structure:* Comparison (how alike) and contrast (how different). One strategy is to describe one magazine or newspaper fully according to subject (such as all the liquor ads) in several paragraphs, followed by several paragraphs treating all the liquor ads in the other magazine. Another option is to choose one part of your subject (such as all the beer and wine ads) and to compare one magazine to another on this part, then to move on to the hard liquor ads, comparing both magazines again in one paragraph. In the case of either strategy, both your thesis and conclusion should bring both periodicals together in one or several generalizations stating what this comparative study has shown you.

Peer Review

Follow up in class by reading your papers to one another in small groups. Bring your magazines to class for your group to examine as you read. Work with partners to rate one another on the extent to which the parameters given above were observed. Rate what is outstanding about the essay.

Readings

MEDIA-SPEAK

Donna Woolfolk Cross

In this reading selection, the author defends her claim that mainstream television offers us a world perspective through the filter of big business. *

---

*Notes to the original reading have not been included here.

> The Establishment is a general term for those people in finance, business, and the professions . . . who hold the principal measure of power and influence in this country. . . . The Establishment has very nearly unchallenged power in deciding what is and what is not respectable in this country.
>
> —Richard Rovere
> *The American Establishment*

. . . Surveys reveal that the average American now watches television for an average of six and one half hours a day. It would be surprising if the effects of what we see and hear for more than one-third of our waking hours did *not* shape our opinions. Yet we seem oddly unaware that much of what we believe to be true derives from television. TV messages have become so familiar to us that they appear to be The Simple Truth. This confirms what propagandists have always known: people accept as true those ideas which are repeated to them most often. 1

In fact, we do not see the world as it is. We see it as television presents it to us. . . . 2

The language of television, which I call Media-speak, is the house we all live in. Media-speak is not merely a way of communicating; it is a way of *perceiving* reality. It provides us with our windows on the world. As Walter Lippmann says, "We do not first see, and then define, we define first and then see. In the great booming, buzzing confusion of the outer world, we pick out what our culture has already defined for us, and we tend to perceive that which we have picked out in the form stereotyped for us by our culture." 3

This phenomenon gives enormous, unprecedented power to media managers: the power to show and tell the rest of us how to live, what to be afraid of, what to be proud of, how to be successful, how to be loved. More than media managers, they are mind managers. 4

Of course, human society has always had mind managers of one sort or another, from witch doctors to kings. The difference today is in the mass media. Never before in human history have so few imposed so much of their thinking on so many. Theodore White has said, "You can take a compass with a one-mile radius and put it down at a corner of Fifth Avenue and 51st Street, and you have . . . 95 percent of the entire opinion and influence in the U.S.A." 5

In America, and throughout the modern world, communication is big business. Like any business, its needs and interests are directed toward increasing profit, not toward promoting the welfare of society as a whole. No less than Adam Smith, the patron saint of modern capitalism, argued that a merchant's necessary self-interest was bound to blind him to "the public interest." Therefore, Smith believed, merchants should never be given monopolistic or governmental power: "The government of an exclusive company of merchants," he said, "is perhaps the worst of all governments." 6

That is, however, a reasonably accurate description of the state of 7
the American mass media today. Network television has been described
by *Advertising Age*, the trade journal of advertising and public relations firms, as being "largely the creation of the one hundred largest
companies in the country." As Jerry Mander points out, this means,
"What we get to see on television is what suits the mentality and purposes of one hundred corporations."

Consider the "public service announcements" regularly offered on 8
network television as one small but representative example of that corporate mentality. These announcements—called PSAs in the trade—
are under the supervision and control of the Advertising Council, a
group of businessmen and advertising agency executives who volun-
teer their time to design and approve messages they judge to be "in the
public interest"—urging people to donate blood to the Red Cross, for
example, or to help prevent forest fires, or to drive carefully. All very
praiseworthy causes. And indeed, the work of the Advertising Council
has been highly praised by government and business alike. Charles E.
Wilson, former president of General Electric, says, "Through the Advertising Council, American business supports more causes, solves more
problems, and serves more people than is possible through any other
single organization."

A closer look at PSAs might lead us to question whose problems are 9
really being solved and whose interests are really being served. Recently I watched an anti-pollution PSA that featured an American Indian mournfully regarding a badly littered highway. "People start pollution; people can stop it," the caption read. "Next time you see someone
polluting, point it out." As the caption rolled, a single tear trickled down
from the corner of the Indian's eye.

It was a very effective ad. I, for one, vowed never again to throw 10
another candy wrapper on the ground.

Only later did I realize how perfectly that ad served the purposes of 11
the business interest that had created it. My attention had been directed
entirely toward small individual acts of pollution and away from other
more important sources. The vast amounts of industrial waste dumped
in the nation's rivers, the massive disposal problems created by the bil-
lions of nonreturnable bottles and cans produced each year—these
were not mentioned. The business interest who designed this PSA may
not have deliberately sought to influence public opinion to their own
advantage; nonetheless the focus of the ad was hardly surprising, considering that those responsible for producing and passing approval on
the PSA spots included executives from the American Can Company,
the National Soft Drink Association, the United States Brewers Association, Pepsi-Cola, and Coca-Cola.

Similarly, PSAs on the subject of crime invariably stress personal 12
precautionary measures such as not leaving keys in the car or carrying
a whistle to blow in case of mugging. Fundamental anti-crime measures

that might raise taxes on profits are ignored. After one series of anti-delinquency spots, a United Auto Workers spokesman commented: "This is wonderful, and good-hearted people are inclined to applaud this public-spirited action, but when you look at the directors of the Advertising Council, you find that they . . . stand four-square against federal aid to education, against a federal housing program, and against city improvements that would tend to cut the breeding ground out from under juvenile delinquency."

Business crime is not addressed either. Recently, oil companies   13
operating on "the honor system" underreported by $650 million the royalties due the government for oil taken from public lands. That shortfall in federal revenues has to be made up by taking someone else's $650 million—and that someone else is you and me. There have never been public service announcements alerting us to *this* form of theft.

The situation is much the same in other media. Magazines, depen-   14
dent on advertising revenues, are easily influenced by business interests. When, for example, a bill designed to end deceptive pricing and weighing practices in food packaging was under consideration in the Senate, the president of the Grocery Manufacturers of America met with the publishers of sixteen national magazines. As he tells it, "We suggested to the publishers that the day was here when their editorial department and business department might better understand their interdependency relationships . . . how their operations may affect the advertiser . . . their bread and butter." Later, he pointed out with pleasure how well most of the publishers had "responded" to this not so subtle threat. At the same time, Senator Philip Hart, who sponsored the bill, had a scheduled television appearance canceled because sponsors objected.

Newspapers, also dependent on advertising revenues, rely increas-   15
ingly on public relations releases as sources of news stories. An American business magazine has noted that "PR plays a unique and quite startling role in the whole flow of communications. . . . This role is often glossed over, but the simple fact is that much of the current news coverage of business by the American press . . . is subsidized by company PR efforts." One study group has concluded that "the portion of the contents of our newspapers that is originated from public relations offices . . . is probably quite remarkable."

Business domination of the media exerts a clear and unmistak-   16
able influence on the nature of the communication we receive. "The mass media everywhere are organs of the Establishment," says Pulitzer Prize-winning journalist Harry Ashmore. "In a Communist country, it is their function to defend and propagate the official faith; in a capitalist society they enjoy guarantees against state control and are expected to perform a critical role, but their economic dependence upon the prevailing system fixes limits to the range of dissent."

Business has a natural and understandable inclination to support 17
the status quo. Most business executives are members of a high-income
social group and the status quo is perfectly fine with them. They are
properly appreciative of the system that has put them where they are,
and their view of the world supports, justifies, even glamorizes that
system.

This is, you might say, only to be expected. Why should any group 18
act against its own interests? But the question is, do other social groups
get an equivalent opportunity to support, justify, and glamorize *their*
ideas about society?

Media critic James Monaco comments, "Whole classes of people 19
are effectively prevented from using the media to record and dissemi-
nate their own versions of myth and history, and even those few dis-
senting views that do get through are subtly, but significantly, attenu-
ated." Alternative ways of looking at things cease to be considered,
because the mass media teach us, through their omission, that such
views are not worth considering.

Surrounded by an abundance of media, we believe we have an 20
abundance of choice. We can choose to subscribe to *Playboy* or *Pent-
house; Good Housekeeping, Redbook,* or *Ladies Home Journal;
Reader's Digest* or *Life; Newsweek* or *Time.* We can tune in to ABC,
NBC, CBS, PBS, or any of a host of cable and pay-TV stations. We can
listen to over 6,700 different commercial radio stations. We can see a
different movie each day of the week. Merely reciting these statistics
tends to reassure us that we are indeed subjected to a wide and representative spectrum of opinion. It is all too easy to confuse the sheer
quantity of media with a diversity of viewpoint. We do not notice that
essentially the same messages are being repeated. As Herbert Schiller
says, "The fact of the matter is that . . . most Americans are basically,
though unconsciously, trapped in what amounts to a no-choice informa-
tional bind. Variety of opinion . . . scarcely exists in the media." He
adds, "It is not so much that the medium is the message, but that *all* the
media transmit the same message."

A thorough examination of all the media is beyond the scope of this 21
book. Instead, I hope by focusing on a single medium to explore the
character of its messages in some detail.

Television is the obvious choice. It is the most seductive, the most 22
pervasive, the most influential form of mass communication today. We
don't seem to *like* it very much—most of us would probably agree with
Fred Allen's comment that "Television is called a medium because anything good on it is rare"—but we watch it. More significantly, we trust
it. Recent Roper reports show that we believe television's picture of the
world more than any other. Years of conditioning to the kinds of ideas
TV sanctions have fortified us against contrary ideas. "The average
American," says Schiller, "will accept information which affirms the

consumer society and reject material which views it critically. When an American has been properly 'prepared,' he or she is relatively invulnerable to dissonant messages, however accurate they may be." Herbert Marcuse takes this line of reasoning one step further: there is no need for Moscow-style government repression in this country, he says, because the mass media have shaped our consciousness so successfully that we no longer conceive of ideas or values that contradict the established political order.

We can hardly be expected to defend ourselves against propaganda 23 if we aren't even aware that it is being used. Our society surrounds us, a fundamental part of our lives. We function within it and cannot conceive of functioning anywhere else. As philosophers are fond of pointing out, we cannot be sure who first explored the various properties of water, but we do know that it wasn't a fish. . . .

From Donna Woolfolk Cross, *Media-Speak: How Television Makes Up Your Mind.* New York: Mentor, 1983. Copyright © 1983 by Donna Woolfolk Cross. Used with permission of The Putnam Publishing Group.

STUDY QUESTIONS

1. Why does the author begin with a quotation defining the Establishment?

2. Have you found it to be true that people accept those ideas repeated to them most often? Give examples to back your answer.

3. Explain this statement: "Media-speak is not merely a way of communicating; it is a way of *perceiving* reality."

4. Do you think the author offers convincing evidence of public mind control by the corporations that own the media? Why or why not?

5. How does she support her claim that although we have an abundance of media, we do not have an abundance of choice?

6. What is the author's thesis and how does her last analogy about the fish in water reinforce it?

BLACK BOY

Richard Wright

It may be difficult for the present generation to realize that it was only sixty years ago when black people in the southern United States were denied literacy skills and access to libraries. This excerpt is

Chapter 13 of Wright's Black Boy, *an autobiographical account of his youth. The author describes discovering alternative viewpoints and discovering how words and writing could offer him liberation and power.*

One morning I arrived early at work and went into the bank lobby where the Negro porter was mopping. I stood at a counter and picked up the Memphis *Commercial Appeal* and began my free reading of the press. I came finally to the editorial page and saw an article dealing with one H. L. Mencken. I knew by hearsay that he was the editor of the *American Mercury*, but aside from that I knew nothing about him. The article was a furious denunciation of Mencken, concluding with one, hot, short sentence: Mencken is a fool. 1

I wondered what on earth this Mencken had done to call down upon him the scorn of the South. The only people I had ever heard denounced in the South were Negroes, and this man was not a Negro. Then what ideas did Mencken hold that made a newspaper like the *Commercial Appeal* castigate him publicly? Undoubtedly he must be advocating ideas that the South did not like. Were there, then, people other than Negroes who criticized the South? I knew that during the Civil War the South had hated northern whites, but I had not encountered such hate during my life. Knowing no more of Mencken than I did at that moment, I felt a vague sympathy for him. Had not the South, which had assigned me the role of a non-man, cast at him its hardest words? 2

Now, how could I find out about this Mencken? There was a huge library near the riverfront, but I knew that Negroes were not allowed to patronize its shelves any more than they were the parks and play-grounds of the city. I had gone into the library several times to get books for the white men on the job. Which of them would now help me to get books? And how could I read them without causing concern to the white men with whom I worked? I had so far been successful in hiding my thoughts and feelings from them, but I knew that I would create hostility if I went about this business of reading in a clumsy way. 3

I weighed the personalities of the men on the job. There was Don, a Jew; but I distrusted him. His position was not much better than mine and I knew that he was uneasy and insecure; he had always treated me in an offhand, bantering way that barely concealed his contempt. I was afraid to ask him to help me to get books; his frantic desire to demonstrate a racial solidarity with the whites against Negroes might make him betray me. 4

Then how about the boss? No, he was a Baptist and I had the suspicion that he would not be quite able to comprehend why a black boy would want to read Mencken. There were other white men on the job whose attitudes showed clearly that they were Kluxers or sympathizers, and they were out of the question. 5

There remained only one man whose attitude did not fit into an 6 anti-Negro category, for I had heard the white men refer to him as a "Pope lover." He was an Irish Catholic and was hated by the white Southerners. I knew that he read books, because I had got him volumes from the library several times. Since he, too, was an object of hatred, I felt that he might refuse me but would hardly betray me. I hesitated, weighing and balancing the imponderable realities.

One morning I paused before the Catholic fellow's desk.   7

"I want to ask you a favor," I whispered to him.   8

"What is it?"   9

"I want to read. I can't get books from the library. I wonder if you'd   10
let me use your card?"

He looked at me suspiciously.   11

"My card is full most of the time," he said.   12

"I see," I said and waited, posing my question silently.   13

"You're not trying to get me into trouble, are you, boy?" he asked,   14
staring at me.

"Oh, no, sir."   15

"What book do you want?"   16

"A book by H. L. Mencken."   17

"Which one?"   18

"I don't know. Has he written more than one?"   19

"He has written several."   20

"I didn't know that."   21

"What makes you want to read Mencken?"   22

"Oh, I just saw his name in the newspaper," I said.   23

"It's good of you to want to read," he said. "But you ought to read   24
the right things."

I said nothing. Would he want to supervise my reading?   25

"Let me think," he said. "I'll figure out something."   26

I turned from him and he called me back. He stared at me   27
quizzically.

"Richard, don't mention this to the other white men," he said.   28

"I understand," I said. "I won't say a word."   29

A few days later he called me to him.   30

"I've got a card in my wife's name," he said. "Here's mine."   31

"Thank you, sir."   32

"Do you think you can manage it?"   33

"I'll manage fine," I said.   34

"If they suspect you, you'll get in trouble," he said.   35

"I'll write the same kind of notes to the library that you wrote when   36
you sent me for books," I told him. "I'll sign your name."

He laughed.   37

"Go ahead. Let me see what you get," he said.   38

That afternoon I addressed myself to forging a note. Now, what   39
were the names of books written by H. L. Mencken? I did not know any

of them. I finally wrote what I thought would be a foolproof note: *Dear Madam: Will you please let this nigger boy*—I used the word "nigger" to make the librarian feel that I could not possibly be the author of the note—*have some books by H. L. Mencken?* I forged the white man's name.

I entered the library as I had always done when on errands for whites, but I felt that I would somehow slip up and betray myself. I doffed my hat, stood a respectful distance from the desk, looked as un-bookish as possible, and waited for the white patrons to be taken care of. When the desk was clear of people, I still waited. The white librarian looked at me. 40

"What do you want, boy?" 41

As though I did not possess the power of speech, I stepped forward and simply handed her the forged note, not parting my lips. 42

"What books by Mencken does he want?" she asked. 43

"I don't know, ma'am," I said, avoiding her eyes. 44

"Who gave you this card?" 45

"Mr. Falk," I said. 46

"Where is he?" 47

"He's at work, at the M—— Optical Company," I said. "I've been in here for him before." 48

"I remember," the woman said. "But he never wrote notes like this." 49

Oh, God, she's suspicious. Perhaps she would not let me have the books? If she had turned her back at that moment, I would have ducked out the door and never gone back. Then I thought of a bold idea. 50

"You can call him up, ma'am," I said, my heart pounding. 51

"You're not using these books, are you?" she asked pointedly. 52

"Oh, no, ma'am. I can't read." 53

"I don't know what he wants by Mencken," she said under her breath. 54

I knew now that I had won; she was thinking of other things and the race question had gone out of her mind. She went to the shelves. Once or twice she looked over her shoulder at me, as though she was still doubtful. Finally she came forward with two books in her hand. 55

"I'm sending him two books," she said. "But tell Mr. Falk to come in next time, or send me the names of the books he wants. I don't know what he wants to read." 56

I said nothing. She stamped the card and handed me the books. Not daring to glance at them, I went out of the library, fearing that the woman would call me back for further questioning. A block away from the library I opened one of the books and read a title: *A Book of Prefaces.* I was nearing my nineteenth birthday and I did not know how to pronounce the word "preface." I thumbed the pages and saw strange words and strange names. I shook my head, disappointed. I looked at the other book; it was called *Prejudices.* I knew what that word meant; 57

I had heard it all my life. And right off I was on guard against Mencken's books. Why would a man want to call a book *Prejudices?* The word was so stained with all my memories of racial hate that I could not conceive of anybody using it for a title. Perhaps I had made a mistake about Mencken? A man who had prejudices must be wrong.

When I showed the books to Mr. Falk, he looked at me and frowned. 58

"That librarian might telephone you," I warned him. 59

"That's all right," he said. "But when you're through reading those 60 books, I want you to tell me what you get out of them."

That night in my rented room, while letting the hot water run over 61 my can of pork and beans in the sink, I opened *A Book of Prefaces* and began to read. I was jarred and shocked by the style, the clear, clean, sweeping sentences. Why did he write like that? And how did one write like that? I pictured the man as a raging demon, slashing with his pen, consumed with hate, denouncing everything American, extolling everything European or German, laughing at the weaknesses of people, mocking God, authority. What was this? I stood up, trying to realize what reality lay behind the meaning of the words . . . Yes, this man was fighting, fighting with words. He was using words as a weapon, using them as one would use a club. Could words be weapons? Well, yes, for here they were. Then, maybe, perhaps, I could use them as a weapon? No. It frightened me. I read on and what amazed me was not what he said, but how on earth anybody had the courage to say it.

Occasionally I glanced up to reassure myself that I was alone in the 62 room. Who were these men about whom Mencken was talking so passionately? Who was Anatole France? Joseph Conrad? Sinclair Lewis, Sherwood Anderson, Dostoevski, George Moore, Gustave Flaubert, Maupassant, Tolstoy, Frank Harris, Mark Twain, Thomas Hardy, Arnold Bennett, Stephen Crane, Zola, Norris, Gorky, Bergson, Ibsen, Balzac, Bernard Shaw, Dumas, Poe, Thomas Mann, O. Henry, Dreiser, H. G. Wells, Gogol, T. S. Eliot, Gide, Baudelaire, Edgar Lee Masters, Stendahl, Turgenev, Huneker, Nietzsche, and scores of others? Were these men real? Did they exist or had they existed? And how did one pronounce their names?

I ran across many words whose meanings I did not know, and I ei- 63 ther looked them up in a dictionary or, before I had a chance to do that, encountered the word in a context that made its meaning clear. But what strange world was this? I concluded the book with the conviction that I had somehow overlooked something terribly important in life. I had once tried to write, had once reveled in feeling, had let my crude imagination roam, but the impulse to dream had been slowly beaten out of me by experience. Now it surged up again and I hungered for books, new ways of looking and seeing. It was not a matter of believing or disbelieving what I read, but of feeling something new, of being affected by something that made the look of the world different.

As dawn broke I ate my pork and beans, feeling dopey, sleepy. I 64
went to work, but the mood of the book would not die; it lingered, col-
oring everything I saw, heard, did. I now felt that I knew what the white
men were feeling. Merely because I had read a book that had spoken of
how they lived and thought, I identified myself with that book. I felt
vaguely guilty. Would I, filled with bookish notions, act in a manner that
would make the whites dislike me?

I forged more notes and my trips to the library became frequent. 65
Reading grew into a passion. My first serious novel was Sinclair Lewis's
Main Street. It made me see my boss, Mr. Gerald, and identify him as an
American type. I would smile when I saw him lugging his golf bags into
the office. I had always felt a vast distance separating me from the boss,
and now I felt closer to him, though still distant. I felt now that I knew
him, that I could feel the very limits of his narrow life. And this had
happened because I had read a novel about a mythical man called
George F. Babbitt.

The plots and stories in the novels did not interest me so much as 66
the point of view revealed. I gave myself over to each novel without reserve, without trying to criticize it; it was enough for me to see and feel
something different. Reading was like a drug, a dope. The novels created moods in which I lived for days. But I could not conquer my sense
of guilt, my feeling that the white men around me knew that I was
changing, that I had begun to regard them differently.

Whenever I brought a book to the job, I wrapped it in newspaper— 67
a habit that was to persist for years in other cities and under other circumstances. But some of the white men pried into my packages when I
was absent and they questioned me.

"Boy, what are you reading those books for?" 68
"Oh, I don't know, sir." 69
"That's deep stuff you're reading, boy." 70
"I'm just killing time, sir." 71
"You'll addle your brains if you don't watch out." 72

I read Dreiser's *Jennie Gerhardt* and *Sister Carrie* and they re- 73
vived in me a vivid sense of my mother's suffering; I was overwhelmed. I
grew silent, wondering about the life around me. It would have been
impossible for me to have told anyone what I derived from these novels, for it was nothing less than a sense of life itself. All my life had
shaped me for the realism, the naturalism of the modern novel, and I
could not read enough of them.

Steeped in new moods and ideas, I bought a ream of paper and tried 74
to write; but nothing would come, or what did come was flat beyond
telling. I discovered that more than desire and feeling were necessary
to write and I dropped the idea. Yet I still wondered how it was possible
to know people sufficiently to write about them? Could I ever learn
about life and people? To me, with my vast ignorance, my Jim Crow sta-

tion in life, it seemed a task impossible of achievement. I now knew what being a Negro meant. I could endure the hunger. I had learned to live with hate. But to feel that there were feelings denied me, that the very breath of life itself was beyond my reach, that more than anything else hurt, wounded me. I had a new hunger.

In buoying me up, reading also cast me down, made me see what 75 was possible, what I had missed. My tension returned, new, terrible, bitter, surging, almost too great to be contained. I no longer *felt* that the world about me was hostile, killing; I *knew* it. A million times I asked myself what I could do to save myself, and there were no answers. I seemed forever condemned, ringed by walls.

I did not discuss my reading with Mr. Falk, who had lent me his li- 76 brary card; it would have meant talking about myself and that would have been too painful. I smiled each day, fighting desperately to maintain my old behavior, to keep my disposition seemingly sunny. But some of the white men discerned that I had begun to brood.

"Wake up there, boy!" Mr. Olin said one day. 77

"Sir!" I answered for the lack of a better word. 78

"You act like you've stolen something," he said. 79

I laughed in the way I knew he expected me to laugh, but I resolved 80 to be more conscious of myself, to watch my every act, to guard and hide the new knowledge that was dawning within me.

If I went north, would it be possible for me to build a new life then? 81 But how could a man build a life upon vague, unformed yearnings? I wanted to write and I did not even know the English language. I bought English grammars and found them dull. I felt that I was getting a better sense of the language from novels than from grammars. I read hard, discarding a writer as soon as I felt that I had grasped his point of view. At night the printed page stood before my eyes in sleep.

Mrs. Moss, my landlady, asked me one Sunday morning: 82

"Son, what is this you keep on reading?" 83

"Oh, nothing. Just novels." 84

"What you get out of 'em?" 85

"I'm just killing time," I said. 86

"I hope you know your own mind," she said in a tone which implied 87 that she doubted if I had a mind.

I knew of no Negroes who read the books I liked and I wondered if 88 any Negroes ever thought of them. I knew that there were Negro doctors, lawyers, newspapermen, but I never saw any of them. When I read a Negro newspaper I never caught the faintest echo of my preoccupation in its pages. I felt trapped and occasionally, for a few days, I would stop reading. But a vague hunger would come over me for books, books that opened up new avenues of feeling and seeing, and again I would forge another note to the white librarian. Again I would read and wonder as only the naïve and unlettered can read and wonder, feeling that I carried a secret, criminal burden about with me each day.

That winter my mother and brother came and we set up housekeep-   89
ing, buying furniture on the installment plan, being cheated and yet knowing no way to avoid it. I began to eat warm food and to my surprise found that regular meals enabled me to read faster. I may have lived through many illnesses and survived them, never suspecting that I was ill. My brother obtained a job and we began to save toward the trip north, plotting our time, setting tentative dates for departure. I told none of the white men on the job that I was planning to go north; I knew that the moment they felt I was thinking of the North they would change toward me. It would have made them feel that I did not like the life I was living, and because my life was completely conditioned by what they said or did, it would have been tantamount to challenging them.

I could calculate my chances for life in the South as a Negro fairly   90
clearly now.

I could fight the southern whites by organizing with other Negroes,   91
as my grandfather had done. But I knew that I could never win that way; there were many whites and there were but few blacks. They were strong and we were weak. Outright black rebellion could never win. If I fought openly I would die and I did not want to die. News of lynchings were frequent.

I could submit and live the life of a genial slave, but that was impos-   92
sible. All of my life had shaped me to live by my own feelings and thoughts. I could make up to Bess and marry her and inherit the house. But that, too, would be the life of a slave; if I did that, I would crush to death something within me, and I would hate myself as much as I knew the whites already hated those who had submitted. Neither could I ever willingly present myself to be kicked, as Shorty had done. I would rather have died than do that.

I could drain off my restlessness by fighting with Shorty and Har-   93
rison. I had seen many Negroes solve the problem of being black by transferring their hatred of themselves to others with a black skin and fighting them. I would have to be cold to do that, and I was not cold and I could never be.

I could, of course, forget what I had read, thrust the whites out of   94
my mind, forget them; and find release from anxiety and longing in sex and alcohol. But the memory of how my father had conducted himself made that course repugnant. If I did not want others to violate my life, how could I voluntarily violate it myself?

I had no hope whatever of being a professional man. Not only had I   95
been so conditioned that I did not desire it, but the fulfillment of such an ambition was beyond my capabilities. Well-to-do Negroes lived in a world that was almost as alien to me as the world inhabited by whites.

What, then, was there? I held my life in my mind, in my conscious- 96
ness each day, feeling at times that I would stumble and drop it, spill it
forever. My reading had created a vast sense of distance between me
and the world in which I lived and tried to make a living, and that sense
of distance was increasing each day. My days and nights were one long,
quiet, continuously contained dream of terror, tension, and anxiety. I
wondered how long I could bear it.

From Richard Wright, *Black Boy.* Copyright 1937, 1942, 1944, 1945 by Richard Wright.
Used with permission of Harper & Row, Publishers, Inc.

STUDY QUESTIONS

1. What would you guess to be the viewpoint of the 1920s Memphis
   newspaper that denounced Mencken?

2. Why does Richard Wright become so interested in Mencken?

3. After Wright decides to get a library card, he weighs the viewpoints and possible reactions of several individuals. Why does he
   choose Mr. Falk, the Irish Catholic?

4. When Wright forges Mr. Falk's message for the librarian, he an-
   ticipates her viewpoint by referring to himself as "nigger boy."
   Was this anticipation or inference correct? Explain.

5. What did the author mean when he wrote, "The plots and stories
   in the novels did not interest me so much as the point of view
   revealed"?

6. How did reading change Wright?

7. Why did the southern whites threaten or discourage blacks from
   reading?

8. What major discovery did Wright make about what the South
   had denied him?

9. Reread the conclusion of the chapter and describe the reasoning
   that totally changed his life.

For Further Reading

Anderson, Walter Truett. *Rethinking Liberalism.* New York: Avon, 1983.

Bagdikian, Ben. *The Media Monopoly.* Boston: Beacon Press, 1983. See Chapter
1, "The Endless Chain"; Chapter 2, "Public Information as Industrial By-
product"; Chapter 10, "Democracy and the Media."

Gans, Herbert J. *Deciding What's News.* New York: Vintage Books, 1980. See
Chapter 2, "Values and the News"; Chapter 8, "Pressures, Censorship and
Self-Censorship."

Kosinski, Jerzy. *Being There.* New York: Bantam, 1970.

Lee, Martin, and Norman Soloman. *Unreliable Sources.* New York: Lyle Stuart, 1990.

Moffett, James, and Kenneth McElheny. *Points of View: An Anthology of Short Stories.* New York: Mentor, 1966.

Research Skills

"Notice all the computations, theoretical scribblings, and lab equipment, Norm. . . . Yes, curiosity killed these cats."

Cartoon by Gary Larson. Used with permission of Universal Press Syndicate.

Too much curiosity could kill any cat. This cartoon illustrates the frustration and exhaustion of undirected investigation. Chapter 9 offers a plan for research paper writing designed to help you meet your deadline without killing yourself. It reviews the kind of thinking needed to meet the four trials of research: (1) knowing what a research paper is and what you are supposed to do; (2) narrowing down your topic to a thesis that can be adequately supported; (3) staying in charge of your sources without being overwhelmed by them; (4) following a schedule that gives you the flexibility you need.

This chapter does not try to tell you all you would ever need to know about research. Instead it puts you to work in *researching how to research.* Two exercises lead you to a research paper assignment that should not only challenge your research skills, but enable you to practice and demonstrate everything you have been learning about critical thinking.

Discovery Exercise

A COLLABORATIVE LEARNING OPPORTUNITY

**Knowing What a Research Paper Is
and What You Are Supposed to Do**

For this exercise you (or you and your partner) will need two dictionaries and an English handbook. If you do not have a handbook, ask your instructor to put several on reserve in your college library.*

When you have these reference materials before you, write down their definitions of the following words:

research paper	claim
subject	support
topic	documentation
thesis	plagiarism
thesis statement	quote
thesis sentence	paraphrase
controlling idea	summary
working thesis	outline
issue	

---

*Some useful sources are *New English Handbook* by Hans Guth (Wadsworth, 1990); *Harbrace Handbook* by John C. Hodges and Mary E. Whitten (Harcourt, 1984); *The Prentice-Hall Guide for College Writers* by Stephen Reid (Prentice-Hall, 1989).

CLASS DISCUSSION

Answer these questions in writing in preparation for class discussion.

1. Did you find that your sources agreed in their definitions of all these terms? Were there differences?

2. How did you find *research paper* defined in your sources?

3. Does a research paper only investigate and explain ideas or does it also engage in evaluating, problem solving, and arguing about issues?

4. Did you find the terms *subject, topic,* and *issue* to be used interchangeably? Did some authors say to move from the subject to the topic whereas others said to move from the topic to the subject?

5. Were *thesis* and *controlling idea* and *thesis statement* and *thesis sentence* used interchangeably?

6. What is documentation and what is its purpose?

7. How confident are you of your ability to quote, summarize, paraphrase, and outline one written paragraph? Do you need to ask for more practice in doing any of these?

8. Are you confused about any of the terms you were asked to define?

LEARNING THROUGH DEFINING: UNDERSTANDING THE RESEARCH PAPER'S CHALLENGE

Before we can think clearly about a subject, we need to have a clear understanding of its terminology. How do we arrive at this understanding? By making a serious study of any word that we're not sure about. This is the practice you have been encouraged to follow through exercises at the beginning of every chapter in this book. In your dictionary and handbook study of the words related to research skills, the task of achieving clarity may have been more difficult than you had first anticipated. You may have been surprised to find a lack of definition agreement and uniformity. The words *subject, topic,* and *issue* are sometimes used interchangeably as synonyms and sometimes given distinct meanings. Similarly, *thesis, thesis statement,* and *controlling idea* may represent three different concepts or one.

This lack of vocabulary precision tends to hinder, rather than assist, the primary thinking task involved in research paper writing: that of *narrowing down* the essay's focus. Because a paper with too broad or narrow a focus leads to a failed endeavor, we may end up doing a lot of work for nothing. Even a fifty-page paper with wonderful language, examples, ideas, great typing, and no sentence errors will not pass muster without a clear thesis governing an essay that is adequately supported.

The irony is that the thinking needed to accomplish this essential maneuver of narrowing down is not very difficult. It is only necessary to assign clear definitions to a vocabulary that can instruct you in what to do. Agreements about these definitions can lead you through this first trial of research paper writing.

What Is a Research Paper?

You probably discovered from your definition studies that *research* is derived from the French *recerchier* meaning to seek out or search again. When we research something, we inspect more closely something that interests us: we study it, ask questions, investigate, gather facts and opinions about it, then evaluate this information for truth and accuracy. Research papers are written not only by students for college courses, but also by professionals, career men and women, and laypeople. These are the reports or studies that we read or hear about in the news every day. A group of citizens, protesting plans to build a waste burning plant in their neighborhood, goes before the City Council to read from an environmental impact study. A governor quotes an engineering firm's report of freeway earthquake hazards as the basis for his plea for more renovation funds. A high school graduate lands a job on a newspaper after writing a report on topics of interest to potential youth readers. In each of these cases, a written report helped individuals attract attention and influence decisions.

The written form of the research paper depends on its audience and its purpose. If it is meant merely to give an account of a subject and explain it, its form is called *expository*. If its author chooses to argue for a position on a subject, its form is *argumentative*. (Some sources say that a research paper *only* uses exposition, whereas others do not insist on this limitation.) You wrote your first expository essay in Chapter 2, an essay of definition, in which you defined, explained, analyzed, and clarified the meaning of a word. As expository essays, research papers are much longer, ranging from ten to five hundred pages.

Another characteristic of a research paper is that it uses outside sources to explain, support, or authenticate its ideas, which are clearly documented in the paper. A research paper cites its sources—or accurately notes such data as names, titles, publication information, and page numbers—for three reasons: (1) as proof of fact or authority; (2) to give credit where credit is due, clearly separating the writer's ideas from ideas from other sources; (3) to enable the reader to verify this information and study the subject further.

Narrowing Down: Moving from Subject to Topic to Thesis

The term *subject* describes the largest class of information or ideas from which your *topic* is selected. In the example research paper that you will find at the end of this chapter, the final selected *topic,* "Driving Under the Influence: The Long-Term Picture," was derived from the following *subject* headings:

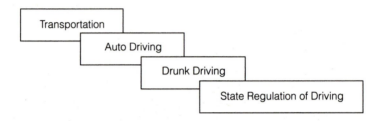

For a college student in search of a topic suitable for a fifteen-page research paper, deciding to write on any of these subjects would be naïve. It would be unwise to tackle a subject area so large that it would require several years' research and a book-length manuscript to cover adequately. Here the standard of *adequately* is crucial. A college research paper is not a scrapbook or a random collage of encyclopedia and magazine articles. It is an essay that thoroughly explains, argues, or proves a single main idea of the writer. All sources used are subservient to this one purpose. To take on too large a subject, such as Auto Driving, would only lead to superficial treatment. Therefore, differentiating a subject from a topic is important in the first stage of your preparation.

Topic is what essentially becomes the title of your paper. It is the final subclass of your subject, although it still provides a kind of superior heading or umbrella for your thesis. In the example research paper, the topic given in the title extends the subcategory boxes as follows:

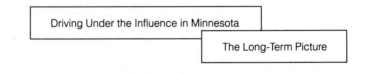

The term *issue* means a topic that is in dispute, a debatable question that elicits propositions pro and con. Here, the implicit issue is "Is drunk driving a critical problem in Minnesota?" A narrower, more controversial issue is "Should Minnesota permanently revoke the license of anyone cited for drunk driving?"

The word *thesis* was defined earlier as the idea that the essay intends to prove. In the example paper the thesis is "Drunk driving in the state of Minnesota is a critical problem that must be more strongly addressed by state and local governments." Because the thesis controls the entire content of an essay of any length, it is also called the *controlling idea.*

The terms *thesis statement* and *thesis sentence* come from one academic tradition that says the thesis should be stated in a single declarative assertion. Although this tradition is often ignored by professional writers, stating the thesis clearly in the first paragraph provides a good test of focused thinking both for the writer and the reader. It clarifies the paper's intention as well as its limitations and organization. Furthermore, it serves as an organization and research guide.

Again, as with the topic sentence, how the essay reads is different from the way in which it is conceived and researched. To be objective, research cannot begin with a conclusion (and your thesis is your conclusion) but usually begins with a hunch, or working thesis. (In the next chapter you will be looking at it as a hypothesis.) This working thesis also guides the organization and direction of your research which can be revised as your evidence indicates. You may decide to change your thesis after calibrating whether you have taken on too broad or too narrow a topic. You might have decided first to limit your study to drunk driving arrests in downtown Virginia, Minnesota, only to discover there were too few arrests there to be typical of the area; this could mean that you have confined yourself to too narrow a topic. Or you may have initially intended to prove that drunk driving was *not* a critical problem in Minnesota, only to have your evidence completely change your mind and your thesis.

The final formulation of the thesis continues the narrowing down process. Here we find a progression to three more subcategories:

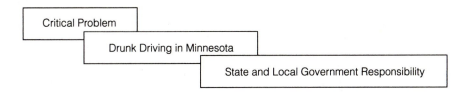

The Working Outline

Once the working thesis has been formulated, we can develop from that a *working outline.* This outline can be revised on a daily basis, depending on the evidence discovered together with the revision, if any, of the thesis.

In the example paper, the final outline became a list of recommendations. These recommendations also inform the reader of the essay's organizational outline: the need for stronger reinforcement, more severe punishment, and more education. Here three categories appear under the heading Recommendations:

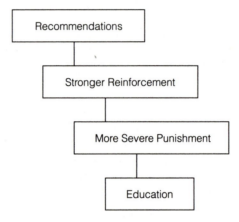

Summary of the First Trials of Research Paper Writing

Once you know what a research paper is, have chosen its subject and topic, and have sketched out a working thesis and working outline, you have finished the first major thinking maneuvers required by research paper writing. This task may take from fifteen minutes to two days. It can save you hours and hours of needless labor spent on the selection of a topic or thesis too broad for adequate coverage or too narrow for treatment in the number of pages assigned.

Discovery Exercise

From Subject to Working Thesis to Working Outline

1. Choose one of the following words as a subject area word or supply one of your own: *jeans, cars, Japan, shoes.*
2. Make a cluster with this word, discovering your associations connected with it.
3. Diagram in boxes, as above, a topic for this subject, then a working thesis and working outline suitable for an eight-page essay. (Allow yourself first to play with several topics and theses before you make your final selection.)
4. Repeat this process with another subject word, working until you can do this rapidly and confidently.

5.   Finally, narrow down one topic one step too far, so that there wouldn't be enough information about it for an eight-page essay.

SORTING OUT THE
RESEARCH PAPER TERMINOLOGY

A research paper, or any kind of essay, consists of two parts: *the claims* and *the support.* Understanding these terms clearly can make the organization of a paper seem quite simple. When we state the thesis, we are making a *claim, which is an assertion that something is true or false.* We can do this with a neutral, detached attitude or with an argumentative attitude. We can combine both attitudes in the claim that drunk driving is a critical problem in Minnesota. We then make further claims in the form of recommendations for changing this situation.

Support is defined as the information, evidence, facts, inferences, opinions, or arguments given to uphold a claim. As good professional writers know, claims asserted without support will not impress a critical reader. The best writing *shows* rather than *says,* convincing through the power of its evidence. There are also standards for the quality of evidence: support needs to be both sufficient and credible, as well as authoritative, recent, primary, and unbiased. Thus in the example research paper, the effective use of primary sources—such as interviews, a survey, and government reports—provides convincing support for the thesis claim. The longer the paper, the more support is required.

Documentation is also a hallmark of the research paper; supplying it requires time and work not only in the research stage but in the final writing. In the example, the MLA style of citation is evident in the bibliography and in the parenthetical references to authors and dates. This research paper example shows you how the final product evolved from keeping careful records about names, dates, titles, and publication data. Learning how to do this is not difficult but it needs to begin in the earliest stage of your work, not the night you start writing your paper when the library may be closed.

A Review Before the Research and Writing Begin

If we review the definitions just covered, we can see a kind of checklist for preliminary organization of a research paper.

1.   Am I clear about what is meant by a research paper?
2.   Am I starting with a subject, topic, or thesis? Given the number of pages I must write, how far must I narrow down in order to

arrive at a working thesis? (For this answer, clustering, mapping, diagramming, or preliminary research may be needed.)

3. What claims or arguments could I make on this topic? Can I find sufficient material in local libraries or from other data sources to support my topic? Or do I have the problem of selecting from too much material?

4. Will my purpose be mainly to explain, analyze, define, clarify, or argue my thesis?

5. Do I understand how to document my sources? Do I have a system for keeping a clear record of my notes and sources?

STAYING IN CHARGE AND ON SCHEDULE

Midway in their research paper writing, many students begin to feel overwhelmed by their source materials. They compare themselves unfavorably to those authors who demonstrate both professional authority and writing skills. Or they may feel uncertain about how to evaluate which information would best support their thesis. If these doubts continue, such students may shift from being writers to being "data dumpers" who merely compile information for the reader to organize. The best remedy for this tendency is self-recognition in its early stages followed by a conference with the instructor.

Data dump papers can also result from too much time spent in the practice of writing out notecards by hand. This tradition, still the stock-in-trade recommendation of all English handbooks, developed before the invention of the photocopy machine and laptop computer. Certainly it is important to have a clear method for keeping careful records of supportive information, quotations, citations, and bibliographies; however, with time limitations, making a notebook of photocopied materials can be more efficient than writing out everything by hand, including summaries or paraphrases that may not even be used in the final product. Photocopying can save more time for the actual composing process, and in this writing stage, the work of selecting and shaping source materials for quotation, paraphrase, or summary can be done more realistically. Investing less time in the note-taking process could also make it less tempting for a student to claim to have "paid his dues" by collecting research only. The rule for research writing is to keep your own thinking and objectives in charge of your source materials. *Your* thinking creates the essay, not your sources. After all, research writers were not meant to be file clerks or collage artists!

A research writer is also not a plagiarist. What this word means also requires honest definition and discussion among students and instructors. A question appearing in the following exercise will give you an opportunity to do just that. Plagiarism can also be related to the feeling of being overwhelmed by sources; it can result from assuming that one's own ideas are not as significant as those in print, from not understanding ideas as property, from not knowing when and how to quote, from not knowing how to paraphrase or summarize properly. Research writing truly challenges the writer to understand the nature of ideas and how to use them with integrity.

Planning a reasonable writing schedule that can expand for the unexpected is the last major trial of research paper writing. This means starting early and working on a regular basis before the final pressure develops. This is a familiar resolution, rarely kept; for although a short essay might blossom from time pressure, research writing's thinking, investigating, and checking for details proceed better when not hurried. The problem is that when you are hurried, you may find yourself unable to handle unexpected problems, like having to revise your thesis to fit some new evidence, or having to go out to the library one more time for additional research.

Altogether, passing the trials of research writing requires that you know yourself. Even the advice written for you on these pages will probably not offer you much help. *Information or advice that is given to you, even when thoroughly understood, is far harder to remember and use than what you discover for yourself.* The following exercises are offered with this principle in mind. They provide a preliminary research project designed to help you acknowledge what you know and to motivate you to learn what you do not know. Both exercises are optional. Look through the questions, confer with your instructor, then decide if you need to go through all or some of them. Then proceed to the Writing Application instructions to begin your research paper essay.

Discovery Exercises

A COLLABORATIVE LEARNING OPPORTUNITY

Research About Writing a Research Paper

Research paper writing might be quite new to some of you, whereas for others, instruction on this subject has been offered every year since junior high school. How much do you know and how much have you applied? This is a survey designed to help you take an honest look at yourself, to recognize what you need to know, to remember where you have succeeded, where you failed, what you might adapt to improve. Answer these questions in writing. If possible, use them for class discussion with your instructor.

1. Your instructor has given you one month in which to choose your topic, do your research, and write a fifteen-page paper. Into what stages would you divide your work and how many days would you give to each stage?

2. What methods do you use for deciding on a topic or issue?

3. When do you formulate your thesis: before, during, or after your research?

4. Your instructor might suggest that you build a cluster, try looping, or use freewriting to get going on a subject. Do you understand what each of these terms means? How well do they work for you?

5. Your instructor asks you to do both primary and secondary research. Define each and give examples to show how you have used both.

6. You need a system for keeping a good record of your notes. What method have you used in the past? What could improve it: a laptop computer, notecards in a card box, a research notebook? What are the advantages of each? Which system would you like to know more about?

7. When you are doing research, do you write down your own ideas as they come, or do you wait until you have collected all your sources first?

8. When you write a research paper, do your sources tend to overpower you, like a car without a driver? What do you do when this starts happening?

9. When do you outline your paper? Do you always stick to that same outline, or do you keep revising it depending on what new ideas or research have turned up?

10. Do you use your outline to show you what claims or support may be missing, what is irrelevant, or what may be overemphasized?

11. What do you have to do to get yourself down to the actual writing of a paper?

12. After you finish your first draft, can you manage your scheduling to allow yourself a one- or two-day interval of rest, so that you reread what you have written with a fresh perspective. Do you ask others to let you read it aloud to them? (Having a listener

not only helps both of you detect errors and gaps in communication, but can also provide you with insights to write into your revision.)

13. Can you allow enough time before the due date to proofread for errors, check for complete bibliographical information, and rewrite a final draft if necessary?

14. Give a definition and example of plagiarism.

Peer Review

Bring your survey answers to class to share with small groups of six to eight people or with the whole class. See if you can classify what you have to say under the following:

1. Ideal scheduling for the stages of writing; dealing with time pressures.

2. Moving from subject to topic to thesis.

3. Keeping good records of your research.

4. Staying in control through your purpose as writer.

5. What causes students to plagiarize?

Research About Gathering Research: How Much Do You Know?

The following questions may require about an hour in the library. Work with a partner or alone as your instructor decides.

1. How can you use the library to help you decide on a topic? After you have chosen your topic, what plan do you follow in using the library to help get information?

2. Does your library have card catalogues or is it computerized? What questions do you have about using either system?

3. If you were writing on drunk driving, would you look in the encyclopedia first? Why or why not?

4. If you were writing on Abraham Lincoln's childhood, would you look in the encyclopedia first?

5. Suppose you decide to write on drunk driving and want to start with a bibliography of readings to study. Where would you turn for this information?

6. What is microfilm, what is it used for, and how does it differ from microfiche?

7. The *Readers' Guide to Periodical Literature* covers two hundred popular mass-circulated magazines and journals. Your library may have *InfoTrac.;* its software offers several larger indexes, including a general periodicals index of seven hundred periodicals. In book form, many specialized indexes also exist, such as the *New York Times Index* and *Consumers Index.* Study at least three indexes that are new to you and write down what you learned about working with each.

8. Does your library carry newspaper, periodical, and book review abstracts? How can this information help you in research?

9. Your instructor says you should use the MLA style of documentation in your paper. Where would you find information about this format to guide you? Would you need this information only while doing the final draft of your paper, or would you need it as you compile your research?

10. If you are given an appointment of only fifteen minutes in which to interview some authority on your research topic, how would you prepare yourself?

11. List other sources in addition to the library and personal interviews that could give you information about a topic.

Peer Review

Bring your survey answers to class for discussion in small groups. Summarize, orally or in writing, your results using the following:

1. This is what I learned about how the library can help me in my research.

2. This is the source I will consult to follow the MLA style of source citation.

3. This is the way in which I will keep my notes in order to maintain a good record of information and citations.

4. Aside from the library, these are the other sources I could use for gathering research information.

Writing Application

The Research Proposal and Project

This chapter centers around one assignment that can be done individually or collectively. It requires that you take a conscious look at investigative or research skills, working with both primary and secondary sources. The assignment begins with a research proposal that must be approved by your instructor before you get too far into the project itself.*

YOUR RESEARCH PROPOSAL

1. Select a topic about which you (or your partner) know something and want to know more.
2. Build clusters that show your thinking associations on this topic.
3. List the types of people who may have an interest in reading about this topic.
4. List places, events, and people you might observe to gather information about your topic.
5. List people you might interview for information about your topic. Select people with a wide range of experiences, knowledge, and opinions. (Check phone books, newspapers, libraries, and other people for possible names.)
6. Prepare a set of open-ended interview questions (not just questions to which one might answer *yes* or *no*).
7. List possible sources of printed information.
8. List other sources.

RESEARCH PROJECT REQUIREMENTS

1. One page of personal observations on this subject for each writer of the project paper. These may be interwoven into your final essay or attached in separate narrative form.
2. A minimum of two interviews. You may have more. Summaries of these interviews should appear attached to your final essay.

---

*The author is indebted to Sue Sixberry, English instructor at Mesabi Community College, who designed this assignment, gave permission for its adaptation, and supplied the student research paper on pp. 279–290, which is used with permission of Donna Schley and James Kochevar.

3. Three printed sources. At least two of these must be of different types (for example, books, pamphlets, newspapers, magazines). In your paper you must use MLA format to document your sources. Photocopies of the materials used must be attached to your final paper.

4. The length of the essay itself should be a minimum of seven typed double-spaced pages.

5. This essay must have a title page, table of contents, and a bibliography.

6. Use an expository or argumentative style, or a mixture of both, as your instructor recommends.

DUI: THE LONG-TERM PICTURE

Donna Schley
James Kochevar
English 112

Table of Contents

I. Introduction: Background of the Issue

On May 3, 1980, Cari Lightner, age thirteen, was struck and killed by a drunk driver. This was the second time a drunk driver had hit her. The first time both she and her twin sister were injured as car passengers, although not seriously. This time Cari was walking with a friend to a school carnival; a car jumped the curb, hit her from behind, and threw her 125 feet through the air. Then amidst the cries, shrieks, and the dust, the driver sped off. Cari died an hour later. After four days, the driver of the car was arrested and charged with felony manslaughter, felony hit-and-run, and felony drunk driving. Adding to the anguish she already felt, Cari's mother discovered that when the driver hit Cari, he was out on bail for a hit-and-run committed just two days earlier. Moreover, she discovered that he had been arrested for drunk driving four times before and that he had a valid California driver's license when he was arrested (Harakas C4).

II. Thesis: Organizing Claim and Three Supporting Claims

Although the above incident happened in California, many similar episodes have happened in our state. Drunk driving in the state of Minnesota is a critical problem which must be more strongly addressed by state and local governments. The need for stronger enforcement, more severe punishment, and education is essential.

1

III. Need for
Stronger En-
forcement.
Support for
Claim

A. Current
Procedures

The recent heightening of public awareness in the problem of drunk driving has led to a recognition of the need
for stronger enforcement. In a recent interview, Anthony
Delzotto, the chief of police in Gilbert, Minnesota, stated that
this trend has naturally caused law enforcement officials to
be more conscientious in their dealings with drunk driving.
In turn, public awareness has caused some drivers to alter
their drinking and driving habits. Delzotto admitted that the
number of drunk driving arrests in Gilbert has decreased in
the last two years, a fact he attributed to stronger emphasis
on enforcement over the past five years (Delzotto interview,
1988).

B. Problems
Inherent in
System

However, according to Mr. Robert Flood, Deputy Court
Administrator in Virginia, Minnesota, arrests have been on
the increase in recent years. Flood points out that although
more arrests are helping to address the problem, this practice only scratches the surface of this enormously complex
issue (Flood interview, 1988). Law enforcement and safety
officials estimate that on any typical Friday or Saturday
night, there are between 20,000 and 30,000 drunk drivers
on Minnesota roads (Mn. Dept. Pub. Safety 1). Mr. Flood estimates that of these 20,000 to 30,000 drunk drivers, only 200
are arrested for driving under the influence. He says this is

2

due to the limited number of officers on duty in relation to the number of drunk drivers as well as to the time it takes to process an arrest. Basically, by the time an officer makes an arrest, processes it, and returns to make further arrests, most drunk drivers have already left the highways for the evening (Flood interview, 1988).

C. Suggested Improvements

One suggested solution has been to add more officers during peak hours. This, however, would make only a small improvement, as one officer is able to make only one or two arrests per evening and the cost of hiring 20,000 to 30,000 officers would be prohibitive (Flood interview, 1988). This is not to say that officials should discontinue stricter enforcement. By continuing to emphasize the importance of not drinking and driving, officials strengthen their own position and prevent complacency in the public at the same time.

IV. Need for More Severe Punishments. Support for Claim

Along with the need for stronger enforcement, the need for more severe punishments has also become accepted. Currently in Minnesota, if a person is convicted of a DUI, he/she

A. Current Minnesota Penalties

may be imprisoned up to 90 days or fined up to $700 or both. A person may have his/her driver's license revoked for not less than 30 days. If the violation involves injury or death, the individual could be imprisoned, fined, and/or receive at least 90 additional days of revocation (Mn. Dept. Pub. Safety 4).

3

These penalties may vary; some are stronger, some weaker. In Virginia, Minnesota, District Court Judge Donovan Frank sees the severity of the problem and strongly feels the need for more stringent punishment. For the typical first-offender DUI arrest, Judge Frank gives the maximum penalties, plus two years of probation. However, on the condition that the offender attend the DUI clinic, the sentence may be reduced and the imprisonment stayed (Frank interview, 1988).

B. Dilemma of Repeat Offenders

Within the whole DUI picture, the major problem seems to be that of repeat offenders. Even though the penalties and costs of a DUI conviction increase with every violation, there continues to be a high rate of repeat offenses. According to Judge Donovan Frank, that rate is as high as 25 percent of the first-time offenders. He further states that 90 percent of all repeat offenders are chemically dependent. Therefore, along with strong penalties, treatment for these dependencies is essential (Frank interview, 1988).

C. Case for Change

Several different organizations have made many efforts to strengthen the laws against drunk driving. Although these efforts have succeeded to a certain extent, further legislation is required. Some of the newer ideas for punishment include the use of bumper stickers which carry the message that drunk driving is wrong or that the offender is a drunk

4

driver, identification of drunk drivers by their license plates, mandatory jail sentences for first-time offenders, automatic jail sentences at the time of arrest, and the overall strengthening of fines and penalties (Frank interview, 1988). In view of the fact that some countries have mandatory death penalties for first-time offenders, none of the proposed suggestions seems too severe.

V. Need for Education. Support for Claim

Over and above the need for stronger enforcement and the need for more severe punishment, the real need appears to lie in the area of education. Some of the current programs

A. Current Programs

used to educate people on the problems of drunk driving include the use of advertising in all forms of media, the dissemination of information by organizations such as Mothers Against Drunk Driving and Students Against Driving Drunk, the use of DUI clinics, and the educating of young people in drivers' training classes.

B. Environmental Attitudes

But are we educating early enough and/or thoroughly enough? According to the Search Institute in Minneapolis, Minnesota, 61 percent of twelfth graders report driving after drinking once or more during the "last 12 months" (Search Institute 2). A survey of 77 people conducted by these writers in the Iron Range area of northeastern Minnesota found that 95 percent of the respondents were aware

5

of the penalties for a DUI, yet 49 percent of them continue to drink and drive (Appendix). The tradition of drinking and driving is an old one in the Iron Range, and the reasoning behind stricter laws and enforcement may still not be fully recognized. Interestingly enough, however, another 49 percent plan ahead by providing for a sober driver when they go out drinking. This, at least, would indicate that recent efforts to educate the public on this matter have had some effect (Appendix).

C. Seeking Social Responsibilities

According to Mr. Robert Flood, 65 people are killed each day on U.S. highways as a result of drunk drivers. Is this acceptable? Most people would say that even one unnecessary death is one too many. When this number of people are killed in a plane crash, immediate cries go out to make the airlines safer. Yet, most deaths caused by drunk drivers go unheeded (Flood interview, 1988). So where does the responsibility lie? Does it lie with our government officials, with our law enforcement officials, or with society as a whole? The aforementioned survey revealed that 18 percent of the people think that the penalties are too strict already (Appendix). This would appear to indicate that nearly one out of five people think that either drunk driving is all right and that the killing of 65 people a day on U.S. highways by drunk

6

drivers is acceptable, or that drunk driving is not a serious enough problem to address with stricter enforcement and higher penalties. At the very least, this would suggest the need for more segments of society to take responsibility for the problem. A massive public education drive is needed. The issues of drunk driving should be discussed in grade school and high school health classes, become a more comprehensive part of drivers' education, and find more emphasis in alcohol abuse counseling. It should be a subject for discussion in political campaigns, be featured in public service announcements and at health fairs, and involve the participation of multiple civic and grassroots organizations. More Americans need to look squarely at the statistics of an average of 25,000 alcohol-related U.S. traffic fatalities a year that includes 8,500 teenagers dead. An additional 40,000 are disfigured (De Vore 11). All of us need to ask ourselves how we could have come to accept so much needless suffering.

VI. Summary and Conclusion

Yet, ultimately the issue of drunk driving is so pervasive and complex that solutions will not quickly be found nor will they be comprehensive in their scope. But it is critical that we continue to seek answers to the problem. It is important that we strive for stronger enforcement and more severe punishments. But the most important thing we have to do is

7

educate the public. Only through education will we be able to effect the kind of long-term change of attitude that results in long-term change in behavior.

Herbert Spencer of Alcoholics Anonymous summed it up best when he said, "There is a principle which opposes all information, which is proof against all argument, and cannot fail to keep man in every last ignorance--that principle is contempt prior to investigation" (1976). Here the word contempt seems not only to include the idea of scornful indifference, but the denial that has made us tolerate an intolerable problem for too long.

VII. Opinions

Opinion
James Kochevar

This research paper, aside from its intention (to learn how to conduct research and how to write a research paper), has taught me many new things. Of all people, I, a recovering alcoholic, should be aware of the consequences of drunk driving. Although I have never had a DUI myself, I certainly have driven drunk. I've had several accidents because of my drinking and have driven many times in a "black out," not remembering a thing the next day. Although it's been over six years since my last drink, I guess that I've become rather complacent regarding my responsibilities in this matter.

8

Only once have I offered to drive someone home who had
been drinking. Moreover, I have never taken any action to
help any of the organizations concerned with this matter, to
help further their causes. To sum up what I've learned about
this problem, I would have to say I learned that just because
I no longer drink or drive drunk doesn't mean that I'm
immune to those who do.

Opinion
Donna Schley

As a result of conducting the research on the problems
of drinking and driving, I have discovered how really severe
this problem is. Before doing this research project, I was an
occasional drunk driver. Seeing the severity of this widespread problem, I have vowed to myself that I will never
again drive drunk. I also plan to share my thoughts with my
friends. By pitching in and helping, I hope to save one or
more lives. I have never taken someone else's life because of
my carelessness or stupidity. Nor do I ever want to. I hope
more of the public soon will be as enlightened as I have been.

9

VIII. Appen-
dix—Survey
In April 1988, seventy-seven individuals were asked the following questions at Mesabi Community College and in some Iron Range, Minnesota, bars.

Appendix--Survey

1. Do you drink and drive?

   yes 38 (49%)   no 39 (51%)

2. Do you and your friends plan ahead for a sober driver when you go out drinking?

   yes 38 (49%)   no 39 (51%)

3. If not, when you have had too much to drink do you let someone else drive if they ask?

   yes 64 (83%)   no 13 (17%)

4. Are you aware of the penalties for a DUI?

   yes 73 (95%)   no 4 (5%)

5. Have you ever been arrested for a DUI?

   yes 8 (10%)   no 69 (90%)

6. Were you ever convicted?

   yes 7   no 1

7. How many DUI arrests have you had?

   7 had 1   1 had 2

8. How many convictions have you had on these arrests?

   6 had 1   1 had 2   1 had 0

10

9. Do you predict that you will get arrested again?

   yes 2   no 6

10. Do you feel the laws are strict enough? Too strict?

    yes 36 (47%)   no 27 (35%)   too strict 14 (18%)

11. Have you ever been involved in an accident while you were under the influence of alcohol or any other substance?

    yes 13 (17%)   no 64 (83%)

12. Were there any injuries? Any fatalities? no

    yes 4   no 9

IX. Bibliography

Bibliography

Delzotto, Anthony. Chief of Police in Gilbert, Minnesota. Personal Interview. 19 Feb. 1988.

De Vore, S. "The Deadly Combination of Drinking and Driving." Current Health Sept. 1988: 11–13.

Flood, Robert. Deputy Court Administrator in Virginia, Minnesota. Personal Interview. 18 Feb. 1988.

Frank, Donovan. District Court Judge in Virginia, Minnesota. Personal Interview. 18 Feb. 1988.

Harakas, Margo. "One Mother's Furious Fight." Palm Beach Post 26 July 1981: C4.

Minnesota Department of Public Safety. Drinking Drivers Lose: Minnesota DUI Laws. DDL 4321.

Search Institute. Highlights from 1983 Minnesota Survey Drug Use and Drug-Related Attitudes. 1983.

Spencer, Herbert. Alcoholics Anonymous. Third Edition. New York City: Alcoholics Anonymous World Services, Inc., 1976.

11

Forms and Standards of Critical Thinking

This final section of the book builds on your experienced understanding of critical thinking as an internal process. Now is the time to look more systematically and abstractly at the forms of thinking called induction and deduction, viewing them as subjects for study with their special vocabularies and rules.

Chapters 10 and 11 explain the structures and rules for inductive and deductive thinking. Each chapter is divided into two parts for easier study of the logical fallacies involved. Should your course time not be sufficient to cover these chapters in detail, they can also be used for reference.

The final chapter offers you some practical guidelines for analyzing arguments as you encounter them in everyday life. This chapter ends with an assignment that tests everything you have learned in this book.

10

Inductive Reasoning and Inductive Fallacies

"I forget . . . What are we making again?"

© 1984. Reprinted courtesy of Bill Hoest and Parade Magazine.

The kids in this cartoon are not following an architectural drawing or a definite mental plan, but are working by trial and error. Creating as they go along, sometimes forgetting their original plan, their reasoning is haphazard and unsystematic.

Inductive reasoning is a method used to discover new information or to supply missing information. We could use it to guess what the kids are building. And the kids could use it to learn that nails alone will not keep the structure standing. When we use inductive reasoning, we observe, test, and check things out in some systematic fashion.

Inductive reasoning is useful when an examination of all data would be an impossible or impractical task. For instance, through samplings or extrapolation we could estimate how many voters nationwide favor a particular candidate, how many needles there are in a haystack, or how many stars there are in the universe.

This chapter is about inductive reasoning. Although inductive reasoning might be called an open-ended method of learning and discovering, it is not hit and miss, or trial and error, but has its own rules for arriving at answers. And it can be fun.

Discovery Exercises

A COLLABORATIVE LEARNING OPPORTUNITY

Defining Key Terms

Using at least two dictionaries, write down definitions of the following words:

1. induce
2. induction
3. reasoning
4. empirical
5. scientific method
6. inductive reasoning

Answering a Survey on Test Performance

Write your answers to the following questions in preparation for discussion. Take notes, also, on the way in which you must reason in order to reply.

1. Do you consistently do well on school tests?
2. Think of a time when you made a high score on a challenging test. What steps did you go through to prepare yourself mentally, physically, and in actual study?
3. Think of a time when you did poorly on a challenging test. How did you prepare? What did you fail to do?
4. What insights did you gain through answering these questions?
5. Do you think this information might be applied to improve your test performance in the future?

Now discuss the following questions in class.

1. Explain how you were reasoning in order to answer these questions. Was this inductive reasoning?
2. How was this reasoning similar to, or different from, the way you worked mentally to describe the vegetable, fruit, shoes, or tool in the first chapter.

LOOKING AT INDUCTIVE REASONING

In this past exercise, as well as in the descriptive work you did earlier in the book, you used inductive reasoning. In this work, you first sensed, observed, and gathered data, then drew inferences about patterns, configurations, and meanings. This method of gathering data and letting it speak for itself is also called *empirical* research, or the *scientific method.* It was the approach, you will remember, used by Samuel Scudder.

In the descriptive exercises you completed, your main concern was with developing the discipline of careful observation without preconceptions or prior judgments. At this point, we are going to look more abstractly at the nature and structure of inductive reasoning in order to learn more about the rules devised to obtain the most reliable results.

Induction comes from the Latin *in* = in, and *ducere* = to lead. Induction is a way of reasoning from evidence about *some* members of a class to form a conclusion about *all* members of that class. This can be done through sensory observation, enumeration, analogous reasoning, causal reasoning, and from pattern recognition. We have already explored sensory observation at some length; we will now define and explain the other modes of inductive reasoning.

ENUMERATION

Induction can be based on enumeration, which includes simple counting as well as statistical analysis of data from a controlled sampling. With numerical information, sometimes a trend can be predicted, or *extrapolated,* from that point on. If you have a car that has run without any repairs for six years, and then suddenly you have one or two major repair problems every six months, you can extrapolate a trend that may well continue until all parts are replaced. The process of such reasoning can be formally demonstrated by a series of sentences followed by a line separating the evidence from a conclusion drawn about it. The conclusion in this case is sometimes preceded by the symbol ∆, which means therefore. In this text, this symbol will be omitted as well as the word *therefore,* and the line will be used to indicate their equivalence.

Here are two examples.

This can of Chock Nuts contains exactly 485 peanuts.

This second can of Chock Nuts contains exactly 485 peanuts.

This third can of Chock Nuts contains exactly 485 peanuts.

(Therefore)all cans of Chock Nuts must contain exactly 485 peanuts.

I got shoes.

You got shoes.

All God's chillen' got shoes.

In the case of example #2, the sampling might be said to be insufficient to warrant the conclusion, but the song carries a wonderful feeling anyway.

ANALOGIES

Inductive reasoning can also be based on analogies. An analogy is the comparison of something familiar to something unfamiliar in order to find or explain a common principle. To argue inductively through analogies is to proceed on the assumption that if two things are similar in some respects, then they are probably similar in other respects.

Here are two examples of analogous reasoning.

1. Bats are blind and yet can move, through the use of reflected sound, without hitting obstacles. By analogy, the development of

sonar devices for blind humans might also help them move safely through public places.

2. Ben Franklin proved by a simple experiment that materials of different colors absorb heat differently. He put squares of cloth of different colors on some snowbanks and left them in the sun. In a few hours he noticed that a black piece had sunk into the snow the deepest, lighter-colored pieces less, and a white piece not at all. From this Franklin reasoned that dark colors absorb the sun's heat more readily than paler ones, which reflect part of the sun's radiation. By analogous reasoning, he decided that people who live in tropical climates should wear white clothing.

DISCOVERY OF PATTERNS

Inductive reasoning seeks to discover patterns in the evidence that suggest a configuration, a tendency, or a trend that could explain or give a name to the entire situation or problem. In this case, the evidence might be called the *parts* and the explanation the *whole*. In medicine, the name given to the whole is called the *diagnosis*.

For example, a child is brought to the doctor with the following symptoms: fever, cough, and eye inflammation. Small red spots with white centers are found on the insides of her cheeks. The doctor says that if a rash appears first on her neck and then on the rest of her body within three to five days, with a diminution of the fever, then he can be sure of a diagnosis of common measles. In the experience of this doctor and his colleagues, this pattern of symptoms has always indicated common measles and nothing else. In this situation, therefore, the doctor uses induction to diagnose what may become common measles—provided all these symptoms do appear, and no others. Other symptoms, or the lack of all these symptoms, could suggest another diagnosis.

CONCERN WITH CAUSES

Induction, as well as other forms of reasoning, seeks causes to explain events. For instance, on the simplest level of using induction to determine causation, you could reason thus:

When I put on a red dress I get attention.

When I don't wear red, I don't get attention.

Wearing red must get me attention.

"Miss California already, don't you, Humphrey . . .?"

Used with permission of the *Minneapolis Star and Tribune.*

Sometimes causes can never be fully determined, but are expressed in the form of speculations or hypotheses. In October of 1985 a humpback whale, later affectionately called Humphrey, made an unprecedented visit to San Francisco Bay, and from there to the Sacramento River Delta region, where he remained for twenty-four days. It took $50,000 and the combined efforts of many individuals to persuade him to return from the brackish water of the Delta to the safety of his natural habitat in the ocean. A great many speculations were discussed in the press as to the cause of his visit and reluctance to leave. They included (1) he was feeding on the wealth of fish he found there; (2) he was insane or suicidal; (3) he was confused and lost; (4) he was plagued by parasites and moving into fresh water to kill them; (5) "he" was a "she" and pregnant, seeking a place for birthing.

CLASS DISCUSSION

Inductive reasoning, whether using enumeration, analogies, pattern recognition, or guesses about causation, has its own rules or standards for producing the most reliable or probable conclusions. See if you can discover whether the following examples use inductive reasoning correctly or poorly. Give your reasons for your evaluation in each case.

1. The leaves on our maple tree turn red in October.

   Some years it is cold in October, and some years it is warm through October. No matter what the temperature, our tree always turns in October.

   October makes the leaves of maple trees turn red.

2. I always get a cold after I go swimming.
   I only get a cold when I go swimming.

   The cause of my colds is swimming.

3. The last ten times I flipped this coin, it came up tails.

   The next time I flip it, it is certain to be tails.

4. I get nervous when I drink coffee.
   I get nervous when I drink tea.
   I get nervous when I drink cola.

   All drinks make me nervous.

5. Jules and Jim like the same dogs.
   Jules and Jim like the same foods.

   Jules and Jim must like the same people.

6. My lover promised to come see me at 8:00 P.M.
   I have waited until 4:00 A.M.

   He is not coming.

7. When I stopped smoking, I gained ten pounds. Smoking keeps my weight down.

8. My wife and I know how beneficial fresh garlic can be to health, but we worried about the smell. Then we found a solution. We chop up pieces of garlic and put them inside a banana to share just before going to bed. Afterward I have never noticed any garlic on the breath. Even the next morning, there is no garlic smell. We believe we have discovered a cure for garlic breath.

9. I had a wart that was protruding and sore. I decided to try vitamin E. I applied the oil about two or three times a day, and in less than ten days the wart was gone. This proves that vitamin E cures warts.

HYPOTHESES

A conclusion derived from inductive reasoning is called a hypothesis. You found a number of them in the story of Humphrey the whale. In the example you just read about warts, the hypothesis was that vitamin E cures warts. Thus, a hypothesis is a theory, or a working assumption, used consciously as a vehicle for finding more facts or evidence. The conclusions given in all of the preceding examples, whether correctly reasoned or not, were hypotheses. Thus, the conclusion derived from inductive reasoning is characteristically a tentative one. Indeed, such an inductive generalization can be less certain than the evidence itself.

The discovery of more evidence always requires that the hypothesis be tested again, when it may have to be revised or even discarded. Even the discovery of one counterexample challenges the truth of a hypothesis. In the case of the claim for vitamin E as a cure for warts, if one other person faithfully applied vitamin E two or three times a day but still had a wart six months later, this alone would challenge the claim that vitamin E is a cure for warts. However, neither case could be considered as proving or disproving the claim of a cure because these "experiments" lack *control of variables.* Moreover, the sampling of only two people is obviously insufficient evidence.

To repeat, a conclusion derived from the inductive process is a hypothesis. Only after time and continuous testing can a hypothesis be established as a final conclusion or as a fact. This was true, for instance, of the discovery that a vaccination could prevent smallpox. It took the interweaving of many hypotheses and many tests to establish this fact, which when put into practice has now succeeded in nearly eradicating the disease.

The following two examples show how hypotheses serve as imaginative guides for inductive reasoning and become modified or reinforced through their interaction with the emerging evidence.

1. When a child developed a high fever and complained of pains in the kidney area, a kidney infection was diagnosed by the doctor (first hypothesis). However, an examination of the child's mouth and throat revealed enlarged and swollen tonsils (new evidence), and it seemed more likely at this point that the fever and kidney pains were due to the infected tonsils (new hypothesis).

2. In the eighteenth century, European experiments began to explore the nature of electricity. The similarity between lightning and electric sparks was observed, and it was conjectured that lightning was simply a big electric spark. Ben Franklin decided to test this hypothesis. Using analogous reasoning, he noticed that both lightning and electric sparks were similar in color and

"Offhand, I'd say its diet goes a long way toward explaining
the lack of reported sightings."

From *Gahan Wilson's America.* Copyright © 1985 by Gahan Wilson.
Used with permission of Simon & Schuster, Inc.

in shape, and that they traveled at about the same speed and
both killed animals. Franklin published a proposal suggesting
that a "sentry box" be built on a high tower with a man inside on
an insulated platform who would draw sparks from passing
clouds with a long pointed iron rod (test for a hypothesis). Before Franklin got around to trying out this experiment himself, it
was conducted in France, and it was proved that clouds are elec-
trified (proof of the hypothesis). Franklin then found a way to
verify his hypothesis again, using his well-known kite experiment. He fixed a sharp-pointed wire to the top of a kite, then
knotted a large iron key between the kite string and a length of
ribbon used for insulation. When a storm cloud passed by, Franklin saw the fibers of the kite string stand on end and drew a spark
from the key with his knuckle (second proof of the hypothesis in
an experiment conducted under different conditions).

CONSCIOUS PROBLEM SOLVING
THROUGH INDUCTIVE REASONING

"He had just been graduated from college. . . . In the long summer afternoons, he sits in the orchard which still stands near the old gray stone house; on one memorable day, an apple falls with a slight thud at his feet. It was a trifling incident which has been idly noticed thousands of times; but now, like the click of some small switch which starts a great machine in operation, it proved to be the job which awoke his mind to action. As in a vision, he saw that if the mysterious pull of the earth can act through space as far as the top of a tree, of a mountain, and even to a bird soaring high in the air, or to the clouds, so it might even reach so far as the moon. . . ."

Question: How did Isaac Newton use inductive reasoning to observe an event that occurred repetitively, then generalize from it to form a hypothesis about its cause? What was the event? What was his hypothesis?

From L. T. More, *Isaac Newton: A Biography.* New York: Scribner's, 1934.

Identifying a Hypothesis

In the following example, underline the hypothesis. Also circle the statement that shows a plan to test the hypothesis and the statement that indicates the hypothesis was disproven.

> A study of high school students in ten major U.S. cities showed that four out of every five were *not* coffee drinkers. It was conjectured that this statistic could be due to the fact that our TV commercials show only older people or married couples drinking coffee. A new advertising promotional scheme was planned showing teenagers enjoying coffee at athletic events, during class breaks, and at lunch hour to see if it might change this ratio. One year and $4 million later, another study was conducted that showed four out of five American high school students still were not coffee drinkers.

STATISTICS AND PROBABILITY
IN INDUCTIVE REASONING

Inductive reasoning can work with statistical samplings (a form of enumeration) and make predictions on the basis of an estimate of probabilities. For example, the payoffs for betting on the winners of horse races are determined by inductive reasoning. Suppose you read in the papers that today at Green Meadows racetrack, the following horses will run with the odds as listed: Post Flag 9.90 to 1; Bru Ha Ha 3.40 to 1; Plane Fast 6.80 to 1; En-Durance 5.20 to 1. These odds are based on the Racing Association's estimates of each horse's chance of winning. Bettors will be paid a multiple of the first number in each of these odds for each dollar bet.

The field of mathematics known as statistics is a science that seeks to make accurate predictions about a whole from a sampling of its parts. Probability and statistics have yielded some basic rules for evaluating the reliability of conclusions drawn by inductive reasoning from statistical samplings. For the purposes of our introduction to the subject, there are five basic rules:

1. The *greater* the size of the *sample* (or number of study subjects), the greater is the probability of that sample being representative of the whole of a *class* (or group it is supposed to represent).

    The results of a survey of the coffee-drinking habits of students in one high school based on questioning only ten students would obviously not be as reliable as the results of a survey of the whole student body. However, samplings are made for the sake of convenience or necessity, and the same information as for a full population sampling can be extrapolated when some rules for size, margin of error, and random selection are followed. These rules are taught in the study of statistics. Yet, without knowing all these rules, you can still estimate that a survey of ten students could not speak for a whole high school, or one high school for all U.S. high schools.

2. The *more representative* the sample is of a class, the more likely it is that accurate conclusions will be drawn about the class from the sample.

    In a poll seeking a representative sampling of menopausal women in Illinois, the most representative respondents would probably be Illinois women between the ages of forty and sixty. Less likely to be representative would be women under the age of thirty. Moreover, a survey limited to women in their forties would also not be representative, nor would a survey of women in the city of Chicago only.

3. One *counterexample* can refute a generalization arrived at through inductive reasoning.

    If you complain that your friend *always* comes late and is *never* reliable, and then one day your friend arrives early, you have a counterexample that refutes your generalization.

4. If statistical evidence is offered, it should be offered in *sufficient detail* to permit verification. Sources or background material

about the researchers should also be cited so others can determine their reputation and independence from vested interests in the study's outcome.

In the following example, consider the vague references to "independent laboratory tests" as well as to the research data used to support the claims.

> FATOFF has been proven to cause weight loss. After years of research and expensive experimentation, an independent *laboratory* with *expertise* in biotechnology has finally uncovered a naturally occurring substance that can be taken orally in tablet form. Now it is being made available to millions of overweight men and women who are losing as much as 10 lbs. a month. It has taken over *15 years of research and over 200 medically documented studies* to produce FATOFF. But there is only one catch: FATOFF is expensive to produce.

5.   When polls are taken, it is important to know not only whether a *reputable organization* or agency (such as Gallup, Roper, or Harris) took the poll but also the *exact formulation* of the question.

Compare the following questions:

(a)   Do you favor a constitutional amendment that declares, The English language shall be the official language of the United States?

(b)   English is the language of the United States by custom, although not by law. In order to avoid the political upheavals over language that have torn apart Canada, Belgium, Sri Lanka (Ceylon), India, and other nations, would you favor legislation designating English the official language of the United States?

The first question might elicit quite a different response than the second. When you hear or read about polls, be sure to see if the exact wording of the question is given so that you can analyze it for bias. Also, do not accept without question results from polls identified only vaguely as "a recent poll." If the pollster's name is given, consider whether it was an independent source or a source filtering information to represent its own political or commercial interests. You need to be able to determine whether the source was unbiased and whether the results are verifiable.

CLASS DISCUSSION

The following examples offer statistical evidence. Rate the statistics given in each as *reliable* or *not reliable* and then state what rule or standard you used in making your judgment.

1.   *Study Shows Major Role of Alcohol in Crime*
     "More than half of jail inmates convicted of violent crimes had been drinking before committing the offenses, the government

said yesterday. . . . A report by the Bureau of Justice showed that more than half of convicted jail inmates who admitted they had been drinking said they felt 'pretty drunk' or 'very drunk' just before committing the crimes for which they were convicted.

"Altogether, 54 percent of 32,112 people convicted of violent crimes had been drinking, the survey said. . . .

"Nearly seven out of ten people convicted of manslaughter— 68 percent—had been drinking before the offense, while 62 percent of those convicted of assault had been drinking. The survey found that 49 percent of those convicted of murder or attempted murder had been drinking.

"The findings were based on personal interviews with a random sample of 5,785 jail inmates convicted of crimes from some 400 local jails around the country. The sample was designed to be representative of the more than 223,500 people housed in the nation's 3,338 local jails during the time of the survey in 1983." (Associated Press; reported in the *Oakland Tribune,* 4 November 1985)

2. "I would guess that the average office female makes 509 visits to the lavatory to a male's 230, and spends 10.7 minutes there to a male's 2.5. What management is going to put up with this 'primp time' featherbedding at equal pay?" (Edgar Berman, guest columnist, *USA Today*)

3. "It was May 1971 when Russell Bliss, a waste hauler, sprayed oil at Judy Piatt's stables in Moscow Mills, Mo., to help control the dust. A few days later hundreds of birds nesting in the stable's rafters fell to the ground and died. Soon, more than 20 of her cats went bald and died, as did 62 horses over the next three and a half years. Piatt herself developed headaches, chest pains and diarrhea, and one of her daughters started hemorrhaging. In 1974 the federal Centers for Disease Control in Atlanta identified the culprit as dioxin and traced it to Bliss's oil, which contained wastes from a defunct hexachlorophene plant that had paid him to dispose of it. Bliss, it turned out, had sprayed the waste-oil mixture on horse arenas, streets, parking lots and farms throughout the state, leaving what state Assistant Attorney General Edward F. Downey called 'a trail of sickness and death.'" (*Newsweek,* 7 March 1983)

4. *Ann Burford Was a Good Administrator*
   "In every program area at the Environmental Protection Agency, Anne Gorsuch Burford had a solid record of achievement. We who worked with her and knew her well are very disappointed that she is leaving. By every measure that can be quantified, EPA's performance has improved in the two years that she has been administrator. For example, the number of guidelines EPA

issued for plant effluents increased from just one in the previous administration to 19 under her leadership. The number of inspections of hazardous waste sites has increased fourfold since 1980. The number of air quality standards issued has also increased. The agency's record for productivity has never been better—you can prove that by measuring almost anything you can put a pencil to. Not only has productivity increased, but greater efficiency has been achieved by spending fewer federal tax dollars. . . . (Steve Durham, who served with Anne Burford in the Colorado legislature, is an EPA regional administrator.)" (*USA Today,* 11 March 1983)

Writing Application

Working from Facts to Inferences to Hypotheses

Follow these steps in this assignment:

1. Skim through books that list facts, such as *The Information Please Almanac, The Book of Lists, the People's Almanac, Government Statistical Abstracts.*

2. Find a group of related facts on one subject and write them down.

3. Draw all the inferences you can that would explain what these facts mean. Write them down as a list of possible conclusions.

4. From these select one conclusion that seems to you to be the most likely hypothesis to explain the facts' meaning.

5. Discuss this hypothesis and list what further facts you would need to determine whether or not it were true.

6. Make this a short essay assignment of from one to two pages.

7. Title your paper with a question your hypothesis seeks to answer.

8. Make your thesis the answer to that question.

Here is an example of one student's outline preparation for her essay:

WHY DON'T AMERICANS VOTE?

1. *Facts:* "In the 1984 presidential election, only 53.3 percent of eligible voters cast their ballots, the smallest percentage of eligibles voting in any democracy. Comparisons to West Germany

show that its latest general election sent 89.1 percent to the polls; Britain, 72.7 percent; in France, 85.85 percent voted in its presidential election; Spain drew 79.6 percent to cast their votes in its most recent election; and Italy 89 percent. In the past 28 years, U.S. voter turnout in presidential years has dropped from 62.8 to 53.3 percent (in spite of increased voter registration drives)." (Richard L. Strout, *Christian Science Monitor*, 11 January 1985)

2. *Possible conclusions:*

   (a)   Americans have become disillusioned and apathetic.

   (b)   Americans don't vote because they don't have laws requiring them to vote as in some other countries.

   (c)   The existing political parties in the U.S. do not actually represent the views of many Americans.

   (d)   Growing TV publicity promotion of the presidential elections trivializes them to passive entertainment.

3. *Most likely hypothesis:* All of these are probably contributing factors. However, I would say that the most likely item for testing would be the second one: *Americans don't vote because they are not required to by law.* (This becomes the thesis.)

4. *Supporting argument for the thesis:* If Americans were required to vote, they would have to turn out, and then perhaps they would take more interest in the elections. They also might begin to demand more from the candidates or the parties representing their interests. This would handle the problems of apathy and indifference. It might also make them more critical of paid political propaganda coming from the media. The only way in which this hypothesis could be tested would be for a required voting law to be passed, enforced, and then evaluated over a period of time. This would then provide us more facts with which to test this hypothesis. If this did not succeed, then we would at least know more than before, and thus possibly be on the way to a solution.

SUMMARY: INDUCTIVE REASONING

1. Inductive reasoning is the process of thinking that you used in describing the tool in Chapter 1, when you began by not knowing the name or function of the object.

2. The inductive method is the same as the scientific method used by Samuel Scudder.

3. Induction reasons from evidence about some members of a class in order to form a conclusion about all members of that class.

4. Induction can be done through sensory observation, enumeration, analogous reasoning, causal reasoning, and from pattern recognition.

5. A conclusion derived through inductive reasoning is called a hypothesis and is always less certain than the evidence itself.

6. Inductive reasoning is used when examining all data would be an impossible task. In this case, induction uses statistical samplings (a form of enumeration) and extrapolations.

7. The five basic rules for evaluating the reliability of hypotheses based on statistical samplings are as follows:

    (a) The greater the size of the sample, the greater is its probability of being representative of the whole of a class.

    (b) A sampling must be representative in order to lead to reliable results.

    (c) One counterexample can refute a generalization arrived at through inductive reasoning.

    (d) Statistical evidence should be offered in sufficient detail for verification.

    (e) When evaluating the results of polls, it is important to examine both the polling agency and the polling question for bias.

Quiz: Inductive Reasoning

Rate the following statements as *true* or *false*. Justify your answers.

_____ 1. Inductive reasoning is also known as the scientific method.

_____ 2. You know that some fish with sharp teeth are predatory. You have to decide quickly whether the fish swimming around you with sharp teeth might also be predatory. Your decision will be based on what is known as analogous reasoning.

_____ 3. You could use inductive reasoning to put together a picture puzzle if all the pieces were available, even if there were no box cover to show what the whole picture would look like when it was finished.

_____ 4. There is a contest to guess how many gumballs are in a jar. You can use inductive reasoning to figure this out.

_____ 5. Inductive reasoning could help you cook a new dish by carefully following instructions from a cookbook.

_____   6.   Inductive reasoning can extrapolate reliable predictions from only one or two examples of a phenomenon.

_____   7.   Counterexamples can test or refute theories or generalizations.

_____   8.   A hypothesis is a theory that can lead to new facts and discoveries, but the hypothesis itself is not a certainty.

_____   9.   Statistical evidence is always reliable regardless of the attitudes of the people who research and present the information.

_____ 10.   *USA Today* conducted a random survey of 1,217 people in one week and found that 43 percent said the United States could win a nuclear war. This finding shows us that the United States could win a nuclear war.

INTRODUCTION TO THE LOGICAL FALLACIES OF INDUCTIVE REASONING

If the senator depicted in the cartoon on page 310 were to use a mass mailing to convince his constituents of an absurdity, how do you think the argument would read? What signs suggest the defense of a lie? What clues reveal an unfair argument? How do you know when public consent is being "manufactured" rather than earned through sound argument? These are some of the questions we will consider as we study the logical fallacies of inductive reasoning in this half of Chapter 10 and those of deductive reasoning in Chapter 11.

An argument that is *fallacious* (or a *fallacy*) is one that appears to be reasonable but is not. It can fail to be reasonable because of errors in either its form or its content. We have been looking at standards for the forms of inductive reasoning and learning to recognize errors that could occur in these *forms.* Now we will focus on the logical fallacies that are errors of *content.*

As we make a separate study of the logical fallacies of induction and deduction, we need to remember that making this distinction between the two is somewhat arbitrary and mainly for the sake of convenience. In addition, these chapters cover many, but by no means all, of the logical fallacies. (If you wish to continue your study of this lively subject, a list of recommended texts appears at the end of Chapter 11.)

Learning logical fallacies requires work with memory. In order to get off to the best start, pause now to review and reinforce what you have learned about inductive reasoning from reviewing the summary and quiz

Reprinted with permission of the Copley News Service, San Diego.
Copyright 1985 San Diego Union.

on pages 307–309. Then be sure to review and practice recognizing the logical fallacies of this chapter repeatedly before going into those of deductive logic. Learning and reviewing segments in this manner will greatly aid your learning.

Discovery Exercise

Recognizing Logical Fallacies

Read the statement given below and answer in writing or discussion the questions that follow.

> Who will shape the future of America? Will it be Jerry Falwell and a rabble of racists, warmongers, bigots, and money-grubbers? Or will it be a majority of caring, sensitive Americans who stand for social justice, constitutional rights, and world peace?

1. Does this statement appeal to your own bias or not?
2. Is the argument fair and well reasoned?

3. What exactly is right or wrong about the argument?

4. If you are familiar with some logical fallacies, do any of the following apply: loaded question, begging the question, poisoning the well, personal attack, either-or fallacy, bandwagon, appeal to fear, slanted language, use of semantic ambiguities?

LOGICAL FALLACIES
OF INDUCTIVE REASONING

In studying the material and completing the exercises in the first part of this chapter, you developed some standards for inductive reasoning and saw some examples of fallacious inductive reasoning. Now we will more clearly define some of the fallacies to which inductive reasoning is subject:

1. The hasty generalization
2. The either-or fallacy
3. The unknowable statistic
4. Inconsistencies and contradictions
5. The loaded question
6. The false analogy
7. False cause
8. The slippery slope

The Hasty Generalization

The hasty generalization is the fallacy that occurs most often in inductive reasoning. A hasty generalization is a conclusion reached prematurely without sufficient study of the evidence. Often the haste is motivated by feelings too strong to allow for a fair and objective survey of the data.

1. I waited half an hour for him to get dressed. All men are really more vain than women.

2. Everyone that I talked to in my neighborhood said that they had guns. This whole town is armed.

In these two cases, the sampling was too small to justify the conclusions made. Seen objectively, the irrationality of such claims is self-evident, yet in the heat of conviction, they can carry some persuasiveness.

Sometimes hasty generalizations are based on biased or careless interpretations of the data: "I read recently in a survey of medical students that it cost them, on the average, $30,000 each to get through medical school. This means that only the wealthy can still make it into the medical profession." This is a hasty generalization because there is no data about the financial status of the students, and no information about the percentage who have scholarships or loans. An assumption is made, and the data interpreted to fit the assumption.

To avoid hasty generalizations, be very careful in your use of the words *all, every, everyone,* and *no.* These are all *quantifiers.* Test to see if what you actually mean are the *qualifiers* such as *in this case, in some cases,* or *it appears* or *seems* or *suggests that.* A careful use of quantifiers and qualifiers can often make the difference between an accurate statement and a fallacious one.

CLASS DISCUSSION

Which of the following are hasty generalizations?

1. Most poor black people who live in cities are anti-Semitic. That's because their landlords are Jewish.

2. Every woman in the military that I ever met was a lesbian. They are all either lesbians or about to become lesbians.

3. Because Asian students are now becoming the majority ethnic group accepted for math and science studies into West Coast graduate schools, this suggests that Asians may be either genetically gifted in abstract thinking and/or culturally encouraged in it.

4. "Americans like to feel that they are leaders—particularly in areas of science and social programs. Yet a recently released National Academy of Sciences report tells us that we are decades behind Europe in the development of contraceptives. . . . Europeans have many more forms of birth control available, including contraceptive implants, injectable contraceptives and other approaches that are easier to use, work longer and fail less often." (*San Francisco Chronicle,* 15 February 1990)

The Either-Or Fallacy, or False Dilemma

An argument that presumes that there are only two ways of looking at a situation—or that only one of two choices can be made—when actually other alternatives do exist, is guilty of the either-or fallacy, or false dilemma. Sometimes these false dilemmas appear in those frustrating questions on personality assessment tests:

1. When you see a person coming toward you on the street, do you rush forward to greet the person or do you cross to the other side?

2.   Do you act impulsively rather than deliberately?

3.   Do you have only a few friends or a large circle of friends?

More often false dilemmas appear in poll questions: "Are you for or against churches providing sanctuaries for refugees from Central America?" Such questions are convenient for tabulation purposes, but do not allow for weighed discriminations that reflect actual opinion. When confronted with either-or questions, a thoughtful person is faced with another dilemma: that of refusing either choice or of compromising with an answer that plays into the questioner's assumption and bias.

The false dilemma is often an assertion of an argument that oversimplifies or seeks to intimidate:

1.   Better dead than red.

2.   America. Love it or leave it.

3.   When you have a headache, all you can do is reach for aspirin.

4.   Are you with me or against me?

5.   When we outlaw guns, only outlaws will have guns.

6.   The Cougar convertible: you'll either own one or want one.

In each of these cases, the dilemma is built into the argument, simplifying the situation to fit premeditated terms or assumptions. Sometimes, as in these slogans and commercial appeals, this is an intentional ploy to negate resistance. More often, false dilemmas are based on convictions strong enough to suppress any willingness to think the problem through carefully. To seek to persuade through the use of false dilemmas is to try to force others to agree to an oversimplification.

Here is an example of such an oversimplification: "Mothers of young children can either have careers or stay at home. But they can't expect both to have careers and to raise happy children." This argument is based on many assumptions. The first is that the children are happier with the mother at home. Another is that the father's part is unimportant. And many alternative possibilities are not considered by the speaker. What if a mother has a business in her home? What if she is so successful in her career that she only has to work ten hours a week? What if she is a single parent who must work, but who runs a janitorial service in which her children also work with her? A false dilemma assumes that there is only one choice, when imaginative thought could produce many more options.

CLASS DISCUSSION

Analyze the false dilemmas just given and offer reasons for your agreement or disagreement with designating them as such.

The Unknowable Statistic

Inductive reasoning requires some knowledge of statistics and how statistics can be used or misused as evidence. As you learned earlier, to evaluate whether statistics are used fairly, you need to look for such things as the size of the sample, whether it was representative and random, and whether a margin for error was considered. These are only some of the basic technicalities involved in interpreting statistics for reliability. The fallacy of the unknowable statistic refers to confusion or deception in the use of statistics and to citing figures that would be actually impossible to obtain.

Recall this use of statistics, quoted earlier: "I would guess that the average office female makes 509 visits to the lavatory to a male's 230, and spends 10.7 minutes there to a male's 2.5. What management is going to put up with this 'primp time' featherbedding at equal pay?" In this case, the author is lightly mocking the use of statistics, implying that even if the statistics are inaccurate, his feelings really speak the truth; and at the same time, he seems to be implying that "everyone knows" his figures are probably accurate.

Statistics carry so much weight as "facts" in arguments that they are sometimes sprinkled on like salt and pepper to add instant authority. We should therefore slow down when reading statistical evidence and always examine it critically.

CLASS DISCUSSION

Are statistics used fairly in the following statements?

1. Only 106 of an estimated 895 cases of rape that occurred in New England last year were reported.

2. "If it is elitist to say that 30 percent of the American people are dumb in the sense of uninstructed, then I'm an elitist. But it's true." (William Buckley)

3. It is a known fact that people use only 10 percent of their actual potential.

4. "If the *Roe* v. *Wade* decision remains in force until the beginning of the twenty-first century, our nation will be missing more than 40 million citizens, of whom approximately 8 million would have been men of military age." (From "It's 'Life for a Life'" quoted in "Notes from the Fringe," *Harper's* magazine, June 1985)

Inconsistencies and Contradictions

Inconsistencies and contradictions appear in both inductive and deductive reasoning. To say "All men are equal, it is just that some are more equal than others" is to reason deductively with two contradictory premises. In this case, one of the premises has to be false. The following student description of a photo, based on inductive reasoning, contains inconsistencies and contradictions. What observations do you find here that would seem to contradict the conclusion found in the topic sentence?

> This photograph shows two students seated on a bench reading in a school library, while in the foreground a woman bends down on the floor to change her baby's diapers. A stack of books about yoga appear on a bench to her right. She must have put them down there on her way to the checkout counter. One curious thing is that all the library books appear to be new paperbacks, and none have call numbers written on their spines.

In this example the writer has backed herself into a corner. How can she explain a library of all new paperbacks uncoded for shelving or borrowing purposes? And isn't it unusual for a student to bring her baby with her to a school library? And do most libraries have benches by the shelves for browsing? These inconsistencies should at least challenge her to reconsider her hypothesis that the photograph shows a school library. Doing this, of course, would mean throwing out a carefully worded paragraph and starting all over again. But exercising such discipline in the name of truth is what it takes both in science and good writing. Thus, an alert response to contradictions can lead us to truth.

Contradictions often appear in political reasoning. Sometimes they can be detected within statements, sometimes between different articles or speeches, and sometimes between statements and actions. If you want to please as many people as possible, discrepancies often become the consequence. Here are two examples of contradictions within statements:

1. "Of course I cannot approve of hecklers disrupting my opponent's speeches. However, I would also say that in a democracy, they also have the right to be heard as much as the speaker."

2. "At present the Administration is gently prodding Israel toward peace talks with Jordanian and Palestinian negotiators. U.S. officials are trying to clear the way for a $1 billion U.S. arms sale to Jordan for advanced fighter planes, anti-aircraft defenses, and other military equipment. The arms sale has been made contingent on Jordan's agreement not to use them except in self-defense."

The first example illustrates what is more commonly known as double-talk. Obviously, in a democracy no one can be heard if speakers are capriciously interrupted by others. This is also known as the fallacy of misapplied generalization: all people who want to speak should be allowed to speak in a democracy. Hecklers are people who want to speak.

Therefore, hecklers should be permitted to (prevent others from speaking in order to) speak themselves.

The second example describes foreign policy decisions that seem to run counter to one another's purposes. The reader wonders how the United States can persuade Israel to agree to peace when the United States has already announced its intention to arm Jordan, Israel's neighboring adversary, with a billion dollars' worth of military equipment. One wonders how the United States can expect to exercise any control over Jordan's interpretation of the word *self-defense*. And finally, one wonders what the U.S. government is doing in the weapons sales business.

CLASS DISCUSSION

List the contradictions you find in the following examples.

1. I love mankind, it's just that I can't stand people.

2. "The Nuclear Regulatory Commission has imposed strict penalties for employees at nuclear plants found to be stoned from illicit drug use on the job; but no penalties were prescribed for workers discovered to be drunk at the nuclear controls. Asked about the more lenient approach to alcohol, an NRC spokesman said: 'The implications are less horrendous.' But a meltdown by any other name . . ." (David Freudberg, KCBS Radio, February 16, 1990)

3. "China will no longer classify as secret the new national laws that local citizens and foreigners are obliged to obey, China's official newspapers reported yesterday." (*New York Times*, November 9, 1989)

4. "National drug policy director William Bennett, who last year prodded the Bush administration to ban importation of military-style assault rifles (because of its proliferation in the hands of drug traffickers), yesterday adamantly rejected any further gun curbs and said he no longer spends much time thinking about the issue." (*Washington Post*, February 15, 1990)

The Loaded Question

Loaded questions occur often in polls, as discussed earlier, in order to create a bias toward a certain answer: "Do you believe pornography should be brought into every home through television?" We are all familiar with the loaded questions "Have you stopped beating your wife?" and "Are you still a heavy drinker?" In such cases, the guilt is assumed and not proven, and a reply to the question traps the respondent into either an admission of guilt or a protest that could be interpreted as a guilty defense. Loaded questions are related to the fallacy of begging the question, where conclusions are asserted without evidence or premises to support them.

CLASS DISCUSSION

Are the following questions loaded? If so, how?

1. Are you in favor of electing a president who stood before a rally and said, "Long Live Fidel Castro! Long Live Cuba"?
2. Are you in favor of electing a president who will permit his Supreme Court judges to be selected by a fundamentalist minister?

The False Analogy

As you learned earlier, an analogy is a form of reasoning in which two things are compared to one another and shown to have a ratio. (The word from which *analogy* is derived, the Greek *analogos,* means according to ratio.) A good analogy often compares some abstract principle that is difficult to understand to a concrete familiar experience in order to make the abstract principle clearer. A good or sound analogy must compare two things or ideas that have major parallels in the aspects under consideration. If one uses the analogy of a pump to explain the heart, the heart does not have to physically look like a metal pump with a handle, but it should at least function on the same principles. Here is an analogy taken from physics about the nature of subatomic particles: "If you wish to understand subatomic particles, think of them as empty space that is distorted, pinched up, concentrated into pointlike ripples of energy." Here the appearance is the essential parallel that permits a visualization of something invisible to us.

In a false analogy, however, important differences that may invalidate the "logic" of the analogy are either overlooked or willfully disregarded. How do we identify a false analogy? A recommended technique is to first write out the equation that the analogy offers, and then list characteristics of the compared items in two columns headed Similarities and Differences. Study the following example.

Claim: "There is no convincing evidence to show that cigarette smoking is harmful. Too much of anything is harmful. Too much applesauce is harmful." (Cigarette manufacturer)

Equation: too much cigarette smoking = too much applesauce

When we see the equation, we sense that something is not right here. For a further check, make a list of the similarities and differences between each. If the differences far outweigh the similarities, you have a false analogy.

Similarities	*Differences*
1. Ingested into body	1. One ingested through lungs first and is not digestible
	2. One a food, other not a food
	3. One addictive, other not
	4. Both don't affect body and consciousness in same way
	5. No evidence applesauce causes cancer, but evidence that cigarette smoking does

Discovery Exercise

Evaluating Analogies

Use the procedure just demonstrated to analyze the two analogies that follow.

1. "There are no grounds for the claim that the incidence of lung cancer is higher in this county because of the presence of our oil refineries. Cancer can be caused by all kinds of things. People don't stop eating peanut butter because it causes cancer, do they?" (Biologist working for an oil refinery)

2. "Guns, I believe, are not America's Number One Problem, or even America's Number Two or Number Ten Problem. Cars, cancer, accidents in the kitchen or bathroom, all kill far more people than guns do." (Advertisement for National Rifle Association of America)

CLASS DISCUSSION

Rate the following examples as either good analogies or false analogies and tell why.

1. Drug testing of employees could be an infringement of civil liberties but is necessary for the preservation of law and order. For the sake of survival, we often have to agree to the invasion of privacy and to limitations on free speech. Baggage and passengers must pass through metal detectors before boarding aircrafts. It is illegal to joke about explosives or guns when passing through security to board an airplane.

2. "People and politicians, who really . . . don't know enough about the issue of acid rain have been brainwashed by the media and

environmentalists into believing that we, in Ohio, are the primary cause of the decay. The biggest killers of human life in the U.S. are automobiles, cigarettes and alcohol. Yet none of these products have been banned. Americans, and no Americans more than we in the coal fields, want to see a healthy and safe environment for all generations to come, but we just cannot accept legislation such as this without a scientific basis. . . ." (Hon. Douglas Applegate, D-Ohio, speaking against a House bill to require federally mandated emission limitations on the largest sources of sulphur dioxide)

3. Analogy to the dilemma of the arms race: "Imagine a room awash with gasoline. In it are two opponents, each with a supply of thousands of matches. One opponent says, 'If you strike your match, I'll also strike mine. And besides, you should be afraid, because I can always manufacture more matches than you.'"

False Cause

An argument that insists on a causal connection between events that cannot reasonably be connected, or interprets causation in an oversimplistic manner without evidence, contains the fallacy of false cause. In the Sufi teaching stories, translated by Idries Shah, examples of false cause appear often in the thinking of the comic character Nasrudin. These very old stories, designed to provoke and teach good thinking habits, are best when they are read aloud. Read them now and discuss how the fallacy of false cause appears in each instance.

> Nasrudin was throwing handfuls of crumbs around his house.
> "What are you doing?" someone asked him.
> "Keeping the tigers away."
> "But there are no tigers in these parts."
> "That's right. Effective, isn't it?"

> "When I was in the desert," said Nasrudin one day, "I caused an entire tribe of horrible and bloodthirsty Bedouins to run."
> "However did you do it?"
> "Easy. I just ran, and they ran after me."

> Two men were quarrelling outside Nasrudin's window at dead of night. Nasrudin got up, wrapped his only blanket around himself, and ran out to try to stop the noise. When he tried to reason with the drunks, one snatched his blanket and both ran away.
> "What were they arguing about?" asked his wife when he went in.
> "It must have been the blanket. When they got that, the fight broke up."

From *The Exploits of the Incomparable Mulla Nasrudin*, by Idries Shah, New York: Dutton, 1972. Reprinted with permission of The Octagon Press, Ltd., London.

CLASS DISCUSSION

False or questionable cause is a fallacy that is often found in political arguments. Analyze the following statements. Decide if you agree or disagree that they are examples of the fallacy of false cause and state why.

1. "As a white nation, we wish to survive in freedom in our own fatherland, and we demand to be governed by our own people. South Africa must retain the fatherland given us by God." (Andries P. Treurnicht, leader, far-right conservative party, South Africa; speech reported in *Los Angeles Times*, 28 May 1986)

2. The corruption of American youth has been caused by rock and roll music. Its rhythms and lyrics together with the role models provided by its singers and musicians have encouraged experimentation with drugs and promiscuity.

3. Malnutrition has been largely eliminated in China, which is quite an achievement for a country that supports one in five of humankind. This has been accomplished by intensive land use, the recycling of wastes, widespread irrigation, and abundant human labor.

4. Americans buy Japanese cars, cameras, and stereos because they are unpatriotic. An ad campaign appealing to their patriotism could reverse this trend.

The Slippery Slope

The slippery slope is another fallacy that deals with causation. In this case the claim is made that permitting one event to occur would set off an uncontrollable chain reaction. In politics this is also called the domino theory—namely that if one country falls, so will all the rest like a line of dominoes. This argument was often given as a reason why the United States should stay in Vietnam—if Vietnam fell to the communists, then China would take over all the rest of Asia. The same argument has been cited for the U.S. presence in El Salvador: if El Salvador falls to the guerrillas, then so will all Central America and Mexico, thus jeopardizing the whole Western hemisphere. In such cases, the predictions of doom could have proved warranted in time, but as arguments they are fallacious in that they urge agreement on the basis of "logic" for a position that involves so many variables and unknowns. (Indeed, now we have the inverse of this domino theory with communism collapsing in Eastern Europe and the USSR.)

Here are three examples of arguments built on the fallacy of the slippery slope:

1. If you offer people unemployment insurance, they will become lazy and expect the government to support them for life.

2.   Sex education in the schools leads to promiscuity, unwanted pregnancies, and cheating in marriages.

3.   "If you teach critical thinking in an Indian university, the young people would go home and question, then disobey their parents. Their families would quarrel and break up. Then they would question their bosses and everyone else. The next thing you know the whole country would fall apart." (Comment made by a University of Bombay professor)

CLASS DISCUSSION

Analyze the following argument. How does it set up a slippery slope?

> The U.S. Constitution guarantees the right to bear arms. It doesn't spell out what type of armed weapons—it says "the right to bear arms." If the legislators start with the banning of assault weapons, where will it end? One day it might be illegal to own a knife. If our rights are taken away one by one, we are really no better off than in a communist state with Big Brother looking over our shoulder at every move we make.

SUMMARY: FALLACIES OF INDUCTIVE REASONING

1.   Hasty generalization is the fallacy of basing a conclusion on insufficient evidence.

2.   The either-or fallacy or false dilemma is an argument that oversimplifies a situation, asserting that there are only two choices, when actually other alternatives exist.

3.   The unknowable statistic is the fallacy of citing statistics that would be impossible to gather.

4.   Inconsistency in evidence is the fallacy of offering evidence that contradicts the conclusion.

5.   The loaded question is the use of a biased question that seeks to obtain a predetermined answer.

6.   The false analogy is a comparison between two things that have some similarities but also significant differences that are ignored for the sake of the argument.

7.   False cause is the fallacy of insisting on a causal connection between events without reasonable evidence to support the claim.

8.   The slippery slope is the fallacy of claiming that permitting one event to occur would lead to a chain reaction that could not be stopped. It urges agreement on the basis of "logic" for a position that involves many variables or unknowns.

Quiz: Fallacies of Inductive Reasoning

Identify the following arguments either as NF for *not fallacious* or by the name of one of the fallacies of inductive reasoning covered in this chapter.

_____ 1. All riders on the buses in a Boston suburb now pay for their rides with special credit cards. All buses are equipped with electronic scanners that record account number, route, time, and date. The American public is being conditioned for the complete Big Brother totalitarian surveillance of the future.

_____ 2. When survivors emerged from the earthquake ruins, they said the quake was due to the anger of the gods.

_____ 3. The present administration cares about the poor and needy, about women and minorities, and has not received all the credit it deserves for its concern in these areas. It is just that it does not support the ERA, abortions by free choice, welfare programs, or civil rights legislation.

_____ 4. A woman college graduate can expect, over a lifetime, to make one million six hundred dollars less than her male counterpart.

_____ 5. Is it raining outside today?

_____ 6. "More than any other time in history, mankind faces a crossroads. One path leads to despair and utter hopelessness. The other, to total extinction. Let us pray we have the wisdom to choose correctly." (Woody Allen, "My Speech to the Graduates")

_____ 7. Are you still getting into the movies without paying?

_____ 8. You can either be an artist or make money but not both.

_____ 9. I want a pleasant, quiet place to study.

_____ 10. Are you still fooling around with that guy?

_____ 11. My wife left me with the kids; which goes to show you, all women are no good!

_____ 12. People shouldn't allow their children to read books written by cult leaders anymore than they should allow them to eat contaminated food.

_____ 13. The reason that we lost the war in Vietnam was because of the treasonous protests going on here at home.

_____ 14. If the baseball players start using drugs, then so will the managers, and the next thing you know all the games will be fixed and baseball will no longer be a real American sport.

_____ 15. "The Strategic Defense Initiative will not make us any safer."
(Senator William Proxmire)

_____ 16. "Reagan's hope is to create [in Star Wars] a space-based defensive umbrella that would zap enemy missiles with lasers or particle beams almost as soon as they were launched. Indeed, if the U.S. can build a foolproof nuclear shield, Reagan proposes sharing the technology with the Soviets." (*Time* magazine, 26 November 1984, p. 18)

_____ 17. "Is two months' salary too much to spend for something that lasts forever?" (Ad for diamonds)

_____ 18. I was turned down in two job interviews. I guess I just don't have what it takes.

_____ 19. *Black Social Pathology*

The leading cause of death among black males ages 15 to 24 in the U.S. is . . . murder by other blacks. More than one out of every three blacks who die in that age group is the victim of a homocide. . . . More than 40 per cent of all the nation's murder victims are black, and 94 per cent of those who commit these murders are black.

". . . There exists a library of academic literature on all of this, but the root seems to be . . . the disintegration of the family structure, which normally functions to convey values and provide role models. There is also plenty of evidence that welfare dependency traps its recipients at the lowest levels of society." (*National Review,* 18 October 1985)

_____ 20. Women, like rugs, need a good beating occasionally.

Writing Application

Detecting Logical Fallacies in an Argument

This is an assignment that you can begin now and complete when you have finished the logical fallacies of deductive reasoning in the next chapter.

So far you have been examining logical fallacies in examples abstracted from the context in which they appear. The purpose of this assignment is to give you the opportunity to search for logical fallacies in an argument, to extract them, and to discuss the manner in which they affect the argument as a whole. This is a research assignment. *You will need to find a short argument: a good source for short arguments that often contain logical fallacies is letters to editors.* Comb newspapers and magazines for your choice and photocopy it to accompany your analysis. Your parameters will be as follows:

1. *Topic:* Logical fallacies in an argument.
2. *Approach:* Critical analysis.
3. *Form:* Exposition and argumentation. Identify the fallacies involved and explain if they affect or do not affect the soundness of the argument.
4. *Length:* Two typed pages, plus a one-page photocopy of the argument.

Reading

THE FAILURE OF OBJECTIVITY

William Broad
Nicholas Wade

How many of you have been told that your intelligence was a fixed, inherited trait and that there was little you could do to change it? This erroneous idea, which held sway over American and British education for decades, was based on a fraudulent study. How Sir Cyril Burt misused the scientific method to make his claim, and how scientific method was used to uncover fraudulence in his research, is the subject of this reading excerpt. Both authors work for the New York Times. *Broad is a science reporter, and Wade is an editorial writer.* *

Cyril Burt, one of the pioneers of applied psychology in England, was a man of brilliance and great culture. He became professor of psychology at University College, London, and was the first psychologist to receive a knighthood for his services. The American Psychological Association gave him its Thorndike prize in 1971, the first time that the high honor had been awarded to a foreigner. When he died, the same year, the obituaries proclaimed him "Britain's most eminent educational psychologist" and even "dean of the world's psychologists." "Everything about the man," wrote Arthur Jensen of Stanford University, "—his fine, sturdy appearance; his aura of vitality; his urbane manner; his unflagging enthusiasm for research, analysis and criticism; . . . and, of course, especially his notably sharp intellect and vast erudi-

1

---

* Notes to the original reading have not been included here.

tion—all together leave a total impression of immense quality, of a born nobleman."

But the man who impressed Jensen with his nobility of intellect   2
possessed a grievous intellectual flaw: he was a cheat. He invented data out of whole cloth to support his own theories and confound his critics. He used his mastery of statistics and gift of lucid exposition to bamboozle alike his bitterest detractors and those who acclaimed his greatness as a psychologist.

What was more remarkable still, Burt attained a great part of his   3
eminence in the field of IQ testing not because of any thoroughgoing program of research, of which he did little worth the name, but through his skills of *rhetoric*. If a real scientist is one who wants to discover the truth, Burt was no scientist, because he already knew the truth. He used the scientific method with great effect, but not as an approach to understanding the world. In Burt's hands the scientific method can be seen most clearly for its utility as a purely rhetorical device, a method of argument with which to assume a position of moral superiority, to pretend to greater learning or diligence. According to his biographer L. S. Hearnshaw, "He was fond of accusing his opponents of basing their criticisms 'not on any fresh evidence or new researches of their own, but chiefly on armchair articles from general principles.' 'My co-workers and I,' on the other hand, were engaged in on-going research. It was a powerful argument with which to belabor the environmentalists; but to sustain it there had to be co-workers, and these co-workers had to be currently engaged in data collection." But there were no new data, and no co-workers. The lonely and embattled Burt sat in his armchair, summoned both data and co-workers from the vasty deep of his tormented imagination, and clothed them so well in the semblance of scientific argument that the illusion fooled all his fellow scientists for as much as thirty years.

Burt's work was influential, in different ways, on both sides of the   4
Atlantic. In England, he served as a consultant to a series of blue-ribbon committees that restructured the English educational system after the Second World War. The crux of the new system was a test applied to children at the age of eleven, the results of which determined their assignment to a higher- or lower-quality education. The 11+ exam, as it was called, was based on the assumption that a child's educability and future potential can fairly be assessed at that age. Burt cannot be held responsible for the 11+ exam, which was the decision of many people, but his persuasive insistence that intelligence is more than 75 percent a fixed, inherited ability was certainly influential in shaping the climate of opinion among English educators from which the 11+ was born.

The 11+ exam and the selective system of education that was   5
based on it began to come under heavy attack in the 1950's, after Burt had retired from his professorship at University College, London. To

defend his theory against the critics, Burt started to publish a series of articles in which striking new evidence for the hereditarian view was produced. The new evidence, Burt explained, had mostly been gathered during the 1920's and 1930's when he was the psychologist for the London school system. It had been updated with the help of his co-workers, Miss Margaret Howard and Miss J. Conway. The pearl of Burt's impressive IQ data was that derived from separated identical twins, the largest single such collection in the world. With the same heredity but different environments, separated identical twins afford uniquely ideal subjects for testing the interplay of the two effects on intelligence. Burt's data on twins and other kinship relations "were widely quoted, widely accepted as valid, and were among the strongest piece of evidence for the preponderantly genetic determination of intelligence," says Hearnshaw.

6   In 1969, after the 11+ had been abolished and England's selective education replaced with a comprehensive system, Burt published an article purporting to document a decline in educational standards. The intention of the article was clearly to influence educational policy.

7   Meanwhile, the authority and crispness of Burt's new twin data was attracting the eager attention of hereditarian psychologists in the United States. Arthur Jensen made considerable use of Burt's findings in his 1969 article in the *Harvard Educational Review*, a furiously debated tract in which he argued that since the genetic factor determines 80 percent of intelligence, programs of compensatory education addressed to lower-class black and white children were useless and should be scrapped. Burt's twin data were relied on even more heavily by Richard Herrnstein of Harvard in his September 1971 article in *The Atlantic* arguing that social class is based in part on inherited differences in intelligence. "The measurement of intelligence," the Harvard psychologist proclaimed in his widely influential article, "is psychology's most telling accomplishment to date." Pride of place was given to Burt's twin studies.

8   When Burt died in October 1971, at the age of eighty-eight, his theories were at the peak of their influence in the United States, even if educational policy in Britain had turned away from them. His oeuvre crumbled only after his death, and the collapse was quite sudden, because the edifice was a mere façade of scholarship. The man who had eyes to see the emperor's outrageous state of undress was Leon Kamin, a Princeton University psychologist who had never ventured into the IQ field until a student urged him to read one of Burt's papers in 1972. "The immediate conclusion I came to after 10 minutes of reading was that Burt was a fraud," says Kamin.

9   Kamin noticed first that Burt's papers are largely innocent of the elementary trappings of scholarship, such as precise details of who had administered what tests to which children and when. This peculiar

vagueness is evident in Burt's first major summary of his IQ and kinship studies, an article published in 1943, and continues thereafter. But in Burt's twin studies, Kamin spotted something much more serious.

Burt published the first full report on the IQ of his separated identical twins in 1955, when he claimed to have located twenty-one pairs. A second report in 1958 mentioned "over 30" pairs, and the final accounting in 1966 cited fifty-three pairs, by far the largest collection in the world. The correlation between the IQ scores of the separated twins, Kamin noticed, was given as 0.771—*in all three studies.* For a correlation coefficient to remain unchanged, to three decimal places, while new members are added to the sample on two occasions, is highly improbable. But it was not the only case. The correlation in IQ of identical twins reared together stuck at 0.944 through three sample sizes. All together there were twenty such coincidences in a table of sixty correlations. Kamin summarized his study of Burt's work in a book published in 1974. His review was biting, ironic, and devastating. He concluded, in words that will always be part of the history of psychometrics, "The absence of procedural description in Burt's reports vitiates their scientific utility. . . . The marvelous consistency of his data supporting the hereditarian position often taxes credibility; and on analysis, the data are found to contain implausible effects consistent with an effort to prove the hereditarian case. The conclusion cannot be avoided. The numbers left behind by Professor Burt are simply not worthy of our current scientific attention. . . ." 10

Despite the unchallenged statements published by Kamin and Jensen two years earlier, the actual charge of fraud evoked spasms of indignation from psychologists on both sides of the Atlantic. The very suggestion, said Herrnstein, "is so outrageous that I find it hard to stay in my chair. Burt was a towering figure of 20th century psychology. I think it is a crime to cast such doubt over a man's career." Hans Eysenck, a leading IQ expert at the Institute of Psychiatry in London, wrote to Burt's sister that the whole affair "is just a determined effort on the part of some very left-wing environmentalists determined to play a political game with scientific facts. I am sure the future will uphold the honour and integrity of Sir Cyril without any question." 11

In effect, the task of deciding exactly what had gone wrong was left to Leslie Hearnshaw, professor of psychology at the University of Liverpool. Hearnshaw, an admirer of Burt's, had given the eulogy at his funeral, as a result of which he had been commissioned by Burt's sister to write a biography. To his growing amazement as he continued his research, Hearnshaw found that Burt had indeed invented data in several of his crucial papers. "As I read Burt's correspondence I was surprised, and shocked, by his contradictions and demonstrable lies—lies which were not benign, but clearly cover-ups," Hearnshaw says. The evidence from Burt's detailed personal diaries showed that he had not carried 12 out the research he claimed to have done. "The verdict must be, therefore, that at any rate in three instances, beyond reasonable doubt, Burt was guilty of deception," his official biographer concluded.

Published in 1979, Hearnshaw's study of Burt is a sympathetic and   13
subtly drawn portrait. It shows a man of great gifts, but with a pathological streak in his character that found expression in his jealous treatment of critics, rivals, and even former students. Introverted, private, ambitious, there was a duality in Burt's nature that allowed his talents to be bent to demeaning ends. His twin data are at least partly spurious, Hearnshaw believes, because he could not have added twins to his collection after his retirement in 1950, yet the papers of 1958 and 1966 state this to be the case. Burt may once have worked with the elusive Misses Conway and Howard, but not in this period: he had no co-workers and did no research. For the same reason, his paper of 1969 purporting to document a decline in educational standards over the period 1914 to 1965 must also be fictitious, at least in part. The third case of proven falsification, in Hearnshaw's view, lies in Burt's claim to have invented the technique of factor analysis. Although Kamin suspects that possibly everything Burt did was fraudulent, right from his first research paper in 1909, Hearnshaw believes that the earliest work there is any reason to doubt dates from 1943. "From 1943 onwards Burt's research reports must be regarded with suspicion," he concludes.

"The gifts which made Burt an effective applied psychologist," observes Hearnshaw, ". . . militated against his scientific work. Neither by   14
temperament nor by training was he a scientist. He was overconfident, too much in a hurry, too eager for final results, too ready to adjust and paper over, to be a good scientist. His work often had the appearance of science, but not always the substance." How could a man who had only the appearance of being a scientist rise to the height of his academic profession, to the senior chair of psychology in Britain? If science is a self-policing, self-correcting community of scholars, always checking one another's work with rigorous and impartial skepticism, how could Burt get so far and stay undetected for so long?

If Burt's fraud is taken as starting in 1943, he remained undetected   15
for thirty-one years, until Kamin's book of 1974. For psychology as a discipline, the point is not so much that the fraud itself passed unnoticed, but that the glaring procedural and statistical errors—there for whatever reason—were not picked up earlier. During the sixteen years that Burt was editor of the *British Journal of Statistical Psychology*, numerous articles signed by pseudonyms (such as Conway) appeared and in unmistakably Burtian style heaped praise on Burt and criticism of his opponents. At least from 1969 onward, his data occupied a central position in controversy, in a subject that is presumably no less rigorous than other disciplines. Why did journal editors and referees not require

that he report his results in scientific form? Why did scholars reading his papers not spot the flaws? . . .

16 The most plausible answer . . . is that many scientific communities do not behave in the way they are supposed to. Science is not self-policing. Scholars do not always read the scientific literature carefully. Science is not a perfectly objective process. Dogma and prejudice, when suitably garbed, creep into science just as easily as into any other human enterprise, and maybe more easily since their entry is unexpected. Burt, with the mere appearance of being a scientist, worked his way to the top of the academic ladder, to a position of power and influence in both science and the world beyond. He used the scientific method as a purely rhetorical tool to force the acceptance of his own dogmatic ideas. Against such weapons, the scientific community that harbored him was defenseless. Against rhetoric and appearance, the scientific method and the scientific ethos proved helpless. Against dogma disguised as science, objectivity failed.

From William Broad and Nicholas Wade, *Betrayers of the Truth: Fraud and Deceit in the Halls of Science.* New York: Simon & Schuster, 1982. Copyright © 1982 by William Broad & Nicholas Wade. Used with permission of Simon & Schuster, Inc.

STUDY QUESTIONS

1. Why is this reading called "The Failure of Objectivity"?
2. Why do these authors say that Burt was not a scientist?
3. Explain Burt's influence on the origin of the English 11+ exam and the significance it had for English schoolchildren for over a decade.
4. Who was Arthur Jensen and how did he use Burt's data?
5. Who first realized that Burt was a fraud? What circumstances and data brought him to this conclusion?
6. Who confirmed Kamin's findings and how?
7. Why, according to the authors, did Burt remain undetected for so long in a scientific community?
8. What main purpose, do you think, shaped this essay?

For Further Reading

Caney, Steven. *Invention Book.* New York: Workman, 1985.

Feynman, Richard P. *"Surely You're Joking, Mr. Feynman!" Adventures of a Curious Character.* New York: Bantam Books, 1985.

Haack, Dennis. *Statistical Literacy: A Guide to Interpretations.* North Scituate, Mass.: Duxbury Press, 1979.

Huff, Darrell, *How to Lie with Statistics.* New York: Norton, 1954.

Roberts, Royston M. *Serendipity: Accidental Discoveries in Science.* New York: John Wiley, 1989.

CHAPTER

11

Deductive Reasoning and Deductive Fallacies

Used with permission of Chronicle Features, San Francisco.

In this cartoon the cook is using deductive reasoning to ponder his dilemma. He wonders if his first premise—that "the cook always goes down with the ship"—is really true. The pattern of his reasoning goes like this:

(All) cooks go down with their ships.

I am a cook.

(Therefore) I will go down with the ship.

Deduction begins with principles and seeks to apply them to specific situations. In this case, we can wonder if the cook will let this form of reasoning dictate his destiny, or whether he will use his instincts and jump.

The main objective of this chapter is to guide you through some of the basics of deductive reasoning to enable you to recognize deduction when it occurs in your own thoughts and in those of others. It is also meant to offer you some rules for correct reasoning and to point out some forms of incorrect reasoning. Nevertheless, this discussion is only the briefest preliminary to this complex subject.

Discovery Exercises

A COLLABORATIVE LEARNING OPPORTUNITY

What Is Deductive Reasoning?

Using at least two dictionaries, look up the terms *deduction, deductive,* and *reasoning.* In your own words what is deductive reasoning?

Evaluating Deductive Arguments

Study the following short deductive arguments. Which of these seem to you to be based on good reasoning and which do not? Explain the basis for your decision in each case.

1. America believes all people should be free. Therefore, whenever America intervenes in the politics of other countries, it is in order to make them free.

2. God made men to serve women. Therefore, men should obey their women.

3. Warts are caused by touching toads. This child has a wart on her finger. This child has touched a toad.

4. "The Supreme Court's Miranda ruling (giving defendants the right to have a lawyer present during questioning) is wrong and only helps guilty defendants. Suspects who are innocent of a crime should be able to have a lawyer present before police questioning. But the thing is you don't have many suspects who are innocent of a crime. That's contradictory. If a person is innocent of a crime, then he is not a suspect." (Attorney General Edwin Meese, quoted in the *Oakland Tribune,* 6 October 1985)

5. If she was the last person to leave the house, she would have locked the door. However, the door was unlocked. Therefore, she was not the last person to leave the house.

6. If the temperature goes below freezing, the orange crop will be lost. The temperature went below freezing. The orange crop will be lost.

Now write down your answers to the following questions in preparation for class discussion.

1. Which of the preceding arguments contain statements that are false?

2. In the examples with the false statements, are the inferences nevertheless reasonable?

3. Are there any that may contain true statements but seem illogical in their reasoning?

4. Are there any that both contain statements that are true and also seem well reasoned?

5. Can you infer any rules for deductive reasoning from what you have learned here?

ABOUT DEDUCTIVE REASONING

Deduction is the subject of formal logic. It is called *formal* because its main concern is with creating *forms* that serve as models to demonstrate both correct and incorrect reasoning. Unlike induction, where an inference is drawn from an accumulation of evidence, deduction is a process that reasons from a series of carefully worded statements, each proceeding in order from the one before. These statements are about relationships between classes, characteristics, and individuals. The first statement is typically about all or some members of a class: "All crocodiles are reptiles." The second statement identifies something or someone as either belonging or not belonging to that class: "Coco is a crocodile." At this point, the two statements lead to an inference that becomes the conclusion: "Coco is a reptile."

Compared to the inductive method, which always remains open to more discoveries that could alter the conclusion, deduction proceeds toward an inevitable conclusion within a closed framework. A conclusion reached through deduction is not a hypothesis: its objective is not to generalize about evidence, but simply to draw a conclusion based on the preceding statements. In our example, since Coco has been identified as a crocodile, then she *must* be a reptile.

Deduction begins with a generalization ("All crocodiles are reptiles") often derived by induction. In this case, the generalization that all crocodiles are members of the reptile family is a conclusion based on inductive observations repeatedly confirmed. Deduction also works with generalizations not necessarily derived from inductive reasoning. For instance, it can begin with a belief: "All crocodiles are sacred animals." Indeed, deduction starts with any statement that makes a claim. And a claim, which is an assertion that something is true or that it exists, can be worked with logically, whether it is true or not. This is possible because *deduction's main concern is not with sorting out evidence for truth, but with studying the implications of a generalization applied to a specific situation.* Its focus is on logic, or the rules of reasoning.

Consider, for instance, the logic of the following belief:

All sacred animals should be worshiped.

The crocodile is a sacred animal.

The crocodile should be worshiped.

Here the conclusion naturally follows from the claims made. Logic can work with claims such as these—or any kind of claim—because it regards them all as *assumptions*. The truth of a statement is important in logic, but when a logician wants to gauge truth, he or she uses memory and experience, not the sampling and testing of the inductive method. Moreover, a logician finds it intriguing that false statements can be made to follow one another reasonably:

All crocodiles are spiders.

All spiders have wings.

All crocodiles have wings.

The purpose of deductive logic is to help us reason well with the information we *have* rather than to *research* information. It offers us models, guidelines, and rules for correct reasoning that can lead us to reliable conclusions with that information. Thus *logic,* by definition, is the science of reasoning or the science of inference.

One major barrier to understanding logic is its technical vocabulary. This vocabulary is needed to identify the components of deductive arguments and to convey its rules for correct usage. However, for the student, the initial task of mastering this terminology can become so formidable that it can prove to be an obstacle to understanding what the subject of deductive logic is all about. The definitions that follow should give you a basis for understanding.

THE VOCABULARY OF LOGIC

The following are key terms in logic: *proposition, argument, reasoning, syllogism, premise* (major and minor), *conclusion, validity, soundness.* We will define and discuss them one at a time.

Proposition.   In logic, a statement that makes a claim about something is called a *proposition.* This may either be an assertion that states, "This is so," or a denial that states, "This is not so." It may be a true claim: "All dollars are green." Or it may be a false claim: "No dollars are green." Propositions can be premises as well as conclusions.

Argument.   In logic, the term *argument* does not mean a quarrel, as in everyday language. *Argument* in logic refers to a series of statements that support claims within a logical structure. Arguments appear in both deductive and inductive forms. As we have seen before, deductive arguments involve one or more statements (claims, assertions, or propositions) that lead to a conclusion:

All people who flirt are showing interest in someone.
She is flirting with me.

She is showing interest in me.

Inductive arguments also establish claims through reasoning, but in this case, the claims are based on experiences, analogies, samples, and general evidence. Compare the following example to the preceding deductive argument.

This woman seeks me out whenever she sees me having my lunch on the lawn. She comes over and sits next to me. She asks for a sip of my coffee. She teases me and makes me laugh a lot.

She is interested in me.

Reasoning. Both of these arguments use reasoning to arrive at a conclusion. *Reasoning* can be defined as the drawing of conclusions, judgments, or inferences from facts or premises. Deductive arguments start with one or more propositions or premises and then investigate what conclusions necessarily follow from them. Sometimes these premises appear in long chains of reasoning.

(1) If I am nice to him, he'll think I am flirting. (2) And if he thinks I'm flirting, he'll come on to me. (3) And if he comes on to me, I'll have to reject him. (4) And if I reject him, he'll be hurt. (5) I don't want him to be hurt.

Therefore, I won't be nice to him.

Syllogism. Logic arranges deductive arguments in standardized forms that make the structure of the argument clearly visible for study and review. These forms are called *syllogisms*. We do not speak in syllogisms, which sound awkward and redundant, but they are useful constructs for testing the reliability of a deduction according to the rules of logic.

Premises and Conclusion. A syllogism contains two statements, or premises, and a conclusion. The first statement is called the *major premise* and the second is called the *minor premise*.

Major premise: No flirts are cross and mean.

Minor premise: This man is cross and mean.

Conclusion: This man is not a flirt.

In deduction, the reasoning "leads away" (Latin *deductus*) from a generalization about a class to identify a specific member belonging to that class—or it can lead to a generalization about another class. In the preceding deductive argument, the major premise states a generalization about the class of flirts: none are cross and mean. Then it determines through reasoning that a specific individual does not belong to that class: *because* he is cross and mean, he *must* not be a flirt. Between the word *because* and the word *must* lies the inference and the logic. Such reasoning can be checked for reliability through outlining the argument in the strict form of the syllogism.

Validity and Soundness. The standards used for testing reliability are based on some specific rules that determine an argument's *validity* and *soundness*. A deductive argument is said to be valid when the inference correctly follows from the premises. The rule in deductive logic is that *if* the premises are true, then their conclusion cannot be false. The following syllogism constitutes a valid argument:

All fathers are males.

Jose is a father.

Jose is a male.

An argument can also be valid *even though the premises are not true:*

All fathers are baseball fans.

All baseball fans like beer.

All fathers like beer.

Similarly, it is possible for an *invalid* deductive argument to be based on *true* premises:

All fathers are males.

Jose is a male.

Jose is a father.

Thus, the logician makes a distinction between the truth or falseness of statements in an argument and the validity of the entire argument. The term *sound* is used to signify that an argument is valid and the premises are true. The rule for determining soundness is that if the premises are both true, and the argument is valid, then the conclusion must also be true.

To summarize, deductive argument is structured or cast into a unit that allows the application of standards to information acquired through reasoning. With this basic understanding of the vocabulary of logic, we can now consider in greater detail the unit of deductive argumentation—the syllogism.

SYLLOGISMS AS STANDARDIZED FORMS

To review, syllogisms consist of propositions, which are claims that can be either true or false. Within the syllogism, the proposition is called a premise; a syllogism states relationships between two premises and a conclusion derived from the premises to gain new insights about these relationships through reasoning.

Standardized forms for phrasing the premises have been developed to show us whether the reasoning fits into the deductive reasoning framework: these forms also make reasoning errors clearly visible. Five of these standardized forms for expressing major premises are as follows:

1. All _____ are _____.
2. No _____ are _____.
3. Some _____ are _____.
4. Some _____ are not _____.
5. If _____, then _____.

You will notice that in the first four forms, each of the blanks offers space for a noun or noun phrase and each is connected by forms of the verb *to be* expressed in the present tense. This simplification allows a reduction of everyday language into verbal mathematics.

Compare the following translations from natural to standardized language.

Natural Language

1. Ice cream always tastes sweet.
2. Cats never take baths.
3. Some airlines have lower fares.
4. If she is over seventy, she must be retired.

Standardized Language

1. All ice cream food is sweet food.
2. No cats are animals that take baths.
3. Some airlines are lower-fare transport, and some airlines are not lower-fare transport.
4. If she is a person over seventy, then she is a retired person.

Discovery Exercise

Practice in Constructing Syllogisms*

1. Rephrase each of the following sentences into a standard major premise. Then see if you can also add a minor premise and a conclusion.

   (a) All horses have exactly four legs.

   (b) Everybody's got needs.

---

*For the style and method used in these exercises, I am indebted to the example provided by Lipman, Sharp, and Oscanyan in their work *Philosophical Inquiry: An Instructional Manual to Accompany Harry Stottlemeier's Discovery*. Second edition. Published by The Institute for the Advancement of Philosophy for Children, Upper Montclair, N.J., 1979.

(c) All coal miners are poor.

(d) Many eighteen-year-olds are college students.

(e) No eight-year-old is a college student.

(f) Lead is poisonous.

(g) If he's late, he'll be sorry.

2. Fill in the blanks in the following sentences so that the syllogisms are all valid.

(a) All horses are mammals.

   All _____ are animals.
   _____

   All horses are animals.

(b) All horses are living things.

   All living things are things that reproduce.
   _____

   All _____ are things that reproduce.

(c) No horses are creatures that sleep in beds.

   This creature is sleeping in a bed.
   _____

   Therefore this creature is _____.

(d) If today is Tuesday, this must be Belgium.

   This is _____.
   _____

   This must be _____.

3. Choose the correct answer in each of the following cases.

(a) All beers are liquids.
   It therefore follows that:

   (1) All liquids are beers.

   (2) No liquids are beers.

   (3) Neither (1) nor (2).

(b) Florida is next to Georgia.
   Georgia is next to South Carolina.

   (1) Florida is next to South Carolina.

   (2) South Carolina is next to Florida.

   (3) Neither (1) nor (2).

(c) Ruth is shorter than Margaret.
   Margaret is shorter than Rosie.
   It therefore follows that:

(1)   Ruth is shorter than Rosie.

(2)   Margaret is shorter than Ruth.

(3)   Ruth is taller than Rosie.

WHAT SYLLOGISMS DO

The logician has a number of purposes for phrasing arguments in syllogisms: (1) to find out exactly what is being said and thus to be able to judge whether each statement is true or false; (2) to discover and expose any hidden premises; and (3) to find out if one thought follows logically from another—or if the inference drawn makes sense. Let's look at each of these purposes in greater detail.

What Is Said, and Is It True?

To find out exactly what is being said—or claimed—is actually not always easy, yet this step is crucial before we can judge whether or not something is true. For instance, consider the statement "Of course she's guilty; didn't she threaten to take revenge?" Translated into a syllogism, the reasoning of the entire argument is exposed to show that it consists of the following:

All people who threaten revenge are people guilty of taking revenge.

She threatened revenge.

She is guilty of taking revenge.

In this case, exposure through the outline of the syllogism reveals a hidden major premise: all people who threaten revenge take revenge. This method of displaying the argument's structure tells us what the assumption is and also reveals its exaggeration and lack of truth through the extent of the claim covered by the word *all.*

Consider the following statement: "She is an actress. How can you expect her to understand politics?" When expressed as a syllogism, the argument appears as follows:

No actress understands politics.

She is an actress.

She does not understand politics.

Here the reasoning is valid, but again the major premise is too broad a generalization to be true, and therefore the conclusion also becomes questionable.

Is There a Hidden Premise?

A major advantage in the use of syllogisms is that it reveals hidden premises—as you learned in the preceding two examples. Consider the following further examples:

1. Senator Jones is a hawk. Don't expect him to be in favor of arms control.

    All hawks are individuals not in favor of arms control. (hidden premise)

    Senator Jones is a hawk.

    Senator Jones is not in favor of arms control.

2. Do I think he's sexy? Well, he drives a truck, doesn't he?

    All those who drive trucks are sexy. (hidden premise)

    He drives a truck.

    He is sexy. (implied conclusion)

In the previous example, both the major premise and the conclusion are hidden or implied. Often this happens in advertising slogans: "The burgers are bigger at Burger John's." As a syllogism this reads:

Bigger burgers are better burgers. (hidden premise)
Burger John's burgers are bigger.

Burger John's burgers are better. (hidden conclusion)
You should buy Burger John's burgers. (additional hidden conclusion)

Does One Thought Follow Logically from the Other?

Here the logician is concerned with validity. Does one thought follow logically from the other? Does the inference drawn in the conclusion make sense?

If you are a suspect, then you are questioned by the police.
You were questioned by the police.

You are a suspect.

"Of course if $\int_r^x \sqrt{}^{\,4}\,du = \lim_{a\to\infty} \sum_{i=1}^{n} \left(\frac{1}{n^x}\right)^4 \cdot \frac{x}{n}$, we're sunk."

From *I Paint What I see.* Copyright © 1971 by Gahan Wilson.
Used with permission of Simon & Schuster, Inc.

Here, even if both the premises were true, the conclusion could still be false. (Maybe you were a witness or questioned about something else.) The argument is invalid because the conclusion is not implied by its premises. The illogic of the reasoning here can be recognized intuitively, but its exposure in the syllogism shows how it is illogical.

The next argument is obviously valid:

She is either married or single.

She is married.

_____

Therefore she is not single.

Here, if the two premises are true, logic compels us to accept the conclusion as true. The inference follows: it makes sense. The syllogism makes this even clearer to us.

CONSCIOUS PROBLEM SOLVING THROUGH DEDUCTIVE REASONING

"I would agree with St. Augustine that 'an unjust law is no law at all.' . . . How does one determine whether a law is just or unjust? A just law is a man-made code that is out of harmony with the moral law. To put it in the terms of St. Thomas Aquinas: an unjust law is a human law that is not rooted in eternal law and natural law. Any law that uplifts human personality is just. Any law that degrades human personality is unjust. All segregation statutes are unjust because segregation distorts the soul and damages the personality. It gives the segregator a false sense of superiority and the segregated a false sense of inferiority. Segregation, to use the terminology of the Jewish philosopher Martin Buber, substitutes an 'I-it' relationship for an 'I-thou' relationship and ends up relegating persons to the status of things. Hence segregation is not only politically, economically, and sociologically unsound, it is morally wrong and sinful. Paul Tillich has said that sin is separation. Is not segregation an existential expression of man's tragic separation, his awful estrangement, his terrible sinfulness? Thus it is that I can urge men to obey the 1954 decision of the Supreme Court, for it is morally right, and I can urge them to disobey segregation ordinances, for they are morally wrong."

Questions:

1. How does King define each of the terms in his argument?

2. Notice how he draws major premises from statements by authorities and reasons for these premises. Write out one syllogism that he uses to advance his claims.

From Martin Luther King, Jr., "Letter from the Birmingham Jail," 1963.

Writing Application

Reviewing the Vocabulary of Logic

Work with a classmate to write down the definitions you can remember of the following words: *logic, reasoning, deductive* and *inductive reasoning, proposition, premise* (major and minor), *conclusion, argument, syllogism, true statement, valid argument, sound argument,*

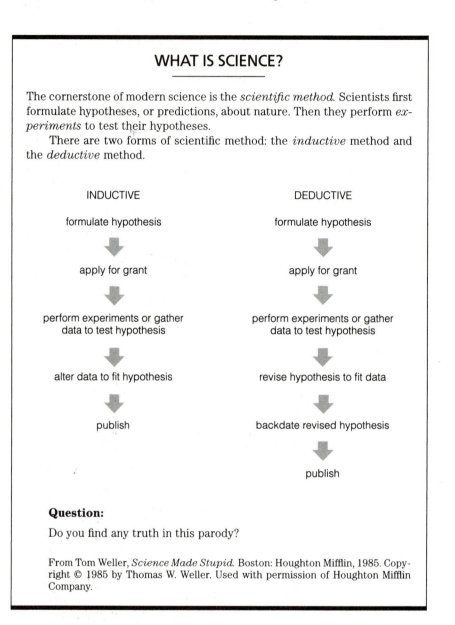

WHAT IS SCIENCE?

The cornerstone of modern science is the *scientific method.* Scientists first formulate hypotheses, or predictions, about nature. Then they perform *experiments* to test their hypotheses.

There are two forms of scientific method: the *inductive* method and the *deductive* method.

INDUCTIVE	DEDUCTIVE
formulate hypothesis	formulate hypothesis
⬇	⬇
apply for grant	apply for grant
⬇	⬇
perform experiments or gather data to test hypothesis	perform experiments or gather data to test hypothesis
⬇	⬇
alter data to fit hypothesis	revise hypothesis to fit data
⬇	⬇
publish	backdate revised hypothesis
	⬇
	publish

Question:

Do you find any truth in this parody?

From Tom Weller, *Science Made Stupid.* Boston: Houghton Mifflin, 1985. Copyright © 1985 by Thomas W. Weller. Used with permission of Houghton Mifflin Company.

hidden premise, hidden conclusion. When you have finished, compare your definitions with the vocabulary summary on pages 356–357. If there is a discrepancy, or if any of the definitions are still unclear to you, review the text discussion until you can explain the term to your partner.

THE FORMAL FALLACIES

Syllogisms simplify deductive arguments into structures with a complex system of rules. These rules enable us to understand and analyze examples of valid as well as invalid reasoning. The latter are called the *formal fallacies* because they represent errors in the *form* deductive reasoning must follow. A few of the most common formal fallacies are demonstrated in the following pages. The nature of each fallacy can be explained in technical terms that require some time to master.

Some of the formal fallacies are first presented to you in Discovery Exercises without the use of any technical terminology. Here you are given an opportunity to study models of valid and invalid reasoning to see if you can discover the rules for yourself before reading any more about them. Technical explanations of each fallacy folllow.

Discovery Exercises

Looking at Some Formal Fallacies

The following are four sets of valid and invalid arguments. To the right of or below them are diagrams that show the relationship described by the syllogism. The asterisk (*) in these diagrams shows that at least one case can be found in the area where the asterisk appears. Study each set and see if you can explain to a class partner why some syllogisms are valid whereas others are not. When you have finished all four sets, go on to the next exercise, where you will match these models to other syllogisms.

SET 1

    A. Valid argument

        All rock stars are musicians.

        Bruce Springsteen is a rock star.

        Bruce Springsteen is a musician.

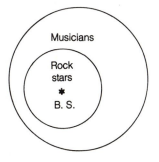

B. Invalid argument

All rock stars are musicians.
Bruce Springsteen is a poet.

Bruce Springsteen is a musician.

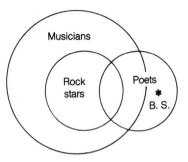

C. Invalid argument

All rock stars are musicians.
Bruce Springsteen is a musician.

Bruce Springsteen is a rock star.

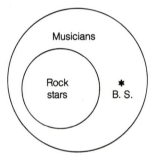

SET 2

A. Valid argument

No rock star is an amateur.
Tina Turner is a rock star.

Tina Turner is not an amateur.

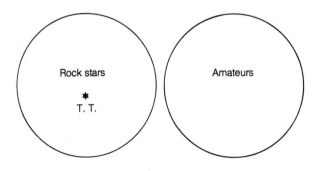

B. Invalid argument

No rock star is an amateur.

Richard Nixon is not a rock star.

Richard Nixon is an amateur.

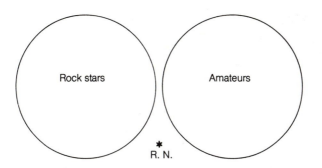

SET 3

A. Valid argument

All rock stars are musicians.

Some women are rock stars.

Some women are musicians.

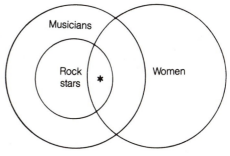

B. Invalid argument

All rock stars are musicians.

Some women are rock stars.

All women are musicians.

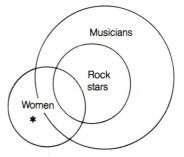

SET 4

A. Valid argument

If Bruce Springsteen is a rock star, then he is a musician.
Bruce Springsteen is a rock star.

Bruce Springsteen is a musician.

B. Invalid argument

If Stevie Wonder is a rock star, then he is a musician.
Stevie Wonder is not a rock star.

Stevie Wonder is not a musician.

C. Invalid argument

If Stevie Wonder is a rock star, then he is a musician.
Stevie Wonder is a musician.

Stevie Wonder is a rock star.

Identifying Formal Fallacies by Type

To check how well you understand the various types of fallacies exemplified in the preceding exercise, see if you can match the invalid arguments that follow to the same type of argument in the preceding sets. After you have assigned them the numbers of their corresponding models, consult the answers supplied at the end of this exercise.

1. If I finish this autobiography, I shall die.
   I will not finish this autobiography.

   I will not die.

2. If he is a right-winger, then he is a Republican.
   He is a Republican.

   He is a right-winger.

3. No person is perfect.
   Our pet is not a person.

   Our pet is perfect.

4. All Democrats are big spenders.
   Some women are Democrats.

   _____

   All women are big spenders.

5. All women are big spenders.
   Peggy is a stockbroker.

   _____

   Peggy is a big spender.

6. All communists are atheists.
   Oscar is an atheist.

   _____

   Oscar is a communist.

ANSWERS

1. 4B   2. 4C   3. 2B   4. 3B   5. 1B   6. 1C

_____

TECHNICAL NAMES FOR
THE FALLACIES, WITH THEIR RULES

By completing the Discovery Exercises, you've probably begun to get a feel for the different types of fallacies that are possible in syllogisms, and for why they render arguments invalid. We want to look now at the names of some common formal fallacies, as exemplified in the Discovery Exercises, and to learn the rules that govern them. The formal fallacies we will consider here are the following:

1. The fallacy of four terms
2. The fallacy of the undistributed middle term
3. The fallacy of faulty exclusions
4. The fallacy of illicit distribution
5. The invalid hypothetical syllogism

The Fallacy of Four Terms

The fallacy of four terms was exemplified by 1B in the first Discovery Exercise:

All rock stars (middle term) are musicians (major term).

Bruce Springsteen (minor term) is a poet (fourth term).

_____

Bruce Springsteen (minor) is a musician (major).

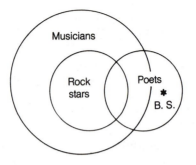

The rule violated by this fallacy is: *A syllogism must have exactly three terms, each used twice.* This invalid syllogism has a fourth term— *poet*—and only the term *musician* is used twice.

The word *term* refers to nouns or classes used in the proposition. Syllogisms have a *major term,* appearing in the predicate of the conclusion, a *minor term,* appearing as the subject of the conclusion, and a *middle term,* which links the major and minor terms in the premises, but which does not appear in the conclusion. The information that Bruce Springsteen is a poet does not relate him to the class of rock stars; hence, the first premise does not apply to him and the conclusion that he is a musician cannot be drawn from the information given.

In the diagram (called an Euler diagram), the asterisk (*) marks the minor term. In the case of invalid arguments, the asterisk shows us that the conclusion may be false when the premises are true. Bruce Springsteen may be a poet, but not necessarily for that reason also a rock star and a musician.

The Fallacy of the Undistributed Middle Term

The fallacy of the undistributed middle term was exemplified by invalid argument 1C earlier:

All rock stars (major term) are musicians (middle term).
Bruce Springsteen (minor term) is a musician.

Bruce Springsteen is a rock star.

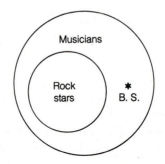

The rule that applies to this fallacy is: *The middle term must be distributed at least once.* In our example, the middle term (musicians) is undistributed.

If a term is *distributed, all* members of the class it refers to are covered by an assertion. If one says, "All rock stars are musicians," or "No rock stars are musicians," the term *rock stars* is distributed: one knows in both cases that *all rock stars* are either included or excluded from the larger category of musicians.

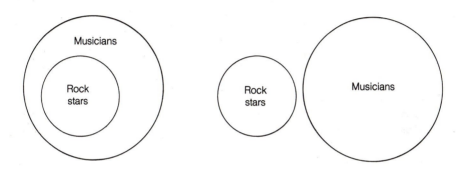

If one says, "Some rock stars are musicians," the term *rock stars* is undistributed, because only some rock stars can be accounted for within the class of musicians.

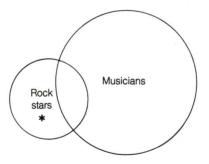

In the proposition "All rock stars are musicians" the term *musicians* is undistributed, because the statement does not make an assertion about the whole class of musicians. There are many other kinds of musicians besides rock stars. Therefore, although the premise states that Bruce Springsteen is a musician, he could be in the subclass of musicians who are not rock stars. We cannot reason on the basis of this information alone that Bruce Springsteen is a rock star. This is more apparent if we substitute for the name Bruce Springsteen the name of a musician who is clearly not in actuality a rock star.

All rock stars are musicians.
Chick Corea is a musician.

Chick Corea is a rock star.

The Fallacy of Faulty Exclusions

The fallacy of faulty exclusions was exemplified by invalid argument 2B:

No rock star is an amateur.
Richard Nixon is not a rock star.

Richard Nixon is an amateur.

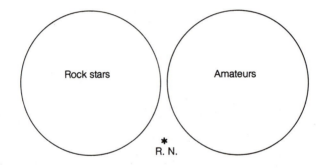

The rule violated by this fallacy is: *A syllogism must have either no exclusion or two exclusions, one of which must appear in the conclusion.* In the invalid argument, we have two exclusions in the premises but none in the conclusion.

Exclusions are terms that are not included in a class; *inclusions* are terms that are part of another class. In the valid argument that follows, the term *rock stars* is excluded from the class of amateurs, and in the conclusion Tina Turner is excluded from the class of amateurs. The syllogism thus follows the rule.

No rock star is an amateur.
Tina Turner is a rock star.

Tina Turner is not an amateur.

In contrast, the reasoning in the invalid argument is obviously false. If no rock star is an amateur, then any person who is not a rock star may be, or may not be, an amateur.

The Fallacy of Illicit Distribution

The fallacy of illicit distribution was exemplified by invalid argument 3B:

All rock stars are musicians.

Some women are rock stars.

_____

All women are musicians.

The rule violated by this fallacy is: *Any term distributed in the conclusion must be distributed in the premise in which it appears.* In our invalid argument, *women* is distributed in the conclusion, but not in the premise in which it appears.

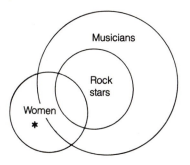

Illicit distribution means that a term cannot claim to represent part of a class in one of the premises and then the entire class in the conclusion. In our example, we know from the minor premise that *some women* are rock stars, but although we know all rock stars are included in the class of musicians, we cannot conclude from this line of reasoning that all women are.

The Invalid Hypothetical Syllogism

The invalid hypothetical syllogism was exemplified by invalid arguments 4B and 4C:

If Stevie Wonder is a rock star, then he is a musician.

Stevie Wonder is not a rock star.

_____

Stevie Wonder is not a musician.

If Stevie Wonder is a rock star, then he is a musician.

Stevie Wonder is a musician.

_____

Stevie Wonder is a rock star.

The rule violated by this fallacy is: *The minor premise must affirm the antecedent or deny the consequent.* In the first example, the minor premise denies the *antecedent;* in the second, the minor premise affirms the *consequent.*

The *antecedent* is the statement "If Stevie Wonder is a rock star," which comes before the *consequent,* or "he is a musician." The rule says that the minor premise (or second premise) either must claim that the antecedent is true or has occurred or must assert that the consequent is false. If, on the other hand, the minor premise denies the antecedent or affirms the consequent, then it offers information beyond the scope of the major premise. If we say Stevie Wonder is not a rock star, and therefore is not a musician, we are mocking the syllogism. The same is true if we claim that he is a musician and therefore a rock star.

Reviewing the Vocabulary of Formal Fallacies

If you wish to study this subject more closely, review the definitions of the following words by writing down what you can remember of them: *major, middle,* and *minor terms, major premise, minor premise, exclusion, inclusion, distributed, illicit distribution, affirm, deny, antecedent, consequent.* Check your definitions against the text.

CLASS DISCUSSION

Write down your answers to the following questions, in preparation for a class discussion.

1. The following syllogisms illustrate the fallacy of four terms. Identify the fourth term for each.

   (a)   All musicians are music lovers.

   Raymond is a violinist.

   Raymond is a music lover.

   (b)   An expert swimmer could cross the channel.

   Nadine is a swimmer.

   Nadine could cross the channel.

2. These syllogisms have faulty exclusions. Explain how this happens in each case.

   (a)   A good pianist would not make that mistake.

   Loretta is not a good pianist.

   Loretta would not make that mistake.

(b) Gold investors are not wise.
Mr. Hill is not wise.

Mr. Hill is a gold investor.

3. These syllogisms have undistributed middle terms. Explain why.

(a) Some baseball players are drug-takers.
Peter is a baseball player.

Peter is a drug-taker.

(b) All Woody Allen's films are funny.
Getting It On is funny.

***Getting it On* is by Woody Allen.**

4. This syllogism illustrates illicit distribution. Explain why.

(a) All who go on picnics are happy.
Many children go on picnics.

All children are happy.

5. The following are invalid hypothetical syllogisms. Explain why.

(a) If he studied, he passed; but because he didn't study, he didn't pass.

(b) If she studied, she passed. She did pass. Therefore she studied.

Writing Application

Writing a Deductive Argument

Write a deductive argument within the following parameters.

1. *Topic:* Application of an aphorism, or wise saying, to life.
2. *Approach:* (a) Explain the aphorism; (b) define its terms; (c) illustrate it; (d) choose to agree, disagree, or both.
3. *Form:* Exposition and argumentation—explain, justify, and persuade through logic, reasoning, and example.
4. *Length:* Concise two pages.
5. *Subject:* Choose your own aphorism or select one of the following:

(a) The most savage controversies are about those matters as to which there is no evidence either way." (Bertrand Russell)

(b) "Man is a social animal who dislikes his fellow men." (Delacroix)

(c) "Competition brings out the best in products and the worst in people." (David Sarnoff)

(d) "Failure is when you stop trying."

(e) "People get the kind of government they deserve."

(f) "Prejudice is never easy unless it can pass itself off as reason." (William Hazlitt)

(g) "Life was meant to be lived, and curiosity must be kept alive. One must never, for whatever reason, turn his back on life." (Eleanor Roosevelt)

(h) "The unleashed power of the atom has changed everything save our modes of thinking and thus we drift toward unparalleled catastrophe." (Albert Einstein)

(i) "Even though a situation is catastrophic, that still does not mean it has to be taken seriously." (Austrian saying)

(j) "People are basically of two kinds: those who lean and those who lift." (unknown source)

(k) "When two persons quarrel, always both are in the wrong." (The Mother of the sri Aurobindo Ashram, India)

SUMMARY: DEDUCTIVE REASONING

1. Deductive reasoning is the process of starting with one or more statements called premises and investigating what conclusions necessarily follow from these premises.

2. Deduction is the subject of formal logic, whose main concern is with creating forms that demonstrate reasoning.

3. Logic has its own technical vocabulary. The following is a summary of the definitions of key terms.

Argument: An assertion with statements that support it.

Claim: Assertion or statement that maintains that something is true or false that is put forward for questioning and testing.

Conclusion: The last step in a reasoning process. It is a statement of decision or judgment based on evidence and reasoning.

In logic, a conclusion is an inference derived from the premises of an argument.

Hidden Premise or Conclusion: A premise or conclusion that is not stated but implied in an argument. When the argument is cast in a syllogism, the missing premise or conclusion is expressed.

Hypothesis: A theory, explanation, or tentative conclusion derived through inductive reasoning based on a limited view of facts or events. A *working hypothesis* can be used as a guide for further investigation to see if it leads to new facts or verification. Many hypotheses can be used and discarded one after the other until one is found that explains and aligns all the data and stands up to all testing and verification.

Inductive reasoning: The process of noting particular facts and drawing a conclusion about them.

Logic: The science of reasoning; also called the science of inference.

Premises: Statements or assumptions offered to support a position.

Propositions: Claims, statements, or assertions used in an argument. They can be either premises or conclusions and either true or false statements.

Reasoning: The act or process of arriving at conclusions, judgments, or inferences from facts or premises.

Sound: A sound argument is one in which all the premises are true and the reasoning is valid.

Syllogism: The formalized structure of a deductive argument, usually written, in which the conclusion is supported by two premises. (Greek *syllogiz* = to reason.)

True: Corresponding to reality.

Valid: A valid argument is one in which the reasoning follows correctly from the premises to the conclusion. An argument can be valid without the premises or conclusion being true.

4. The standardized language of syllogisms allows a reduction of everyday language into verbal mathematics.

5. Syllogisms allow logicians to determine what is being said, to identify hidden premises, and to find out if the argument makes sense.

6. Formal fallacies are violations of the rules governing the forms of valid reasoning. The study of formal fallacies is a subject of formal logic.

7. It is possible to infer the rules of valid and invalid reasoning from the study of models.

8. A study of formal fallacies involves an understanding of such words as *major, middle,* and *minor terms; exclusion, inclusion, distributed, illicit distribution, affirm, deny, antecedent, consequent;* and *major* and *minor premise.*

Quiz: Deductive Reasoning

Rate the following statements as *true* or *false*. Justify your answers.

_____ 1. A proposition is a claim about something.

_____ 2. Syllogisms are used in logic because logicians like to make their knowledge arcane, or hidden and secret.

_____ 3. Logic is less concerned with truth than with whether one statement follows reasonably from another.

_____ 4. Reasoning only occurs in deduction—not in induction.

_____ 5. A generalization reached through induction can become a premise used in a deductive syllogism.

_____ 6. "All homeowners are taxpayers. He is a property owner. Therefore he is a taxpayer." This is a valid argument.

_____ 7. "Bloodletting reduces fever. This patient has fever. This patient needs bloodletting." This syllogism shows valid reasoning although both premises may not be true.

_____ 8. "White-skinned people are superior to dark-skinned people. Therefore it is the manifest destiny of white-skinned people to rule dark-skinned people." No country would ever accept such fallacious reasoning as this.

State whether the reasoning in each of the following syllogisms is correct or incorrect.

9. If the two parties agree, then there is no strike.

   The two parties agree.
   _____

   Therefore, there is no strike.

10. If the two parties agree, then there is no strike.

    There is no strike.
    _____

    Therefore the two parties agree.

11.   If the two parties agree, then there is no strike.
      The two parties do not agree.

      _____

      Therefore, there is a strike.

12.   If the two parties agree, then there is no strike.
      There is a strike.

      _____

      Therefore, the two parties do not agree.

After you have decided, compare your answers to those given below. Explain why these answers are correct.

   9. correct   10. incorrect   11. incorrect   12. correct

INTRODUCTION TO THE INFORMAL FALLACIES OF DEDUCTIVE REASONING

You will probably find the informal fallacies of deductive reasoning to be less difficult to remember than the formal fallacies, partially because they can be so funny. Before continuing into this section, however, take out some time to review the summary and quiz on deductive reasoning on pages 356–359.

INFORMAL FALLACIES OF DEDUCTIVE REASONING

This section of the chapter will examine the following informal fallacies that are especially applicable to deductive reasoning.

   1.   Misapplied generalization
   2.   Begging the question
   3.   Fallacies of ambiguity (semantic ambiguity, euphemisms, equivocation)
   4.   Covert persuasion (slanted language; emotional appeals to fear, pity, authority, bandwagon; personal attack; poisoning the well)
   5.   Diversion into other issues (red herring, pointing to another wrong)

Misapplied Generalization

An argument that states a generalization with the insistence that it has no exceptions and should be applied even to atypical situations is guilty of the misapplied generalization. An earlier example of the misapplied generalization was discussed in the argument about hecklers. It maintained that hecklers should be allowed to interrupt speakers for the sake of free speech. Here are some other examples:

1. Milk is good for everybody. You can't be allergic to milk. You should drink at least one glass a day.
2. Rachael reads books all day, every day, and sometimes through the night. She uses her time well.

Most of us would agree that these examples obviously misapply the generalization to the situation. However, in many cases the designation *misapplied generalization* depends entirely on values and viewpoint. The generalization, law, or rule that one person might go to great lengths to uphold could appear to someone else to be a misapplied generalization.

CLASS DISCUSSION

Consider the examples that follow and discuss whether you find them to be (1) valid applications of a law or rule to a situation or (2) generalizations misapplied to exceptional circumstances.

1. No lives should be taken through abortions. Therefore, even in cases of rape and incest, the fetus should have a right to life.
2. When you take the blood of someone else into you, that is a form of cannibalism. Therefore, under no circumstances would I have a blood transfusion.
3. Resorting to doctors and medicine means a lack of faith in God and the kind of healing that can only come through a spiritual crisis. Therefore, we will not permit our children to have doctors or medicine.
4. War is evil under all circumstances. Therefore, I will never agree to serve in the armed forces of any country, even if I have to go to jail.
5. Those protestors who slashed the tires of workers' cars while the workers were driving through their picket lines into the nuclear installation should be subject to the same laws that protect any citizen's property from vandalism.

Misapplication of Wise Sayings. Sometimes misapplied generalizations are based on an application of wise sayings to support personal opinions. Thus, when misapplied, the wise saying is taken as an absolute law without exceptions. This provides a kind of stereotyping mechanism that makes further careful discriminations unnecessary.

Consider the following examples:

1. You can't make a silk purse out of a sow's ear. You'll never make it as a ballet dancer.

2. The grass always looks greener on the other side of the fence. You should give up the idea of looking for another job.

3. There will always be wars and rumors of wars. There is no use putting any faith in peace talks.

4. You can't have your cake and eat it too. You have to be either married or single.

CLASS DISCUSSION

1. Can you think of any generalizations that you or others apply indiscriminately to your lives?

2. Think of the task of a judge and jury as one of seeking to apply laws to specific cases. Can you think of historical examples of decisions that you felt were misapplied generalizations?

Begging the Question

The fallacy of begging the question occurs in an argument in which *no* argument is really offered in the premises; the conclusion is only asserted and then reasserted, as though it were an explanation. The person arguing does not *earn* your agreement through evidence and reasoning, but *begs* for it through insistence and repetition. This fallacy is also called circular reasoning because it says, "A is true because A is true." Here are some examples:

1. Union bosses are a menace to this country because they control millions of workers. (This is saying that union bosses are a menace because they are doing the work of union bosses. The whole argument also hinges on the ambiguity of the word *control*.)

2. Elect Wallace Brown supervisor—a Korean War pilot. (What makes a jet pilot a good supervisor?)

3. White supremacy is a justifiable tradition in South Africa because the blacks there are not able to govern themselves. (White supremacy is justified because it succeeds in doing well what it does.)

4. Aerobic exercise promotes good health. If you want to be healthy, you should do aerobics. (Aerobics is good for you because aerobics is good for you.)

5. The Koran is the word of Allah. It says so in the Koran. (The Koran is the word of Allah because the Koran says it is the word of Allah.)

6. The new space weapons will be good for the security of this country. Isn't it obvious that when we have space-based ballistic missle defense, we will have security? (Space weapons provide security because they provide security.)

CLASS DISCUSSION

1. Challenge the preceding statements.

2. Provide reasons for the conclusions given and make them into sound arguments.

Fallacies of Ambiguity

As you have often seen emphasized in this book, all the words in an argument need to be clearly defined and understood for a dialogue to proceed without confusion. The logical fallacies of ambiguity make arguments unsound when the arguments contain words that could be understood in more than one way. Again, this ambiguity could be due either to carelessness or to calculated intention. The three fallacies of ambiguity that we will consider here are semantic ambiguity, euphemisms, and equivocation.

Semantic Ambiguity. The fallacy of semantic ambiguity involves the choice of a word that is never defined, or is left purposely unclear. "We should treat drug use as a private right that harms no one but the user." Here, what is meant by *drug* is left to the reader to guess. Does the author mean heroin or aspirin? Depending on the definition, the issue of harm to others would vary.

Ambiguous words are often chosen by advertisers to lure buyers into projecting their own desires and hopes on advertising claims. For advertisers, the advantage of this approach is that they can later deny responsibility for the buyer's interpretations. Such ambiguities may take the form of such "weasel words" as *helps,* as in "Helps prevent cavities," or *as much as,* as in "Saves as much as one gallon of gas." A few other familiar weasel words appear in the following ads.

1. Save on typewriters from a leading maker! SALE! SALE! $200! Made to sell for $495! (Here the word *sale* only tells you the store has something to sell. Perhaps it was overpriced in the first place.)

2. Women's coats—$54. A $75 value. (The word *value* is relative. Perhaps the store bought the coats especially for the sale and set the previous value arbitrarily.)

3. These blouses have the feel of silk. (If an item has the *feel* of silk, that does not mean it is silk.)

4. Come see our sheepskin-look seat covers. (Remember, they are not saying that the items *are* sheepskin.)

CLASS DISCUSSION

Identify the ambiguous words in the following sentences by underlining the words and stating how they function for persuasion.

1. All ingredients in this ice cream are natural and nutritious.
2. These pies are made from locally grown cherries and have that old-fashioned country taste.
3. Ace aspirin provides relief up to eight hours.
4. Ida Insect Spray helps fight mosquitoes.
5. Tony's Tonic helps you feel and look ten years younger.
6. You can save as much as one quart of oil a day.
7. Wear a jacket that has the feel of leather.
8. Cults enslave people.
9. The federal government has too much power.
10. You should be willing to do anything for love.

Euphemisms. The word *euphemism* comes from the Greek word meaning good voice, or to use words of good omen. Euphemisms are inoffensive words used in place of others that might be considered distasteful or offensive. We say *remains* for *corpse, pass away* for *die, bathroom* or *restroom* for *toilet*. Euphemisms are not only used in polite society to keep life more formal and free of inconvenient feelings, but also politically for propaganda purposes.

In political life, euphemisms perform the task of public relations where neutral words are used to camouflage actions, things, or events that are unacceptable in light of professed values. The result is a distortion of truth and meaning. In George Orwell's novel *1984*, such distortions of language are grimly parodied in his creation of a state built on the slogans "War Is Peace," "Freedom Is Slavery," "Ignorance Is Strength." Here the government ministries include the Ministry of Truth (which produces lies and propaganda), the Ministry of Love (which practices imprisonment, brainwashing, and torture), and the Ministry of Peace (which concerns itself with war).

Following is a list of a few neutral euphemisms being used in American life today. New ones keep arriving all the time. See if you can add some more.

Neutralized Term	Accurate Term
entry device	bomb
deploy a missle	set up to fire
enhanced radiation device	neutron bomb
vaporize	blow up and kill
neutralize	kill
de-escalate	withdraw
incomplete success	failed mission
strategic redeployment	surrender
"The Peacekeeper"	MX missile
"Star Wars"—Strategic Defense Initiative	futuristic weapons system using lasers and nonnuclear missiles
security assistance	sending weapons and soldiers to another country
credibility gap	government lying
disinformation	lies planted for media releases
expendable resources	soldiers in war
casualties	dead soldiers
chemically dependent	drug addicted
political unparticipants	unregistered minority voters
withdrawal of enthusiasm	boycott of products

CLASS DISCUSSION

1. In the novel *1984*, George Orwell predicts the development of a totalitarian government that will purposefully corrupt language in order to control thought. Do you feel that the use of the kind of political double-talk we just focused on actually deceives Americans, or do you think these expressions are generally recognized with humor?

2. The following is an excerpt from an article that appeared in the 1982 annual issue of the *Harvard Lampoon,* which parodied *Newsweek* magazine. This article, reported in the *Lampoon*'s version of *Newsweek* style, describes life inside the USSR. Note how the article parodies familiar Soviet rhetoric in its double-talk, defensiveness, and use of neutralized euphemisms. Read the article and underline for discussion all the euphemisms that appear there.

Russia Swings at 65

There has never been a stronger or happier Russia. The one potential sore thumb remains the controversial prison camp system. . . . Party officials categorically deny that these gulags exist at all and, if they ever did, were not particularly astringent or cruel. "They are not worse than Stalag 13 on your American 'Hogan's Heroes' show," says a former prisoner who now works for the government.

Today the government claims that prisoners are not punished, but rehabilitated. Living in prisons with names such as Archipelago Sunshine Park in Siberia, prisoners learn the joys of life under the Red Flag. During their stay at these rehabilitation centers, inmates are given a chance to "shape up and slim down" with one of the most rigorous physical culture programs and specialized diets in the world. Those inmates who suffer from bouts of alienation, "unhealthy religious fervor," and "perverse opposition to the State" benefit from . . . a combination of group therapy and one-on-one counseling Soviet style. Says Dr. Yuri Aivazian, chief administrator of chemical readjustment therapy, "Our patients are much more happy when they finish the program. They see the world with a new childlike wonder." As evidence of this Aivazian points to a group of smiling, glassy-eyed patients strapped onto the "Twirling Cups and Saucers" amusement ride recently built on park grounds.

Harvard Lampoon, Fall 1982. Used with permission of the publisher.

Equivocation. The word *equivocation* comes from the Latin word meaning equal voice. In general, to equivocate is to use ambiguous words purposely in order to mislead or deceive or hedge. "Equal voice" is giving the same voice accent to saying something meaningless as to saying something meaningful. Often we hear this when a person confronted with accountability for an event uses the phrase "to the best of my knowledge" to deny that something did occur or did not occur, implying both (1) "I know everything," and (2) "I could be wrong." Another evasion is the phrase "as far as I know," which can serve the same purpose.

Equivocation can also take the form of going through the formal rhythm of answering questions, with words that could only be translated as "quack, quack, quack, quack, quack."

HE: "Do you love me?"

SHE: "If I didn't, would I be here with you now?"

HE: "But will you marry me?"

SHE: "I will marry you when—everything considered—marriage is a commitment that needs careful consideration and responsibility."

In logic, *equivocation* has a different and more specialized meaning from that just described. It means drawing an unwarranted conclusion from premises containing a term that *shifts* in its meaning within the argument. The following syllogism illustrates this:

Only *man* is rational.

No woman is a *man*.

No woman is rational.

Here the first premise uses the word *man* to mean a human, whereas the second uses *man* to mean a male. The conclusion, therefore, is unsound.

CLASS DISCUSSION

Some of the following examples of equivocation are old familiars from textbooks on logical fallacies. Show that you can identify the key equivocal words here by underlining them. Write out, for comparison, the definition of each word used twice, to show their differences. Then explain how these words create elusive shifts within the argument.

1. The laws of gravitation and motion must have a lawmaker for the simple reason that they are laws and all laws have a lawmaker.
2. People say that sexism and racism are forms of discrimination. But what is wrong with discrimination? We discriminate all the time in our choices of food, homes, and friends.
3. Business is business.
4. Sick children should stay in bed, right? Well, I am sick of school!
5. In a cartoon, Margaret Heckler, the former Health and Welfare Secretary, is shown looking unhappy in a press conference with the President. He has just requested her resignation so that she can take a position as ambassador to Ireland. The President commends her for being "one of this administration's greatest assets, far and away."

Covert Persuasion

Slanted language; emotional appeals to fear, pity, authority, bandwagon; personal attack; and poisoning the well are all irrational appeals disguised as rational arguments. They appeal to weaknesses and are most effective when they arouse emotions that are not consciously recognized. They can become insidiously effective in clouding any further rational discussion on an issue. As techniques, they stress material irrelevant to the argument that will make their position hold more dramatic interest. They are used in politics and advertising as propaganda ploys familiar to us all. Indeed, they are so familiar, most of us have even learned to tolerate and live with them. Moreover, in this age of hype and hucksterism, when ideas usually have to enter into sales competition in order to come across, even writers who can construct sound arguments may feel that they have to turn the volume up to be heard.

All of this does not mean that any argument that includes expression of feeling or emotion is invalid. Usually we are not aroused to construct arguments unless motivated by feelings. To be sane on many topics is to feel clear anger, indignation, or grief. However, a fallacious argument is not always clear about its feeling involvement, which might be so great that the argument cannot evolve coherently. If this happens, the writer might be even more tempted to manipulate by composing an argument that would arouse a feeling response in others to agree with his or her own feelings. A fallacious argument constructed on this basis cannot appeal to reason or to rational feeling, but instead appeals to fear, pity, respect for authority, need for popularity, prejudice, and the wish to slander.

Slanted Language.   We touched on slanted language earlier when we discussed connotative words in the chapter on evaluations. To refresh your memory, note the use of language in the following two headlines that appeared in *U.S. News & World Report,* July 1983:

1.   Castro <u>Molds</u> a <u>Breed</u> of Young <u>Zealots</u>.
2.   Next <u>Stop</u>—Central America? <u>No One in Washington</u> Wants to <u>Send</u> America to War. But <u>Events</u> in the Region Could <u>Force Reagan's Hand</u>.

What are the connotations of the underlined words and phrases, and what purpose do they serve in terms of persuasion? (What associations, for instance, do we have with the word *breed?*)

Compare them to the following statements. Do they state the same basic message? Do you think the following statements would attract readers as readily as the previous headlines?

1.   Fidel Castro inspires his young people to be patriotic.
2.   Will the United States invade Central America?

Note the words that you consider to be slanted in the following quotations.

1.   "America's dirty little war in El Salvador has so far been limited to thin transfusions of money and material as well as moral support for murderous regimes." (*Mother Jones,* June/July 1983)

2. *Guerrillas Endanger Caribbean Dominoes*
   "For three years now . . . the United States has been engaged in an effort to stop the advance of communism in Central America by doing what Americans instinctively do best—supporting democracy." (*USA Today*, 8 March 1983)

3. "The Salvadoran army and auxiliary forces are far less interested in fighting the guerrillas than in killing civilians. The State Department, holding its nose to certify progress on human rights, said recently that 'only' 5000 civilians had been butchered last year." (Anthony Lewis, *San Francisco Chronicle*, 8 March 1983)

In these examples, the words chosen are not dishonest or inaccurate, but merely reflect the bias of the speaker; for the speaker in all these cases, the evaluative words may seem to honestly represent the facts. The problem for the critical reader is to recognize the range of connotations in the words chosen and to notice their effects on the argument. If the argument is more loaded with evaluative terms than with facts or objective and valid arguments, then one can only conclude that the argument must be weak to begin with.

CLASS DISCUSSION

How would you evaluate the following arguments?

1. Disdainful of God's eternal laws to the contrary, Planned Parenthood encourages the idea that sexual activity is to be expected and tolerated in our schoolchildren. Then in behavior more befitting the barnyard, they are influenced in a way of life that definitely thwarts their chances of future happiness, or integrity.

2. The rich man's man in the White House, whose feet are planted in cement when they are not stuck in his mouth, only appears to be yielding to the will of the people, but this man is a jingoistic sweet-talker and warmongering disaster.

3. "All that the children of America need is for a few more parents to indoctrinate them into pacifistic blobs and the end of freedom, as we now know it in America, is in sight." (Senator H. L. Richardson, *Your Heritage News*, January 1983)

Emotional Appeals to Fear and Pity. Appeals to fear and pity are two logical fallacies that are staples of commercial advertising. An appeal to fear or pity may be justified in many circumstances, but an argument becomes fallacious when it depends upon this appeal to carry it. Moreover, the attempt to arouse such feelings can be designed to prevent others from ever noticing the lack of a sound argument. The following examples may serve as familiar reminders of the use of appeals to fear.

1. "What your best friends won't tell you . . ."

2. (Picture of a frantic traveler who has lost her traveler's checks.) "Next time be safe with our fast call-in service."

3. (Picture of man in hospital bed in a state of shock after seeing his bill.) "Did you think one insurance coverage plan was enough?"

4. (Picture of burglars breaking into a house.) "Are you still post-poning that alarm system?"

CLASS DISCUSSION

The use of an appeal to anger is not usually listed among the logical falla-cies; using this type of appeal to arouse others out of a state of indif-ference is often assumed to be legitimate in argumentation. Listed below are some appeals to fear, pity, and anger over alleged cases of victimiza-tion. Read the arguments and decide which you think are fallacious (in that the situation is exaggerated) and which you feel are appropriate calls for fear or pity. Again, this may depend on personal values. Defend your answers.

1. "We are dragging heaven into hell. Our nation and the Soviet Union are turning the vast reach of space into a battlefield for new and terrifying machines of destruction." (Appeal letter from the Union of Concerned Scientists)

2. "The continent of Africa is in the grip of one of the worst droughts in its history. . . . Thousands have already died. Entire regions are at risk. And hundreds of thousands have left their homes, trekking for weeks, often to other countries, to find food and water. Oxfam America is providing emergency assistance and relief to those affected by the drought." (Oxfam America ap-peal letter)

3. "Dear Fellow Taxpayer: You can calculate your actual savings on property taxes because of Proposition 13. Without these savings, many thousands of Californians would have *lost their homes* years ago." (Howard Jarvis, in a political advertisement for a proposition to further lower property taxes)

4. These are our beliefs. During your life you can accept them or not. If you do, you will be saved. Otherwise you will go to hell for eternity.

5. "Dear Fellow American,
   "The National Rifle Association is once again thumbing its nose at you.

"In the lingering aftermath of the slaughter at a McDonald's restaurant in California, where 21 people were viciously gunned down, the NRA is spending freely from its $55 million political war chest to (1) defend the sale of 'assault' weapons like the Uzi used in the San Ysidro massacre, and (2) permit the sale of Teflon-coated 'cop-killer' bullets, which can rip through bullet-proof vests." (Appeal letter from Handgun Control)

6. "'We are God in Here . . .' That's what the guards in an Argentine prison taunted Grace Guena with as they applied electrical shocks to her body while she lay handcuffed to the springs of a metal bed. Her cries were echoed by the screams of other victims and the laughter of their torturers." (Appeal letter from Amnesty International USA)

Appeal to Authority. An appeal to authority is a fallacious argument that attempts to overwhelm an opponent's reliance on his or her own judgment by appealing to the superior wisdom of famous people, traditions, or beliefs. The citing of authority as evidence can be valid when the authority has expertise relevant to the issue at hand. But it is fallacious to appeal to irrelevant or nonspecific authorities, or to vague sentiment that urges conformity. (Remember Solomon Asch's experiment?)

CLASS DISCUSSION

Explain how the following statements are different kinds of appeals to authority. Which are fallacious? Which legitimate?

1. My doctor says that I should take a nap every afternoon.

2. A ten-year study by leading scientists has found that Tuff toothpaste prevents decay in four out of five cases.

3. Buzz Bonanza, star of stage and screen, drives a Macho Motorcycle.

4. I read it in the newspapers.

5. Interviewer: "Vice President Quayle, do you feel domestic assault rifles should be banned?" Quayle: "My viewpoint is always in agreement with the President's. And I am sure that if he felt we should have a ban on them, we'd have one."

6. The 1990 Nicaragua election in which Daniel Ortega was defeated by Violeta Chamorro was a fair election expressing a popular mandate. This was voiced by Ortega himself in his concession speech and substantiated by Jimmy Carter's Council of Freely Elected Heads of Government.

7. "Women have babies and men provide the support. If you don't like the way we're made you've got to take it up with God." (Phyllis Schlafly)

8. For over a quarter of a century our teachers have been committed to the idea that the best way to teach students is to withhold criticisms and build self-esteem. But both Alfred Binet, the father of intelligence testing, and Sigmund Freud, the father of psychoanalysis, described the development of self-criticism, which we learn from the criticisms of others, as the essence of intelligence.

Appeal to Popularity or Bandwagon.   An argument that appeals to the comfort of joining the crowd and coming over to the winning side is also fallacious. It is another version of an appeal to authority: this time the authority is a vague group or mass of "others." It also promises the exhilaration of being swept up in an irrepressible momentum of instinctive wisdom.

Here are some examples of appeals to the bandwagon:

1. Don't vote for Proposition 9. The polls show it will lose 5 to 1.
2. Everyone else does it; why can't I?
3. Last year over ten million people switched to Buckaroo Trucks!
4. Buddy Springs! America's Beer!
5. Millions of Americans are now buying personal computers for their children. Give your children a head start in school with their personal home computer today!

Personal Attack.   The fallacy of personal attack is familiar enough to us all at election time. This fallacy, also known under the Latin name of *ad hominem,* consists in using name calling and even abuse of an opponent as a diversionary tactic, rather than discussing the issues of disagreement. Here an attack is made on the individual *person* rather than on the *argument.*

1. This particular senator, whom I shall not name, is a known cocaine user, and yet he has dared to take a stand against our Central American policy.
2. My opponent in this election, Adam Marks, is a deadbeat politician and a liar who chiseled a former business associate.
3. I will not say what I call this woman candidate, but the word rhymes with *rich.*

CLASS DISCUSSION

Do you think that name calling is persuasive in an argument or that it usually boomerangs?

Poisoning the Well.   In the fallacy known as poisoning the well, the argument seeks to create prejudice and to discredit opponents before their viewpoints can be heard. "Don't listen to anything that senator has to say: he's a warmonger." Thus, this ploy seeks to "poison the well" before anyone can drink from it.

Poisoning the well is most effective when the allegations have no proven connection to the issue at hand, as in the following example: "Upset by federal aid cutbacks, American students have blindly taken revenge by holding sit-ins and demonstrations for divestiture of their universities' investments in South Africa." No evidence is offered for this implied cause-and-effect connection between students' being "upset by federal aid cutbacks" and students' participating in South Africa divestment rallies. But this juxtaposition minimizes and discredits the students' actions. It poisons the well, prejudicing the reader from hearing what the students have to say about divestiture.

The following example offers a more literal example of poisoning the well, or to use an older expression, of blackballing.

An EPA "Hit List" of Scientists

A "hit list" of EPA scientific advisors that brands some as liberals or environmentalists and urges their dismissal was given yesterday to several congressional subcommittees. The list was provided by an unidentified Environmental Protection Agency employee. It labels one advisor an "extreme anti-nuclear type" and says: "Get him out fast." "Deep-six him" is the notation next to another name, while a third man is rated a "bleeding heart liberal." (From the *Oakland Tribune,* November 1983)

CLASS DISCUSSION

The Freedom of Information Act is one that promises to give people access to information that might be poison in their own well. Do you feel that this act was needed?

Diversion into Other Issues

Those who use the fallacies of the red herring and pointing to another wrong sidestep their own arguments to divert attention to other issues. This can be quite effective as a ploy, and if skillfully done, the diversion can offer so much appeal that the argument will get off track without its being noticed.

The Red Herring.   The term *red herring* comes from the ruse used by prison escapees of smearing themselves with herring to throw dogs off the scent of their tracks. The red herring in argumentation succeeds in being most distracting when it proves a point other than the one being addressed. Its purpose is to sidetrack opponents into irrelevancies and to divert them from concentrating on the issue at hand.

CLASS DISCUSSION

Study the following examples of red herring arguments. Write out (1) the issue and (2) the diversion.

1. Guns are not America's major problem, or even high on the list of our problems. Cars, cancer, accidents in the kitchen all kill far more people than guns do. It is not *guns* that we should be frightened of, but the effects of poverty, lack of education, a judicial system that sends criminals and psychopaths back out into the streets. Guns are not a solution, but they are not the problem, either!

2. TV can't be harmful to children, because it occupies their attention for hours and keeps them off the streets. (Taken from S. Morris Engel's *With Good Reason,* St. Martin's Press, 1982)

3. Marijuana smoking is not all that bad. I would feel safer driving with a marijuana smoker than with a driver under the influence of liquor any day.

4. Those who are so ferociously involved in Mothers Against Drunk Driving would better spend their time in working with A.A. to help alcoholics.

5. Why are you always nagging at me about the way I drive?

Pointing to Another Wrong.   The fallacy of pointing to another wrong is also called "two wrongs make a right." Again, it introduces an irrelevancy, or an irresponsibility, however you choose to see it, into an argument. It is an attempt to justify an action considered objectionable by appealing to similar instances that went unnoticed, unjudged, or unpunished.

Consider these examples of pointing to another wrong:

1. Student to instructor: "Why are you getting after me for being late to class? You never say anything to that pretty coed who comes late to class every day."

2. Motorist to police officer: "Why are you giving me a ticket for going the wrong way on a one-way street? Didn't you see that red sedan I was following doing the same thing?"

3.   Why do we lay so much blame on Nixon for the Watergate coverup? He was only doing the same thing that Kennedy and his men did.

4.   "I never saw President Carter's briefing book. Besides, what difference would it make since it never got to me as a debater. And even if it was stolen, it probably wasn't too much different from the press rushing into print with the Pentagon papers, which were stolen."

CLASS DISCUSSION

Have you ever used a red herring argument yourself? Did it work?

SUMMARY: FALLACIES
OF DEDUCTIVE REASONING

1.   Misapplied generalization is the application of a generalization to an exception or atypical example.

2.   Begging the question is the assertion or repeated assertion of a conclusion with the insistence that the conclusion is a reason.

3.   Ambiguous language is the fallacy in an argument that uses and takes advantage of key words that could be interpreted in more than one way.

4.   Euphemisms are words that mask meaning by enveloping an idea with a more positive or neutral connotation. Use of euphemisms is fallacious when done to mislead understanding or disarm objections.

5.   Equivocation, in the general sense of the word, is creating a verbal smoke screen that seems to be saying something while saying nothing. As a logical fallacy, equivocation is drawing an unwarranted conclusion from an argument that contains a term that has more than one meaning, under the pretense that it has only one meaning. This shift in meaning occurs between the premises and the conclusion.

6.   Slanted language persuades through the use of loaded words that pretend or appear to convey objective information.

7.   Appeals to fear and pity persuade through emotional appeals that prevent rational analysis of an argument's merits and therefore make construction of a rational argument unnecessary.

8.   Appeal to authority seeks to influence others to agree to an argument through appealing to an irrelevant authority. This authority can be not only a person, but also a tradition.

9. Appeal to bandwagon is another example of the appeal to authority, but in this case the authority is an amorphous mass, offering the exhilarating momentum of the herd instinct. This fallacy is also called mob appeal.

10. Personal attack is the fallacy of not offering a rational argument, but instead getting into emotional irrelevance through the use of abuse or name calling.

11. Poisoning the well prejudices others against an opponent so that he or she will not be heard objectively.

12. Red herring is a ploy of distraction. It brings up one issue, then minimizes or diverts attention from it by emphasizing other issues that are irrelevant. Those following this line of argument will soon find themselves off the track.

13. Pointing to another wrong is also called "two wrongs make a right." It says, "Don't look at me; he did it too!"

Quiz: Fallacies of Deductive Reasoning

Identify the following arguments either as NF for *not fallacious,* or by the name of one of the fallacies of deductive reasoning defined in this chapter. In some cases you may find that more than one fallacy applies; choose the one you feel to be most appropriate. Be prepared to defend your answers.

_____ 1. It was announced today that our troops, who have been shelled for some weeks now in Lebanon, have made a *strategic transfer* to their ships offshore of that country.

_____ 2. All boys like baseball. Put down those books and get out and play!

_____ 3. Eating meats and dairy foods contaminates the spirit, according to my religion. Therefore, even though I have anemia, which my doctor says is caused by a low protein diet, I must adhere to my religious teachings.

_____ 4. Children are supposed to have rights like everyone else, aren't they? Well, then I am right in not wanting to go to bed.

_____ 5. Five million people have already seen this movie. Shouldn't you?

_____ 6. Why do I think the President's program is sound? Because the polls show that the vast majority supports it.

_____ 7. By a margin of two to one, shoppers prefer Brand X to any of the leading competitors. Reason enough to buy Brand X.

_____ 8. What if your bank fails and takes your life savings? Buy diamonds—the safe investment.

_____ 9. Repressive environmentalists and economic zero-growthers have attacked the Environmental Protection Agency. Those stop-all-progress destructionists have nothing under their thick skulls.

_____ 10. A spokesman for a chemical industrial firm, when charged and fined for disposing of toxic wastes in the lakes of Illinois, protested, "Thousands of other industries are doing the same thing."

_____ 11. Good thinking depends on clear perception.

_____ 12. Democrats are captives of an anti-growth dinosaur mentality that offers nothing for the future but repeating their failed past. If the big spenders get their way, they'll charge everything on your Taxpayers' Express Card.

_____ 13. There is _virtually no tar_ in these cigarettes.

_____ 14. The Soviet Union does not have a _government_ but a _regime,_ and instead of an FBI, they have a "dread secret police." (Adapted from an Art Hoppe parody, _San Francisco Chronicle,_ 27 May 1984)

_____ 15. In Ethel Rae Cosmetics we don't call ourselves "salespeople" but "teachers." We teach people how to take better care of their skins.

_____ 16. Using hidden notes on a test is not unethical; our professors wouldn't be where they are today if they hadn't done the same thing.

_____ 17. Maybe I do cheat on income tax, but so does everyone else.

_____ 18. Those people so fanatical about protesting in front of the nuclear plants would be better involved in voter registration and voter education.

_____ 19. Don't support the American Civil Liberties Union. They want nothing but criminals' rights.

_____ 20. Why are you wasting your time reading that radical right-wing newspaper? They are nothing but a bunch of fuddy-duddy old-timers and little old ladies in tennis shoes.

_____ 21. There are plenty of people out there on the streets waiting to get your job. If you go on strike, you may find yourself out there with them.

_____ 22. Elijah Jones was the tenth victim of police brutality this year. Arrested for murdering his two children in a fit of insanity due to the pressures of his ghetto existence, he had hoped, on release from a mental institution through the help of the drug thorazine, to make a new life for himself. But Sunday he was shot down mercilessly by the Pigs when he attacked a police officer after robbing a liquor store.

_____ 23. The *natural* way to relieve muscular pain is through our vitamin ointment. It *relieves* pain from burns, stiff neck, backache, swelling, and so forth.

_____ 24. Ice cream may provide some nutrition, but lots of fat and calories, too.

_____ 25. American educators, in a recent survey, unanimously agreed that longer school days, more homework, and longer school years would only penalize children and not necessarily result in better learning.

_____ 26. The President of the United States says that the problems of illiteracy can be solved only by longer school days, more homework, and longer school years.

_____ 27. In China, Europe, and Brazil, efforts are being made to defuse the population time bomb that adds one billion more people every decade.

_____ 28. Sanity is about to prevail in New Zealand, where the government is about to take a firm hand against its radical troublemakers who have been protesting the docking of nuclear ships in its ports.

Readings

THE DECLARATION OF INDEPENDENCE

Thomas Jefferson

Based on a clear line of deductive reasoning, this great historical document written in 1776 is also an enduring work of literature. Jefferson begins by stating some "self-evident truths," or axioms, which set off a revolution and formed the ideological basis for the laws of a new government. Study this document as a structure of reasoning. Outline the whole into four parts. What is the function of each part?

When in the Course of human events, it becomes necessary for one 1 people to dissolve the political bands which have connected them with another, and to assume among the powers of the earth, the separate and equal station to which the Laws of Nature and of Nature's God entitle them, a decent respect to the opinions of mankind requires that they should declare the causes which impel them to the separation.

We hold these truths to be self-evident, that all men are created   2
equal, that they are endowed by their Creator with certain unalienable
Rights, that among these are Life, Liberty and the pursuit of Happiness.
That to secure these rights, Governments are instituted among Men, deriving their just powers from the consent of the governed, That whenever any Form of Government becomes destructive of these ends it is
the Right of the People to alter or to abolish it, and to institute new
Government, laying its foundation on such principles and organizing its
powers in such form, as to them shall seem most likely to effect their
Safety and Happiness. Prudence, indeed, will dictate that Governments
long established should not be changed for light and transient causes;
and accordingly all experience has shewn, that mankind are more dis-
posed to suffer, while evils are sufferable, than to right themselves by
abolishing the forms to which they are accustomed. But when a long
train of abuses and usurpations, pursuing invariably the same Object
evinces a design to reduce them under absolute Despotism, it is their
right, it is their duty, to throw off such Government, and to provide new
Guards for their future security. Such has been the patient sufferance of
these Colonies; and such is now the necessity which constrains them to
alter their former Systems of Government. The history of the present
King of Great Britain is a history of repeated injuries and usurpations,
all having in direct object the establishment of an absolute Tyranny
over these States. To prove this, let Facts be submitted to a candid
world.

He has refused his Assent to Laws, the most wholesome and neces-   3
sary for the public good.

He has forbidden his Governors to pass Laws of immediate and   4
pressing importance, unless suspended in their operation till his Assent
should be obtained; and when so suspended, he has utterly neglected to
attend to them. He has refused to pass other Laws for the accommodation of large districts of people, unless those people would relinquish
the right of Representation in the Legislature, a right inestimable to
them and formidable to tyrants only.

He has called together legislative bodies at places unusual, uncom-   5
fortable, and distant from the depository of their public Records, for
the sole purpose of fatiguing them into compliance with his measures.

He has dissolved Representative Houses repeatedly, for opposing   6
with manly firmness his invasions on the rights of the people.

He has refused for a long time, after such dissolutions, to cause   7
others to be elected; whereby the Legislative powers, incapable of An-
nihilation, have returned to the People at large for their exercise, the
State remaining in the mean time exposed to all the dangers of invasion
from without, and convulsions within.

He has endeavoured to prevent the population of these States; for   8
that purpose obstructing the Laws for Naturalization of Foreigners; re-

fusing to pass others to encourage their migrations hither, and raising the conditions of new Appropriations of Lands.

He has obstructed the Administration of Justice, by refusing his Assent to Laws for establishing Judiciary powers.   9

He has made Judges dependent on his Will alone, for the tenure of their offices, and the amount and payment of their salaries.   10

He has erected a multitude of New Offices, and sent hither swarms of Officers to harass our People, and eat out their substance.   11

He has kept among us, in times of peace, standing Armies without the Consent of our legislatures.   12

He has affected to render the Military independent of and superior to the Civil power.   13

He has combined with others to subject us to a jurisdiction foreign to our constitution, and unacknowledged by our laws; giving his Assent to their Acts of pretended Legislation: 14

For Quartering large bodies of armed troops among us: 15

For protecting them, by a mock Trial, from punishment for any Murders which they should commit on the Inhabitants of these States: 16

For cutting off our Trade with all parts of the world: 17

For imposing Taxes on us without our Consent: 18

For depriving us in many cases of the benefits of Trial by Jury: 19

For transporting us beyond Seas to be tried for pretended offences: 20

For abolishing the free System of English Laws in a neighbouring Province, establishing therein an Arbitrary government, and enlarging its Boundaries so as to render it at once an example and fit instrument for introducing the same absolute rule into these Colonies: 21

For taking away our Charters, abolishing our most valuable Laws, and altering fundamentally the Forms of our Governments: 22

For suspending our own Legislatures, and declaring themselves invested with power to legislate for us in all cases whatsoever.   23

He has abdicated Government here, by declaring us out of his Protection and waging War against us.   24

He has plundered our seas, ravaged our Coasts, burnt our towns, and destroyed the Lives of our people.   25

He is at this time transporting large Armies of foreign Mercenaries to compleat the works of death, desolation and tyranny, already begun with circumstances of Cruelty & perfidy scarcely paralleled in the most barbarous ages, and totally unworthy the Head of a civilized nation.   26

He has constrained our fellow Citizens taken Captive on the high Seas to bear Arms against their Country, to become the executioners of their friends and Brethren, or to fall themselves by their Hands.   27

He has excited domestic insurrections amongst us, and has endeavoured to bring on the inhabitants of our frontiers, merciless Indian Savages, whose known rule of warfare, is an undistinguished destruction of all ages, sexes and conditions.   28

In every stage of these Oppressions We have Petitioned for Redress   29
in the most humble terms: Our repeated Petitions have been answered
only by repeated injury. A Prince, whose character is thus marked by
every act which may define a Tyrant, is unfit to be the ruler of a free
people.

Nor have We been wanting in attentions to our British brethren. We   30
have warned them from time to time of attempts by their legislature to
extend an unwarrantable jurisdiction over us. We have reminded them
of the circumstances of our emigration and settlement here. We have
appealed to their native justice and magnanimity, and we have conjured
them by the ties of our common kindred to disavow these usurpations,
which would inevitably interrupt our connections and correspondence.
They too have been deaf to the voice of Justice and of consanguinity.
We must, therefore, acquiesce in the necessity, which denounces our
Separation, and hold them, as we hold the rest of mankind, Enemies in
War, in Peace Friends.

We, therefore, the Representatives of the united States of America,   31
in General Congress, Assembled, appealing to the Supreme Judge of the
world for the rectitude of our intentions, do, in the Name, and by Authority of the good People of these Colonies, solemnly publish and declare, That these United Colonies are, and of Right ought to be Free and
Independent States; that they are absolved from all Allegiance to the
British Crown, and that all political connection between them and the
State of Great Britain, is and ought to be totally dissolved; and that as
Free and Independent States, they have full Power to levy War, conclude Peace, contract Alliances, establish Commerce, and to do all
other Acts and Things which Independent States may of right do. And
for the support of this Declaration, with a firm reliance on the protection of divine Providence, we mutually pledge to each other our Lives,
our Fortunes and our sacred Honor.

STUDY QUESTIONS

1. In the first sentence it is stated that people are entitled by "the
    Laws of Nature and Nature's God" to separate and equal sta-
    tions. What does this mean? Is there any evidence offered to
    back this claim?

2. Outline the deductive reasoning offered in the second para-
    graph. Which truths does Jefferson claim to be self-evident?
    What is the purpose of governments? From where do they derive
    their power?

3. How does Jefferson anticipate the argument that this kind of
    reasoning would allow people to overthrow governments "for
    light and transient causes"?

4. What are some of the complaints listed by Jefferson to justify a declaration of independence from England? Are some more evaluative than factual?

5. In the last paragraph, in the name of what authorities does he make the declaration?

6. The reasoning in this document opens with a deductive framework citing self-evident truths. Do you think the recognition of such truths preceded the abuses listed or were they born out of them?

THE RABBITS WHO CAUSED ALL THE TROUBLE

James Thurber

James Thurber is a beloved American essayist, short-story writer, humorist, and artist. He was a contributor to The New Yorker *for many years, and did much to set the tone and style of that magazine.*

Within the memory of the youngest child there was a family of rabbits who lived near a pack of wolves. The wolves announced that they did not like the way the rabbits were living. (The wolves were crazy about the way they themselves were living, because it was the only way to live.) One night several wolves were killed in an earthquake and this was blamed on the rabbits, for it is well known that rabbits pound on the ground with their hind legs and cause earthquakes. On another night one of the wolves was killed by a bolt of lightning and this was also blamed on the rabbits, for it is well known that lettuce-eaters cause lightning. The wolves threatened to civilize the rabbits if they didn't behave, and the rabbits decided to run away to a desert island. But the other animals, who lived at a great distance, shamed them, saying, "You must stay where you are and be brave. This is no world for escapists. If the wolves attack you, we will come to your aid, in all probability." So the rabbits continued to live near the wolves and one day there was a terrible flood which drowned a great many wolves. This was blamed on the rabbits, for it is well known that carrot-nibblers with long ears cause floods. The wolves descended on the rabbits, for their own good, and imprisoned them in a dark cave, for their own protection. 1

When nothing was heard about the rabbits for some weeks, the other animals demanded to know what had happened to them. The wolves replied that the rabbits had been eaten and since they had been 2 eaten the affair was a purely internal matter. But the other animals warned that they might possibly unite against the wolves unless some reason was given for the destruction of the rabbits. So the wolves gave them one. "They were trying to escape," said the wolves, "and, as you know, this is no world for escapists."

Moral: Run, don't walk, to the nearest desert island. 3

STUDY QUESTIONS

1. Write out the syllogism that concludes this fable.
2. Is there an equivocation in the syllogism?
3. What fallacy do you find in the wolves' reasoning about the cause of earthquakes?
4. Discuss the use of the following expressions:
   (a) it is well known that
   (b) to civilize
   (c) escapists
   (d) for their own good
   (e) for their own protection
   (f) the affair was a purely internal matter
5. Why did the animals ask the wolves for a reason for destroying the rabbits? Do you think any answer would have satisfied them?
6. Does this all sound familiar? Describe some historical events that carry parallels.
7. Are there any desert islands left to go to?

For Further Reading

If you want to know more about logic, or to study it on your own, the following texts are suggested.

Barry, Vincent. *Invitation to Critical Thinking.* New York: Holt, Rinehart & Winston, 1984.

Kahane, Howard. *Logic and Philosophy,* 4th ed. Belmont, Calif.: Wadsworth, 1982.

Missimer, Connie. *Good Arguments: An Introduction to Critical Thinking.* Englewood Cliffs, N.J.: Prentice-Hall, 1986.

Thomas, Stephen. *Practical Reasoning in Natural Language,* 2nd ed. Englewood Cliffs, N.J.: Prentice-Hall, 1981.

The following are excellent sources for learning about logical fallacies:

Barry, Vincent. *Good Reason for Writing.* Belmont, Calif.: Wadsworth, 1983.

————. *Invitation to Critical Thinking.* New York: Holt, Rinehart & Winston, 1984.

Damer, T. Edward. *Attacking Faulty Reasoning.* Belmont, Calif.: Wadsworth, 1980.

Engel, S. Morris. *With Good Reason: An Introduction to Informal Fallacies,* 3rd ed. New York: St. Martin's Press, 1986.

Kahane, Howard. *Logic and Contemporary Rhetoric,* 4th ed. Belmont, Calif.: Wadsworth, 1984.

Shulman, Max. "Love Is a Fallacy." In *Tall Short Stories.* Ed. Erik Duthie. New York: Simon & Schuster, 1959.

Critical Analysis of Argumentation

Used with permission of Ben Dib.

Fighting may be easier than arguing, but even fighting can't proceed without stopping to reason when viewpoints and ideologies get so entangled.

This chapter shows you how to disentangle before the fighting starts, or better, to make the fighting unnecessary. It offers some techniques for working with arguments with more speed, clarity, certainty, and sanity. In the way of basic skills, this chapter teaches the following: (1) how to read arguments; (2) how to judge arguments; (3) how to write arguments; (4) how to write a critical analysis of an argument; and (5) how to write an argumentative essay.

Discovery Exercise

A COLLABORATIVE LEARNING OPPORTUNITY

Reading and Judging Arguments

Read the six points of view offered here on a controversial subject. Then answer the questions that follow in writing.

VIEWPOINT 1

None of us here at U.S. English [an organization whose goal is to make English the official language of the United States] wants the newcomers to deny their roots, or even to lose their native tongue. To remember, and celebrate, the folkways, the festivals, the food of the old country . . . enriches the variety of American life. . . . But the day that the immigrant's native tongue becomes the first language of any community or—God forbid—a State, the American experiment will be on its way to breaking up into a collection of feuding German republics, with several Quebecs in our future.

> Alistair Cooke, author, broadcaster, member of Board of Advisors for U.S. English. From an undated promotional newsletter.

VIEWPOINT 2

As you know, I have been outspoken in my opposition to the English Only movement. I have pledged to veto any bill that came before me calling for establishing English as the official language of our State. It appears my opposition to this legislation has led U.S. English to concentrate on destroying the outstanding bilingual education programs offered by school districts throughout New York State.

Bilingual education has been extremely successful in helping students to learn English. In fact, a national study conducted by the U.S.

Department of Education found that students in bilingual classes had more success in learning English than students in English only immersion classes. . . .

Mario M. Cuomo, Governor of New York State. Letter to Tom Sobol, Commissioner of Education for New York State, July 27, 1989.

VIEWPOINT 3

But the point of officializing English is to strengthen our common bond, not to obliterate our individual identities. For millions of Americans, ethnicity and language are linked. Communicating in an ancestral tongue is a means of maintaining ties with the past. . . . Ethnic diversity is one of the greatest strengths of the United States. English should be our official language, but it should not be our only language.

Barbara Mujica, Associate Professor of Spanish, Georgetown University. *Dallas News*, June 24, 1989.

VIEWPOINT 4

Our nation and the English language have done quite well with Chinese spoken in California, German in Pennsylvania, Italian in New York, Swedish in Minnesota, and Spanish in the Southwest. I fail to see the cause for alarm now.

Arizona Senator John McCain. From *Time*, December 5, 1988.

VIEWPOINT 5

Those who watched the Democratic convention in July 1988 may remember that it was the first at which the nominee gave his acceptance speech in two languages. Years from now, we may well remember this event was a turning point, a time and place at which the seeds of disunity were still more deeply planted across the land.

Gerda Bikales, consultant on public policy in Washington, D.C., and former executive director of U.S. English. *Dallas Morning News*, November 2, 1988.

VIEWPOINT 6

Most unfortunate of all is that advocates of the English Language Amendment send a plain message to minority-language groups: return to that age of less dignified status—to that time when your children were linguistically excluded from the classroom, to a time when language barred you from voting, to a time when you were unable to understand court proceedings because you could not speak English. To minority-language group members, the picture is clear. The ELA has little to do with language; it has everything to do with oppression.

> Roseann Duenas Gonzales, Alice A. Schott, and Victoria F. Vasquez, professors, University of Arizona. "The English Language Amendment: Examining Myths," *English Journal*, March 1988.

QUESTIONS

1. How would you describe each of the viewpoints given here?
2. What is the basic position, pro or con, taken by each? How do you know this position?
3. Take one viewpoint for analysis. What reasons are given to support its position?
4. Which do you find to be the most persuasive?
5. How did you decide?

CRITICAL ANALYSIS IN READING

As you will remember from the discussion in the word skills chapter, good critical reading does not begin with criticism, but with accurate comprehension of the material. Yet, even accurate comprehension depends on an attitude of mental *receptivity*. If we cannot remain open (as we learned in the chapter on observation skills), we mentally alter or distort whatever appears before us. Receptive reading does not substitute different words or ideas for those present, but faithfully and accurately records the message, regardless of whether or not it agrees with our own values, experiences, or world views.

In reading or hearing arguments, maintaining receptivity can sometimes become a particularly difficult requirement. This is especially true when we meet views that differ from our own; indeed, it can even feel painful to hear them out. All of us know that we tend to accept what agrees with our own opinions and preconceptions and to resist and criticize what does not. Both effort and discipline are needed to stay objective. And it can be even more difficult to remain neutral about what we favor than what we would reject. In reading the viewpoints on "English only" that opened this chapter, you may well have found yourself carefully reading and rereading those viewpoints that agreed with your own and feeling impatient or angry about those you disagreed with.

Objectivity is never a perfect achievement, but as a standard it may be defined as the ability to hold off personal reactions and take their influence into account while regarding a situation. Objectivity does not mean that you have eradicated your own feeling reactions, or that they will necessarily change, but it does mean that they have been taken consciously into account and weighed for their potential bias. Objectivity, moreover, is not a feeling of apathy, or a passive acceptance of everything. Apathy begins with the suppression of disagreements or questions, and eventually leads to the feeling that it just takes too much effort to think or react at all. Critical reading is always an active endeavor, requiring conscious focus, even in the first stage of reading for simple comprehension of content.

Critical reading cannot be hurried; it is a slow, careful process accompanied by many questions. Nevertheless, it must always begin with an accurate mental reproduction of the message. Of course, all of this holds true for conversations or discussions as well. We cannot be critical or skeptical and receptive at the same time. When we are critical too soon, we get an inaccurate reading of the material. And a criticism of information or argument based on an inaccurate reading is a waste of time for everyone involved.

The definition of *critical* given in the beginning of this book traces the original ideas of this term back to the words *sift* and *separate*. When one reads critically, one sifts out words and ideas, separates content from structure, questions and reflects. In critical reading the reader *interacts* with the material, is *involved* with what is said, and *questions* and *evaluates* what is said. Critical reading may begin by absorption of content, but it does not remain there; instead, it begins to formulate questions such as the following: Who wrote this? What values, perspectives, or vested interests lie behind the message? What is the argument? What does the author want from me?

Although critical reading should waive premature evaluations, its final objective is to judge an argument according to some traditional standards that test truth and reliability. A description of these standards has actually been a large measure of what this whole book has been about. By way of a systematic review, these standards can be summarized in the form of the five following questions:

1. What *viewpoint* and what *values* or *interests* have shaped this argument?

2. How is the argument structured in terms of *reasons* and *conclusions?*

3. Is it an *argument?* Or is it a *report?* Or is it a combination of both?

4.   What is the *issue* of controversy?

5.   What are the *strengths* and *weaknesses* of this argument?

WHAT VIEWPOINT, INTERESTS, AND VALUES SHAPED THIS ARGUMENT?

This question was treated in depth in Chapter 8, on viewpoints. By the time you finished the exercises in that chapter, together with the periodicals assignment, you should have discovered how different it can be to both read material and consider its viewpoint, interests, and values at the same time. If you enjoyed doing this, perhaps it was automatic for you to do the same in analyzing the viewpoints on English as the official language of the United States that opened this chapter. However, if you feel a little hazy on this subject after having gone through the intervening chapters, you might stop now to review Chapter 8 briefly. The crucial point to remember is the first question of critical reading: What viewpoint, values, and interests shaped the content of this argument?

HOW IS THE ARGUMENT STRUCTURED IN TERMS OF REASONS AND CONCLUSIONS?

A fair and honest argument is not always the most persuasive argument, yet it remains a standard for sanity. For those who are more conscious of how feelings and reasoning operate in themselves and others, a sound argument is a persuasive argument. And what are the standards for a sound argument? A sound argument is a clear statement of a claim supported by true evidence, true statements, and valid reasoning.

In the last chapters we studied some structures used to test or ensure the soundness of arguments arrived at by both inductive and deductive reasoning. With induction we used this form:

Data

Data

Data

Data
_____

Hypothesis or generalization → conclusion

And with deduction we used this form (the syllogism):

Major Premise

Minor Premise
_____

Conclusion

Yet, these structures serve only as artificial models, abstracted from the arguments we hear and use throughout a day. We do not speak in syllogisms or expect to read them in newspaper editorials or hear them in presidential debates on television or from a used car salesman. However, in order to argue, we have to know what point we want to make and how it can be supported. And when we hear the arguments of others, we need to be able to size up these components very quickly, abstracting the argument's core from the form in which it appears. Thus, when reading the "English only" arguments earlier in this chapter, you may have sensed that some of them were better reasoned than others, but you may not have been really sure how to explain why or why not.

The next couple of pages offer a method for explaining whether an argument is well reasoned or not. This method can also make the construction of arguments easier. This method is known as the analysis of arguments in terms of *reasons* and *conclusions*. The main advantage of this method is that it applies to both inductive and deductive arguments. The term *reasons* can be used to include both the premises of deduction as well as the factual evidence of induction, and the term *conclusion* to include inductive hypotheses as well as deductive conclusions. This portion of the chapter will offer a great deal of practice in identifying and analyzing arguments in terms of their reasons and conclusions. And the final research writing assignment will challenge you to demonstrate this skill.

Identifying the Conclusion of an Argument

The key to understanding any written argument is finding its conclusion. Although a conclusion is generally defined as a summary statement that comes last in any kind of spoken or written statement (or *discourse*), an argument's conclusion is not necessarily an ending point or summary, but a statement of a kind of thesis, or decision, or judgment. Usually, but not always, it is also a statement that one wants to convince others to believe.

In the formal reasoning of induction and deduction, a conclusion is the *last* step in a reasoning process. In everyday spoken or written argumentation, a conclusion may be stated *at any time* during the argument—or never stated at all but only implied.

Inductive

Yesterday I was happy singing.

Last week I was happy singing.

Everytime in my life I sing, I feel happy.

Conclusion: Singing makes me happy.

Deductive

Singing makes me happy.

I am singing.

Conclusion: I am happy.

Implied

I would rather sing than do anything else.

Singing is my favorite pastime.

Conclusions, however, need not be single or separate, but may be arrived at in rapid succession, one leading to another and another. If, for instance, your pleasure in singing led you to join a college chorus, that decision could have been based on several prior conclusions such as "I want to sing with others" and "I prefer a college chorus to a church choir." Considered as an argument, your final conclusion could have been based on a series of *reasons* such as the following: (1) the chorus has a good musical reputation; (2) the tuition cost is low; (3) the sign-up for the semester is next week. Thus in an argument, a conclusion is the bottom line, which carries with it a sense of finality. And the reasons are the thinking considerations that lead to this point of decision.

However, even though we can *feel* our own conclusions, it is not always that easy to find them in written arguments, where the reasons may also sound like conclusions.

> Those who watched the Democratic convention in July 1988 may remember that it was the first at which the nominee gave his acceptance speech in two languages. [reason in form of evidence leading to next reason] Years from now, we may well remember this event was a turning point, a time and place at which the seeds of disunity were still more deeply planted across the land. [reason supporting the implied conclusion]

In this case, both of the reasons offered could have served as conclusions in another context. But here they support a conclusion that is not stated: I am in favor of "official" English.

Conclusions can sometimes be easily recognized by the so-called *inference indicator words* that precede them. Such indicator words include the following: *therefore, so, in fact, the truth of the matter is, in short, it follows that, shows that, indicates that, suggests that, proves that, we may deduce that, points to the conclusion that, in my opinion,* and *the most obvious explanation is.*

1. *The truth of the matter is* that "official" English is based on xenophobia.

2. *In my opinion* "official" English will help, not hurt, immigrants.

3. *It all goes to show* that the United States is becoming like Germany in the 1930s, where arguments for the purity of the Aryan race and the German language were made with the same reasoned logic as those being made for "English only" today.

Identifying Reasons

Reasons are statements of opinion, propositions, premises, or statements of evidence offered to explain, justify, or support conclusions.

1. I am not in favor of "official" English. [conclusion] *Such laws would oppress minorities.* [reason] *Such laws would create problems where there are no problems.* [reason]

2. *"But the point of officializing English is to strengthen our common bond, not to obliterate our individual identities. . . .* [reason] English should be our official language, but it should not be our only language." [conclusion]

When we are giving our *own* reasons for an argument, they are self-evident. But it is not always easy to distinguish the reasons from the conclusions offered in someone else's argument. Yet, this must be done if we would know exactly what another is trying to prove and whether or not adequate reasons are given in its support. This means we have to take the argument apart, and the best strategy for analysis is to find the conclusion first, and thus extricate it from the whole. This method is rather like finding the leader of a group to communicate with, rather than trying to talk to everyone in the group at once. Thus, once the conclusion is found, the reasons are simply what remain.

Another technique for finding reasons is to look for the so-called inference indicator words that often introduce reasons: *because, first . . . second, since, for, for one thing, in view of the fact that, for the reason that, is supported by, for example, also.*

> I am in favor of officializing English [conclusion] *first because* it would avert cultural separatism [reason] *and secondly* because this would make us stronger as a nation. [reason]

Exercise

Identifying Reasons and Conclusions

In the following statements, underline the conclusions and number the reasons.

1. I am going to become an engineer because I see more advertisements in the newspapers for engineers than for any other profession.

2. By the study of different religions we find that in essence they are one. All are concerned with revelations or breakthrough experiences that can redirect lives and empower them toward good.

3. I am not pro-abortion at all. I think that people nowadays use abortion as an easy form of birth control. It's also against my religion. . . . I kept my baby because that's what I wanted to do.

4. Guns kill people; that's why handguns should be banned.

5. Deep fat frying can greatly increase the calories of foods such as fish, chicken, and potatoes. Therefore, it is better to bake, boil, or steam foods.

6. "It is important that individual citizens equip themselves with a baloney detection kit to determine whether politicians, scientists, or religious leaders are lying—it's an important part of becoming a citizen of the world." (Carl Sagan)

7. America should put a freeze on immigration. Its first duty is to take better care of its own disadvantaged, poor, and unemployed.

8. Marijuana laws are lenient in California and will probably not be changed. This is because those with the strongest economic interest—the commercial growers—would be out of business. After all, it's the third largest agricultural business in the state of California.

9. The U.S. policy on the use of chemical weapons is to protest their production by other nations while producing them ourselves. This is supported by the content of our negotiations on the one hand, and our military budget allocations for binary nerve gas on the other.

10. I don't drink because alcohol gives a brief high followed by a longer depression.

More on Distinguishing Reasons from Conclusions

Discovering the structure of arguments in general reading can involve some complexities that take a little practice to untangle. For instance, sometimes the conclusion is not stated at all but merely implied. In the fourth viewpoint on officializing English, Senator McCain's disapproval of the idea is stated only in terms of his reasons.

> Our nation and the English language have done quite well with Chinese spoken in California, German in Pennsylvania, Italian in New York, Swedish in Minnesota and Spanish in the Southwest. I fail to see the cause for alarm now.

Here the implied conclusion of the Senator's statement, "I am opposed to officializing English," is obvious. In some arguments, however, the missing conclusion may be more difficult to formulate.

> If you spend a billion dollars on retail trade, you generate 65,000 jobs. If you spend it on education, you generate 62,000 jobs; on hospitals, 48,000 jobs; on guided missiles and ordinance, 14,000 jobs. When you move money from the Department of Education to the Pentagon, for instance, or from a state like Michigan which would spend it on education, you are destroying jobs at about a three to one ratio.
>
> Marion Anderson, testimony before special congressional ad hoc hearings on the full implications of the military budget, January 1982; quoted by Ronald Dellums in *Defense Sense.*

In this case the speaker's conclusion might be stated as *"Contrary to popular belief, defense destroys more jobs than it creates."*

Sometimes a series of conclusions can be offered as reasons for an implied conclusion. In the following quotation, the speaker is offering a parody of the reasons given in the Preamble to the Constitution for the creation of that Constitution. These conclusions serve as his argument's reasons.

> The arms race does not form a more perfect union. The arms race does not insure domestic tranquility. The arms race does not provide for the common defense. The arms race does not promote the general welfare. And finally, the arms race does not secure the blessings of liberty to ourselves and to our posterity.
>
> Bishop Walter F. Sullivan, testimony before special congressional ad hoc hearings on the full implications of the military budget, January 1982; quoted by Ronald Dellums in *Defense Sense.*

Conclusions do not always appear at the end of an argument: sometimes they appear in the beginning, as in newspaper headlines.

> *Lifeline Banking Idea Unlikely to Take Hold at Banks*
>
> Aside from the heated debate over whether the nation's banks, like public utilities, should have to provide low-cost, low-use "lifeline service" to the poor, there's some doubt about whether they would, and more about whether they will.
>
> *Oakland Tribune,* 22 October 1984.

Sometimes a conclusion appears in the middle of a series of statements.

> Groups such as Public Advocates may be asking for the impossible or for something no longer possible, ignoring valid possibilities already in place. *Nevertheless, banks might be wise to move faster in coming up with spe-*

cial services not just appropriate, but actively promoted for low-income groups. [conclusion]

One reason might be the good of society. Those who live a cash-only life cost everyone time and money. It costs Pacific Bell $1.98, for example, to process a cash payment personally delivered and only 9 cents to process a mailed-in check.

Another reason suggested is the good of the bank, which could enjoy some public relations advantage in offering special services for the poor.

Oakland Tribune, 22 October 1984.

As we stated earlier, the first problem to address in analyzing arguments is to identify the conclusion, separating it from the reasons given in its support. This action prepares the way for us to question whether or not the reasons are adequate to support the conclusion. Indeed, we cannot answer such questions until we have unveiled the structure of the argument and clearly identified for study the offered conclusion and reasons. Obviously, we need to determine clearly *exactly what the author is claiming to prove* before becoming involved in a reaction of agreement or disagreement. By identifying the conclusion, we know the author's exact position on an issue. We may agree or disagree with this position—but first we must know what it is. If we should mistake one of the reasons for the conclusion, we may find ourselves going off on a wrong track in our analysis and rebuttal. But once we have identified the conclusion, then we can easily determine the reasons and isolate them for examination.

The other advantage of learning how to identify conclusions and reasons is that it enables us to refute or dismiss arguments that are fallacious. Such a process of elimination can then free us to spend more time with arguments that can really instruct us or challenge our thinking. Moreover, when we are writing our own arguments, we have a clear structural model to keep in mind that will help us build and test our arguments at their core.

Exercises

More Practice in Identifying Reasons and Conclusions

Analyze the following arguments by underlining the conclusions, or by supplying the conclusion in writing if it is only implied. Note that sometimes a conclusion may be part of a sentence, or the conclusion may be offered alone without any reasons attached.

1. Frequent snacks of high-energy food are not harmful to backpackers. Indeed, hikers are found to have more energy and less weariness if they snack every hour.

2. The American people have been brainwashed to turn away from Israel, its oldest ally, to sympathetic support for the Palestinian Arabs. The Arabs have accomplished this by depicting Israel in the media as a bully colonial power oppressing them as underdogs.

3. "The 1980s will be a revolutionary time, because the whole structure of society does not correspond with the world view emerging from scientific thought." (Fritjof Capra)

4. "I have come to believe that sound is God." (Ravi Shankar)

5. There's nothing like the taste of fresh, hot brownies. Bake your own the easy way with Brownlee's Brownie Mix!

6. No doctor should have the right to allow a patient to die. No doctor is God.

7. Videos are a good way to entertain children. You can control what they watch, and there are many worthwhile films to choose from.

8. Life is fast-paced in Japan but its citizens do not have as high a rate of coronary heart disease as those in the northeast cities of the United States. This may be due to their cultural habit of not associating hard work with competitiveness the way we do.

9. Since the 1920s, sperm counts have declined among American men. The underlying causes are uncertain, but the factors of stress and toxic chemicals are being considered.

10. If only 1 percent of the car owners in America would not use their cars for one day a week, it would save 42 million gallons of gas a year and keep 840 million pounds of CO_2 out of the atmosphere.

11. It takes twenty long years to make Freddy Scotch. It has every right to be expensive.

12. "Three of the core principles of the Green Party in West Germany—ecological wisdom, grass-roots democracy, and non-violence—were expressly borrowed from the citizens' movements in the United States. . . ." (Charlene Spretnak, "It Can Happen Here," *Utne Reader,* Summer 1984)

13. Because of their greater use of prescription drugs, women turn up in hospital emergency rooms with drug problems more frequently than men. (FDA Consumer Report)

14. "Our role is no longer that of an imperial power, as it was for 30 years after World War II. We have become progressively recolonialized. Our economy is increasingly controlled by outside powers—not governments, but by foreign ownership and con-

trol of our industry and finance. This is occurring through multi-national corporations, some of which have taken on the characteristics of sovereign states, and by heavy direct investments here by foreigners." (Eugene J. McCarthy, *USA Today,* 19 November 1984)

15. "I feel proud because in our democracy movement we were thinking for ourselves in a way that really distinguished us from the older generation." (Shen Tong, Chinese student leader at Tiananmen Square, now in exile in the United States)

A COLLABORATIVE LEARNING OPPORTUNITY

Finding Reasons and Conclusions in Newspapers

Study some newspapers to find concise arguments on several subjects. If you are working alone, find two arguments; if you are working with a partner, find four. Cut out or photocopy your selections, underlining the conclusions in red. Glue each or several to a page. Then on a separate sheet, write out these conclusions. List, underneath each conclusion, the reasons given. Bring this to class for sharing or to turn in for a grade.

Writing Application

Writing a Letter of Complaint

Write a letter in which you express a complaint about an injustice. Address the letter to a specific individual: to a friend, a parent, an elected official, a newspaper editor—in short, to anyone who has the power to do something about the situation. It may take some research to determine who this person should be, but don't just address your letter "To Whom It May Concern."

As you outline the draft of your letter, state exactly (1) what the situation is; (2) what is unfair about it; and (3) what you want done to rectify the situation. Use reasoning and evidence to support your case. Be clear about your conclusions and your reasons.

As you consider your topic, try to select one that really *feels* unjust to you. The more emotion you feel on the subject, the greater will be your challenge to argue your case through sound and persuasive reasoning. If you feel overwhelmed by the topic, write freely for an hour until you blow off steam. When you feel more collected, discard what you have done and compose your argument. After you have finished your first draft, ask yourself if your purpose has become one of trying to make the other party feel ashamed or wrong. This objective may make *you* feel better, but will not necessarily help you get yourself heard or your demands met. Most people when made to feel guilty are not likely to be open to hearing complaints or demands, much less to cooperate to change or amend a situation. Be quite specific about how you see the problem and what you want understood or done, but respect the person you are addressing and make your demands within range of the other party's capacity for reasonable acceptance.

Peer Review

To follow up on this exercise in class, exchange your letter or essay with a partner and do the following:

1. Underline the conclusion and circle the reasons.
2. Answer these questions on a sheet to attach to your partner's work:
   (a) Which reasons clearly support, justify, or explain the conclusion? Which do not?
   (b) Are more reasons needed? Explain.
3. If any portion is not clear to you, circle that in the work and ask your partner to explain it to you.

When you receive your work back, consider the comments. If you cannot agree with the critique, seek another partner and go through the same process verbally. If you find the criticisms helpful, revise your work accordingly.

If this exercise stimulated your interest in making yourself heard to achieve change, you may be interested in reading this publication:

Tell It to Washington: A Guide for Citizen Action, Including a Congressional Directory. Pub. no. 349. Available for $1.00 from the League of Women Voters of the U.S., 1730 M Street NW, Washington, D.C. 20036.

Discovery Exercise

Distinguishing Arguments from Reports

The following article is a *report* that explains some facts about an event and an issue. Read it and answer the question that follows.

Changing Our National Anthem

Indiana Congressman Andrew Jacobs has introduced a bill that would change the national anthem to "America the Beautiful." He says that both musicians and the general public agree that "The Star-Spangled Banner" is just too difficult to sing correctly. However, although everyone might agree with him on this score, winning public support for the change might not be so easy. According to a recent telephone poll conducted by *Time* magazine, 67 percent were against this replacement.

The idea of changing our national anthem is a controversial proposal. Why is this a report on the subject and not an argument?

The following is an *argument* and not a report. Read it and then write down what makes it an argument.

I am in favor of replacing "The Star-Spangled Banner" with "America the Beautiful." Our present anthem, with its incredible range of octaves, makes it difficult even for an opera singer to perform. As a result, most of us can only hum along. Moreover, the content of the lyrics is antiquated, hard to remember, and warmongering. "America the Beautiful" spares us all these problems.

Define *argument* and *report.*

IS IT AN ARGUMENT
OR A REPORT OR BOTH?

Because reports and arguments are each evaluated by different criteria in critical reading, it is essential to recognize the difference between them. The main purpose of *reports* is to offer information; this can be done through relating events or by offering facts or findings. Reports follow the rules of inductive reasoning. *Arguments,* on the other hand, only *use* information to reason toward an objective—to explain an idea, to justify it, or to persuade others to accept it. A report can relate an event, as in the first example, "Changing Our National Anthem"; it can offer findings, by interviewing supporters and detractors; and it can offer a hypothesis to predict what the final outcome may be.

But as often as not, a report leaves the conclusions up to the reader. It does not argue to prove a point. *One cannot, therefore, analyze a report as though it were an argument.*

This distinction may not always be so simple, however, because there are also *arguments disguised as reports*. These are particularly prevalent in many of the so-called news magazines that publish "reports" that are so slanted in their language, selection of information, and emphasis that they actually function as disguised arguments. Compare the following report to the example on page 399.

Oh, Say Can You Sing It?

> To put audiences out of their pregame misery, many stadiums resort to canned versions of error-free performances of ["The Star-Spangled Banner"] ... But a taped version takes away the thrill of victory and the agony of defeat inherent in every live performance, as well as the singers' inalienable right to get it wrong.
>
> *Time*, 12 February 1990, p. 27.

And reports and arguments are not always entirely separate entities. Often, we find the two combined, with report information serving as evidence or reasons to back up an argument.

> Today Indiana Congressman Andrew Jacobs introduced a bill that would change the national anthem to "America the Beautiful." He'll never get very far with that idea. We have enough trouble hanging onto our traditions, and, for better or worse, "The Star-Spangled Banner" holds too many of our shared memories for us to part with no matter how difficult it may be to sing.

CLASS DISCUSSION: REPORTS, ARGUMENTS, OR BOTH?

Identify the following as either reports or arguments, or as mixtures of both. Remember that an argument usually tries to persuade others to accept an idea by justifying and explaining it. A report simply presents the facts and suggests hypotheses, records conclusions made by several sources, or even lets the readers draw their own conclusions. Slanted reports, on the other hand, seek to sway others toward their own biases.

1. "Americans receive almost *2 million tons of* junk mail every year. About 44% of the junk mail is never even opened and read. Nonetheless, the average American still spends 8 full months of his or her life just opening junk mail." (*50 Simple Things You Can Do to Save the Earth*, Earthworks Press, 1989)

2. "Conservation to some people once implied sacrifice, deprivation and lower living standards. Now even many of them recog-

nize that *conserving energy is the cheapest, safest, cleanest and fastest way to avoid future energy crises.*" (Senator Alan Cranston, newsletter to constituents, November 1984)

3. "Too often the American economic system is looked upon as being a kind of battlefield between two opposing sides—consumers and the business/industrial community. This is a misguided but widely held viewpoint. *It is wrong to believe that consumers are at the mercy of business and industry.* The individual consumer is sovereign in the free market economy. . . . All of us are part of free enterprise, and what is good for business is good for the consumer." (Robert Bearce, "Free Enterprise," *Your Heritage News,* May 1984)

4. "Handguns caused about 10,000 deaths in the U.S. last year. The British, with a quarter the population, had 40. In 1978, 18,714 Americans were murdered, nearly two-thirds with handguns. In that year there were more killings with pistols and revolvers by children ten and under in America than the British total for killers of all ages. In Japan, with half the U.S. population, the 1979 total of crimes involving handguns was 171; in West Germany it was 69.

   "Americans seem unable or unwilling to acknowledge the simple truth that nations such as Australia, Britain, Canada, Japan, Germany, and Sweden have strict gun control and far less mayhem. It cannot be a coincidence." (Christopher Reed, "The Age," *Worldpress,* May 1984)

5. *Noriega's Surrender*
   "Noriega was a mere shadow of the machete-waving, gringo-hating dictator who once vowed that the Americans would have to kill him to get him out. . . . But Noriega, the master of psychological warfare, met his match in . . . a wily Spanish priest who persuaded the fugitive to put his faith in due process." (*Newsweek,* 15 January 1990)

6. *Making Suicide Pay*
   "There is finally good news for Mr. Milo Stevens, the 26-year-old incompetent who botched a suicide attempt in 1977 during which he launched himself into the path of a New York Transit Authority subway train. He has won a $650,000 negligence settlement and is still free to try again." (*American Spectator,* March 1984)

7. "The number of annual visitors to the U.S. will increase more than 75 percent by the end of the decade from last year's 38 million visitors, the Commerce Department said." (*New York Times,* 6 February 1990)

WHAT IS THE ISSUE OF CONTROVERSY?

Arguments are based on *issues.* An issue is a controversial question or problem that evokes different points of view with arguments to support those views. In the report offered earlier about visitors to the United States, no issue was raised. One could say that the number of tourists was the *topic* written as a report. However, this topic could be turned into an *issue* by raising the question, Should the United States try to encourage more visitors?

When we read arguments, issues are usually not stated as such and require some thinking from us to articulate. In the last exercise about arguments and reports, numbers 2, 3, and 4 were arguments. In none of these cases was the issue stated. If formulated as questions, their issues might be stated as follows:

2. Is conserving energy the best way to avoid future energy crises?
3. Are consumers at the mercy of business and industry?
4. Should handguns be outlawed in the United States?

If we have difficulty expressing the issue of an argument, one way we can do it is to formulate it into a question—just as debaters do—showing that several positions could be taken on the subject. Stating the issue in neutral terms like this requires a careful choice of words for their connotations. (Remember the discussion of how to examine polling questions for bias?)

Take, for instance, the following issue statement. Should the United States withdraw from any intervention in Central America? Here the question is prefaced by the word *should,* suggesting that it is open to argument; it also suggests that viewpoints will probably be based on personal values and ethics. The term *intervention* is also intended here to be neutral, although that might be challenged. Again, depending on viewpoint, such terms as *an imperialist colonialist policy* or *protecting our own interests* might be preferred. Nevertheless, to state an issue, an effort has to be made to make it as neutral as possible.

CLASS DISCUSSION: STATING ISSUES

Read the following arguments and for each formulate a statement of the issue in your own words.

1. "They're [the major media] ethnocentric. They seldom focus on how revolutions, natural disasters, military coups affect the people where these events happen. They focus on how it affects 'American interests.'" ("An Interview with Jeff Cohen," head of FAIR [Fairness & Accuracy in Reporting], Newsletter, 1989)

2. "I have heard the questions often. Have you no sense of social obligation? the Liberals ask. Have you no concern for people who are out of work? for sick people who lack medical care? for children in overcrowded schools? Are you unmoved by the problems of the aged and disabled? Are you *against* human welfare? The answer to all these questions is, of course, no. But a simple 'no' is not enough. I feel certain that Conservatism is through unless Conservatives can demonstrate and communicate the difference between being concerned with these problems and believing that the federal government is the proper agent for their solution." (Barry Goldwater, "The Welfare State," from *The Conscience of a Conservative,* 1960)

3. "The State is a means to an end. This end is the preservation and advancement of a community of physically and spiritually homogeneous living creatures." (Adolph Hitler, *Mein Kampf II*)

4. "The Bush administration is still more concerned about polluters' profits than protecting the Earth from global warming." (Daniel Becker, Sierra Club spokesman, *San Francisco Chronicle,* 2 February 1990)

5. "Concerning the Soviet-led reforms in Eastern Europe, we must guard against overconfidence. Many of the changes that have taken place there are reversible." (Dan Quayle, speaking at the Hoover Institution at Stanford, 18 January 1990)

6. "A national anthem is like the Constitution: one should not change it as one changes one's shirt, particularly when the change is dictated by fashion" (Unidentified opinion on editorial page, *San Francisco Chronicle,* 30 November 1989)

WHAT ARE THE STRENGTHS AND WEAKNESSES OF THIS ARGUMENT?

To make a list of standards for judging the strengths and weaknesses of an argument would mean reviewing most of the material covered in the past several chapters of this text. The seven following questions summarize such standards:

1. Are the reasons adequate to support the conclusion?
2. Is the reasoning sound—are the premises true and the reasoning valid?
3. Are there any hidden premises or assumptions crucial to the argument?
4. Are any central words ambiguous?
5. Are there logical fallacies?
6. Is any important information or evidence omitted?
7. Is any information false, contradictory, or irreconcilable?

All but the final two questions have already been discussed in this text.

Detecting Missing Information

Detecting missing information is not so difficult when we are familiar with the basic facts about a subject. In the final exam research assignment to follow, you will be asked to analyze three different points of view on a subject of controversy. As you go through the period of researching this assignment, you will gradually accumulate a sense of all the facts that this controversy entails. As this knowledge increases, so will your ability to judge how different arguments use this information: which information is given the most emphasis, which is minimized, and which is omitted altogether.

It is not this easy, however, to detect missing information in arguments about unfamiliar subjects. Here we have to depend on our ability to observe, read carefully, and ask questions. Looking for the most important missing elements under three categories—missing definitions, missing premises and conclusions, and missing information—can be helpful.

These categories, which also function as standards, have already been discussed in this text. The importance of definitions was stressed in the second chapter, where you learned how their absence confuses argumentation as well as general understanding. In the chapter on deductive reasoning was an explanation of missing premises and conclusions. In your work on photograph description and on report writing, you encountered the problems caused by missing pertinent information, which could also be described as missing data.

Discovering missing data takes active concentration and thinking. Because data are invisible when missing, their absence has to be detected with the searchlight of questions and imagination. Sometimes the absence of essential information can only be traced through the confusion we feel while reading. For instance, consider the following advertisement:

Our highest rate for five years. Guaranteed. Now for a limited time only you can lock into our highest rate for up to five years with an Iowa Federal five-year C.D. If you're retired, think about what this could mean. You won't have to worry about dropping interest rates for a long time. And it's FSLIC insured. Completely safe.

If you don't feel tempted to rush right down to invest, you might realize that the actual interest rate is never mentioned. And here you are being asked to "lock into" it for a period of five years! Thus, it may be true after all that you won't have to worry about dropping interest rates: you may spend more time regretting missing the higher ones. To forget to read carefully for missing information may result in later being unhappily reminded of the adage "Let the buyer beware."

CLASS DISCUSSION

What questions would you ask of the writers or speakers who said the following?

1. *Weight problem?* You've tried every kind of diet, exercise, pills and if you do lose a pound or two, it's back in no time. Everybody offers their advice, which is even more frustrating. Your weight problem is taking over your life. At our Health Spa, health specialists will work to take your weight off for good. Call us. Toll free. Georgetown Hospital Health Spa.

2. You are invited to my twenty-first birthday party. Prizes will be given for those who arrive Friday evening exactly at 7:07 P.M. in the Sigma Delta Dormitory lounge.

3. He hit me first.

4. Oh, honey, by the way, my former boyfriend came into town today and gave me a call.

5. I have to go out now and take care of some business.

6. The government should subsidize tobacco growers more than it does. If American tobacco growers are unable to meet production costs, they will be forced to quit growing tobacco, and we will be entirely dependent on foreign sources. Besides, tobacco farmers are making lower profits today than they were ten years ago.

7. Our religion forbids sexual misconduct.

8. *Nuclear Power Is Cheaper Energy for Tomorrow*
   "The price of electricity from fossil fuel plants will always depend heavily on the cost of fuel, which is unpredictable. The cost of nuclear fuel is more stable; its supply is within our control; and there's plenty of it. As a nuclear plant's construction costs

are paid for, its lower fuel costs *hold down* the price of the electricity. Eventually, the lower cost of fuel more than makes up for the higher cost of construction." (Advertisement, U.S. Committee for Energy Awareness)

Detecting False, Contradictory, or Irreconcilable Information

A final subject for critical concern is the detection of false information or false assertions in an argument. As critical readers, we cannot hold court hearings to prove lies, but we can remember to watch for any discrepancies or contradictions that might suggest the presence of lies. A sound argument that is both true and well reasoned does not contain contradictions.

Of course, the distinction exists between contradictions based upon insufficient thinking (as discussed in "Inconsistencies and Contradictions" in Chapter 10) and contradictions denoting an imperfect structure of lies. However, for our purposes as critical thinkers, ascertaining the distinction is not usually the issue. What matters is to recognize that whenever contradictions appear, the argument or claim is unsound. The argument, at best, has to be placed "on hold" mentally, awaiting further evidence or study.

And this policy applies not only to discrepancies found in arguments, but to inconsistencies appearing between words and action, between evidence and denials, between different testimonies, between differing accounts of facts, between claims and consequences, and between what we are told and what we know to be true. In any case, no discrepancy ever appears with the label *discrepancy* marked clearly on it; its detection results only from alert perception and thinking.

CLASS DISCUSSION

The following selection is a series of statements of fact taken from a review of three new books on the Dalkon Shield. Read it carefully and then answer the questions that follow either in writing or discussion. Make a list as you read of any contradictions you notice.

The Dalkon Shield is a contraceptive device marketed between 1971 and 1974 by the A. H. Robins Company of Richmond, Virginia. Marketed as a safe contraceptive, it led to complications in pregnancies as well as uterine infections for thousands, resulting in septic abortions, deaths for 20 mothers, and children born with birth defects. After the Shield was taken off the market in 1974, it was shipped overseas to Third World nations where 700,000 were distributed. By June 1985, 14,000 American women had filed suits against the company, which made payment of $378.3 million to settle 9,230 claims. Recently the Robins company filed for bankruptcy with thousands of claims still pending. The Robins company still insists that there is nothing wrong with the Shield.

Information taken from a review by Ann Jones called "Books Uncover Hidden Truth of Dalkon Shield," *Oakland Tribune*, 27 November 1985.

1. What contradictions appear here?

2. Do you think that the women victimized by the Dalkon Shield might have been more cautious if they had been trained in critical thinking skills?

3. Can you think of any other public scandals in which there were early warning signs of information being falsified or withheld from the public?

CHAPTER SUMMARY

1. The critical reading of arguments is an active endeavor that requires involvement, interaction with questions, and evaluation.

2. The questions asked in the critical reading of arguments are:

   (a) What viewpoint or values shaped this argument?

   (b) Where is the conclusion of this argument? What reasons support it?

   (c) Is it an argument or a report or both?

   (d) What is the issue of controversy?

   (e) What are the argument's strengths and weaknesses?

3. The analysis of arguments in terms of their reasons and conclusions applies to both inductive and deductive arguments. Reasons include data, evidence, and premises, while conclusions include those deductively drawn as well as hypotheses.

4. The conclusion of an argument is the last step in a reasoning process. However, it may be stated at any time during an argument or not at all.

5. Reasons support conclusions. They may be generalizations that could function as conclusions in another context. Once the argument's main conclusion is uncovered, the identification of generalizations as support becomes clear.

6. Arguments state and defend a claim. Usually they also attempt to persuade. Arguments disguised as reports slant the facts and language toward a bias.

7. Reports that only relate events or state facts cannot be analyzed as though they were arguments.

8. An issue is a selected aspect of a topic of controversy upon which positions may be taken either pro or con. Issues are stated in neutral terms often beginning with the word *should* and ending with a question.

9. The following questions can serve as guidelines for analyzing the strengths and weaknesses of arguments:

    (a) Are the reasons adequate to support the conclusion?

    (b) Is the reasoning sound?

    (c) Are there any hidden premises or assumptions?

    (d) Are any central words ambiguous?

    (e) Are there logical fallacies?

    (f) Is any important information missing?

    (g) Is any information false, contradictory, or irreconcilable?

Take-Home Final Research Exam

This is an assignment that will ask you to demonstrate all the knowledge and skills you have learned while studying this book. The following is a list of these skills. Use this list to assess your strengths and weaknesses, and as an overall guideline for your research and writing of this assignment.

The final research exam tests these skills:

1. The ability to isolate a controversial issue

2. The ability to do research necessary to find three arguments representing three different viewpoints on that issue

3. The ability to identify the political and social orientation of a viewpoint

4. The ability to extricate the core of an argument from a whole article and to analyze the argument's structure, strengths, and weaknesses according to standards learned in this text

5. The ability to objectively compare, evaluate, and summarize all three arguments before drawing your own conclusions

6. The ability to follow instructions and to communicate your findings clearly

Choose one subject of contemporary controversy that interests you. Browse in the library; study magazines and newspapers representing all points of view to stimulate your thinking.

Once you have selected your topic, narrow it down to one issue related to that topic. For instance, if you were interested in the subject of women in the military, you would only work with one question, such as *Should women serve in combat?*

Select and photocopy three different articles representing three different social or political positions on your chosen issue. These articles should be short, not more than four paragraphs. If you want to work with some passages taken out of the context of an article several pages long, photocopy the whole and highlight the section you intend to analyze. Newspaper editorials and letters to editors can also serve as short-length materials to cover. If you are working on a political subject, try to find three different views from the political spectrum that come from three different published sources. If you have an issue of sociological interest, such as the right to die, find three different perspectives concerning it, such as a doctor's view, a clergywoman's view, and the view of someone who has made a mercy-killing pact with a spouse.

Photocopy each argument on a separate sheet of paper to hand in with your analysis. Taking these arguments one at a time, begin your analysis by listing the following information at the top of the page: (1) the article's title, (2) magazine or newspaper source, (3) date of publication, and (4) whether it is argumentation or report/argumentation. (*Remember not to use reports for analysis.*)

Underneath this information, write your critique. Use the following outline.

1. Label the viewpoint as leaning more right or left if it is political. If it is sociological, find some appropriate label (as, for instance, "a minority view").

2. State the argument's conclusion. (You may have to put this in your own words.)

3. List the argument's reasons. (Again, this may have to be in your own words. Be sure not to quote what you do not understand as a substitute for trying to understand it.)

4. Review the article according to the following criteria. Discuss each systematically. Remember also that this is not just an exercise in finding flaws; you may find much to commend in the argument.

    (a) How well is the argument structured? Is the conclusion clear, and are there sound and sufficient reasons offered in its support?

    (b) Are any central words ambiguous? What and how?

    (c) Are there logical fallacies? If so, describe the examples involved.

    (d) Are there hidden assumptions? How do they affect the argument?

(e)   Is any important information missing?

(f)   Is any information false, irreconcilable, or contradictory?

Critique each of the three arguments. Then on a final page, write a paragraph that contrasts the arguments you selected. Look for the following: Do you find contradictory evidence among them? Which viewpoint do you find to be the most persuasive and why? (Note that you are not asked to defend your own viewpoint on this subject, but only to show why you find one of the three to be the most persuasive and well-reasoned argument. Your choice of the best argument could even represent a viewpoint different from your own.)

Follow your instructor's directions for the form in which to present this paper. You might put it together in a notebook of about ten pages with a title and table of contents combined on one page. Take pride in giving your work a professional appearance.

Practice Exercise

To practice for the final exam, complete this exercise in class. The following are three articles representing three different points of view on the issue *Should we aid Ethiopia?* The first article has been critiqued to serve as a model for you. For your own practice and class discussion, follow the same procedure for the other two, extricating the argument's conclusion and its reasons, followed by your critique. On a final page, write your comparison of the three articles, state your preference, and explain why.

Issue: Should We Aid Ethiopia? Three Views

SAVE AFRICAN CHILDREN

Ralph Diaz
(*UNICEF Regional Office for East Africa*)

DIRE DAWA, Ethiopia—I feel ashamed now remembering that 1 when I first saw death among the children laying on the cold earth I did not want to be affected by it. I held my breath, lest I too inhale death. Close by, I noticed that others, much stronger than myself, touched, and even smiled at, death. "See," one of them seemed to say to me, "I can touch death and life takes on more vigor in me to bring life to others."

Me? I was afraid to touch those small skeleton hands. I feared that 2 the reverse process would take place, that death would flow into life.

All my knowledge of human development was useless at that moment when I faced death. There I was, standing, unable to move, wanting to go away, to wake up in a different reality, in Geneva or Nairobi or some other place far from death and the clutch of fear. So my mind started to rationalize. "What can you do anyway? You are just one person representing one organization. It has airlifted 30,000 tons of wheat flour to a storage place nearby. Then what? It's too late for most of the children, isn't it?"

The child nearby closed her eyes for the last time with a smile on   3
her lips, still holding the hands of the lady who dared to defy death. The lady had managed to give something very precious to the child who had just died: "You are dying as a person," she told her, "and not as an animal."

Moisture gathered in my eyes. The lady faced me. She read my   4
thoughts. She told me: "You are wrong. Not everyone is near death here. The force of life is unbelievably strong in persons. With your help, many more children, their mothers and others can be saved." Why had I not realized it before? First fear, then rationalization: these are both instruments of death. I must break away from them.

Let us do something now in Africa with our African brothers and   5
sisters. Together let us form a life bridge. Let us reverse death's harvest. There is still time left for many children to be fully restored to life. Are you afraid? If so, you too will become an instrument of death. Will you act now? If so, you too can be a force of life.

(*New York Times*, 6 January 1985)

From *U.N. Chronicle*, Vol. XXII, No. 1 (1985), p. 20. Used with permission of the publisher.

Critique

Article's title: "Save the African Children"

Magazine Source: U.N. Chronicle (reprinted from the *New York Times*, 6 January 1985)

Date: Volume XXII, 1985

Form: Argument

Viewpoint: Left liberal

Conclusion: Save African Children (the title)

Reasons:

1. The death of children is not an abstraction but a personal encounter in Ethiopia.

2. More aid can prevent these deaths.
3. There is still time to act.
4. If you are afraid to act, you are an instrument of death.
5. You can become a force of life if you act now.

Critique:

1. The final paragraph offers reasoned arguments. The first paragraphs lead logically into the arguments through an effective personal narrative dramatizing the themes of life and death, and contrasting the author's own fears with the example of the "lady" who holds and comforts the dying. The language used in this story is rather old-fashioned romantic, using some clichés, such as "cold earth," "small skeleton hands," and "closed her eyes for the last time with a smile on her lips."

2. Two central ambiguous words are *act* and *aid*. What is needed? Money? Food? People? And to what source? UNICEF? And how? All this comes under the category of missing as well as practical information.

3. As for logical fallacies, there is a strong appeal to emotion, especially pity and guilt, but this would seem to be justified in terms of Christian, left liberal, or "one world" values. For someone with less sympathy, who felt the Ethiopians brought this situation upon themselves, this appeal, especially with its selected focus on children, might seem to be an irrelevant "pulling of the heart strings" in the liberal paternalistic tradition of rescuing "victims."

4. The main hidden assumption is a value assumption that this is one world in which we are all responsible for one another, most especially for innocent children. This assumption is not expressed, but the whole argumen is based on this premise.

5. There is a lot of missing information in this argument:
   (a) How did this crisis come about? (The author assumes you have been reading about this crisis for months, which seems justifiable.)
   (b) Why is the 30,000 tons of wheat in a storage place "nearby" (vague reference) "too late" (vague) for most of the children?
   (c) Is UNICEF the best source to contribute to?
   (d) What exactly is needed? More transport? More grain? All these are important practical questions, but the author seems to have omitted the answers in order to keep the romantic, feeling tone of his appeal.

A MEDIA EVENT:
TREATING AFRICAN AFFAIRS WITH CYNICISM

Peter Enahoro

Humanity should stand united when the elements invade us with 1
their worst excesses. Those who are able to render aid should feel no
self-congratulatory satisfaction that they do so. This is why one feels
outraged at the manner in which relief for Ethiopians has been conducted, as though it were an international contest for a media award.

We must not minimize the value of the contributions of all donors. 2
But we must be bold enough to examine the timing of their arrival and
even the selection of Ethiopia for attention.

Twenty-four African countries are now drought-stricken. Although 3
half of these are in the Sahel belt, the ravages of the continuous lack of
rain have spread as far south as Mozambique and Zimbabwe. Concentrating attention almost exclusively on Ethiopia because that is where
the cameras are is grievous cynicism.

For the past fifteen years, Africa has been blighted by unrelieved 4
widespread drought. Where has the rest of the world been? Oh, yes, ac-
ademicians have been writing and speaking about the "desertification"
in Africa; unctuous official voices have expressed concern; we have
played host to high-profile "experts" and "observers."

These migratory persons fly into the capital of an afflicted country, 5
carefully avoiding a visit to the disaster areas, and then leave to trum-
pet their predictable deduction that Africa's food crisis stems from corruption in high places. Others make the astonishing claim that the food
shortage is the consequence of the better-off using the better land to
grow cash crops instead of food.

Through these interventions Africa has acquired a stereotyped im- 6
age: It is a continent that cannot feed itself because its politicians are
corrupt, its soldiers are permanently on a rampage, and its planners are
innately stupid.

Africa has unwittingly forged an alliance between those who have 7
never forgiven us for seeking independence from European rule and
those do-gooders who forget that we fought for and won our independence precisely because we wished to assume responsibility for
ourselves. What both groups have done is divert attention from the
root causes of Africa's problems. While a prolonged drought slowly destroys Africa we have the neo-imperialists, on the one hand, who tell
the world that Africans cannot manage their own affairs and, on the
other, the liberals who would have us believe that our troubles are
others' responsibility. . . .

We must wonder where the donors will be tomorrow, when the   8
story dies and the cameras depart. The Soviet Union, the U.S., and the
European Economic Community countries should establish a tripartite
body and launch a permanent scientific research and practical aid
group to confront this challenge. This plea is not the same as carrying
the begging bowl that many consider our right to hold out to the richer
nations. It is simply to remind those nations that have the resources
that the desertification of Africa is a continuing natural disaster—perhaps the most prolonged natural disaster in the history of humanity.

> Excerpted from an article by Peter Enahoro, publisher of *Africa Now*, reprinted in
> *World Press Review*, February 1985, p. 41. Used with permission of *World Press
> Review*.

WE AREN'T THE WORLD

The best way to experience the charity mega-hit "We Are the   1
World" is by means of the video, on which you can actually watch the
collection of 45 pop stars, ranging from the hot (Bruce Springsteen) to
the dead (Bob Dylan) to the seemingly eternal (Ray Charles), shaking
and singing for the relief of Ethiopia. Musically, it's a good tune, as-
tonishingly good for a committee effort; and morally, it is better that the
millions of dollars be raised with the intention of feeding the starving
than of paying for the next few cocaine deals.

Intellectually, though, the musical effort leaves some things to be   2
desired. The last wave of concern for African misery, ten years ago, was
stimulated by the grinding Sahel drought. That drought was not an act
of God. It was caused, in large part, by overgrazing; which occurred because the nomads had increased the size of their herds; which became
possible because the local governments, acting on the advice of Western "experts," had dotted the landscape with wells (which also, inci-
dentally, lowered the water table). The suffering, in other words, was
caused by misguided efforts to help. Since 20 percent of the profits of
"We Are the World" is supposed to go for "long-term development," the
Sahel experience is not academic.

Or it would not be academic if the Marxist government of Ethiopia   3
were genuinely interested in ending the famine—which it is not. Most
of the dying are "rebels," and Addis Ababa is content to take food for its
own hungry, and let the rest eat sand. Relief organizations have been
trying, with difficulty, to get around the problem: by feeding refugees in
the Sudan; by going into rebel areas illegally. But you won't learn this
from "We Are the World." Men eat. They also think; sometimes their

thoughts lead them to cruelties not dreamt of in Bruce Springsteen's philosophy. We aren't the world, and not all the world is like us.

Study Checklist in Preparation for Your Take-Home Final

If you find that you cannot answer any of the questions given below, re-study this chapter or arrange for a conference with your instructor or tutor.

1. What is your topic?
2. What is your issue? (Remember you have to decide on your issue in order to limit the scope of your research and also to determine whether you have three different points of view that address the same issue.)
3. Can you label the viewpoints of the arguments you have selected? (If they are political, you may need some assistance. But remember, they may also be social, ethnic, or role-related.)
4. Are you sure you have arguments to work with and not just reports?
5. If you have found a long argument extending over many pages, have you selected a suitable portion to handle in depth for your analysis?
6. Give an example of a conclusion from one of your arguments.
7. Give an example of a reason that supports this conclusion.
8. Can you apply each critique question in turn to your analysis of each argument?

Writing Application

Writing an Argumentative Research Essay

Here is an opportunity for you to express and defend your own view on the issue you researched in your take-home final. Write an argumentative essay, following these steps:

1. Shape your view of the issue you researched into a thesis.
2. Use whatever research sources you used for the final exam and shape them to support your argument. Also use your own expe-

rience or any other applicable research you wish to pursue or are familiar with.

3. Outline your argument first, beginning with your main conclusion, or thesis, followed by a list of your reasons. Study this outline. Notice where you need to acquire more evidence or examples, and where you already have more than enough material to write a total of from eight to ten typed pages.

4. Keep your outline before you as you write. Make sure that each part of the essay relates to your thesis.

5. Check over your work and rewrite it as necessary to improve coherency and correct errors.

6. Use the MLA format and include a bibliography of your sources at the end.

7. Present your essay in a form that shows pride in your work.

INDEX

417